# Legal Issues of Mobile Apps

# Legal Issues of Mobile Apps

## A Practical Guide

Edited by

Ioannis Iglezakis

Wolters Kluwer

*Published by:*
Kluwer Law International B.V.
PO Box 316
2400 AH Alphen aan den Rijn
The Netherlands
E-mail: international-sales@wolterskluwer.com
Website: lrus.wolterskluwer.com

*Sold and distributed in North, Central and South America by:*
Wolters Kluwer Legal & Regulatory U.S.
7201 McKinney Circle
Frederick, MD 21704
United States of America
Email: customer.service@wolterskluwer.com

*Sold and distributed in all other countries by:*
Air Business Subscriptions
Rockwood House
Haywards Heath
West Sussex
RH16 3DH
United Kingdom
Email: international-customerservice@wolterskluwer.com

ISBN 978-94-035-2240-1

e-Book: ISBN 978-94-035-2243-2
web-PDF: ISBN 978-94-035-2252-4

# Editor

**Ioannis Iglezakis** is Professor of Law and Informatics at the School of Law in the Aristotle University in Thessaloniki (Greece) and an attorney-at-law at the Thessaloniki Bar Association. He is currently Director in the Postgraduate Department of Legal Theory and Interdisciplinary Law Studies and a Member of the Office of the Dean of the School of Law of Thessaloniki.

He has widely published in Greece and has authored many studies in international legal reviews. His research interests include IT law, legal informatics, media law, economic and EU law. He is a member of the editorial team of Greek legal journals. He has published eleven books and over 160 articles, in Greek, German and English, and has also edited several books published in English: Legal and Socioeconomic Aspects of Intrusion, IGI (2009); E-Publishing and Digital Libraries: Legal and Organizational Issues, IGI (2010); Values and Freedoms in Modern Information Law & Ethics. Proceedings of the 4th International Conference on Information Law and Ethics (2011); Proceedings of the 6th International Conference on Information Law and Ethics (2015); Cyberlaw in Greece, Kluwer Law International (2015); Legal Regulation of Cyber Attacks, Kluwer Law International (2016); Digital Tools for Computer Production and distribution, IGI Publishing (2016), Media Law in Greece, Kluwer Law International (2016).

# Contributors

**Philippe Jougleux** is Associate Professor at the Law School of European University Cyprus, where he teaches Cypriot tort law and contract law, legal methodology, EU copyright law and EU internet law. He wrote numerous articles in Greek and English, mainly on topics related to new technologies (online copyright law, data protection, cybercrime). He published five books, is a founding member of the Cypriot organization for the promotion of copyright law (EDPI) and he is chief editor of the law Journal "ENTHA".

**Dr. Georgios Matsos, LLM** lectures on domestic and international tax law at the Aristotle University of Thessaloniki and at the International Hellenic University, Thessaloniki. He is author of many publications on tax law, on accounting law and on public finances. He has been an invited speaker in many international and domestic conferences and also a guest lecturer at many international Universities. He is head of Matsos & Associates Law Office, Thessaloniki.

**Eleftheria Papadimitriou** is a PhD candidate in Information Technology Law. She is specialized in Privacy, e-Commerce, Consumer Protection and Intellectual Property issues. She is an accredited Mediator and Trainer for Mediators and International Online Dispute Resolution Mediator (Consumer, Commercial, Personal Data and Intellectual Property disputes). She is the founder of "Ria Papadimitriou and Associates Law Office" and Founder and General Director of "startADR", an Alternative Dispute Resolution Institute (startadr.org).

**Anastasios Papathanasiou** is a PhD candidate in Information Security and Technology Law, in Aristotle University in Thessaloniki (Greece). He holds a bachelor degree (BSc) in Computer Science from University of Piraeus and a master degree (MSc) in Techno-economic Management & Security of Digital Systems from the Department of Digital Systems, University of Piraeus. Additionally, he holds a second master degree (MSc) in Law Science from the Faculty of Law of the National and Kapodistrian University of Athens and he holds a third master degree (MSc) in Criminology at the same University. He has published his research and academic papers in a variety of information technology and security-related academic journals and academic conferences and has lectured extensively on the need to integrate social science and computer science when addressing high-tech crime.

**Paschalis Paschalidis, LLM** is an attorney-at-law at the Thessaloniki Bar Association and a post-graduate researcher. He is a graduate of the Faculty of Law of the Aristotle University of Thessaloniki and possesses an LLM degree on Public Law and Political Science from the same University. His academic interests include constitutional law, administrative law, tax law, political science and political philosophy.

**Vasiliki Samartzi, PhD, LLM (UCL),** is PhD in information technology law, from the Centre for Commercial Law Studies (CCLS), Queen Mary, University of London. She graduated from the Faculty of Law of the National and Kapodistrian University of Athens (Greece) (LLB) and holds an LLM in Commercial Law from the University of Bristol (UK) and an LLM in Computer & Communications Law from the University College London (UCL). Vasiliki has considerable professional experience as an IT-specialized lawyer and also considerable academic experience having taught law courses in top-tier law schools & having published several peer-reviewed articles in internationally acclaimed law journals.

**Dr. Maria K. Sheppard** was lecturer in the field of "New Medical Technologies and the Law" at Queen Mary University of London covering areas such as remote and technology enabled healthcare, 3D printing and medical device regulation. As a post-doctoral researcher she worked on an EU funded interdisciplinary project for a proposed clinical trial using maternal gene therapy. She continues lecturing and publishing in the field of new medical technologies.

**Evgenia Smyrnaki** is a PhD candidate in Computer Law at the University of Thessaloniki, Greece. She has graduated from the Law Department of the University of Athens and holds a Master's Degree in "Bioethics" (University of Crete) and a degree in Information and Communication Law (LLM in Computer and Communications Law – Queen Mary University of London). She has participated in national and European projects related to the availability and exploitation of open data sets, the development of open academic courses and free software and open source software (EL/LAC).

**Efmorfia (Efi) Tziva** is Associate Professor of Commercial Law at the School of Law in the Aristotle University in Thessaloniki (Greece). Her research concentrates on insurance, consumer protection, company law, medical and e-commerce law. She is a member of the Office of the Dean of the School of Law of Thessaloniki. She published three monographs and many articles in Greek and English on the topics referred above. She has participated in many congresses held in Greece and abroad as a representative conference speaker and she has given lectures and seminars in many universities and scientific organizations.

**Eleni Tzoulia** is a PhD and currently a post-doctoral researcher on commercial law. She has attended master studies in the field of European Economic law at the

Ruprecht-Karls University of Heidelberg in Germany and has participated in two EU traineeship programs at the premises of the European Parliament in Brussels and the European Ombudsman in Strasbourg respectively. Since 2018, she has been serving as an adjunct lecturer for commercial law at the Aristotle University of Thessaloniki.

# Summary of Contents

# Table of Contents

CHAPTER 1

# Definitions, Economic and Technical Aspects of Apps

*Ioannis Iglezakis*

*Mobile applications or (mobile) apps have gained a significant segment of the market of information technology products. These are software specifically designed for mobile devices, such as smartphones, tablets, etc. Mobile apps are widely used for a variety of tasks, e.g., social networking, gaming, general productivity, information retrieval, web browsing, email, maps and GPS, calendar, weather forecasting, etc. In this chapter we provide an overview of apps' technology, their functionality and technical characteristics, as well as technical aspects and also, of app stores, through which apps are being distributed. Particular reference is made to the economic importance of apps, to their distribution and pricing. Security issues related to apps are also reviewed, as there are various threats and security risks in the apps ecosystem.*

## §1.01 OVERVIEW

### [A] Mobile Internet and Smartphones

The Digital Revolution which led to the rise in the use of computers worldwide also introduced the concept of mobile computing that includes portability, connectivity and ubiquitous computing.[1] Technological advances in the semiconductor device fabrication, as transistors became smaller with decreasing power consumption, enabled the development of portable smart devices. Additionally, technological innovation sparked

1. *See, e.g.*, L. Hamill, "Introduction: Digital Revolution—Mobile Revolution?," in: L. Hamill, A. Lasen and D. Diaper (eds.) *Mobile World. Computer Supported Cooperative Work*. Springer, 2005.

the development of digital wireless mobile networks and, this enabled the proliferation of mobile devices such as smartphones.

The first portable devices were personal digital assistants (PDAs), which had the functionality of handheld PCs and were first produced in the 1980s, but they differed from PCs in that they had a touchscreen and a few buttons, while some had a stylus. In the 1990s PDAs acquired full telephone capabilities, with companies such as IBM and Nokia leading the way. Apart from these hybrid phones, mobile phones were developed first in Japan, in 1999, and later, in the US business professionals started adopted Blackberry smartphones and devices with Windows Mobile, but the adoption of smartphones from the general public was limited. The breakthrough came with the introduction of the iPhone by Apple in January 2007, which was the first smartphone designed for mass adoption. A huge advance was also the addition of App Store, an application that allowed direct wireless downloading of software by third-party developers.

In the ensuing years, touchscreen smartphones gained popularity and superseded ordinary mobile phones. The existence of mobile apps made available via app stores contributed greatly in this development, as they provide efficiency of use and portability.

### [B] Apps

Mobile applications or (mobile) apps have gained a significant segment of the market of information technology products. Mobile apps are computer programs specifically designed for mobile devices such as mobile phones, tablets or watches. Some apps are preinstalled on mobile devices, so, e.g., web browser, email, calendar, maps, media players, and lately, health apps. These apps which are preinstalled cannot always be removed and must be rooted to be uninstalled and leave storage space for other uses.[2]

Users of mobile devices may download apps through official distribution platforms, such as the Apple App Store,[3] Google Play,[4] Windows Phone Store,[5] and BlackBerry App World,[6] or independent platforms, such as Cydia,[7] i.e., an app store containing jailbreak apps and other content not available on Apple App Store, GetJar,[8] which is an open app store for Android and F-Droid,[9] which is an installable catalog of free and open source software applications for the Android platform.

Since the first launch in 2008, mobile apps have found widespread application and are now used not only for general productivity, information retrieval, web browsing, email, maps and GPS, calendar, weather forecasting, and other auxiliary

2. *See* Wikipedia, *Mobile App*, https://en.wikipedia.org/wiki/Mobile_app.
3. www.appstore.com.
4. Play.google.com.
5. https://www.microsoft.com/en-us/store/apps/windows-phone.
6. https://appworld.blackberry.com/.
7. https://cydia-app.com/.
8. https://www.getjar.com/.
9. https://f-droid.org/.

services, but also for purposes normally handled by desktop application software packages.[10]

These include many popular uses of mobile devices such as social networks, including not only favorite social networking services such as Facebook, Instagram and Twitter, but also apps for various purposes, e.g., gaming, listening radio and/or music, video chat, capturing videos and photos, photo editing, e-banking, messaging, cloud storage, news services and watching videos. Many apps are mobile versions of popular internet services, such as flight and hotel booking services, traveler reviews, videoconferencing, ridesharing, home-sharing, etc.

The evolvement of apps is surging, as there were 12 million mobile app developers worldwide as of October 7, 2016, and this number represents almost half of the total global developer community. The total number of app developers is forecasted to reach 14 million by 2020.[11]

Mobile apps are expected to generate USD 189 billion in revenue by 2020, whereas 21% of Millennials open an app 50 + times per day and 49% of users open an app 11 + times each day. Concurrently, and as mobile app usage grows in popularity, the number of app downloads worldwide increases as well (*see* Figure 1.1).[12]

*Figure 1.1 Annual App Downloads in Billions*

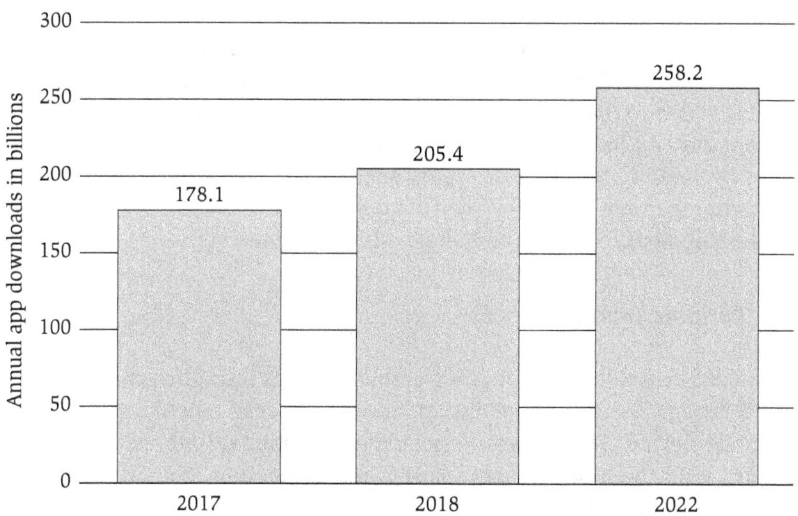


Mobile apps are designed for and can be installed in smart devices, i.e., electronic devices with internet connectivity and exhibiting properties of ubiquitous computing, such as the following:

10. Wikipedia, *supra*.
11. Mobile Developer Population Reaches 12M Worldwide, Expected to Top 14M by 2020, available online at: https://evansdata.com/press/viewRelease.php?pressID = 244.
12. https://buildfire.com/app-statistics/.

- Smartphones;
- Tablets, phablets;
- iPads, iPods;
- Smart TV;
- Smartwatches;
- Activity trackers (smart bands);
- Other wearables (smart soles, etc.);
- Drones;
- Smart cars;
- Mobile Virtual Reality;
- IoT devices,[13] etc.

## [C] Apps Functionality

Mobile apps have a significant added value as they perform tasks which are transformative for mobile devices, providing them with features that exceed their potential, given the fact that they are not as powerful as desktop computers or laptops.[14]

### *[1] Apps as Substitutes for Various Devices*

Apps are computer applications, that is, software, but as they are integrated into portable devices which have several sensors, they have the potential to replace other devices. This is due to the fact that it is more practical to carry one lightweight device rather than many. As the technology is developing, many devices and equipment are substituted by mobile devices with apps, such as digital video cameras, navigation systems, radio, gaming consoles, calculators, music players, scanners, and also non-digital equipment, e.g., thermometers, chronometers, etc.

### *[2] Portable Libraries*

Apps transform smartphones and other mobile devices into powerful portable mediums for file storage. What is more important, one can read e-books and magazines in his/her mobile device. This proves very efficient in holidays where app users do not need to carry with them books, newspapers and magazines, but can buy online and download them in their device.

13. *See, e.g.*, https://www.softwaretestinghelp.com/iot-devices/.
14. Denker, Hartl and Denker, in: C. Solmeck, J. Taeger and T. Feldmann, *Mobile Apps. Rechtsfragen und Rechtliche Rahmenbedigungen*. De Gruyter, 2013, p. 4.

#### *[3] Mobile Internet*

Smartphones and tablets are convenient means to access the internet, as mobile broadband has become inexpensive and, thus, widely available.

### [D] App Stores

The existence of app stores has contributed greatly to the development of the mobile app market, since an app store has greater capacity to connect users to apps compared to independent software providers, whereas it provides security of transactions, allowing users to trust a platform from a renowned company such as Google or Apple. As mentioned above, there are other platforms, as well, but we will provide a brief overview of these two, which are the most important ones.

#### *[1] Apple's App Store (iOS)*

App Store[15] (*see* Figure 1.2) was the first distribution platform for mobile apps, which was opened on July 2008 by Apple Inc. Initially, it offered more than 500 apps for use with the new iPhone 3G which entered the market on July 11, 2008. Most apps cost USD 9.99, while about 25% of the total apps were free.[16] It is worthwhile that by January 5, 2017 there were 2,200,000 apps in the App Store and the number of downloads exceeded 130 billion downloads. As of second quarter 2019 the number of available apps for download on App Store was 1,960,000.[17]

App Store allows users to download mobile apps compatible with Apple's iOS. These apps are intended for use on the iPhone smartphone, the iPod Touch handheld computer and the iPad tablet computer, while some can also be transferred to the Apple Watch smartwatch and the Apple TV as extensions of iPhone apps.[18]

Mobile apps on iOS are developed with the iOS SDK (Software Development Kit), which can be downloaded for free by users of Apple's computers, providing developers access to various functions and devices of iOS devices. With the iOS SDK third-party developers can develop native apps for iOS, but they must pay a USD 99 yearly fee for access to Apple's Developer Program, and chose the preferable option to monetize their application.

15. Apple App Store, https://www.apple.com/gr/ios/app-store/.
16. AppleInsider Staff, *Apple's App Store Launches with More Than 500 Apps*, July 10, 2008, https://appleinsider.com/articles/08/07/10/apples_app_store_launches_with_more_than_500_apps.
17. *Number of Apps Available in Leading App Stores as of 2nd Quarter 2019*, https://www.statista.com/statistics/276623/number-of-apps-available-in-leading-app-stores/.
18. *See* https://en.wikipedia.org/wiki/App_Store_(iOS).

*Figure 1.2 Apple's App Store*

### *[2] Google Play*

Google Play (*see* Figure 1.3), which was previously known as Android Market, is a distribution platform for Android apps, operated by Google LLC.[19] It is the official app store for the Android operating system, offering applications developed with the Android SDK and published through Google for download. It also includes other Google services, such as Google Play Book, Google Games, Google Play Movies & TV and Google Play Music, thus operating as a digital media store.[20]

The difference with Apple is that Google has open-sourced the code for the Android operation system, allowing developers to create their own modified version of the operation system. This provides providers of tablets or phones the possibility to adjust the platform to the particular hardware. Nevertheless, modified versions of the Android system are not always compatible with apps developed for the official version of Google's Android system.

Android devices have a preinstalled Play Store app, which provides access to content on the Google Play Store. Android Apps can be downloaded directly on an Android Device through the Play Store mobile app or by installing them to a device from the Google Play website. Play Store offers for download 2,758,211 Android apps as of September 2, 2019.[21] Developers can join the platform after registering for a Google Play Developer Console account. They may, then, control the distribution of an

19. Google Play Store, https://play.google.com.
20. Wikipedia, *Google Play*, https://en.wikipedia.org/wiki/Google_Play.
21. *Number of Android apps on Google Play*, https://www.appbrain.com/stats/number-of-android-apps.

app in various countries, and the pricing for the app and in-app purchases in each country.[22] The operating fees and distribution cost of paid apps amount 30% of the application price.

*Figure 1.3 Google Play*

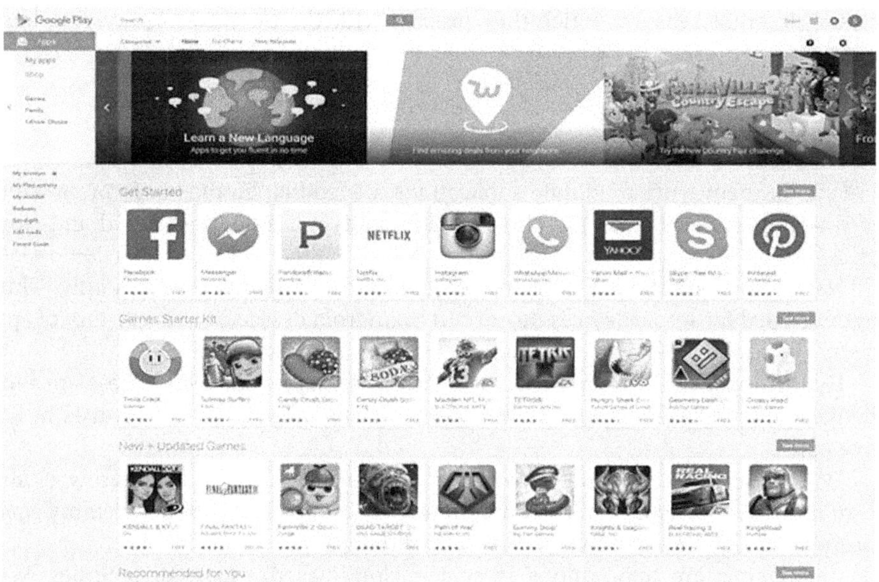


## §1.02 TECHNICAL ASPECTS

### [A] App Development

As mentioned above, apps are developed with software development kits (SDKs or devkits). These are used to create applications for a specific software package and are distinctively employed for specific platforms. To add advanced features, advertisings, etc., app developers implement specific SDKS, while some are used only to develop a platform-specific app. So, e.g., to create an Android app on Java it is required to use a Java Development kit, etc.[23]

SDKs may take the form of application programming interfaces (APIs) used as on-device libraries to interface to a particular programming language or they may be used to control hardware equipment of smartphones, such as cameras, loudspeakers, sensors, etc. SDKs actually make sure that specific functions can only be activated if the user consents to their use.[24]

22. *Supported locations for distribution to Google Play users*, Developer Console Help. Google.
23. *See* Software development kit, Wikipedia, https://en.wikipedia.org/wiki/Software_development_kit.
24. *See* Ewald, in: Baumgartner and Ewald, Apps und Recht, Beck Verlag, 2013, p. 4.

Furthermore, smart devices may be equipped with a multitude of sensors including a gyroscope, digital compass and accelerometer that provide speed and direction of movement, cameras that take photographs and record video, and a microphone, etc. Access to those sensors is provided to apps through APIs, while geolocation services provide the location of smart mobile devices. App developers make use of this connectivity through the APIs to collect data from the device and data from the different sensors, which they process with the purpose of providing tailor made services to users.

### [B] Types of Apps

There are different types of mobile applications, depending on the platform on which they run. In particular, apps are classified into native, hybrid, web-based and cloud apps.

Native apps are those which are designed for a particular platform only. Thus, apps developed for Apple devices do not run in Android devices. Such category of apps performs better and therefore, it is mostly used by businesses.[25]

Hybrid apps, on the other hand, work across multiple platforms. These are a mix of native and web-based apps and are easier to develop, but do not perform as well as native apps.

Web-based apps are applications in which the client runs in a web browser and, thus require internet access to perform properly. These apps use limited memory space in users' devices compared to native and hybrid apps.

Cloud apps are applications in which cloud-based and local modules work together.[26] They rely on remote servers operated by a cloud service provider.

### [C] Actors in the App Ecosystem

A number of different actors are involved in the technical development of apps, which form the ecosystem of apps. At the core of the app ecosystem are the app developers which produce the numerous applications available in app stores and elsewhere, on the internet. The taxonomy of an ecosystem that focusses on the central role of app developers is provided in Figure 1.4.[27] This presents the Android app ecosystem from a technical aspect, but it can be generalized to ecosystems of other app stores.[28]

25. Wikipedia, *supra*.
26. *See* https://searchcloudcomputing.techtarget.com/definition/cloud-application.
27. Y. Acar, M. Backes, S. Bugiel and M. Smith, "SoK: Lessons Learned from Android Security Research for Appified Software Platforms," in *IEEE Symposium on Security and Privacy (SP)*, 2016.
28. ENISA, *Privacy and data protection in mobile applications. A study on the app development ecosystem and the technical implementation of GDPR*, November 2017, p. 26, available online at: www.enisa.europa.eu.

*Figure 1.4 Actors in the Android Ecosystem*

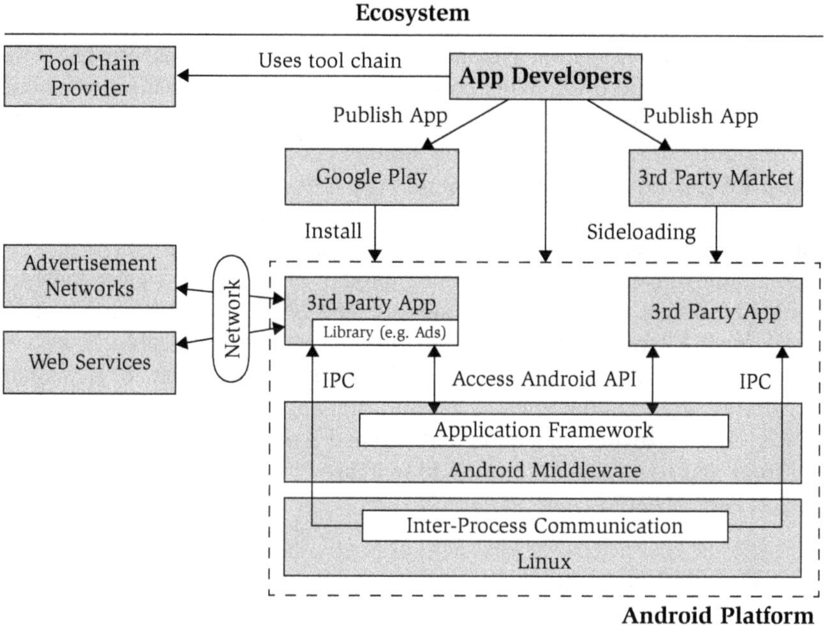


As it is evident, the following actors are included in this representation of an ecosystem:

(1) Operating System (OS) and platform providers: these are the actors that create the platform and the software to run apps. For example, Google provides the Android SDK/OS platform.
(2) Hardware and device manufacturers: these provide and develop the hardware device on which the app will be installed. So, e.g., mobile phone manufacturers use the Android OS or have their own version of the Android OS.
(3) App developers: these are the ones who develop the code of the app. They make available the app directly to end-users or via an app provider.
(4) Tool chain providers: they provide the IDEs which are used to create a mobile app (e.g., Android SDK, Eclipse).
(5) Library providers: these build APIs offering new features such as advertising services or develop APIs replacing platform APIs.
(6) App publishers: these are service providers assisting app developers to publish their apps.
(7) App markets and stores: these are operators that provide a gateway to make apps available to end-users (e.g., Google Play, App Store, etc.).
(8) End-users: the mobile device owns who install and use apps.

## §1.03 ECONOMICS OF APPS

### [A] The Economic Importance of Apps

Mobile apps are evolving into a billion-dollar industry, as apps provide value to smartphone owners and bring many commercial opportunities to businesses and job opportunities for the workforce in the technology sector. It is assumed that apps and mobile computing have become the most rapidly adopted technology in one decade, overtaking other innovations such as the printing press.[29] It is a fact, nonetheless, that the app economy has made a positive impact on economy, as mobile application have brought significant revenue to companies and advanced employment.

The mobile app ecosystem is considered today as one of the biggest industries.[30] The number of mobile app downloads amounted to 197 billion in 2017 and is predicted to rise up to 352.2 billion in 2021. The number of apps available is also rising exponentially. The iOS App Store had only 500 apps on its launch, while in January 2017 it offered 2.2 million apps. The Android app store, that is, Google Play, experienced more growth than Apple and reached 3 million apps by June 2017. The revenue from end-users was forecasted to increase from USD 10.3 billion in 2013 to USD 25.2 billion in 2017.[31]

### [B] Distribution of Apps

As mentioned above, mobile apps are being sold at App stores, such as Google Play and Apple's App Store. App stores have a central importance in the distribution of apps, although one can download an app from the developer's website and install it in his/her mobile device. App stores are repositories of apps and have a central directories in which users can search for a specific, as apps are organized in categories, e.g., books, music, news, education, photo and video, entertainment, finance, productivity, games, shopping, social networking, health & fitness, travel, sports, utilities, etc.[32] Categories are very useful, since they help users to discover new apps to their particular needs.

Each app has a product page, in which the features of the apps are mentioned, as well as info on the app developer and/or provider. One can also read in the product page the description of the app, its content rating, users' assessment and comments and other information (*see, e.g.*, Figure 1.5).

---

29. ACT, *State of the App Economy*, 6th edition, p. 1.
30. http://www.businessofapps.com/data/app-statistics/.
31. A. Ghose and S.P. Han, Estimating Demand for Mobile Applications in the New Economy (January 1, 2014). Management Science, Forthcoming. Available at SSRN: https://ssrn.com/abstract=2378007.
32. *See, e.g.*, App Store's categories, https://developer.apple.com/app-store/categories/.

*Figure 1.5 Product Page of Facebook App*

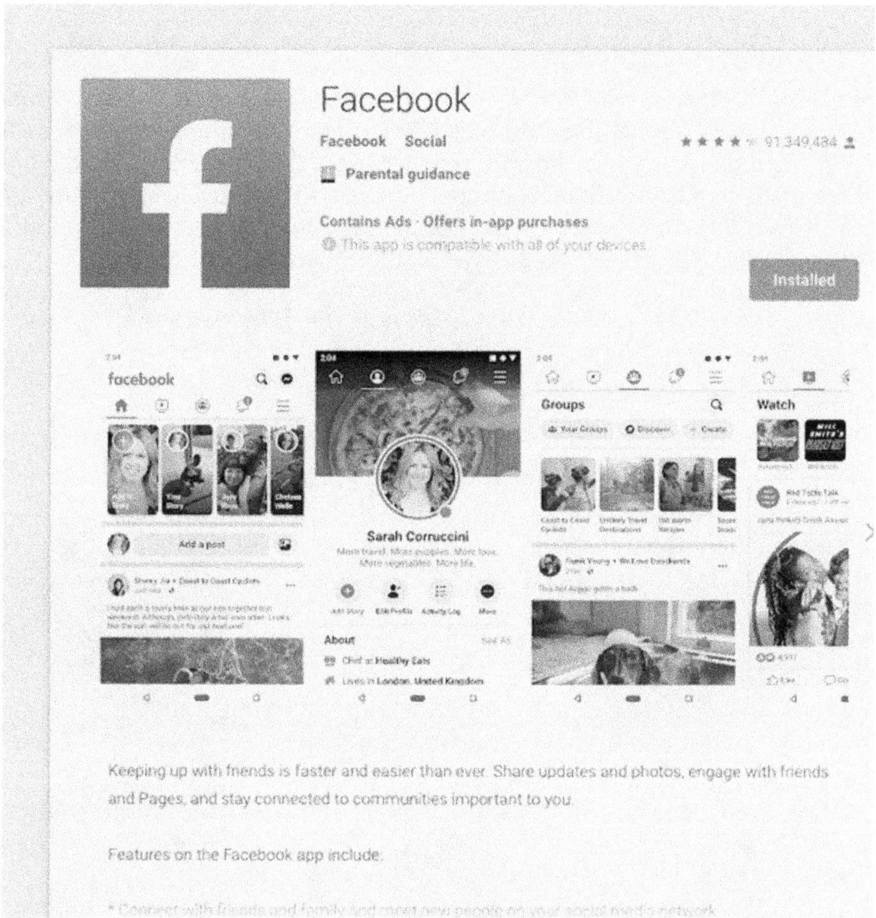


In case an app is chargeable, the user must have already provided his/her credit card's details to the app store. By clicking, then, on the button *buy*, the credit card will be charged by the app store, and the app will be downloaded. Subsequently, the invoice is sent by email to the customer, indicating the app provider as the seller.

When an app is installed, the user controls which capabilities or information the app can access. These are known as permissions, and they are referring to allowing apps to have access to information such as, e.g., device contacts or location. Some apps ask for permission to use information before the installation begins, but in some versions of OS, the user can allow or deny permissions after starting their use. So, e.g., app permissions for Android 6.0 and up include the following: body sensors, calendar, camera, contacts, location, microphone, phone, SMS and storage.[33]

### [C] Pricing

Apps offered on different platforms are either for free or sold at a price which is usually lower than the price of ordinary software. More than 80% of apps are free, as the developer has chosen to offer them for free, while paid apps are those in which the customer pays in advance from the store and received free updates. In those apps which are paid, 20%-30% is disbursed to the app store provider. The average prices for apps in the Apple App Store are 0.88 as of May 2019 (*see* Figure 1.6).[34]

*Figure 1.6 Average Prices for Apps in the Apple App Store*

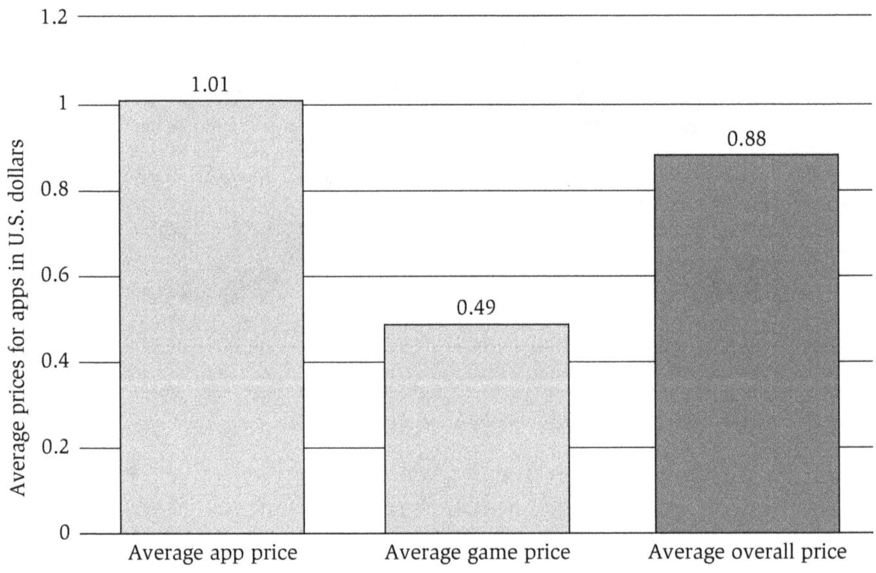


Apps, however, may cost a different price when sold on different mobile platforms. Consumers are divided as to the purchasing of apps, as many only download free apps, whereas others pay for quality apps with more features than apps offered for free. App developers which offer free mobile apps gain revenue from in-app advertising, i.e., advertising in the apps or from in-app purchases, i.e., where users pay for additional digital features and content in the app. In other cases, where apps are offered for free, the developers gain revenue by selling physical goods and services. Hence, app purchasing is not the only source of income for app developers.

33. Control your app permissions on Android 6.0 and up, available at: support.google.com/googleplay.
34. *See* https://www.statista.com/statistics/267346/average-apple-app-store-price-app/.

It should be mentioned that the principal method of monetizing apps for app developers is to offer free apps but including in-app advertising. App stores as well as external providers provide tools for advertising within apps, which is remunerated on the basis of a pay-per-click model. Furthermore, in-app purchasing or micro-transactions within apps are employed to offer apps at premium prices without any advertising.[35]

In addition, there are apps which are free to download, but users can buy auto-renewing subscription inside the app (freemium model).[36] In-app purchases offer customer extra content and features, including premium content, digital goods and subscriptions, directly in the app. Users can buy: (a) different types of consumables, such as lives in a game, which are used only once and can be purchased again; (b) non-consumables, premium features within an app – these are features which are purchased once and do not expire, such as additional filters in a photo app; (c) auto-renewable subscriptions, that is, access to services or periodically updated content, such as subscription to a magazine, and they are charged on a recurring basis, as long as they do not cancel the subscription; and (d) non-renewable subscription, i.e., access to services or content for a limited duration, such as subscription to streaming content.[37]

Finally, there are cross-platform apps which offer digital content for sale within the app, but also allow users to make those purchases on other platforms. In any case, users can consume the content in the app on the device.[38]

## §1.04 THREATS, RISKS AND SECURITY ISSUES

*Anastasios Papathanasiou*

### [A] Introduction

Official app stores tend to have stricter guidelines as to which kinds of apps can be uploaded, as well as how they interact with the device and collect information about users and the device itself. Applications that collect phone numbers, call history, GPS location, Wi-Fi password and other data can be considered as a concern for security.

Apps can sometimes contain malware that may steal important information from the device. Most official app stores have screening processes that detect malicious software and behavior embedded within applications, but these processes are not perfect and there have been instances of suspicious or malicious apps getting through

35. *See* Ghose and Han *supra*.
36. *See* App Store, Using the Freemium-Model, https://developer.apple.com/app-store/freemium-business-model/.
37. *See* App Store, In-App Purchase, https://developer.apple.com/in-app-purchase/.
38. *See* https://www.apple.com/ios/app-store/principles-practices/.

screening and into general availability. Winn Schwartau, Chairman of MobileActive-Defense.com, has mentioned that: "App stores and mobile apps are the greatest hostile code and malware delivery mechanism ever created."[39]

Recently, various reports have shown multiple exploits of app stores via exploiting flaws and zero-day exploits, as well as by installing malicious apps[40] that bypass app store review processes, such as by sideloading, which means installing applications without using the official app store.[41]

The motivations for an end-user to sideload an application from an illegitimate source may vary, such as allowing the use to fine-tune the app experience, giving the ability to work offline, avoiding registration, or login to use the app, remove phoning-home code, or remove in-app advertising. The risk is that the device is then more vulnerable to attacks from applications and that the user accepts all the responsibility that comes with the downloading of the app.

### [B] Approved Applications

Poor implementation of a legitimate application's usage of device information and authentication credentials can thereby expose sensitive data to third parties. Some examples of this sensitive data include location, owner identification (e.g., name, number and device ID), authentication credentials and authorization tokens. Smartphone apps can give automatic access to near-field communications (NFC) payments, SMS, roaming data, premium rate phone calls, etc.

Apps with privileged access to such APIs can allow attackers to take advantage of this to abuse the user's financial resources, with subsequent monetary impact. For example, if an API is able to access the PayPal account details of a user and subsequently use these details to make a purchase from a different device, that proves that the security risks of mobile devices are not limited to just the mobile device.

Data segregation is an approach whereby personal and corporate data are separated, allowing different controls to be applied to each. Although this is less important on corporate-owned devices used only for corporate work, it can be extremely useful in other ownership scenarios, such as personally owned devices which are also used for work.[42]

39. W. Schwartau, Available at: http://www.itsecuritywatch.com/mobile-security/10-great-quotes-aboutmobile-security/.
40. Zero-day exploit lets App Store malware steal OS X and iOS passwords, http://www.macworld.com/article/2937239/zero-day-exploit-lets-app-store-malware-steal-os-x-and-ios-passwords.html.
41. Hacker exploits iOS flaw for free in-app purchases, http://www.macworld.com/article/1167677/hacker_exploits_ios_flaw_for_free_in_app_purchases.html.
42. *See* M.H. Au and K.-K.R. Choo, *Mobile Security and Privacy, Advances, Challenges and Future Research Directions*, 2016.

### [C] Mobile App Risks

With the continuous technological evolution, especially in business, IT auditing and security professionals have to adapt to the changing threat scenario created by mobile applications ahead of risk. To do this, appropriate controls and testing of mobile applications from conception to launch should be put in place.

We could consider the following environment (*see* Figure 1.7) for mobile applications.

*Figure 1.7 Mobile Application Architecture*

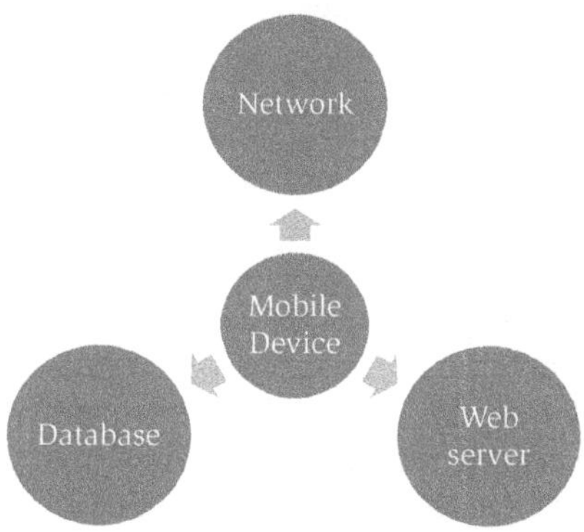


In the center, we identify the mobile device where the app is installed. Then around the device we see the network used by the device to connect to the internet, the web server with which the app is communicating and the databases that the app is accessing.

A recent research has shown the existence of the risks as shown in Table 1.1 which are related to the mobile applications.[43]

*Table 1.1 Mobile Applications' Risks*

| | *Field* | *Risk* |
|---|---|---|
| Mobile Devices | Data storage | Loss and disclosure of data |
| -/- | Data transmission | Loss and disclosure of data |
| -/- | Access and security management application | Unauthorized access and fraud |
| -/- | Take mobile devices outside the business perimeter | Loss or theft of the mobile device, making it possible for unauthorized access to the mobile applications of the device and the fraud of their data |

43. M.J. Khan, *Mobile App Security Audit Framework*, ISACA Journal: mobile apps, no. 4 (2016): 14–17.

| | *Field* | *Risk* |
|---|---|---|
| Network | Wireless connectivity | Data loss and disclosure |
| -/- | Session hijacking | Loss and disclosure of data and unauthorized access |
| Web Server | Access Management | Loss and disclosure of data and unauthorized access |
| -/- | Brute Force Attack | Unauthorized access and fraud, application availability |
| Database | Privileged access | Unauthorized access and fraud |
| -/- | SQL injection | Unauthorized access and fraud |
| -/- | Validation of the application entry (client) | Unauthorized access and fraud |

### [D] Application-Based Threats and Security Issues

Downloadable or preinstalled applications may present various security issues for mobile devices. Preinstalled applications are especially a problem in Android, where bloatware often includes insecure applications which present immediate "out-of-the-box" security and privacy risks. "Malicious apps" may look fine on a download site, but they are designed to handle multiple tasks, such as capture passwords, collect personal information about the end-user without their knowledge, commit fraud, collect information for targeted advertising or facilitate mischief (e.g., exploit a machine to become part of a botnet).

Even some legitimate software can be exploited for fraudulent purposes. Application-based threats generally fit into one or more of the following categories.[44]

(1) Malware

Malware is software that performs malicious actions while installed on your phone. Without your knowledge, malware can make changes to your phone bill, send unsolicited messages to your contact list or give an attacker control over your device.

(2) Malicious Functionality

Malicious functionality include operations such as activity monitoring and data retrieval, unauthorized dialing, SMS, and payments, unauthorized network connectivity.

(3) Electronic Tracking (Spyware or Adware)

- **Spyware** is designed to collect and use private data without your knowledge or approval. Data commonly targeted by spyware includes phone call history,

44. *See* M.H. Au and K.-K.R. Choo, *supra*.

text messages, user location, browser history, contact list, email and private photos. This stolen information could be used for identity theft or financial fraud.

- **Adware** is typically installed unwittingly by the end-user and is a common component of free software such as file sharing applications. It collects information about the user that can be used for targeted advertisements in the form of banners, pop-ups and privacy invasion through the tracking of cookies to correlate online behavior to identify a specific individual, which aids in targeted attacks.

(4) Vulnerable Applications

Vulnerable applications are apps that contain flaws that can be exploited for malicious purposes. Such vulnerabilities allow an attacker to access sensitive information, perform undesirable actions, stop a service from functioning correctly, download apps to a device without the user's knowledge, sensitive data leakage (inadvertent or side channel), unsafe sensitive data storage, unsafe sensitive data transmission or hard-coded password/keys.

(5) Ransomware

Another development is ransomware targeting mobile devices. Examples include Simplocker, CryptoLocker, and since February 2016, Locky. Users will not be able to uninstall the malicious app by traditional uninstall means as one would normally do because the system or even the antivirus (AV) user interface is always "covered" by the malware's user interface.

To protect against these application-based threats, users should consider installing malware, spyware and adware detection software on their mobile devices.[45]

### [E] OWASP: Most Common Security Issues to Mobile Applications

OWASP (Open Web Application Security Project)[46] is an online community of security specialists that have created freely available learning materials, documentation and tools to help build secure web and mobile applications. Among other things, they have compiled a list of ten most common threats to mobile applications (Figure 1.8).

45. *See* the ISACA study at http://www.isaca.org/SiteCollectionDocuments/CSX-Mobile-Payment_whp_eng_0915.pdf.
46. *See* OWASP Mobile Top 10, available at: https://www.owasp.org/index.php/OWASP_Mobile_Top_10.

*Figure 1.8 OWASP Mobile Top 10 Violation Rates*

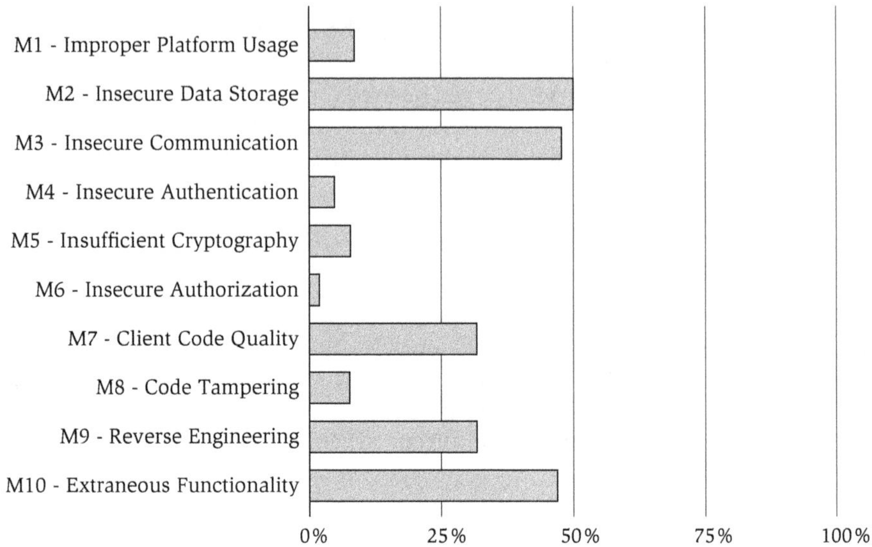


It is difficult for a basic user to understand how these risks can be taken advantage of in the real world and how vulnerable everyday applications can really be. A short overview of the top ten mobile risks and a few examples of real world disclosed vulnerabilities for each risk will be presented below.

Here is the list of *ten most common threats* to mobile applications.[47]

**M1 Improper platform usage**

Misuse of a platform feature or failure to use platform security controls. Might include: android intents, platform permissions, misuse of TouchID, misuse the Keychain, misuse of other security controls.

**M2 Insecure data storage**

This covers insecure data storage and unintended data leakage. Might include: wrong keychain accessibility option, insufficient file data protection, access to privacy resources when using this data incorrectly.

47. *See OWASP Mobile Top 10 Security Risks Explained with Real World Examples*, available at: https://medium.com/swlh/owasp-mobile-top-10-explained-with-real-world-examples-685c2f09e48c.

**M3 Insecure communication**

This might include: poor handshaking/weak negotiation, incorrect SSL versions, cleartext communication of sensitive assets, HTTP instead of HTTPS. For example, the Misafe smart watches where communication was not encrypted and not correctly authenticated.[48]

Attackers could retrieve real-time GPS coordinates of the kids' watches, call the child on their watch, create a covert one-way audio call, spying on the child, send audio messages to the child on the watch, bypassing the approved caller list, retrieve a photo of the child, plus their name, date of birth, gender, weight and height.

**M4 Insecure authentication**

Problems authenticating the end-user or bad session management. Might include: ailing to identify the user at all when that should be required, failure to maintain the user's identity when it is required, weaknesses in session management.

**M5 Insufficient cryptography**

Cryptography was attempted, but insufficient in some way. For example, developer might have used an outdated cryptographic algorithm or written a custom vulnerable algorithm.

**M6 Insecure authorization**

This might include: failures in authorization, (e.g., authorization decisions in the client side, forced browsing, etc.) able to execute over-privileged functionality. It is distinct from authentication issues (e.g., device enrolment, user identification, etc.). For example: Viper smart start.[49] A security researcher discovered that the Viper smart start failed to correctly authorize users. After you log in to the server it was possible to change the id number of the car and gain access among other things the car's location. It was also possible to change data about the car and open the car remotely.

**M7 Client code quality**

Catch-all for code-level implementation problems in the mobile client. It might include: buffer overflows, format string vulnerabilities, various other code-level mistakes where the solution is to rewrite some code that is running on the mobile device. For example: WhatsApp.[50] WhatsApp engineers found that it was possible to create a buffer overflow by sending specially crafted series of packets to WhatsApp when making a

---

48. L. Vaas, Hacking MiSafes' Smartwatches for Kids Is Child's Play, available at: https://nakedsecurity.sophos.com/2018/11/16/hacking-misafes-smartwatches-for-kids-is-childs-play/?source=post_page-----685c2f09e48c----------------------.
49. V. Stykas, *Remote Smart Car Hacking with Just a Phone,* available at: https://medium.com/@evstykas/remote-smart-car-hacking-with-just-a-phone-2fe7ca682162.
50. S. Khandelwal, *Hackers Used WhatsApp 0-Day Flaw to Secretly Install Spyware On Phones,* available at: https://thehackernews.com/2019/05/hack-whatsapp-vulnerability.html?source=post_page-----685c2f09e48c----------------------.

call. For this to work the call does not need to be answered and the adversary can run arbitrary code. It was discovered that the vulnerability was used to install spyware on the phone.[51]

**M8 Code tampering**

It might include binary patching, local resource modification, method hooking and swizzling, and dynamic memory modification.

**M9 Reverse engineering**

It might include analysis of the final core binary to determine its source code, libraries, algorithms and other assets. Reverse engineering makes it easier to exploit other vulnerabilities in the application. It can reveal information about backend servers, cryptographic constants and ciphers, and intellectual property.

**M10 Extraneous functionality**

It might include hidden backdoor functionality and other internal development security controls not intended for production environment.

## §1.05 CONCLUSION

In the recent years we have experienced the exponential growth of smartphones and mobile applications. Since this appeared as an innovation, many users have not been worried about their privacy or the security of their data. However, users of mobile applications become aware of such issues and tend to concern for data security and protection. Thus, for an app developer to build confidence, it is needed to be transparent and clear with the personal data that is collected and with the use made of those data.

Every new information technology platform delivers new benefits and new risks. Applications running on these platforms contribute a large portion of the risk. Mobile applications are no different, and therefore, they should be carefully analyzed for security risks, particularly those identified above as top risks.

51. *See* the ISACA study, available at: http://www.isaca.org/SiteCollectionDocuments/CSX-Mobile-Payment_whp_eng_0915.pdf.

CHAPTER 2

# Contracts

*Evgenia Smyrnaki*

*The purpose of this chapter is to highlight several critical issues concerning the contractual relationships formed between the main key actors (app developers, app providers, platform providers / app stores and end-users) on an app store. The difficulties and uncertainties of applying the existing legal framework in the online app world are illustrated. Predefined answers as to the contract typology cannot be provided, as national contract law still holds a prominent position that is not affected by EU legislation. In addition, the role of app stores as direct counterparties or simple intermediaries is analyzed. Special reference is also made to personal data as a new type of contractual consideration. The research conducted supports the view that the legal approach extensively depends on multiple factors (e.g. type of application, structure and business model of the app store, terms & conditions etc.), which must be considered by the national judge and cannot be handled on an ad hoc basis.*

## §2.01 INTRODUCTION: DEVELOPMENT, DISTRIBUTION AND USE OF APPS: KEY ACTORS

The promotion and sale of applications takes place via online app stores, such as App Store, Galaxy Store, Microsoft Store, Amazon, Google Play etc., or via web pages (with the app stores being the most popular way, though). App stores are online platforms operating as marketplaces,[1] where each application has its own page. The European

1. OECD, An Introduction to Online Platforms and Their Role in the Digital Transformation, May 13, 2019, available online at https://www.oecd.org/innovation/an-introduction-to-online-platforms-and-their-role-in-the-digital-transformation-53e5f593-en.htm.

Commission has defined a platform as "an undertaking operating in two (or multi)-sided markets, which uses the Internet to enable interactions between two or more distinct but interdependent groups of users so as to generate value for at least one of the groups."[2] In the recently adopted Directive (EU) 2019/2161, which amended Directive 2005/29/EU, "'online marketplace' means a service using software, including a website, part of a website or an application, operated by or on behalf of a trader which allows consumers to conclude distance contracts with other traders or consumers."[3]

The four main actors involved in the development, distribution and use of applications via online platforms are the application developers/designers, application providers, platform providers, end-users.[4]

**Application developers** are the entities, either natural (e.g., freelance programmer, student etc.) or legal persons (e.g., software company) to develop and create an application. An application consists of several parts (programming, design, functionalities, web services, etc.). The application downloaded via an app store could be the result of the work of just one person or more than one, working together.

The **application provider** is the supplier of the application to the end-users. The application provider could be the application developer himself or another entity, which has acquired rights to market, sell, license the application. The app provider may have outsourced the services of a developer under an agreement for full transfer of Intellectual property rights.

The **platform providers** provide the marketplace, that would be the virtual online store where the applications are loaded, stored and hosted. In many cases, app stores provide platforms or software development kits used by programmers to develop apps locally on their devices or in the cloud.

The **end-user** (consumer or not) registers in the app store. He interacts with the online marketplace and downloads or is granted access to the application(s), uploaded or made available by the app provider via the app store.

2. Jacques Delors Institut, Berlin, Policy Paper No. 227, Online Platforms and how to regulate them: an EU overview. European Commission, Regulatory environment for platforms, online intermediaries, data and cloud computing and the collaborative economy, Survey document in preparation of a Communication.
3. Article 3 para. 1, Directive (EU) 2019/2161 of the European Parliament and of the Council of 27 November 2019 amending Council Directive 93/13/EEC and Directives 98/6/EC, 2005/29/EC and 2011/83/EU of the European Parliament and of the Council as regards the better enforcement and modernisation of Union consumer protection rules (Text with EEA relevance).
4. Baumgartner/Ewald, *Apps und Recht*, Auflage 2016, pp. 31–32. *See also* Christian Solmecke, Jürgen Taeger and Thorsten Feldmann, *Mobile Apps, Rechtsfragen und rechtliche Rahmenbedingungen*, August 2013, pp. 25 et seq.; Fabian Niemann and Joerg-Alexander Paul (Hrsg), *Rechtsfragen des Cloud Computing, Herausforderungen für die unternehmerische Praxis*, De Gruyter Praxishandbuch, 2014, pp. 160 et seq.

*Figure 2.1 The Relationships Between the Four Basic Actors in the Development, Distribution and Use of Applications*

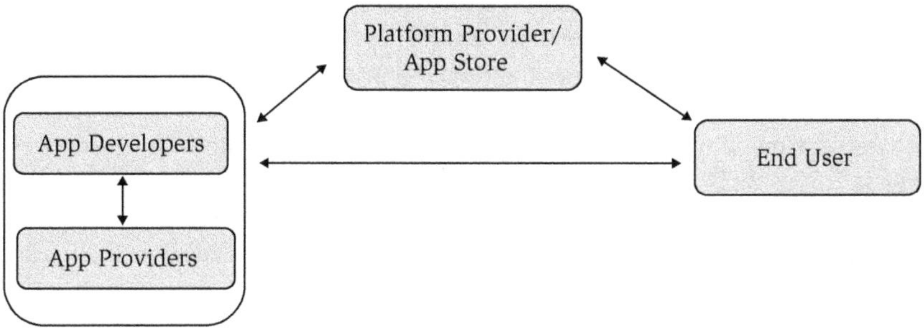


## §2.02 APPLICATION PROVIDERS AND APP DEVELOPERS/DESIGNERS

Apps may be developed by app providers or by another entity (natural or legal person). In case where the app provider engages another person to develop the application under remuneration/payment, a separate legal relationship is created between these parties (app provider and app developer). The application is the result of the personal work of the third party (or third parties), other than the app provider. The third party may be a programmer, designer or any other entity,[5] who may contribute to bringing the application to its final form, ready to be placed on the market.

These parties may work together or separately, and the product of their work shall merge at a later point. The programmer will work on the software, the source code of the application, the functionalities and its operational features. In addition, a graphics designer is needed in order to visualize the interface in a pleasant and attractive way for the targeted audience.

The contractual relationship formed between the app provider and app developer may be qualified either as a contract of services/employment or a contract for services.[6] The classification of the contract into a particular contractual type is the result of a careful consideration of several aspects of their relationship, including the clauses in the relevant agreement concluded between the parties. For instance, the contract is more likely to be considered as a contract of employment rather than a contract for services, where the employer has acquired more control over "what" work is done, "where," "when" and "how" the work is performed.[7] In addition, factors such as the provision of benefits to the developer (e.g., sickness pay), life/health insurance, provision of equipment (e.g., laptops/mobile phones, etc.), may indicate that the

5. Christian Solmecke, Jürgen Taeger and Thorsten Feldmann, *Mobile Apps, Rechtsfragen und rechtliche Rahmenbedingungen*, August 2013, pp. 30 et seq.
6. Mark Freedland FBA and Nicola Kountouris, *The Legal Construction of Personal Work Relationships, Oxford Monograph on Labour Law*, Oxford University Press, 2011, p. 269.
7. In UK the "Control Test" may be applied by the courts in order to determine the contract type. *See* James Holland, Stuart Burnett and Philip Millington, *Employment 2016*, Oxford University Press, 2016, p. 19.

relationship is an employment contract (integration test in common law countries).[8] In such a case, the relationship is subject to labor/employment law provisions. However, if the app provider outsources the services of the app developer and/or designer, who may be a freelancer—independent contractor—the relationship is a contract for works and services.[9] The obligations and rights of the parties largely depend on the clauses included in the software development agreement and the mandatory provisions of the applicable laws.

Classification of the contract between the app provider and app developer/app designer is important, among others, for the ownership/intellectual property rights over the applications developed (software, design, artistic features, etc.). The contract clauses shall be thoroughly considered, especially if the app provider wishes to acquire all Intellectual Property Rights.

## §2.03 APPLICATION PROVIDERS AND APP STORES

App stores, as already mentioned, are online marketplaces where applications are stored, marketed and can be downloaded by the users. App providers have the chance to enjoy a full IT-platform solution offered by the app stores. As a matter of fact, the app stores do not just host the applications, but offer a variety of additional services, such as infrastructure and platform maintenance, auditing, marketing, distribution of apps, payment services. With reference to the contract concluded between app providers and the app store, the multiple technical and operational characteristics and the functionalities of the app store services render it difficult to clearly define the legal role the parties hold. Rather it is the result of a case-by-case approach, depending on the services the app provider has chosen.

Concerning the distribution of the applications, the Google Play store indicates in its Developer Distribution Agreement that the developer/app provider "*appoint[s] Google as [his]* ***Agent*** *or* ***marketplace service provider***."[10] However, such declarations are not the determinants for defining the type of the agreement. Rather, the court seeks to define the real intentions of the contracting parties, by applying contract interpretation rules. Further, Google highlights that "By virtue of Google acting as agent, You acknowledge that the purchase and sale of Your Product(s) is governed by a contract of sale directly between You and users."[11] "Acting as Your agent, and with You acting

8. James Holland, Stuart Burnett and Philip Millington, *Employment 2016*, Oxford University Press, 2016, p. 19.
9. *See, for instance,* Article 631 of the German Civil Code (BGB): "(1) By a contract to produce a work, a contractor is obliged to produce the promised work and the customer is obliged to pay the agreed remuneration. (2) The subject matter of a contract to produce a work may be either the production or alteration of a thing or another result to be achieved by work or by a service." Available online at https://www.gesetze-im-internet.de/englisch_bgb/englisch_bgb.html#p2686.
10. Google Play Developer Distribution Agreement, effective as of November 5, 2019, available online at https://play.google.com/intl/ALL_uk/about/developer-distribution-agreement.html.
11. Play Console Help, Supported locations for developers and merchant registration, available online at https://support.google.com/googleplay/android-developer/answer/9306917?hl=en&visit_id=637144478542897754-630038059&rd=1.

as a principal, Google is the **merchant of record** for Products sold or made available to users in the European Economic Area (EEA) and in the United Kingdom."[12] Google play does not explain the term "merchant of record" in its Definitions Section of the Developer Distribution Agreement. According to the VISA RULES, an entity is classified as a merchant if the entity "represents itself as selling the goods, or the services to the card holder, ... uses its name primarily to identify its Merchant Outlet to the Cardholder, ... provides recourse to the Cardholder in the event of a dispute."[13] A Merchant of Record appears to be the seller in front of the customer.[14] As a matter of fact, in Play Store, Google Commerce Ltd is presented as the direct seller/provider of applications.[15]

In addition, the management and conclusion of payments for the purchase of an application or for in-app purchases is conducted on the app store. The operator of the app store receives a proportion of the price.[16] This payment model facilitates app stores to receive their share from the distribution of applications through their online platform.[17] After all, the engagement of a third-party payment provider, acting independently from the mobile platform, would endanger the economic existence of the mobile platform itself.[18] In addition, an app store provider may offer additional services to the developer, in relation to the building of the applications. Usually, developers are provided with software solutions which enable them to develop applications in conformity with the app store standards.[19] It shall be noted that the app store receives a fee (e.g., annually) from the developers for the provision of these developer program services.[20]

12. Google Play Developer Distribution Agreement, effective as of November 5, 2019, available online at https://play.google.com/intl/ALL_uk/about/developer-distribution-agreement.html.
13. VISA Core Rules and VISA Product and Service Rules, October 19, 2019, available online at usa.visa.com.
14. Evan Minsberg and Andrew Bigart, Venable LLP, *Will the Real Merchant (Of Record) Please Stand Up?*, May 2019, https://www.paymentfacilitator.com/risk-compliance/will-the-real-merchant-of-record-please-stand-up/.
15. "3. Purchases and Payments: Content on Google Play is offered by Google Commerce Limited, and when you download, view, use, or purchase Content on or using Google Play, you will enter into a separate contract based on these Terms (as applicable) with Google Commerce Limited", Google Play Terms of Service for UK, Effective as of January 22, 2019, available online at https://play.google.com/intl/en_uk/about/play-terms/. The same term is included in the relevant Google Play Terms of Service for Germany: "Die Inhalte bei Google Play werden von Google Commerce Limited angeboten und wenn Sie Inhalte bei oder über Google Play herunterladen, ansehen, verwenden oder erwerben, gehen Sie damit einen separaten Vertrag gemäß diesen Nutzungsbedingungen (soweit anwendbar) mit Google Commerce Limited ein", available online at https://play.google.com/intl/de_de/about/play-terms/.
16. Google Play Console Help, Service Fees, available online at https://support.google.com/googleplay/android-developer/answer/112622?hl=en-GB, where it is mentioned that "For apps and in-app products offered through Google Play, the service fee is equivalent to 30% of the price. You receive 70% of the payment. The remaining 30% goes to the distribution partner and operating fees."
17. Jesko Schwarz, *Zugang zu App Stores: Eine Untersuchung des Verhältnisses von App Store-Betreibern und Inhalteanbietern nach Wettbewerbs- und Medienrecht*, NOMOS Verlag, May 2017, pp. 123–124.
18. *Ibid.*
19. *See also* https://developer.apple.com/.
20. *See also* https://developer.apple.com/support/purchase-activation/.

So, as can be reasonably inferred, the contract classification of the relationship between the app store and the app provider highly depends on the specific services offered (e.g., hosting, maintenance, auditing, payment, etc.). The terms governing the versatile relationship between these two actors (app store and app provider) are included in the Developer's Distribution Agreements[21] and are standard and non-negotiable terms. If the contract between the app provider and the app store qualifies as a business-to-business (B2B) relationship, then the protective provisions of consumer law are not applicable, since the app provider is not a consumer.[22] However, app stores which are economically robust international enterprises still hold a more powerful position compared to their non-consumer counterparty (e.g., a freelancer, a small and medium size enterprise, etc.). In an attempt to mediate this imbalance and strengthen trust in the online platform economy, the EU legislator adopted Regulation 1150/2019 on promoting fairness and transparency for business users of online intermediation services (*see* Chapter 11).[23]

## §2.04 APP PROVIDER: APP STORE AND THE END-USER

### [A] Contractual Classification

The activities of the end-users on the app store mainly concern: (a) the access to the online marketplace and (b) the ability to download applications either for free or under a fee. So, by registering in the app store, the user agrees with Terms and Conditions which relate to the use of the marketplace itself. It is common practice that these terms include provisions with the clear tendency to define the different legal relationships created between the app store and the app provider, with reference to the use of the marketplace and the downloading of the applications.

#### *[1] Access to the App Store*

The application(s) is/are uploaded onto the app store by the app provider who may be the developer himself. The user can use the search engine of the app store to find apps of his/her choice. On each app page, he/she is informed mainly about the developer, the entity acting as the trader, the general and special characteristics, price of the applications and comments or reviews from other users of the app. The whole process of acquisition of the application (order, payment, downloading) is concluded via the app store.

21. Google Play, Developer Distribution Agreement, available online at https://play.google.com/about/developer-distribution-agreement.html, Apple Developer Program License Agreement, available online at https://developer.apple.com/terms/.
22. Provided that the applicable laws in the relevant jurisdiction do not indicate otherwise.
23. Regulation (EU) 2019/1150 of the European Parliament and of the Council of 20 June 2019 on promoting fairness and transparency for business users of online intermediation services, available online at https://eur-lex.europa.eu/legal-content/EN/ALL/?uri=CELEX:32019R1150.

First, for downloading an application, the user registers with the app store without any charge (as is the case in most app stores) and is granted access to the online marketplace and the content. Regarding Google Play, the user has to create a Google account and accept the Google Play Terms. The acceptance of the terms is performed at the beginning, before registration is completed. Likewise, in Apple App Store, the user of an iPhone or another Apple device creates an Apple ID. By using the Apple ID, he/she gets access to the app store and accepts the terms and conditions of use. The app store provides the user with a service by offering access to its online environment, hosted on its own servers. In this way, it has been indicated that the legal relationship of app store and app provider with the consumer/end-user of the application falls under the concept of *services contracts.*[24] In terms of private national law, it has been suggested that this relationship is treated according to the law of *mandate.*[25] The end-user is granted access and has the right to use the technical solution of the marketplace for free for a period (usually indefinitely). The services offered include free navigation in the app store and opportunity to engage in further legal transactions by downloading applications.[26]

Application of the "donation" contract type for access and use of the app store is rather rejected.[27] The app store enables the end-user to get access to a service. No gratuitous transfer of ownership takes place.[28]

### *[2] Acquisition of Apps*

The contractual type of the relationship between either the app provider or the app store and the end-user cannot be predefined but is the result of careful analysis of multiple parameters, such as the type of the app, the technical way to acquire the app, the business-payment model and the offered services.

The types of applications available as well as the payment models vary. Applications may be distributed *free of charge,* where the user downloads the application without being charged. If the user can opt for additional functionalities under a fee, then the trader has adopted the so-called *freemium* payment policy. In case of applications offered under a *once fully paid up fee,* the user can download and permanently use the application on his device (tablet, PC, cell phone, etc.). For additional functionalities in the paid apps, the provider may charge extra fees (*in-app purchases*).

It is imperative to clearly identify where the application is offered for free, without any payment/consideration at all. In civil law countries, counter-performance is not a prerequisite for a contract to be formed. Rather it simply affects the classification type of a contract, whether to be considered as a sales, donation (gift), etc. In case

24. Alexander Vorndran, *Die Verwendung Allgemeiner Geschäftsbedingungen beim Vertrieb von Apps*, Duncker & Humblot, Berlin, 2018, p. 236.
25. *Ibid.*, p. 236.
26. *Ibid.*
27. *Ibid.*
28. Part H Donation—1: 101: Contracts Covered, in Principles, Definitions and Model Rules of European Private Law—Draft Common Frame of Reference (DCFR).

of acquisition of free applications, the relationship between the trader and the end-user could be characterized as *donation.*[29] If the acquiring party does not give something in return, then on national law level the provision on donation may apply. The existence or absence of consideration/payment affects the contractual obligations undertaken by the parties. After all in many civil law countries, the donor has limited obligations toward the donee and can be held liable only if specific circumstances are met.[30] For instance, in the German Civil Code, the donor is responsible only for intent and gross negligence.[31] In case where there are legal or material defects, the donee may demand damages for non-performance only in case where the donor fraudulently concealed the defect or was unaware of it due to gross negligence.[32] Needless to say that the gratuitous nature of a contractual relationship (with no consideration at all) may render the Consumer Rights Directive inapplicable. After all, Article 2 paragraphs 5–6 of the Consumer Rights Directive defines that in case of a sales and a services contract, the consumer pays or undertakes to pay a price.

If additional functionalities are purchased (freemium model), the contract type in relation to the additional functionalities, would be that of a *sale contract.* It is obvious that the different performances (free download of an application, purchase of additional functionalities *in the same application*) belong to different contractual types. The contracting parties are the same. In such a case, it should be examined whether the subsequent purchase, affects the initially concluded contract to be considered as a *mixed* one[33] or if the different performances are to be treated as being parts of independent contracts. In order to address the contract type of mixed contracts, the legal theory of absorption or combination may be applied.[34] Thus, if the "principal performance ... 'absorbs' the secondary elements from other contracts,"[35] the rules applicable to the principal performance prevail. This would be the case if the user's main initial intention is to acquire the application with the additional functionality (as a whole) under a consideration,[36] which would mean that the sales provisions would cover the free of charge part of the contract.

However, a parameter which shall be weighted upon is that the applications offered for free may operate independently from the additional features. This means that the mobile user can download and use the basic version of an application, enjoying the functionalities combined with that version. In addition, he does not predetermine that he will opt for the additional paid extensions. He may proceed to acquire them

29. Baumgartner/Ewald, *supra*, pp. 44–45.
30. Janal Ruth, Fishing for an Agreement, Data Access and the Notion of Contract, in Lohsse Sebastian, Schulze Reiner and Staudenmayer Dirk (eds.), *Trading Data in the Digital Economy: Legal Concepts and Tools*, Münster Colloquia on EU Law and the Digital Economy III, NOMOS Hart Publishing, 2017, p. 285.
31. BGB 521.
32. BGB 523, 524.
33. Nils Löflig, *Die App-Ökonomie des Schenkens, Eine rechtsökonomische Analyse zur Haftung von App-Marktplätzen*, 2017, p. 54.
34. Hanoch Dagan and Michael Heller, *The Choice Theory of Contracts*, Cambridge University Press, 2017, p. 172.
35. Michael Stathopoulos, Antonios G. Karampatzos, *Contract Law in Greece*, Kluwer Law International BV, 2017.
36. Nils Löflig, *supra*, p. 54.

under payment at a later time, but he may as well *not*. So, it has been suggested that under such circumstances the performances should be treated as belonging to independent contracts and not a mixed one.[37]

In case of free applications, the app provider may generate revenue by advertisements. However, this does not affect the contract classification between the app provider and the app user as a donation, if the app user does not provide anything as consideration in exchange for the application.[38] The application is still offered free of any charge to the user and the contract cannot be characterized as sales, merely because the provider makes profit out of advertisements.[39]

Where the user is entitled to use the application by paying a one-time (fully paid up) fee (remuneration), the contractual relationship falls within the framework of purchase/sale law.[40] The user downloads the application on his device *permanently* and enjoys functionalities he has paid for. In case an application under a fee offers the possibility of in-app purchases, these shall be treated as different contracts,[41] which will either qualify as sales or lease, depending on the type of service offered.

The approach in the case of cloud or online applications is somehow different. The user simply accesses the application online via his browser or downloads an application on his device. The downloaded application does not function autonomously. Rather, it serves as a tool to gain access to the online service.[42] The use of the application is provided against a periodically or fully paid up fee (monthly, yearly, etc.) for a period of time, and such a contract may be classified as lease.[43] If access to the service is to be terminated, the downloaded application loses any functionality. In cases of online and cloud apps, it is advisable to first identify the offered services. It is commonplace that the trader may offer additional services, such as software maintenance, updates, backups, technical support and helpline,[44] which leads to the formation of a *mixed contract*. While analyzing the mixed contracts, it is important to identify the main/principal contract element which outweighs the others (ancillary services). If the services are of equal value, then the legal provisions pertaining to each separate service shall be applied.[45]

37. *Ibid.*, p. 55.
38. *Ibid.*
39. *Ibid.*
40. Bundesgerichtshof Urt. v. 04.11.1987, Az.: VIII ZR 314/86, available online at https://www.jurion.de/urteile/bgh/1987-11-04/viii-zr-314_86/.
41. Alexander Vorndran, *supra*, p. 114.
42. Baumgartner/Ewald, *supra*, p. 43. *See also*, Alexander Vorndran, *ibid.*, p. 232.
43. Bundesgerichtshof Urt. v. 15.11.2006, Az.: XII ZR 120/04 available online at https://www.jurion.de/urteile/bgh/2006-11-15/xii-zr-120_04/.
44. Christian Solmecke, Jürgen Taeger and Thorsten Feldmann, *Mobile Apps, Rechtsfragen und rechtliche Rahmenbedingungen*, August 2013, p. 111. *See also* Bundesgerichtshof Urt. v. 15.11.2006, *ibid.*
45. *Ibid.*, p. 31.

### [B] App Providers as Prosumers/Hybrid Consumers

An important parameter to define is "who" is the direct counterparty of the end-user in relation to the downloading and use of the applications themselves[46] and in what capacity he interacts with the user. The evolution of digital technology introduced innovative ways of online interactivity and the adoption of a "participatory culture"[47] via online platforms. Private individuals do not only consume services and products available online, but they may as well create services, content and contribute to the online market and digital society.[48] Next to the traditional models of Business to Consumer (B2C) and Business to Business (B2B), comes the **Consumer to Consumer (C2C) model**. As has been aptly put, in the C2C market "some consumers temporarily put on the hat of business and offer their products to other people,"[49] turning into "hybrids acting on different sides of the market"[50] and becoming (producers + consumers = ) prosumers. **Prosumers** are consumers offering products or services on platforms without being professionals themselves.[51] The developer of an application acting also as the provider of the application may not necessarily be a trader having an organized business. The app provider using the app platform could just be a university student, who cannot qualify as a trader, rather as a prosumer. So, the relationship between the app platform and the app provider—prosumer, would be classified as a B2C contract. At the same time, the legal relationship between the application end-user and the app provider/prosumer falls under the Consumer to Consumer (C2C) model.

The legal challenge arising at this point is concerning the applicable regulatory provisions, especially in the framework of consumer protection. In case where the app provider is a prosumer, then the relationship between the app platform (trader) and the prosumer (consumer) is governed by consumer protection laws and the prosumer enjoys the same rights as "traditional consumers."[52] Likewise, where the prosumer does not qualify as "traditional trader" but rather as a consumer himself, the end-user of the application as a counterparty to the prosumer cannot rely on consumer privileges,[53] since the contract between the end-user and the prosumer is classified as a C2C. As a result, the contractual relationship concluded between two consumers (traditional and prosumer) via an online platform is not covered by EU directives on consumer protection, but it is governed by national civil code provisions. EU directives on consumer protection explicitly apply only to any contract concluded between a

46. The access to the online platform (as a service) is differentiated from the acquisition of an application, which is a separate legal relationship formed.
47. Michael Solomon, Rebekah Russell-Bennett and Josephine Previte, *Consumer Behaviour (Buying—Having—Being)*, Pearson Education Inc., 2013, p. 15.
48. *Ibid.*, pp. 15-16.
49. Theresia Theurl and Eric Meye, *Cooperatives in the Age of Sharing*, in Kai Riemer, Stefan Schellhammer and Michaela Meinert (eds), *Collaboration in the Digital Age—How Technology Enables Individuals, Teams and Businesses*, Springer International Publishing AG, 2019, p. 196.
50. *Ibid.*, p. 196.
51. The European Consumer Organization, Ensuring Consumer Protection in the Platform Economy—Position paper, October 02, 2018, available online at https://www.beuc.eu/publications/beuc-x-2018-080_ensuring_consumer_protection_in_the_platform_economy.pdf.
52. Vassilis Hatzopoulos, *The Collaborative Economy and EU Law*, Hart Publishing, 2018, p. 54.
53. *Ibid.*, p. 55.

trader and a consumer. It depends on the Member States' national law whether to extend the consumer protection privileges to cover C2C contracts as well.

So, it is important that clear information is provided to the end-user on whether his counterparty is a consumer/private individual or a trader. The application of the consumer protection laws, applicable law and competent courts depends on such a specification. However, the CJEU judgment in Case C-149/2015 may act as a protection shield for consumers in their capacity as end-users in the online world. The CJEU gives useful guidance by teleologically interpreting the EU Directive 1999/44, to effectively manage the "significant imbalance, concerning information, between the consumer and the professional intermediary, in particular where the consumer is not informed of the fact that the owner of the goods sold, is in reality, a private individual."[54] The Court concluded that by interpretation, the concept of a "seller" in the Directive 1999/44[55] covers also a trader acting as intermediary on behalf of a private individual, which it is for the referring court to determine, taking into consideration all the circumstances of the case.[56]

The case of **dual purpose contracts** is another parameter creating uncertainty as to the applicable legal framework. Dual purpose contracts are contracts concluded for purposes that are partly within and partly outside the person's trade, and where the trade purpose is so limited as not to be predominant in the overall context of the contract.[57] According to Recital 17 of Directive 2019/770, Member States remain free to "determine whether and under which conditions that person should also be considered a consumer." Member States may extend the application of the rules of the directives (Digital Content and Digital Sales) to natural or legal persons, who are **not** consumers (e.g., nongovernmental organizations), start-ups or SMEs.[58] As a result, the directives have been criticized as creating uncertainty at European level. There may be Member States which will adopt a restrictive notion of consumer and not consider that such a person—party to a dual purpose contract—can be classified as one (consumer),[59] whereas there may be Member States which will adopt a different approach.

### [C] Object of the Contract: Goods, Services, Digital Content, Copyright

Mobile apps are of intangible nature. They are mostly downloaded from online stores or preinstalled in smart devices (e.g., phones, tablets, etc.). They are classified as one of the basic categories of software along with operating systems and middleware.[60] In particular, they are "software programs providing functionality focused on a particular

54. C-149/15, 40.
55. Directive 1999/44/EC of the European Parliament and of the Council of 25 May 1999 on certain aspects of the sale of consumer goods and associated guarantees.
56. *See also*, §2.04[E] below.
57. Recital 17 Directive 770/2019.
58. Recital 16 of 2019/770 Directive and Recital 21 of the 2019/771 Directive.
59. Jorge Morais Carvalho, "Sale of Goods and Supply of Digital Content and Digital Services—Overview of Directives 2019/770 and 2019/771," (2019) 5 *EuCML—Journal of European Consumer and Market Law*.
60. Lippoldt C. Douglas and Piotr Stryszowski, *Innovation in the Software Sector*, OECD Publishing, 2009.

task for end users and ... may reside locally on a machine or be delivered remotely."[61] According to existing legislation, applications can be classified as digital content.[62] The digital content can be integrated in products, downloaded (e.g., an application) or even streamed online (music, video applications).

The notion of digital content has already been introduced and regulated in several EU legal instruments. The Consumer Rights Directive (CRD)[63] defines digital content as "any data which are produced and supplied in digital form, such as computer programs, applications, games, music, videos or texts, irrespective of whether they are accessed through downloading or streaming, from a tangible medium or through any other means" (Recital 21 CRD). Although, the above definition is rather broad,[64] it does not expressly cover the case of digital services, which are provided online. As a result, in the initial proposal for the Digital Content Directive[65] (DCD), the definition of digital content was further extended to include both digital content and digital services[66] as well. However, for the purpose of **avoiding inconsistencies** with the definition included in the CRD—which remains in force—, after its adoption the DCD makes a clear distinction between digital content and digital services.[67]

According to Article 2 of the DCD, digital content means "data which are produced and supplied in digital form," whereas "digital services are services which allow the consumer to create, process, store or access data in digital form or a service that allows the sharing of or any other interaction with data in digital form uploaded or created by the consumer or other users of that service." Recital 19 of DCD indicates that "the Directive covers computer programmes, applications, video files, audio files, digital games, e-books, or other e-publications and also digital services which allow the creation, processing of, accessing or storage of data in digital form, including software-as-a-service, such as video and audio sharing and other file hosting, word processing or games offered in the cloud computing environment and social media."

As already mentioned, applications are explicitly characterized as digital content in the DCD. However, not all applications are covered by the scope of the DCD.

61. *Ibid.*
62. DCD 770/2019.
63. Consumer Rights Directive 2011/83/EU.
64. European Commission, DG Justice Guidance Document concerning directive 2011/83/EC, June 2014, p. 64, available online at https://www.cr-online.de/crd_guidance_en.pdf.
65. Proposal for a Directive of the European Parliament and of the Council on certain aspects concerning contracts for the supply of digital content, COM(2015) 634 final, Brussels 9.12.2015, available online at https://eur-lex.europa.eu/legal-content/EN/TXT/PDF/?uri=CELEX:52015PC0634&from=EN.
66. COM (2015) 634 final, *ibid*: "'digital content' means (a) data which is produced and supplied in digital form, for example video, audio, applications, digital games and any other software, (b) a service allowing the creation, processing or storage of data in digital form, where such data is provided by the consumer, and (c) a service allowing sharing of and any other interaction with data in digital form provided by other users of the service."
67. European Parliament, Explanatory Statement, included in the REPORT on the proposal for a directive of the European Parliament and of the Council on certain aspects concerning contracts for the supply of digital content (COM(2015)0634—C8-0394/2015—2015/0287(COD)), 27.11.2017, available online at http://www.europarl.europa.eu/sides/getDoc.do?pubRef=-//EP//NONSGML+REPORT+A8-2017-0375+0+DOC+PDF+V0//EN.

The Directive does not apply in cases where "the main subject matter of the contract is the provision of professional services, such as translation services, architectural services, legal services or other professional advice services, which are often performed personally by the trader, regardless of whether digital means are used by the trader in order to produce the output of the service or to deliver or transmit it to the consumer."[68] In the Proposal of the DCD, the wording used referred to "services performed with a predominant element of human intervention,"[69] indicating that the human intervention and parameter is of central importance.

Embedded software constitutes another type of software,[70] which is "permanently embedded in a given hardware unit,"[71] defines or controls the way of operation of the hardware[72] and is widely used in everyday economies and activities. The interrelationship and level of interdependence of the software and the hardware depends on the functionalities of each specific product.

Characteristic modern examples of applications embedded in goods are the cases of a smartwatch, smart TV or even a smart phone with preinstalled applications in order to function. Many such wearable and smart devices, which operate with the use of applications, are based on a more advanced technology, the Internet of Things (IoT). IoT "refers to an infrastructure in which billions of sensors embedded in common, everyday devices—"things" as such, or things linked to other objects or individuals—are designed to record, process, store and transfer data and, as they are associated with unique identifiers, interact with other devices or systems using networking capabilities."[73] Sensors, cameras, microphones, trackers, GPS, activity counters are "connected" to devices. Data pertaining to the use of the device is collected and transmitted to the manufacturer. In addition, by use of IoT home devices can be controlled over the internet ("Home automation"—Domotics) such as light bulbs, smoke alarms, washing machines, ovens etc.[74] So, IoT offers a technologically advanced way for the provision of a digital service or digital content in combination with hardware.

Where the digital content is "incorporate[d] or inter-connecte[d] with digital content or a digital service in such a way that the absence of that digital content or digital service would prevent the goods from performing their functions" (Recital 21, DCD), then we enter the realm of the Directive 2019/771[75] and of "goods with digital elements." Goods with digital elements refer to "any tangible movable items that

68. Recital 27 in combination with Article 5 para. A of the Digital Content Directive.
69. Proposal for a Directive of the European Parliament and of the Council on certain aspects concerning contracts for the supply of digital content COM/2015/0634 final—2015/0287 (COD) https://eur-lex.europa.eu/legal-content/EN/TXT/?uri=celex%3A52015PC0634.
70. Embedded software is not analyzed in this chapter.
71. Lippoldt C. Douglas and Piotr Stryszowski, *supra*.
72. Bart Broekman and Edwin Notenboom, *Testing Embedded Software*, Addison-Wesley, 2003.
73. WP29, Opinion 8/2014 on the on Recent Developments on the Internet of Things, 16 September 2019.
74. *Ibid*.
75. Directive (EU) 2019/771 of the European Parliament and of the Council of 20 May 2019 on certain aspects concerning contracts for the sale of goods, amending Regulation (EU) 2017/2394 and Directive 2009/22/EC, and repealing Directive 1999/44/EC.

incorporate or are inter-connected with digital content or a digital service in such a way that the absence of the digital content or would prevent goods from performing their functions" (Article 2(3) DCD).

National contract law does not specify whether a digital content contract shall be classified as a **sales** or **services** contract. The answer to this question depends largely on the definition of the type of the digital content either as goods or as services.[76] In addition, there are those who support the view for the creation of a **sui generis** contract.[77] Rights and obligations of traders and consumers vary in relationship to whether digital content provision is considered as "sales" or "goods." CRD indicates that "If digital content is supplied on a tangible medium, such as a CD or a DVD, it should be considered as goods within the meaning of this Directive." In addition "Similarly to contracts for the supply of water, gas or electricity, where they are not put up for sale in a limited volume or set quantity, or of district heating, contracts for digital content which is **not supplied on a tangible medium** should be classified, for the purpose of this Directive, neither as sales contracts nor as service contracts."

In case of ***sales*** contract, one party (called the seller) transfers ***ownership*** of goods to his counterparty, the purchaser/buyer. As indicated by the CJEU, ownership can be on an item not only of tangible property but also of intangible one,[78] thus covering the case of digital items, such as applications which are downloaded online and are not embedded in physical carriers before the sale. The main two attributes of the "sale" are "the permanence of such a transfer and appropriate remuneration obtained by the right holder, usually for an upfront fee."[79] So, if an application is downloaded on a mobile device under a fee permanently, then a *sale* of that specific copy of the application has taken place. Another parameter to be considered is the fact that the downloading of applications from online stores is subject to specific terms included in multi-paged "terms and conditions of use" or "licenses." These terms provide whether the app provider may allow the copy of the application downloaded onto the user mobile device to be used permanently or for a limited time period and the rights conferred upon the user. In case of sale, it is considered that the license and the copy of the work cannot be viewed separately but rather as whole. In the case of computer software downloaded online, the CJEU has already concluded that "the downloading onto the customer's server of a copy of the computer program on the rightsholder's website and the conclusion of a user license agreement for that copy form an indivisible whole which, as a whole, must be classified as a sale."[80]

---

76. Lucie Guibault and Natali Helberger, *Digital Consumers and the Law: Towards a Cohesive European Framework*, Wolters Kluwer, 2012.
77. Natalia Helberger, Marco B.M. Loos, Lucie Guibault, Chantal Mak and Lodewijk Pessers, "Digital Content Contracts for Consumers," (2003) 36 *Journal of Consumer Policy*, available online at https://pure.uva.nl/ws/files/1870764/122561_374238.pdf.
78. C-128/2011, *UsedSoft GmbH v. Oracle International Corp.*: "42. According to a commonly accepted definition, a 'sale' is an agreement by which a person, in return for payment, transfers to another person his rights of ownership in an item of tangible or intangible property belonging to him."
79. Masa Savic, "The Legality of Resale of Digital Content after Usedsoft in Subsequent German and CJEU Law," (2015) 37 *European Intellectual Property Review* 414–429.
80. C-128/2011, *supra*.

This may be so, but at the same time, it is unquestionable that applications are subject to intellectual property, falling under the protection (among others) of copyright laws.[81] Applications are not only software per se. It is rather a mixture of software and artistic works. Software is the fundamental element of an application, but it also consists of interface, audiovisual images, etc. Copyright law differentiates between the protected work itself (an intellectual creation, by definition intangible) and a copy of the work (which can be tangible, e.g., a paper book, or digital, e.g., an e-book).[82]

Sales contracts involve transfer of ownership. So, in case of sale/purchase of application, we need to define the item/property which is transferred. Would it be the intellectual property rights or just the rights to use the specific copy of the application downloaded? It is important to differentiate between the intellectual property rights on the works contained in the application and the copy of the work which is sold.

The relationships between the user and copyright holders are regulated not only by the relevant contract law and contractual clauses but are also subject to applicable copyright provisions. Contracts have an "in personam character" since they are enforceable only against the parties involved in the contract,[83] whereas copyright is a "right against the world" (i.e., in rem),[84] granting exclusive rights.

### [D] Consideration Other than "Traditional" Money

The validity of the formation of a digital content contract depends on the principles of the applicable national law. In order for a contract of sales or services to be concluded, the one party provides the good or service, whereas the other party may be obliged to a counter-performance (most commonly payment in money), if the contract type is not of a gratuitous nature. For instance, in a purchase of a bicycle, the seller transfers ownership of the bicycle and the buyer undertakes to pay the agreed price. In the online app world, the traditional model of money as payment/consideration tends to be substituted by new methods of transactions. Consideration may be anything else other than money as direct payment. It is common practice that the user—consumer contracts with the app provider in order to download an application. The consumer may not have to pay money in order to gain access to and use the application. Rather, he is informed by the app provider that use of the application is possible in exchange for access and use of a large amount of the consumer's personal data (such as contact

81. Rafal Mańko, "Contracts for Supply of Digital Content—A Legal Analysis of the Commission's Proposal for a New Directive," European Parliamentary Research Service. Available online at http://www.europarl.europa.eu/RegData/etudes/IDAN/2016/582048/EPRS_IDA%282016%29582048_EN.pdf. Natalia Helberger, Marco B.M. Loos, Lucie Guibault, Chantal Mak and Lodewijk Pessers, *supra*.
82. Rafal Mańko, *supra*.
83. James G.H. Griffin, "The Interface Between Copyright and Contract: Suggestions for the Future," (2011) 2(1) *European Journal of Law and Technology*, available online at http://ejlt.org/article/view/23/110.
84. *ProCD, Inc. v. Zeidenberg*, 86 F.3d 1447 (7th Cir. 1996), available online at https://www.courtlistener.com/opinion/720542/procd-inc-v-zeidenberg/.

details, friends' list). In other words, the user is asked to "pay" with his/her personal data. By accepting the relevant terms and conditions on his/her phone/tablet screen, he/she grants the app provider the right to use his/her personal data and subsequently, he can download and use the application.

The Consumer Rights Directive in 2011 did not contain any definition of what constitutes a "price" to be paid by the consumer, something which happens almost eight years later in the Digital Content Directive. The EU legislator had understood the urgent need to bring under the umbrella of consumer protection, contractual relationships based on newly introduced revenue/business models (e.g., with payment other than "traditional" currency/money). In addition, Directive 2019/2161/EU amends the CRD extending its scope "to cover also contracts under which the trader supplies or undertakes to supply a digital service to the consumer, and the consumer provides or undertakes to provide personal data."[85]

It is noteworthy, however, that the House of Lords in the UK back in 2015 took into consideration the payment methods which are widely used in the online market and supported by technical means. As a result, the Consumer Rights Act 2015 in the UK applies also to digital content that has been "paid for with a facility, such as a token, virtual currency, or gift voucher, that was originally purchased with money (e.g., a magic sword bought within a computer game that was paid for within the game using 'jewels' but those jewels were originally purchased with money)."[86] The UK legislator in 2015 did not extend the scope of the CRA to cover personal data as consideration. However, he explicitly highlighted that "Government reserves the power to extend the coverage of the digital content provisions to digital content contractually supplied in exchange for something else of value other than money (e.g., in exchange for personal data) in the future, should the Secretary of State be satisfied that there is significant consumer detriment resulting from these sorts of contracts."[87]

The EU legislator acknowledges that such business models (with modern forms of payment—other than "traditional" money) are used in a considerable part of the market.[88] As a result, the term "price" is further construed to include money or a digital representation of value that is due in exchange for the supply of digital content or a

85. Recital 33. *See also* Article 4, 2(b) Amendments to Directive 2011/83/EU: "This Directive shall also apply where the trader supplies or undertakes to supply digital content which is not supplied on a tangible medium or a digital service to the consumer and the consumer provides or undertakes to provide personal data to the trader, except where the personal data provided by the consumer are exclusively processed by the trader for the purpose of supplying the digital content which is not supplied on a tangible medium or digital service in accordance with this Directive or for allowing the trader to comply with legal requirements to which the trader is subject, and the trader does not process those data for any other purpose."
86. Explanatory notes para. 174, Consumer Rights Act 2015, Chapter 3, available online at http://www.legislation.gov.uk/ukpga/2015/15/notes/contents.
87. *Ibid.*
88. Recital 24, Digital Content Directive 770/2019. "Digital content or digital services are often supplied also where the consumer does not pay a price but provides personal data to the trader. Such business models are used in different forms in a considerable part of the market. While fully recognising that the protection of personal data is a fundamental right and that therefore personal data cannot be considered as a commodity, this Directive should ensure that consumers are, in the context of such business models, entitled to contractual remedies. This Directive

digital service (Article 2 paragraph 7).[89] In addition, the DCD also applies where the digital content or service are supplied in exchange for personal data.[90]

The legal question arising is whether personal data can be treated as "consideration" under contract law terms and if such payment models survive ethical standards. The EU Legislator explicitly stated that personal data cannot be considered as a commodity,[91] but at the same he recognizes the wide adoption of such business models and chooses to ensure that consumers are, in the context of such models, entitled to remedies.[92] However, he refrains from enacting rules on the validity of such contracts and underlines the discretionary power of each Member State to determine whether the requirements for the formation, existence and validity of a contract under national law are fulfilled.

Personal data are offered as "consideration" without the user even realizing it. Many online applications are labeled as free. By downloading and making use of them, they indicate that they need access to the personal data in order to improve their services or make their advertising personalized. In case the trader (app provider) has violated data protection law, it remains a question whether the contract is still valid. Under General Data Protection Regulation 679/2016 (GDPR), consent must be freely given, specific and informed. The consent is not freely given if the data subject is unable to refuse or withdraw consent without detriment.[93] The Article 29 Working Party (WP) Guidelines on consent include a characteristic example of withdrawal of consent with detriment, where a user downloads a lifestyle application and the app asks the user for consent to access the phone's accelerometer, something not necessary for the app to work.[94] However, when the user revokes consent, she realizes that the application works to a limited extent.[95] In such a case, as is indicated by the Article 29 WP, the consent was never validly obtained under data protection rules. Would that mean that the contract which has been concluded between the app provider and the app user is also not valid under contract law?

Scholars indicate that consent under GDPR and contract law shall be considered separately.[96] They infer arguments from the legal instrument GDPR 679/2016 itself (Article 7(2) and Article 6(1)(b)). Article 7(2) GDPR mandates that consent under

should, therefore, apply to contracts where the trader supplies, or undertakes to supply, digital content or a digital service to the consumer, and the consumer provides, or undertakes to provide, personal data."

89. Recital 23, Digital Content Directive 770/2019.
90. Recital 24, Digital Content Directive 770/2019.
91. *See* Recital 24 of the Digital Content Directive, available online at https://data.consilium.europa.eu/doc/document/PE-26-2019-INIT/en/pdf.
92. *Ibid*. Recital 24.
93. Recital 42, GDPR.
94. Article 29 Working Party, Guidelines on consent under Regulation 679/2016, 10/04/2018 available online at https://ec.europa.eu/newsroom/article29/item-detail.cfm?item_id=623051.
95. *Ibid*.
96. Martin Schmidt-Kessel, *Part 3—Processing of Personal Data*, in Alberto De Franceschi and Reiner Schulze (eds), *Digital Revolution—New Challenges for Law*, C.H. Beck, NOMOS, 2019, p. 77.

GDPR should be distinguished from consent asked for other matters.[97] Another argument in favor of the above view is that Article 6(1)(b) again separates the two consents. It indicates that if data processing is necessary for the performance of a contract, then consent under GDPR is not essential.[98] If the data processing is a separate act, a separate and clear consent is entailed. However, it has been suggested that such contracts could be rendered void according to the doctrine of illegality.[99] The doctrine of illegality is based on the "Ex turpi causa non oritur actio," meaning that "no cause of action may be founded on an immoral or illegal act."[100] As a result, if data processing is unlawful under data protection law, then the contract which involves the unlawfully processed data is invalid. However, it has been suggested as a counter argument, that data and contract law should still remain independent. Invalidity of such a contract would leave the data subject in an even weaker position toward the app provider, deprived of important legal remedies.[101] In addition, it would add uncertainty to contractual relationships formed.[102] In any case though, it is up to the national judge to decide on the validity of a contract, as explicitly indicated in the DCD.[103]

### [E] Case of Underage/Minor App Store Users

Children constitute a large proportion of the app market in the digital world. Their use of online platforms and applications begins at a very young age and is extremely extensive. They are more familiar than adults with the technical ways the smart devices and online platforms work. Yet they are still the vulnerable and weaker parties in an online transaction,[104] where the user must agree to long, predefined terms and conditions which contain difficult and complicated legal language.

---

97. GDPR 679/2016, Article 7 Conditions for Consent, "2. If the data subject's consent is given in the context of a written declaration which also concerns other matters, the request for consent shall be presented in a manner which is clearly distinguishable from the other matters, in an intelligible and easily accessible form, using clear and plain language. Any part of such a declaration which constitutes an infringement of this Regulation shall not be binding."
98. Schmidt-Kessel, *Part 3—Processing of Personal Data*, in De Franceschi and Schulze, *Digital Revolution—New Challenges for Law, supra*, p. 78.
99. Dr. Philipp Hacker, Regulating the Economic Impact of Data as Counter-Performance: From the Illegality Doctrine to the Unfair Contract Terms Directive, May 2019, available online at https://papers.ssrn.com/sol3/papers.cfm?abstract_id=3391772.
100. Lincoln Caylor and Martin S. Kenney, "In Pari Delicto and Ex Turpi Causa: The Defence of Illegality—Approaches taken in England and Whales, Canada and the US," (2017) 18(3) *Business Law Journal*.
101. Dr. Philipp Hacker, "Regulating the Economic Impact of Data as Counter-Performance: From the Illegality Doctrine to the Unfair Contract Terms Directive," May 2019, available online at https://papers.ssrn.com/sol3/papers.cfm?abstract_id=3391772.
102. *Ibid.*
103. Digital Content Directive, Recital 12: "This Directive should not affect national law to the extent that the matters concerned are not regulated by this Directive, such as national rules on the formation, validity, nullity or effects of contracts or the legality of the digital content or the digital service … ."
104. Marco B.M. Loos, CSECL et al., Final Report—Comparative analysis, Law & Economics analysis, assessment and development of recommendations for possible future rules on digital content contracts, Centre for the Study of European Contract Law (CSECL), Institute for

Legislation on the legal capacity of minors to enter into binding agreements is not harmonized in EU Member States and in other non-EU jurisdictions. The age limits and respective ability to enter into a contract varies around the world. When someone is 18 years old, then generally he is considered an adult and fully capable of contracting,[105] yet not absolute in all jurisdictions. Those who are considered under aged may have limited contractual capacity or not at all, depending on the provisions of each legal system.[106] For instance, in Germany "a minor who has reached the age of seven has limited capacity to contract under sections 107 to 113 [of the German Civil Code].[107] For a declaration of intent as a result of which [the minor] does not receive only a legal benefit, a minor requires the consent of his legal representative."[108] So, if the minor does not acquire only benefits or the contract is not "at least neutral"[109] to the minor's situation, then the consent of the parents is essential. In the French Civil Code, lack of legal capacity to enter a contract renders it ineffective. However, the party who has contracted with the minor, "may defend an action for annulment brought against him by establishing that the act was **useful** to the protected person and was free from substantive inequality, or that he **profited** from it."[110] In English law, contracts with minors are void or voidable. Contracts for necessities and beneficial contracts of service could under circumstances be enforceable.[111]

So, if the minor receives only **benefits** from the contract, then the contract may be regarded as enforceable. It is yet to define what equates "benefit" for the under aged consumer in the online marketplace. In the offline world, "benefit" would be giving the minor a bicycle for free and without the minor having any other obligations.

App stores clearly define in their terms of service, that they do not accept registration for persons who are under 13 years of age. Apple indicates that "You must be age 13 (or equivalent minimum age in your Home Country, as set forth in the registration process) to create an Apple ID and use our Services. Apple IDs for persons under this age can be created by a parent or legal guardian using Family Sharing or by an approved educational institution."[112]

---

Information Law (IViR), Amsterdam Centre for Law and Economics (ACLE), available online at https://dare.uva.nl/search?identifier=7d3d806d-8315-4aa6-8fb6-1fc565d2b557 (p. 134).

105. *See* France, Code civil—Article 388, available online at https://www.legifrance.gouv.fr/affichCodeArticle.do?cidTexte=LEGITEXT000006070721&idArticle=LEGIARTI000006427141&dateTexte=&categorieLien=cid, Germany, Civil Code article 2 and 108 available online at https://www.gesetze-im-internet.de/englisch_bgb/.

106. Marco B.M. Loos, CSECL et al., *supra*, p. 138.

107. Section 106, Limited capacity for minors to contract, German Civil Code available online at https://www.gesetze-im-internet.de/englisch_bgb/englisch_bgb.html#p0321.

108. Section 107, German Civil Code, Consent of legal representative.

109. Basil S. Markesinis, Hannes Unberath and Angus C. Johnston, *The German Law of Contract: A Comparative Treatise*, Second Edition, Hart Publishing, 2006, p. 233.

110. French Civil Code 2016, Article 1151, available online in English at https://www.trans-lex.org/601101/_/french-civil-code-2016/ and in French at https://www.legifrance.gouv.fr/affichCode.do;jsessionid=745F4A1D175E15C4DC773EF1C5723D80.tplgfr21s_2?idSectionTA=LEGISCTA000032008380&cidTexte=LEGITEXT000006070721&dateTexte=20190829.

111. Richard Store, *The Modern Law of Contract*, Sixth Edition, Cavendish Publishing Ltd, 2005, p. 180.

112. https://www.apple.com/legal/internet-services/itunes/us/terms.html.

Taking the above into consideration, the minor can validly create an account in an app store, provided that the creation is considered at least neutral for the minor.[113] Predefined answers do not exist, but it is rather a result of a case-by-case analysis[114] depending on the terms the minor has accepted and the relevant obligations imposed on him. In order to indicate whether the contract is disadvantageous to the minor, close attention must be paid to the consideration provided, especially where data exchange is involved, and to consent related issues. When the minor creates an account, he does not have to pay, but he does have to accept terms, which can be considered as entering into a disadvantageous situation.[115] For instance, the minor user by clicking on the "I agree/accept" option waives certain legal rights or accepts limited liability of the app store provider. The questions about minors entering into app store agreements becomes more complicated, as we shall consider the formation of a contract where the minor/**juvenile** offers as **counter-performance** his/her personal data,[116] which can be considered as disadvantageous situation in terms of contract law.

In addition, (as already mentioned) there are applications which are called freemium and enable for in-app purchases. The user can download and use the application, but in order to enjoy additional functions, he must pay. Financial details such as debit or credit card numbers are stored in the app stores and the purchases can be made instantly. The "buyer" just has to click on the purchase or "get" button/option. What if a minor is using his parent's smart device and concludes a purchase without the parent being aware? The parent appears to have paid, but will he be bound by a contract concluded by his child? One could argue that the parent has not intended to be legally bound by such a contract, especially if no parental authorization preceded the transaction. However, there are jurisdictions where the contract is effective, if the parents ratify/consent to the agreement *after* it has been concluded.[117] In any case, the type of parental consent (explicit or implied) should be examined. After all, if a parent allows the child to use the smart phone, where (he expects that) the child can have access to an app store or to his verification/authentication data,[118] implied consent[119] could be a defense for an app store. This would be a matter of national contract rules and left to the national judge to decide based on the facts of the case.

According to GDPR 679/2016, juveniles may consent to the processing of their data provided that they are over 16 years old. A Member State may provide for lower

113. Samir Buhl, *Der App-Download, Rechtliche Analyse eines Alltagsphänomens unter besonderer Berücksichtigung von Vertragsschluss, Vertragstyp und Vertragsinhalt aus Sicht des Nutzers, Juristische Schriftnreihe*, Band 297, LIT Verlag, 2019, p. 80.

114. *Ibid.*, p. 80.

115. *Ibid.*, p. 81.

116. Dr. Axel Metzger, "Data as Counter-Performance: What Rights and Duties do Parties Have?," (2017) 8(1) *Journal of Intellectual Property, Information Technology and E-Commerce Law*, available online at https://www.jipitec.eu/issues/jipitec-8-1-2017/4528.

117. *See* German Civil Code Article 108, where it is stated that "Section 108: Entry into a contract without consent (1) If the minor enters into a contract without the necessary consent of the legal representative, the effectiveness of the contract is subject to the ratification of the legal representative … ."

118. App stores apply additional authentication measures, which may request from the user to verify his identity by use of his codes (e.g., Apple ID).

119. Samir Buhl, *supra*, p. 86.

age standards (13 years old) by enforcing relevant law. So, there may be conflict at this point, where the juvenile has validly consented to the use of his personal data under GDPR but at the same time ***is not*** legally bound to the contract for the provision of the service due to contract law issues. It has been argued that "the stricter general contract law principles of minor protection must be respected [and] If the parents have not authorized the contract, it must be regarded as void. Still, the consent given by the minor could be regarded as valid based on Art. 8 GDPR."[120] It shall be noted that even the validity of the consent under GDPR could be challenged as not being freely given. Recital 42 indicates that "consent should not be regarded as freely given if the data subject has no genuine or free choice or is unable to refuse or withdraw consent without detriment." If the juvenile withdraws consent and has negative consequences in return (i.e., he/she may have no more access to the service or may not enjoy the same service functionalities as before), then this means that the consent was not validly given. The controller must offer evidence in order to prove that the consent was freely given.[121,122] According to Article 7 paragraph 4 GDPR "When assessing whether consent is freely given, utmost account shall be taken of whether, inter alia, the performance of a contract, including the provision of a service, is **conditional** on consent to the processing of personal data that is **not** necessary for the performance of that contract."[123] As the Article 29 Working Party has underlined, "the GDPR ensures that the processing of personal data for which consent is sought cannot become directly or indirectly the counter-performance of a contract. The two lawful bases for the lawful processing of personal data, i.e. consent and contract cannot be merged and blurred."[124]

## §2.05 MOBILE PLATFORMS / APP STORES

App stores have a dominant position in the app marketplace, leaving the impression to the end-users that they are their actual counterparts and suppliers of the applications or relevant services. The question arising pertains to who the actual provider/trader of the applications is, who has the burden to comply with relevant consumer laws and can be held liable in case of contract violation or defective performance.

120. Dr. Axel Metzger, *supra*.
121. Article 29 Working Party, Guidelines on consent under Regulation 2016/679, adopted on November 28, 2017. As last revised and adopted on April 10, 2018, WP259 rev.01.
122. *See also* Article 29 Working Party Guidelines on consent under Regulation 2016/679 and the characteristic example contained therein (p. 11): "When downloading a lifestyle mobile app, the app asks for consent to access the phone's accelerometer. This is not necessary for the app to work, but it is useful for the controller who wishes to learn more about the movements and activity levels of its users. When the user later revokes that consent, she finds out that the app now only works to a limited extent. This is an example of detriment as meant in Recital 42, which means that consent was never validly obtained (and thus, the controller needs to delete all personal data about users' movements collected this way)."
123. *See also* Recital 43 GDPR: "consent is presumed not to be freely given ... if the performance of a contract, including the provision of a service, is dependent on the consent despite such consent not being necessary for such performance."
124. Article 29 Working Party, Guidelines on consent under Regulation 2016/679, adopted on November 28, 2017. As last revised and adopted on April 10, 2018, WP259 rev.01.

Arguably, Recital 18 of the Digital Content Directive extends its scope to platform providers as traders "if they act for purposes relating to their own business and as the **direct contractual partner** of the consumer for the supply of digital content or a digital service." Member States are free to extend the application of the 2019/770 Directive to platform providers that do not fulfill the requirements for being considered a trader under the Directive. In many cases, the app store makes available its own applications so contractual relationships between the two parties (app store and end-user) are not difficult to be defined and respectively regulated.

However, existing legal framework has been criticized as inadequate to deal with the triangular relationships created on an online platform environment.[125] In-between the traditional seller (e.g., app provider) and buyer (e.g., app user) intervenes the online platform provider (e.g., app store), holding—*at least*—the role of mere facilitator of the transaction. After all, app stores *do* determine the standard terms and other key elements of the contractual relationships with app developers and end-users, and even act as payment service providers.[126]

It shall be noted that literature suggests that the app store may well be acting as a representative of the app supplier/provider.[127] In common law, the principal authorizes the agent to act on his behalf and the agent agrees to do so. The agent has the authority to legally bind the principal by concluding contracts with third parties.[128] In civil law countries, agency is commonly referred to as "representation."[129] Such intent to act on behalf of another shall be evident. Otherwise, the lack of intent on the part of the agent (app store) to act on his own behalf (rather on behalf of the principal/represented) is not taken into consideration[130] and the result is that the app store could be considered as the trader—direct counterparty to the consumer.

As a matter of fact, app stores in their terms and conditions tend to restrict their roles to mere intermediaries or "agents" which do not sell or supply services directly to end-users. For instance, Apple clearly states in its terms and conditions that it does not sell apps directly to the users as it merely holds the role of an "agent" and that it is "not a party to the sales contract or user agreement" between the consumer/user and the app provider.[131]

125. Christoph Busch, Hans Schulte-Nölke, Aneta Wiewiórowska-Domagalska and Fryderyk Zoll, "The Rise of the Platform Economy: A New Challenge for EU Consumer Law?," (2016) 5(1) *Journal of European Consumer and Market Law* p. 4.
126. *Ibid.*
127. Baumgartner/Ewald, *supra.*
128. Hugh Beale et al., *Cases, Materials and Text on Contract Law, Ius Commune Casebooks for the Common Law of Europe*, Second Edition, Hart Publishing, 2010.
129. Study Group on the European Civil Code and Research Group on EC Private Law (Acquis Group), Principles, Definitions and Model Rules of European Private Law—Draft Common Frame of Reference (DCFR), Outline Edition, European Law Publishers GmbH, 2009 (Chapter 6: Representation, p. 205).
130. *Ibid.* DCFR *Chapter 6:106: Representative acting in own name. See also* Artikel 164: Wirkung der Erklärung des Vertreters, Bürgerliches Gesetzbuch (BGB) available online at http://www.gesetze-im-internet.de/bgb/__164.html, Article 212 of the Greek Civil Code.
131. Apple Media Services Terms and Conditions: "Apple acts as an agent for App Providers in providing the App Store and is not a party to the sales contract or user agreement between you and the App Provider." "You acquire Apple Books Content from the third-party provider of such Content (the 'Publisher'), not Apple. Apple acts as an agent for the Publisher in providing

In the Apple Developer Agreement, it is indicated that the relationship between the app developer and Apple shall be that of principal and agent, or principal and commissionaire.[132] The developer as principal accepts responsibility for any claims and liabilities related to the applications.[133] Such or similar written declarations are not the ultimate factor which shall be considered to determine the app store's legal role and such terms can be declared invalid for several reasons.[134]

According to basic principles of contract law, the type of the contract and the relevant duties of the parties are the result of contract interpretation and assessment of multiple parameters and factors. There is a need to define and interpret the intentions of the parties involved, their statements or conduct.[135] In addition, the design of the app store and the technical way of distribution of apps shall also be considered.[136] In most cases, the end-user qualifies as a consumer and the legal relationship is subject to consumer law, where it is clearly stated that the consumer shall be informed in clear and comprehensible manner about the identity of the trader.[137] Yet, even if the trader (app provider) is explicitly named, other features and functionalities of the app store are likely to **mislead** or create **confusion** to the user about the actual entity offering the services. For instance, upon concluding a purchase/acquisition of an application in the Apple App Store, the user receives an email with the subject "Your invoice from Apple." The invoice is not coming from the trader of the application whose name may appear in the app page. So, the first impression the consumer gets, is that Apple may be the counter party in their transaction. In addition, in the body of the same email the following notice is found: "To cancel your purchase within 14 days of receiving this invoice, report a problem or contact us. Learn more about your right of withdrawal." The following phrases/sentences: "report a problem," "contact us" and "Learn more about your right of withdrawal," are hyperlinked. Once you click on the hyperlinked

---

Apple Books Content to you, and therefore Apple is not a party to the Transaction between you and the Publisher," available online at https://www.apple.com/legal/internet-services/itunes/us/terms.html (last updated: May 13, 2019).

132. Schedule 1 Appointment of Agent, Apple Developer Program License Agreement, available at https://developer.apple.com/.

133. *Ibid.*

134. An interesting approach has already been made by the respondents in the *Apple Inc. (petitioner) v. Robbert Pepper (respondents)* even though the case relates to violation of antitrust laws. The respondents indicate that Apple cannot use "the agency label to avoid remedy for anticompetitive conduct." They argue that Apple has control in the relationship between App developers and app users. The prominent role of Apple is supported by the nature of the T&Cs as "take it or leave it," by imposing the policy that all prices "end in 99 cents" and by reserving the right to amend contractual terms any time and at will. *See Apple Inc. (petitioner) v. Robbert Pepper et al. (respondents)*, in the Supreme Court of the United States, Brief for Respondents, available online at https://www.supremecourt.gov/DocketPDF/17/17-204/64643/20180924150810273_17-204bs.pdf.

135. Article 2: 102 "The intention of a party to be legally bound by contract is to be determined from the party's statements or conduct as they were reasonably understood by the other party." Principles of European Contract Law, available online at https://www.trans-lex.org/400200/_/pecl/#head_22.

136. Baumgartner/Ewald, *supra*, p. 49.

137. Article 6, para. 1b, Directive 2011/83/EU of the European Parliament and of the Council of 25 October 2011 on consumer rights, available online at https://eur-lex.europa.eu/legal-content/EN/TXT/?uri=celex%3A32011L0083.

phrases/sentences, you are redirected to webpages which are all run by apple and hosted on the Apple domain.[138] Even the form to exercise the withdrawal right is expressly addressed to Apple and ***not*** the trader of the application—whose name may exist on the app page.

*Table 2.1 Extract of Model Cancellation Form by Apple*[139]

| **Model Cancellation Form** |
| --- |
| - To Apple Distribution International<br>iTunes Store Customer Support<br>Hollyhill Industrial Estate, Hollyhill, Cork, Republic of Ireland:<br>- I hereby give notice that I withdraw from my contract for the following:<br>[INSERT ORDER ID, ITEM, ARTIST AND TYPE]<br>- Ordered on [INSERT DATE] / received on [INSERT DATE]<br>- Name of consumer<br>- Address of consumer<br>- Email address of consumer (optional)<br>- Date |

In relation to the results of cancellation, Apple clearly indicates that "**We** will reimburse you no later than 14 days from the day on which **we** receive your cancellation notice. **We** will use the same means of payment as you used for the transaction, and you will not incur any fees for such reimbursement."[140] In addition, the name of the trader (app provider) again is absent. So, the entire cancellation process is conducted by Apple. They do not refer that they act as agents of the trader in the same email, nor do they indicate that they will inform the trader of the cancellation.

The CJEU[141] in several cases which were brought before it has indicated a methodology to be applied and considered in an attempt to discern the roles of the parties in triangular contractual relationships, where one party insists on just being a simple intermediary and not a direct counter party to a consumer. Characteristic example is the *Uber* case, where the terms and conditions indicated that "Uber UK is not a party to the Transportation Contract and acts as a disclosed agent for the Transportation Provider in communicating the Transportation Provider's agreement to enter into the Transportation Contract."[142] However, the Court indicated that Uber is not a mere platform with the purpose to connect by means of a smart phone application

138. URL in order to report a problem: https://idmsa.apple.com/IDMSWebAuth/signin?appIdKey=6f59402f11d3e2234be5b88bf1c96e1e453a875aec205272add55157582a9f61&path=%2F%3Fa%3D537049275%26s%3D1%26wo%3DMN743LTJQ3%26pli%3D65049537630497&language=US-EN, URL for the contact form: https://support.apple.com/en-gb/contact, URL for the withdrawal form: https://www.apple.com/legal/internet-services/itunes/uk/rightofwithdrawal-uk.pdf.
139. https://www.apple.com/legal/internet-services/itunes/uk/rightofwithdrawal-uk.pdf.
140. *Ibid.*
141. C-149/15, *Sabrina Wathelet v. Garage Bietheres & Fils SPRL*. C-434/2015.
142. Uber Terms and Conditions, last updated: March 14, 2018, available online at https://www.uber.com/legal/terms/gb/.

non-professional drivers with persons who wish to make urban journeys, but was regarded as being inherently linked to a transport service.[143]

It is noteworthy that CJEU in *Sabrina Wathelet v. Garage Bietheres & Fils SPRL* accepted a teleological interpretation of Article 1(2)(c) of the Directive 1999/44 (on certain aspects of the sale of consumer goods and associated guarantees) and concluded that "the sale of consumer goods and associated guarantees, must be interpreted as covering also a trader acting as intermediary on behalf of a private individual, which it is for the referring court to determine, taking into account all the circumstances of the case."[144] The facts of the case are related to Ms Wathelet in her capacity as a consumer, who had purchased a second-hand car from Garage Bietheres. When the car engine failed, Ms Wathelet was asked by the garage to pay the repair costs, but Ms Wathelet refused on the ground that Bietheres garage as the seller should cover such costs. Bietheres garage informed her that they were just intermediaries, not sellers and that they never owned the car, which belonged to another woman, herself a private individual. CJEU accepted that the term "seller" as included in Article 1(2)(c) of the Directive 1999/44 does not cover intermediaries. However, it stated that the overall purpose of consumer protection and Article 169 TFEU justify a teleological interpretation of directive 1999/44 so that the seller's liability can be imposed on an intermediary, "who, by addressing the consumer, creates a likelihood or confusion in the mind of the latter, leading him to believe in its capacity as owner of the goods sold."[145]

The above case is not directly related to the online transactions, rather the sale of goods offline. However, the CJEU approach to define the actual role of an intermediary is of high importance. It took into consideration key factors and parameters, having as reference point of its interpretation the high-level consumer protection afforded by primary EU law. First, one shall examine whether the intermediary creates confusion in the mind of the consumer by giving him false impression that he is acting as the seller[146] or if the consumer is "misled in the light of conditions, in which the sale is carried out."[147] Another parameter is whether the consumer is not aware that the trader is acting as an intermediary on behalf of another entity, especially where the other entity is a *private* individual—which results in the consumer being deprived of his consumer protection rights.[148]

143. CJEU C-434/2015, available online at http://curia.europa.eu/juris/liste.jsf?num=C-434/15, where it is stated "In addition, Uber exercises *decisive influence* over the conditions under which that service is provided by those drivers. On the latter point, it appears, *inter alia*, that Uber *determines at least the maximum fare* by means of the eponymous application, that the company receives that amount from the client before paying part of it to the non-professional driver of the vehicle, and that it exercises *a certain control over the quality* of the vehicles, the drivers and their conduct, which can, in some circumstances, result in their exclusion. (40) That intermediation service must thus be regarded as forming an integral part of an overall service whose main component is a transport service … ."
144. C-149/15.
145. *Ibid.*, 41.
146. *Ibid.*, 34.
147. *Ibid.*, 41.
148. *Ibid.*

The CJEU considers the transparency of transactions as an indispensable element of consumer protection.[149] Transparency requirement is satisfied by providing the consumer with the necessary precontractual information and in a way that does not mislead or confuse him. As a result, statements of intermediary platforms, rejecting any direct contractual relationship with the consumers in the purchase of a product, are not enough to predetermine the platform role. Rather, the courts should rely "not only on the presentation of the platform but also [on] the reasonable perception of the platform activity from the viewpoint of the consumer."[150]

Similar approach was followed by the US Court of Appeals for the Third Circuit in the Opinion filed in July 3, 2019 concerning the case *Heather R. Oberdorf v. Amazon.com INC.*[151] The Court of Appeals decided on the case by analyzing the way the Amazon service is working and the prominent role Amazon holds in the transactions made on its website. The Court concluded that Amazon is a *seller* for purposes of § 402A of the Second Restatement of Torts and thus subject to the Pennsylvania *strict products liability law.* It did not accept Amazon's allegations that it is entitled to immunity under section 230 of the Communications Decency Act which indicates that "[n]o provider or user of an interactive computer service shall be treated as the publisher or speaker of any information provided by another information content provider."

The Court considered and accepted the following factors: (a) the sellers of goods (referred to in the decision as third-party vendors) communicate with the customers only through Amazon, (b) the third-party vendors can conceal themselves from the customer, "leaving customers injured by defective products with no direct recourse to the third-party vendor,"[152] (c) "Amazon exerts substantial control over third-party vendors which grants Amazon "the right in [its] sole discretion to . . . suspend[], prohibit[], or remov[e] any [product] listing," "withhold any payments" to third-party vendors, "impose transaction limits," and "terminate or suspend . . . any Service [to a third-party vendor] for any reason at any time," (d) "Amazon is uniquely positioned to receive reports of defective products, which in turn can lead to such products being removed from circulation,"[153] (e) In its contract with third-party vendors, Amazon already retains the ability to collect customer feedback: "We may use mechanisms that rate, or allow shoppers to rate, Your Products and your performance as a seller and Amazon may make these ratings and feedback publicly available."[154]

So, the court of Appeal accepted that the platform intermediary can be held liable for defective products sold through their website/platform by third parties. This decision creates a new precedent for Amazon, especially where there were already

149. Irina Domurath, "Platforms as Contract Partners: Uber and Beyond," (2018) 25(5) *Maastricht Journal of European and Comparative Law*565–581 (p. 576).
150. *Ibid.*, p. 579.
151. United States Court of Appeal for the Third Circuit No. 18-1041, *Heather R. Oberdorf v. Amazon.com INC*, on Appeal from the United States District Court for the Middle District of Pennsylvania (D.C. Civil No. 4-16-cv-01127), argued October 3, 2018, opinion filed: July 3, 2019, available online at https://www2.ca3.uscourts.gov/opinarch/181041p.pdf.
152. US Court of Appeals, *Heather R. Oberdorf v. Amazon.com INC, ibid.*
153. *Ibid.*
154. *Ibid.*

court decisions which ruled against Amazon being held liable for products sold on its web platform, since it was not considered to be the "seller."[155]

The role of the app store/platform is important not only to the consumer himself but to the platform vendors as well. After all, if the mobile platform is considered as simple intermediary, then it may be exempted (under circumstances) from liability based on the safe harbors of the E-commerce Directive which relate to caching, mere conduit and hosting (Articles 12–14). App stores could be considered as hosting providers, since they *do* provide hosting services—storage for the applications.[156] So, it is important to examine the role of the platform provider as being a traditional intermediary within the scope of the hosting safe harbor or a new type of intermediary not compatible with the E-Commerce Directive hosting category.[157,158]

155. United States District Court of Maryland, *Ryan McDonald v. LG Electronics and Amazon.com Inc*, where the United States District Judge stated that "Amazon's role as the 'platform' for the third party sales does not qualify it as a merchant or a seller under Maryland's UCC," available online at https://cases.justia.com/federal/district-courts/maryland/mddce/1:2016cv01093/347907/21/0.pdf?ts=1478870389. *See also Fox v. Amazon.com Inc. et al.*, 2018, US District Court for the Middle District of Tennesse, available online at https://docs.justia.com/cases/federal/district-courts/tennessee/tnmdce/3:2016cv03013/68712/161. *See also Milo Gabby LCC, Karen Keller v. Amazon.com Inc. et al.*, Decided on 23 May 2017, United States Court of Appeal for the Federal Circuit, where it is indicated that "Amazon operates a website that offers an online marketplace for customers. Although Amazon sells some of the products available on its website, most of the products offered for sale on Amazon's website are offered by third party sellers. … We conclude that Milo & Gabby has failed to show that Amazon was a 'seller' under 17 U.S.C. § 106 based on its actions in this case. Section 2-106 of the U.C.C. defines a 'sale' as consisting of 'passing of title from the seller to the buyer for a price.' U.C.C. § 2-106(1). Section 2-103 defines 'seller' as 'a person who sells or contracts to sell goods.' U.C.C. § 2-103(1)(d). … Amazon, therefore, was not responsible for the actual listing of the product for sale, consummating the sale, or transferring title. Instead, Amazon merely provided an online marketplace that third-party sellers could use to sell their products and then, in some instances when the third-party sellers used the additional Amazon services, shipped the products to the final destination. Thus, while Amazon's services made it easier for third parties to consummate a sale, the third parties remained the sellers … ." Available online at http://www.cafc.uscourts.gov/sites/default/files/opinions-orders/16-1290.Opinion.5-22-2017.1.PDF.

156. Commission Staff Working Document on the existing EU legal framework applicable to lifestyle and wellbeing apps Accompanying the document—Green Paper on mobile Health ("mHealth"), (COM(2014) 219 final), Brussels, 10/04/2014.

157. Center for Democracy & Technology, Mobile Platforms as Intermediaries: Liability protections in the United States, the European Union and Canada, September 2012, available online at https://cdt.org/files/pdfs/Mobile-Platforms-As-Intermediaries.pdf.

158. *See* Chapter 11 of this book, App Stores: Liability Issues and the New Regulatory Framework on Online Platforms.

CHAPTER 3

# Intellectual Property Rights in Mobile Apps

*Vasiliki Samartzi*

*This chapter discusses the protection of mobile apps by means of intellectual property rights and intellectual property law issues pertinent to the development, launch and use of mobile apps. The analysis is heavily based on apps that are distributed via mobile app markets/platforms ('app stores') due to the popularity of such business models and the interesting questions raised from a legal perspective. Copyright analysis is underpinned by the three main sets of legal relationships formed when apps are distributed via app stores, that is, the relationship between (1) app developer and app store, (2) app user and app store, and (3) app developer and app user. Due to the extended scope of the particular subject matter and due to space considerations, database, patent, trademark, and unfair competition law protection considerations are discussed in a more unstructured way in the form of selected issues that the writer thinks might be useful and of special interest in the case of mobile app development and use.*

## §3.01 INTRODUCTION

Mobile apps are digital content as stated in the ToU governing the relationships between App Markets (Apple, Android) and the users.[1] In terms of the scope of the term 'app', according to the Apple Media Services Terms and Conditions: 'the term "App" includes apps, iMessage and Apple Watch apps, in-app purchases, extensions

1. For example, Google Play Terms of Service (Introduction section), 5 February 2018, available at https://play.google.com/about/play-terms/index.html (accessed 1 December 2019) provides that: '[...] the apps (including Android Instant Apps), games, music, movies, books, magazines, or other digital content of services ([are] referred to as "Content") [...]'.

(such as keyboards), stickers and subscriptions made available in an app'.[2] The term 'app' is not defined in a similar manner in the Google Play Terms of Service, where there is only provision for Android Instant Apps (apps one can tap to try them without installing them first and which not take up storage on the device) and for Google Play subscriptions. However, in the Google Play Developer Distribution Agreement, apps are included in the wider term 'products' which includes '[s]oftware, content, digital materials and other items and services as made available by Developers via the Play Console'. Such inclusion is not very helpful from an intellectual property law standpoint when the question is whether apps can be protected under intellectual property law provisions. The lack of a characterization of apps that could be indicative of the kind of intellectual property protection that may be afforded to them does not mean that apps may not be protected by intellectual property laws. On the contrary, the various facets of apps, namely computer programs, images, text, and even sounds or videos, may be protected by a bunch of intellectual property rights (IPRs): Copyright protects computer programs which are the basis for mobile applications and may also protect GUIs. Applications, in their capacity as software, can also be patented to the extent they are functional, i.e., they make phones function in a certain way by running a process on a mobile phone that connects to a remote server containing data that either stores the data or processes it to be used on the mobile phone. Trademark and unfair competition laws may be used to protect GUIs in case GUIs have a great impact on apps' acceptance by users. Accordingly, the importance of intellectual property provisions must not be underestimated when examining the legal treatment of apps.

This chapter discusses the protection of mobile apps by means of intellectual property law provisions. The analysis in this chapter is heavily based on apps that are distributed via mobile app markets/platforms (hereinafter 'app stores') due to the popularity of such business models and due to the interesting questions raised from a legal perspective regarding, in particular, intellectual property. In the case of apps distributed via app stores, three main sets of legal relationships are formed: (1) the relationship between the app developer and the app store, (2) the relationship between the user of the app and the app store, and (3) the relationship between the app developer and the user of the app. These relationships shall underpin the analysis throughout the present chapter.

The relationship between the app developer and the app store is dictated by the fact that two types of apps are can be distributed via an app store, that is the app store's own apps ('native apps') and third-party apps. A native app is developed by a developer that is at the same time the manufacturer of the device the app runs on or the owner of the website that offers it. By way of contrast, third-party apps are created by parties not affiliated with the device or operating system manufacturer or owner of the website offering the app, for example, apps created for the official app stores of Apple and Google by vendors other than Apple or Google. In the case of native apps, the app store itself is the IPR holder, while in the case of third-party apps, the rightholder is the

2. Apple Media Services Terms and Conditions (last updated: 17 September 2018), available at: https://www.apple.com/ca/legal/internet-services/itunes/ca/terms.html (last accessed 10 December 2019).

third party developing the app usually in the context of an employment relationship with the app store or in the context of an agreement for the development of software (so-called developer agreement). In such a case, the IPRs in the app should be contractually cleared.

With regard to the Android operating system, the official app store of which is Google Play, it is an open source platform freely available to app developers. In order to develop an Android app, the developer must follow the Developer Program Policies.[3] Google Play, a publicly available service through which one can distribute his/her apps for Android-powered devices while it offers also services such as in-app billing and licence verification, is an optional service for Android apps, alongside other optional services such as Android Studio, Google Maps Android API, Android Cloud to Device Messaging and Android Backup Service, and has its own special terms and conditions. A developer, in order to distribute his/her apps on Google Play, that is to display and make them available for viewing, download and purchase by users (section 2.1), and use the associated services must agree to the Google Play Developer Distribution Agreement[4] by means of which the developer grants to Google a non-exclusive, worldwide and royalty-free licence to: reproduce, perform, display, analyse and use his apps in connection with (a) the operation and marketing of Google Play, (b) the marketing of devices and services that support the use of the apps, (c) the making of improvements to Google Play, Play Console and Android platform, and (d) the checking of compliance with the Google Play Developer Distribution Agreement and the Developer Programme Policies (section 5.1). Moreover, the developer grants Google a non-exclusive and royalty-free licence to distribute his app in the manner indicated in the Play Console[5] and he 'may not use Google Play to distribute or make available any product which has a purpose that facilitates the distribution of software application and games for use on Android devices outside of Google Play' (section 4.5).

3. Available at https://play.google.com/about/developer-content-policy/ (last accessed 10 December 2019).
4. Available at https://play.google.com/about/developer-distribution-agreement.html (last accessed 10 January 2020).
5. The Play Console terms are available at https://policies.google.com/terms?gl = GR&hl = en-GB (last accessed 10 January 2020). In relation to the use by Google of the content distributed via the Play Console, the following are provided:

> Some of our Services allow you to upload, submit, store, send or receive content You retain ownership of any intellectual property rights that you hold in that content. In short, what belongs to you stays yours. When you upload, submit, store, send or receive content to or through our Services, you give Google (and those we work with) a worldwide licence to use, host, store, reproduce, modify, create derivative works (such as those resulting from translations, adaptations or other changes that we make so that your content works better with our Services), communicate, publish, publicly perform, publicly display and distribute such content. The rights that you grant in this licence are for the limited purpose of operating, promoting and improving our Services, and to develop new ones. This licence continues even if you stop using our Services (for example, for a business listing that you have added to Google Maps). Some Services may offer you ways to access and remove content that has been provided to that Service. Also, in some of our Services, there are terms or settings that narrow the scope of our use of the content submitted in those Services. Make sure that you have the necessary rights to grant us this licence for any content that you submit to our Services.

Except for the licence rights granted by the developer, Google obtains 'no rights, title or interest' in any of the products, 'including any Intellectual Property Rights in those Products' (section 4.4).

With regard to the iOS operating system, the official app store of which is the App Store, it is a closed source system providing developers an application programming interface (API), that is set of tools that let them develop programs for the iPhone, restricting what they have access to. By means of the Apple Developer Agreement, Apple grants the Developer a limited, non-exclusive, personal, revocable, non-sublicensable and non-transferrable licence to use Apple software for developing and testing apps while Apple retains the right to limit the number of devices this software may be installed on. The developer grants to Apple a non-exclusive and royalty-free intellectual property licence to allow for the distribution of the app to end users, including hosting and displaying the app, making copies thereof and allowing end user downloads and also to allow Apple to use excerpts of an app in its promotional materials (unless the developer notifies Apple that the developer itself does not possess these rights due to incorporated third-party intellectual property).

As far as the relationship between the user of the app and the app store is concerned, the following apply: As mentioned in Chapter 1, the principal business distribution model for apps is the free model, including in-app advertising.[6] Other business models are the paid model (users pay and can use all of the app's functionality once it is downloaded), the subscription model (users can make in-app purchases to access content and/or services for renewable or non-renewing duration) and the freemium model (apps are free to download and users can buy auto-renewing subscription inside the app). These business models are made possible since apps are not sold to the user but are licensed instead. Licensing provisions are technically enforced by the use of Technical Protection Measures (TPMs).

With regard to Android operating system, and, in particular, according to the Google Play ToS, apps (including Android Instant Apps) (alongside games, music, movies, books, magazines, or other digital content or services) are referred to as 'Content' (section 1). A user may use Google Play 'to browse, locate, view, stream, or download Content for [his/her] mobile, computer, tv, watch, or other supported device' (section 2). Section 4 provides that the user:

> [a]fter completing a transaction or paying the applicable fees for Content, [...] will have the non-exclusive right, [...] to store, access, view, use, and display copies of the applicable Content on [his/her] Devices or as otherwise authorized as part of the Service for [his/her] personal, non-commercial use only. All rights, title and interest in Google Play and Content not expressly granted to [the user] in the Terms are reserved. [The user's] use of apps and games may be governed by the additional terms and condition of the end user license agreement between [the user] and the Provider.

Section 4 also provides that the user may not:

6. *See* Chapter 1, *Definitions, Economic and Technical Aspects of Apps*.

> display (in part or in whole) the Content as part of any public performance or display even if no fee is charged except (a) where such use would not constitute a copyright infringement or violate any other applicable right or (b) as specifically permitted and only in the exact manner provided; sell, rent, lease, redistribute, broadcast, transmit, communicate, modify, sublicense, transfer, assign any Content to any third party including with regard to any downloads of Content that [the user] may obtain through Google Play except as specifically permitted and only in the exact manner provided; use Google Play or any Content in conjunction with any stream-ripping, stream capture or similar software to record or create a copy of any Content that is presented to [the user] in streaming format; use Content as part of any service for sharing, lending or multi-person use, or for the purpose of any other institution, except as specifically permitted and only in the exact manner provided; attempt to, or assist, authorize or encourage others to circumvent, disable or defeat any of the security features or components that protect, obfuscate or otherwise restrict access to any Content or Google Play; remove any watermarks, labels or other legal or proprietary notices included in any Content, or attempt to modify any Content obtained through Google Play, including any modification for the purpose of disguising or changing any indications of the ownership or source of Content.

With regard to the iOS operating system, according to Apple Media Services ToU (hereinafter 'AMS ToU'), the App Store is one of Apple's services (other services include iTunes Store, Apple Books, Apple music and Apple News). Though these services, one can 'buy, get, license, rent or subscribe to media, apps ('Apps') and other in-app services' all of which are mentioned as 'Content'. AMS ToU governs the use by the user of the aforementioned Apple's services. It is expressly mentioned that apps made available through the App Store are licensed, not sold, to the user. The terms of the End User License Agreements govern any content, materials or services accessible from or purchased within the licensed application, as well as upgrades provided by the licensor that replace or supplement the original licensed application. Apps available in the App Store are licensed to users either by Apple or third-party app providers under either (a) the 'Standard End User License Agreement' ('Standard EULA') or (b) a 'Custom End User License Agreement' ('Custom EULA'). Special mention of AMS ToU is made to the apps that allow the user to purchase access to Content or services on a subscription basis ('Paid Subscriptions') and also to apps that offer content, services or functionality for use within such apps ('In-App Purchases') (which are either consumed during the use of the App or not).

As far as the relationship between the app developer and the user is concerned, it is governed by the terms of the End User Licence Agreements.

In the context of the Android operating system, according to the Google Play Developer Distribution Agreement, the developer grants to the user a non-exclusive, worldwide and perpetual licence to perform, display and use the app.[7] The user's rights to the app are governed by the Google Play Developer Distribution Agreement but if the developer chooses, he may include a separate end user license agreement (EULA) that will govern the user's rights to the app, but, to the extent that EULA conflicts with

7. *See* Google Play Developer Distribution Agreement (effective as of 26 February 2018) available at https://play.google.com/intl/ALL_uk/about/developer-distribution-agreement.html.

Google Play Developer Distribution Agreement, the latter shall supersede the EULA (section 5.3 of the Google Play Developer Distribution Agreement).

In the context of the iOS operating system, Apple Media Services ToU[8] provides that regarding Apple's apps the user is granted by the company either the 'Standard EULA' or the 'Custom EULA'. The first provides that Apple (in its capacity as the app's developer) grants to the user a non-transferable licence to use the app on any Apple-branded products he/she owns or controls and as permitted by the 'Usage Rules' which can be found in Apple Media Services Terms and Conditions. The Usage Rules concern any type of services provided by Apple, including services provided by the App Store, and provide the following: the user may engage only in personal, non-commercial use; no commercial or promotional use rights are transferred to the user; the user can use Content from up to five different Apple IDs on each device; the user is responsible not to lose, destroy or damage Content once downloaded and thus, must do regular back-ups; the user may not tamper with or circumvent any security technology included with the services; the user may access Apple's services only using Apple's software, and may not modify or use modified versions of such software, etc. With regard to App Store content in particular, it is provided that 'the term "App" includes apps for any Apple platform and/or operating system, in-app purchases, extensions (such as keyboards), stickers, and subscriptions made available in an app' and that the user can use Apps on any device that he/she owns or controls. Moreover, special licensing provisions exist for those acting on behalf of a commercial enterprise, governmental organization or educational institution.

## §3.02 COPYRIGHT

Apps consist of computer programs, images, text and even sounds or videos, all of which may be separately protected by copyright. Although it is acknowledged that copyright is protected under national laws of Member States, this chapter discusses the existing extensive European copyright regulation and also highlights, where necessary, any striking differences between common law and civil law countries regarding the issues discussed.

### [A] Subsistence of Copyright

All authorial works, including computer programs, photographs and databases are protected by copyright law. Broadly speaking, copyright subject matter is authorial works, while related rights subject matter are recordings or communications of such authorial works by persons other than authors.

Mobile apps include computer programs within the meaning of Article 1 Software Directive. However, they include other subject matters as well, as already mentioned. Apps are not protected as authorial works in their entirety, but, instead, different

8. Last updated: 13 May 2019, available at https://www.apple.com/legal/internet-services/itunes/us/terms.html.

protection is afforded to their different components. By way of contrast, in the case of video games, the CJEU held in Case C-355/12 *Nintendo Co. Ltd v. PC Box Srl*[9] that they are authorial works and that their 'unique creative value [....] cannot be reduced' to their underlying computer program; accordingly, video games are protected as authorial works under the Information Society Directive (InfoSoc Directive) in addition to the protection their underlying computer programs may attract as authorial works under the Software Directive.[10]

Regarding the protection afforded to computer programs, the Berne Convention for the Protection of Literary and Artistic Works (1986) provides in Article 2(1) that '[t]he expression "literary and artistic works" shall include every production in the literary, scientific and artistic domain, whatever may be the mode or form of its expression, such as books, pamphlets and other writings; [...]'.[11] Similarly, Article 4 of the World Intellectual Property Organization (WIPO) Copyright Treaty (WCT) provides that: '[c]omputer programs are protected as literary works within the meaning of Article 2 of the Berne Convention. Such protection applies to computer programs, whatever may be the mode or form of their expression'.[12] Moreover, Article 10(1) of the Agreement on Trade-Related Aspects of Intellectual Property Rights (TRIPS Agreement) provides that: '[c]omputer programs, whether in source or object code, shall be protected as literary works under the Berne Convention'.[13] Directive 91/250/EEC on software protection (codified by Directive 2009/24/EC on the legal protection of computer programs) states in Article 1(1) that '[...] Member States shall protect computer programs, by copyright, as literary works within the meaning of the Berne Convention for the Protection of Literary and Artistic Works. For the purposes of this Directive, the term "computer programs" shall include their preparatory design material'. Moreover, it states in Recital 6 that:

> [t]he Community's legal framework on the protection of computer programs can accordingly in the first instance be limited to establishing that Member States should accord protection to computer programs under copyright law as literary works and, further, to establishing who and what should be protected, the exclusive rights on which protected persons should be able to rely in order to authorise or prohibit certain acts and for how long the protection should apply.

9. Case C-355/12, *Nintendo Co. Ltd and Others v. PC Box Srl and 9Net Srl.*, EU:C:2014:25.
10. Directive 2009/24/EC of the European Parliament and of the Council of 23 April 2009 on the legal protection of computer programs, OJ L 111, 5.5.2009, pp. 16–22.
11. Berne Convention for the protection of literary and artistic works, of 9 September 1886, completed at Paris on 4 May 1896, revised at Berlin on 13 November 1908, completed at Berne on 20 March 1914, revised at Rome on 2 June 1928, revised at Brussels on 26 June 1948, and revised at Stockholm on 14 July 1967 (Geneva, United International Bureaux for the Protection of Intellectual Property).
12. World Intellectual Property Organization Copyright Treaty (WIPO Copyright Treaty (WCT) (1996)), adopted at Geneva on 20 December 1996.
13. C.M. Correa & A. Yusuf, *Intellectual Property and International Trade: The TRIPs Agreement* (Alphen van den Rijn: Kluwer Law International 2008).

### [B] The Concept of 'Originality'

A work need not be new or novel in order to merit copyright protection and to be considered original. For example, two novelists may write about the same topic, thus the work that is the last to be produced will not be new. However, it may be original if the prerequisites apply. In other words, originality is a subjective concept that is closely linked to the personality of the author.

The originality threshold is determined by legislation and jurisprudence. In terms of EU law, Directive 2009/24/EC on software protection (codifying Directive 91/250/EEC) (hereinafter 'Software Directive')[14] requires Member States to 'protect computer programs, by copyright, as literary works within the meaning of the Berne Convention', provided they are 'original in the sense that [they are] the author's own intellectual creation' (Article 1); Database Directive 96/9/EC[15] requires that databases 'which, by reason of the selection or arrangement of their contents, constitute the author's own intellectual creation [...] be protected as such be copyright' (Article 3(3)); Term Directive 2006/116/EC[16] states that: '[p]hotographs which are original in the sense that they are the author's own intellectual creation' shall merit copyright protection and that '[n]o other criteria shall be applied to determine their eligibility for protection' (Article 6).

Computer programs' mechanical form makes difficult the application of the originality standard to them. In the case of computer programs, although the programmer uses programming languages and algorithms, he exercises his skills and artistic freedom to the extent he chooses to design and build the sequences of action steps necessary for the program to be executed. Originally, the 91/250/EEC on software protection provided for the first time that '[a] computer program shall be protected if it is original in the sense that it is the author's own intellectual creation. No other criteria shall be applied to determine its eligibility for protection' (Article 1(3)). Moreover, Recital 8 of that Directive provided that:

> '[w]hereas, in respect of the criteria to be applied in determining whether or not a computer program is an original work, no tests as to the qualitative or aesthetic merits of the program should be applied'. This phasing was based on the wording of Directive 87/54/EEC on the legal protection of topographies of semiconductor products, that is the 'creator's own intellectual effort'.[17]

Prior to the landmark decision of the Court of Justice of the European Union (CJEU) in *Infopaq*, C-5/08, the EU legislature has only harmonized the originality standard for computer programs, databases and photographs. In the landmark decision

14. Directive 2009/24/EC of the European Parliament and of the Council of 23 April 2009 on the legal protection of computer programs, OJ L 111, 5.5.2009, pp. 16–22.
15. Directive 96/9/EC of the European Parliament and of the Council of 11 March 1996 on the legal protection of databases, OJ L 77, 27.3.1996, pp. 20–28.
16. Directive 2006/116/EC of the European Parliament and of the Council of 12 December 2006 on the term of protection of copyright and certain related rights, OJ L 372, 27.12.2006, pp. 12–18.
17. Council Directive 87/54/EEC of 16 December 1986 on the legal protection of topographies of semiconductor products, OJ L 24, 27.1.1987, pp. 36–40.

of the CJEU in Infopaq[18] the CJEU held that 'originality' as understood in the Software Directive (2009/24), the Database Directive (96/9) and Term Directive (2006/116) forms also the standard under the InfoSoc Directive (2001/29), and it harmonized the EU standard of originality to be met by those works that are their 'author's own intellectual creation'. The CJEU further elaborated upon the notion of 'author's own intellectual creation' in its subsequent decisions in BSA[19] (paragraph 50 states that: 'the components of a graphic user interface do not permit the author to express his creativity in an original manner and achieve a result which is an intellectual creation of that author'), Football Association[20] (paragraph 98 of the decision states that sporting events leave: 'no room for creative freedom for the purposes of copyright'), Football Dataco[21] (paragraphs 38–39 of the decision state that for a database to be original, its author 'through the selection or arrangement of the data which [the database] contains [...] expresses his creativity in an original manner by making free and creative choices' and this is not the case when the setting up of a database is 'dictated by technical considerations, rules or constraints which leave no room for creative freedom') and Painer (paragraph 92 of the decision stated that the creator of a photographic portrait 'can make free and creative choices in several ways at various points in its production' and 'stamp the work with his "personal touch"').[22] Computer programs are protected by copyright provided that they are original, that is, they are their author's own intellectual creation[23] and, accordingly, the originality threshold will usually be met provided the work has not been copied.

If we move to the US, the landmark decision on the concept of originality arguably remains the US Supreme Court judgment in *Feist*,[24] in which the Court rejected the 'sweat of the brow' approach and held that: '[a]s a constitutional matter, copyright protects only those constituent elements of a work that possess more than a de minimis quantum of creativity'.

### *[1] Idea-Expression Doctrine*

According to the so-called idea/expression doctrine, copyright protects only the expression and not the underlying ideas and other non-literal aspects of a work. According to Article 9(2) TRIPS Agreement: '[c]opyright protection shall extend to expressions and not to ideas, procedures, methods of operation or mathematical concepts as such'. In the US, there exists the so-called merger doctrine according to which when the idea and expression are very difficult to separate, they 'merge', and

18. Case C-5/08, *Infopaq International*, [2009] ECR I-6569.
19. Case C-393/09, *BSA v. Ministerstvokulturi*, (2011) 3 ECDR 70.
20. Joined Cases C-403/08 and C-429/08, *Football Association Premier League Ltd, NetMed Hellas SA, Multichoice Hellas SA v. QC Leisure, David Richardson, AV Station plc, Malcolm Chamberlain, Michael Madden, SR Leisure Ltd Philip George Charles Houghton, Derek Owen and Karen Murphy v. Media Protection Services Ltd.*, OJ C 100, 17.4.2010, pp. 10–11.
21. Case C-604/10, *Football Dataco & Others v. Yahoo! & Others*, [2012] 2 CMLR 24.
22. Case C-145/10, *Eva-Maria Painer v. Standard VerlagsGmbH*, [2011] EUECJ.
23. Case C-5/08 *Infopaq International*, para. 35.
24. *Feist Pubs., Inc. v. Rural Tel. Svc. Co., Inc.*, 499 U.S. 340 (1991).

when there is only one or limited number of ways to express an idea, the expression is not protected under copyright law because it has 'merged' with the idea.[25]

It has been argued that the problem with software is that it is at the same time symbolic and functional and cannot be considered 'expressive' in the sense of other copyright works, e.g., books that can be read by human, since is not intended to be used by humans but, instead is intended to be used by machines;[26] therefore, in order to identify the unprotected ideas and concepts behind a computer program, one has to reproduce the computer program (by means of reverse engineering/decompiling the object code that is available on the market).[27]

In case of literal copying of software when apps are concerned, namely the copying of the expression which constitutes an infringement, one can copy either an app's internal aspects/structure (code, architecture and APIs[28]) or an app's external aspects/structure, namely graphical user interfaces – GUIs. GUIs are the 'interaction interface which enable communication between the computer program and the user'.[29] GUIs have been categorized broadly in the literature as falling under one of the following categories: (1) the overall interface/appearance of a desktop, (2) the individual components of the overall interface and (3) the ephemeral and animated effects that usually are the outcome of user interactions with categories (1) and (2).[30]

With regard to non-literal copying, in *SAS Institute, Inc. v. World Programming Limited* (C-406/10), the Court was asked to interpret the Software Directive in a case where a competitor had developed a competing product with similar functionality to an original product. In essence, the case concerned the non-literal copying of the 'structure, sequence and organization' of a computer program. In that instance, WPL was a competitor to SAS which had developed a statistical software. WPL created a competing statistical program without having access to the source or object code of SAS software but merely by studying a version of properly licensed SAS software. SAS claimed copyright infringement in its software and manuals by means of WPL software and manuals. CJEU held that the functionality, programming languages and data file formats are not protectable expression of computer programs under the Software Directive (they may, however, be protectable under the InfoSoc Directive in case they constitute the author's own intellectual creation). The Court stipulated that ideas and principles of a computer program are not protected by copyright and, thus, cannot be

25. The doctrine arose in the case *Baker v. Selden*, 101 U.S. 99 (U.S. 1880) and was later applied to *Morrissey v. Procter & Gamble Co.*, 379 F.2d 675 (1st Cir. Mass. 1967).
26. Noam Shemtov, *Beyond Code: Protection of Non-Textual Features of Software* (Oxford University Press, 1st edition, 2017), pp. 26–28.
27. *Ibid.*, p. 28 where it is noted that '[t]his phenomenon is further compounded in the case of SAAS, where the user has no access to the code to start with, whether in object or source code versions. There is no other example of a work protected by copyright where ideas and concepts that underlie such work are not discoverable upon an examination that does not involve copyright infringement'.
28. For a definition of APIs, *see* Chapter 1, I. Iglezakis, *Definitions, Economic and Technical Aspects of Apps*.
29. Case C-393/09, *BSA v. Ministerstvokulturi* (2011) 3 ECDR 70, OJ C 11, 16.1.2010.
30. Noam Shemtov, *Intellectual Property and Mobile Applications*, WIPO January 2018, available at https://www.wipo.int/export/sites/www/ip-development/en/agenda/pdf/ip_and_mobile_applications_study.pdf, at pp. 39, 49.

licensed and that manuals are protected by copyright to the extent they can are the expression of the author's intellectual creation. The Court expressly stated that: '[t]o accept that the functionality of a computer program can be protected by copyright would amount to making it possible to monopolize ideas, to the detriment of technological progress and industrial development'.[31] Similarly, in the case of apps, copyright in the underlying software of the app will be limited to the source code and shall not extend to the programming language, functionality and structure of data files.

Although the Court in the *SAS Institute* case (C-406/10) held that APIs may be protectable under the InfoSoc Directive in case they constitute the author's own intellectual creation, the decision may be interpreted as stating that within the EU APIs are not protected by copyright because they are functional in nature, that is they fall under the 'idea', rather than the 'expression', part of the dichotomy. At this point, it should be noted that it could be argued that the need not to protect APIs by means of copyright in computer programs is mainly due to the fact that APIs need to be interoperable.[32]

A US case, which originally involved the legal treatment of APIs, is the *Oracle v. Google* case.[33] The Federal Circuit stipulated that if an interface or part thereof could be designed in other ways in order to achieve the same function and is not to be dictated by a certain hardware or software environment, efficiency consideration, standard programming techniques, etc. then the said interface shall be protectable and shall fall under the 'expression', rather than the 'idea', part of the dichotomy.

With regard to the non-literal copying of the 'look and feel' of a computer program, that is certain external aspects of software products such as GUIs, the Court in the *BSA* case (C-393/09)[34] examined whether such 'look and feel' is protected by means of copyright in software and the answer was negative. The 'look and feel' of the program is protected if it is original but independently from the copyright in software and, thus, such external aspects of software products can be protected under the InfoSoc Directive, on condition the requirements of the said Directive for works of authorship are met, rather than the Software Directive. In the context of the said dispute and referral for a preliminary ruling, the ECJ made implicit reference to the idea-expression doctrine by holding that 'where the expression of [the components of the GUI] is dictated by their technical function, the criterion of originality is not met, since the different methods of implementing an idea are so limited that the idea and the expression become indissociable' (paragraph 49 of the decision). In other words, in cases where a particular expression is one of the few ways to achieve functionality then such an expression cannot be considered original and, accordingly, copyrightable.

31. *See* para. 40 of the decision.
32. The importance of interoperability in APIs is also highlighted in the *Communication from the Commission to the European Parliament, the Council, the European Economic and Social Committee and the Committee of the Regions – Online Platforms and the Digital Single Market Opportunities and Challenges for Europe* (COM(2016)288), at pp. 13–14.
33. *Oracle Am., Inc. v. Google, Inc.* (2014) 750 F. 3d 1339, 1364 (Fed. Cir.).
34. Case C-393/09, *BSA v. Ministerstvokulturi,* (2011) 3 ECDR 70, OJ C 11, 16.1.2010.

The *Oracle v. Google* case discussed above, originally concerning the legal treatment of APIs, can be used to infer certain conclusion regarding GUIs as well.[35] Thus, it could be argued that GUIs shall be protectable if they could be designed in different ways in order to achieve the same function, that is their functionality is not dictated by their design.

### *[2] Ownership of Copyright*

Regarding ownership, the IPR rests with the author (as also implied by the InfoSoc Directive that provides that copyright protection is afforded to 'authors, in respect of their works'). Relevant 'exceptions' to this general rule can be found in the Database Directive which defines the author as 'the natural person or group of natural persons who created the base or, where the legislation of the Member States so permits, the legal person designated as the rightholder by that legislation' (Article 4(1)). Moreover, the Software Directive provides that the authors of computer programs are 'all natural or legal persons eligible under national copyright legislation as applied to literary works'. Exceptions to the initial vesting of copyright to the author also arises in the case of computer programs 'created by an employee in the execution of his duties or following the instructions given by his employer' in which case copyright is owned by the author's employer, subject to any contractual provision between the parties to the contrary (Article 2(3) Software Directive). Moreover, in the case of employee-created databases, Recital 29 of the Database Directive leaves the issue of copyright ownership to the discretion of the Member States which have adopted several positions.[36]

Copyright ownership might be complicated if the app development has been outsourced to a vendor, achieved through a joint effort or derived from an open source software (OSS). Where all or part of the development of the app has been outsourced, the vendor agreement should ensure that the party financing the app development has acquired all IPRs to the app's software through a properly drafted 'work for hire' clause. In addition, it is important to bind the vendor with a non-disclosure agreement to ensure strict confidentiality while the app is being developed.

When an app is developed through a partnership, each company owns the IPR only over the piece developed by it, in the absence of an agreement to the contrary. If each party involved in the development wants to further exploit the app for commercial and non-commercial purposes, then the parties should execute an agreement of joint ownership of the app wherein which each party will be required to account to the other of the financial benefit derived from its use of the app.

35. *Oracle Am., Inc. v. Google, Inc.* (2014) 750 F. 3d 1339, 1364 (Fed. Cir.), *supra* n. 33.
36. *See* Justine Pila & Paul Torremans, *European Intellectual Property Law* (Oxford University Press, 2nd edition 2019), at p. 273.

### [3] *Rights Conferred and Limitations to These Rights*

Copyright confers a closed list of exclusive economic rights and lasts until seventy years after the author's death. In particular, the Software Directive confers (a) a reproduction right (Article 4(a) indent 1 refers to 'the permanent or temporary reproduction of a computer program by any means and in any form, in part or in whole'), (b) a right to loading, displaying, running, transmission, or storage necessitating reproduction (Article 4(a) indent 2), (c) a translation, adaptation, arrangement and any other alteration of a computer program and reproduction of the results thereof right (Article 4(1)(b)), (d) a distribution right (Article 4(1)(c) refers to 'any form of distribution to the public, including the rental, of the original computer program or of copies thereof').

The InfoSoc Directive confers (a) a reproduction right (Article 2), (b) a communication to the public right (Article 3(1)); a making available to the public right (Article 3(2)), (c) a distribution right (Article 4). According to Article 5(1) InfoSoc Directive, excluded from the protection afforded to the author by means of the reproduction right is any temporary act of reproduction with no independent economic significance that is transient or incidental and an integral and essential part of a technological process, and whose sole purpose to enable (i) a transmission in a network between third parties by an intermediary or (ii) a lawful use of a work or subject matter to be made.

With regard to the making available to public of a work 'in such a way that members of the public may access [it] from a place and at a time individually chosen by them', it covers several acts of making a work available over the internet such as making available for download, on demand streaming of a work, peer-to-peer (p2p) sharing of works, providing hyperlinks to works hosted on a third party's website for download from that website. As concerns hyperlinking, in particular, the CJEU held that it infringes the making available right when it (the hyperlink) results in making the work or subject matter accessible without the rightholder's authorization[37] or in case the link-provider knew or ought reasonably to have known that the rightholder had not authorized the posting of the work or subject matter on the third party's website, and this will be the case if the provision of the link is profit motivated and the provider did not ascertained the rightholder's consent to the work or subject matter's posting.[38] Over-the-top (OTT) media services accessed via apps on mobile phones, that is internet-based streaming media services inside an app offered directly to viewers via the Internet bypassing the content's traditional controllers/distributors such as cable and satellite television platforms, may also infringe the communication to the public right upon conditions.

For these reasons the importance of the 'communication to the public' right (Article 8) and the 'making available to the pubic' right (Article 6) introduced by the WIPO Copyright Treaty of 1996 (WCT) is incontestable. The right to authorize or prohibit the communication of their works and subject matter to the public is

37. Case C-466/12, *Svensson v. Retriever Sverige AB*, [2014] EUECJ.
38. Case C-527/15, *Stichting Brein v. Wullems (t/a Filmspeler)*, [2017] ECDR 14; Case C-160/15, *GS Media v. Sanoma Media Netherlands BV*, EU:C:2016:644.

implemented in the EU by means of Article 3(1) InfoSoc Directive for works other than databases, as already said, while the right to authorize or prohibit the communication of works and subject matter to the public for databases is implemented in the EU by means of Article 5(d) Database Directive. The right to authorize or prohibit the making available of works to the public 'in such a way that members of the public may access them from a place and at a time individually chosen by them' is implemented by means of Article 3(1) and (2) InfoSoc Directive for works. For works other than computer programs and databases, the right to authorize or prohibit their distribution is implemented by means of Article 4 InfoSoc Directive while for computer programs it is implemented by means of Article 4(1)(c) Software Directive, and for databases it is implemented by means of Article 5(c) Database Directive.

As far as exceptions and limitations are concerned, third parties are not prevented from making temporary and transient or incidental copes of work necessary for the operation of a technological process, such as internet browsing, as already said, in addition to permitting Member States to recognize certain further exceptions to copyright infringement covering such third-party acts as reproducing and communicating parts of a work for purposes such as research, news reporting, criticism or review, study, instruction, quotation or parody.

More specifically, an exhaustive list of mandatory exceptions to the reproduction right (of Article 2 InfoSoc Directive) in the case of authorial works (other than computer programs and databases) can be found in Article 5(1) InfoSoc Directive which excludes from the protection afforded to the author by means of the reproduction right certain temporary acts of reproduction during a technological process, as already discussed. An exhaustive list of non-mandatory exceptions to the reproduction right can be found in Article 5(2) InfoSoc Directive. In this context, an exception is provided to the reproduction right in cases of reproduction 'for private use and for ends that are neither directly nor indirectly commercial, on condition that the rightholders receive fair compensation which takes account of the application or non-application of technological measures ... to the work or subject-matter concerned'. An exhaustive list of non-mandatory exceptions to the communication, making available and distribution rights (of Articles 3 and 4 InfoSoc Directive) can be found in Article 5(3) and (4) InfoSoc Directive; the said Article contains a long list of exempted uses, however only some of them may be relevant in the case of mobile apps. It should be noted that the Digital Single Market Copyright Directive[39] (DSM Directive) extends the list of exceptions and limitations to cover certain additional unauthorized uses of works to facilitate scientific research (Article 3), text and data mining (Article 4), digital and cross-border teaching activities (Article 5) and the preservation of cultural heritage collections (Article 6).

With regard to computer programs, an exhaustive list of mandatory exceptions to the reproduction, alteration and distribution rights (of Article 4(1) Software Directive) can be found in Articles 5 and 6 Software Directive.

39. Directive (EU) 2019/790 of the European Parliament and of the Council of 17 April 2019 on copyright and related rights in the Digital Single Market and amending Directives 96/9/EC and 2001/29/EC.

### *[4] Exhaustion of Rights Doctrine*

Closely linked to the distribution right is so-called exhaustion of rights doctrine and its US-equivalent, the 'first-sale doctrine'. According to the exhaustion of rights doctrine, a work that has been placed on the market in an EU Member State by or with the consent of the rightholder may be resold anywhere in the EU without the need to obtain further permission. The rationale behind the doctrine is that the payment or other consideration received by the rightholder for the transfer of ownership of a product is sufficient for any IPR attaching to that product insofar as that product is concerned; by way of contrast, the restriction by the rightholder of the further exploitation of the product would have restricted the free movement of the product in accordance to Articles 34 and 35 TFEU.[40] Since the doctrine only applies to the redistribution of products, its operation is excluded as far as services are concerned, cloud computing and other online services included (Recital 29 InfoSoc Directive). Reference to the doctrine is made, among other, in Article 4(2) InfoSoc Directive with regard to works, in Article 4(2) Software Directive with regard to computer programs and in Article 5(c) Database Directive with regard to databases.

According to the CJEU decision in *UsedSoft v. Oracle*, digital exhaustion applies in the case of software as well under certain conditions. In that case, the Court held that a person who does not hold a user right in the computer program granted by the rightholder but relies on the exhaustion of the right to distribute a copy of the computer program is a 'lawful acquirer' of that copy within the meaning of Article (5)1 of Software Directive and, thus, benefits from the right of reproduction. However, for digital exhaustion to apply in software and for second-hand software to be permitted, several conditions must cumulatively be met: (1) the copyright holder must have authorized, even free of charge, the downloading of the copy of the computer program from the internet onto a data carrier in the EU, (2) the copyright holder must have conferred, in return for payment of a fee intended to enable him to obtain a remuneration corresponding to the economic value of the copy of the work of which he is the proprietor, a right to use that copy for an unlimited period, and (3) the first lawful acquirer of the computer program must have erased his computer program copy or must no longer use it.

The Court in *UsedSoft* also rejected the argument put forward by Oracle and the Commission that that the making available of a computer program on the copyright holder's website constitutes a 'making available to the public' within the meaning of Article 3(1) InfoSoc Directive, which cannot give rise to the exhaustion of the right of distribution of the copy, as provided for in Article 3(3) of InfoSoc Directive.[41] The

40. Justine Pila & Paul Torremans, *supra* n. 36, at p. 301.
41. Article 3 of Directive 2001/29 provides that:

> 1. Member States shall provide authors with the exclusive right to authorize or prohibit any communication to the public or their works, by wire or wireless means, including the making available to the public of their works in such a way that members of the public may access them from a place and at a time individually chosen by them. [...] 3. The rights referred to in paragraphs 1 and 2 shall not be exhausted by any act of

reason lies in the relationship between the InfoSoc and the Software Directive and, in particular, in Article 1(2)(a) of the InfoSoc Directive which provides that it 'leave[s] intact and ... in no way affect[s] existing ... [European] provisions relating to ... the legal protection of computer programs'. The provisions of the Software Directive and, in particular, Article 4(2), thus, 'constitute a *lex specialis* in relation to the provisions of Directive 2001/29, so that even if the contractual relationship at issue in the main proceedings or an aspect of it might also be covered by the concept of 'communication to the public' within the meaning of Article 3(1) of the latter Directive, the 'first sale ... of a copy of a program' within the meaning of Article 4(2) of Directive 2009/24 would still give rise, in accordance with that provision, to exhaustion of the right of distribution of that copy'.[42]

The Court in the *Aleksandrs Ranks and JurijsVasilevics* case[43] confirmed the application of the digital exhaustion principle to software and also clarified that the exhaustion of right applies to the original copy of the software, not to the back-up copy.

In *UsedSoft*, Oracle submitted that its practice does not constitute sale but, rather, licence, since it submitted that it makes available to its customers, free of charge, on its website a copy of the program concerned, which they can download. The copy downloaded can only be used by the customers if they have concluded a non-exclusive and non-transferable license agreement with Oracle for use of the computer program for an unlimited period. The Court did not accept Oracle's submissions that 'neither the making available of a copy free of charge nor the conclusion of the user license agreement involves a transfer of the right of ownership of that copy'[44] and held that allowing customers to download software from the internet for remuneration which they can use for an unlimited period constitutes 'sale'. In particular, it held that this situation 'examined as a whole, involves the transfer of the right of ownership of the copy of the computer program in question'.[45] Interestingly, the Court said that '[i]t makes no difference ... whether the copy of the computer program was made available to the customer by the rightholder concerned by means of a download from the rightholder's website or by means of a material medium such as a CD-ROM or DVD'[46] and held that both the operation of downloading a computer program from a material medium such as CD-ROM or DVD and the operation of downloading a computer program from the rightholder's website when combined with the conclusion of a

communication to the public or making available to the public as set out in this Article'. Similarly, Recital 29 of Directive 2001/29 provides that 'The question of exhaustion does not arise in the case of services and on-line services in particular. This also applies with regard to a material copy of a work or other subject-matter made by a user of such a service with the consent of the rightholder. Therefore, the same applies to rental and lending of the original and copies of works or other subject-matter which are services by nature. Unlike CD-ROM or CD-I, where the intellectual property is incorporated in a material medium, namely an item of goods, every on-line service is in fact an act which should be subject to authorization where the copyright or related right so provides.

42. Case C-128/11, *UsedSoft GmbH v. Oracle International Corp.*, OJ C 287, 22.9.2012, para. 51.
43. Case C-166/15, *Aleksandrs Ranks and JurijsVasilevics*, [2016] ECLI:EU:C:2016: 762.
44. Case C-128/11, *UsedSoft GmbH v. Oracle International Corp.*, para. 43.
45. *Ibid.*, para. 46.
46. *Ibid.*, para. 47.

licence agreement providing the right to use a copy for an unlimited period in return for payment of a fee must be considered to involve the transfer of the right of ownership of that computer program copy.[47] Most importantly, the Court held that:

> if the term 'sale' with the meaning of Article 4(2) of Directive 2009/24 were not given a broad interpretation as encompassing all forms of product marketing characterized by the grant of a right to use a copy of a computer program, for an unlimited period, in return for payment of a fee designed to enable the copyright holder to obtain a remuneration corresponding to the economic value of the copy of the work of which he is the proprietor, the effectiveness of that provision would be undermined, since suppliers would merely have to call the contract a 'license' rather than a 'sale' in order to circumvent the rule of exhaustion and divest it of all scope.[48]

App stores make clear in their legal agreements with the users that apps made available through them are licensed, not sold, to users. The Apple Media Services Terms and Conditions and the Licensed Application End User License Agreement provide that the user 'may not transfer, redistribute or sublicense the Licensed Application and, if [he] sell[s his] Apple Device to a third party, [he] must remove the Licensed Application from the Apple Device before doing so'.

### *[5] Non-proprietary Software*

This section will examine openness from the perspective of the relationship between Free Software and Open Source Software (FOSS) and App Stores. Open source licensing requires special consideration because the OSS licences (GPL, GNU Lesser General Public Licence (LGPL) or Apache) have specific requirements for attribution, distribution and non-discrimination with respect to the platform. The issue of FOSS will be discussed from two aspects; first, there is the issue of whether the operating system of Android and iOS are open source themselves; second, there is the issue whether open source apps can be available at Google Play and App Store.

#### *[a] Android's Open Source and IOS's Proprietary Operating Systems*

As far as the first issue is concerned, it could be generally argued that Apple's iOS is mainly proprietary software with some open source components.[49] Contrary to iOS, the

47. *Ibid.*, para. 47.
48. *Ibid.*, para. 49.
49. According to Apple: 'Open source software is at the heart of Apple platforms and developer tools, and Apple continues to contribute and release significant quantities of open source code' as stated by the company at: https://developer.apple.com/opensource/; for example, 'ResearchKit is an open source framework that enables an iOS app to become a powerful tool for medical research. It includes a variety of customizable modules that you can build upon and share with the community' (as stated here: https://developer.apple.com/opensource/).

Android operating system is open source, using mainly the Apache licence as well as the GPL for Linux components.[50]

The question of whether the operating system of Android and iOS are open source themselves is closely linked to the need to scrutinize code before making it available as open source as has been highlighted in a longstanding dispute between Oracle and Apple. Oracle is the author of the Java programming language, the language utilized by Google when it acquired Android back in 2005. Google was sued by Oracle claiming Google had copied several Oracle's Java 'API packages' for the development of its Android operating system. The Java API is 'a collection of "pre-written Java source code programs for common and more advanced computer functions." ... These APIs "allow programmers to use the prewritten code to build certain functions into their own programs rather than write their own code to perform those functions from scratch. They are shortcuts."'[51] Although Oracle makes the Java platform freely available to programmers building apps, it has devised a licensing scheme to attract programmers and commercialize the platform.[52] In particular, Oracle offers three different licences, the first of which is the open source GPL which is free of charge and provides that the licensee can use the (declaring and implementing code) packages but must give away any improvements made to the Java community. The second licence is the Specification Licence which provides that: 'the licensee can use the declaring code and organization of Oracle's API packages but must write its own implementing code' while the third licence is the Commercial Licence that can be used by those who 'want to use and customize the full Java code in their commercial products and keep their code secret', and it is offered in exchange for royalties.[53]

Before Android was released all of the Java packages were available for free and open source under the name Open JDK, subject to the terms of a GPL.[54] After copying the Java code, Google replaced the GPL and redistributed Android under the GPL-incompatible permissive Apache open source licence. Google, therefore, not only infringed copyright in Java but also violated the terms of the open source GPL under which Java was distributed. To illustrate the significance of open source licensing, had Google adopted Java under the GPL instead of a permissive open source licence, Google would not have been liable for copyright infringement (GPL allows copying under its specific terms) and also would not have violated the GPL terms under which Java was distributed.

Google did not object to having copied the APIs, but insisted that they did not merit copyright protection in the first place due to their functional character. During a long-term dispute, the US Court of Appeals for the Federal Circuit has issued two

50. *See* https://source.android.com/setup/start/licenses where it is noted that 'Apache License, Version 2.0 (Apache 2.0) is the preferred license for AOSP, and the majority of Android software is licensed with Apache 2.0. While the project strives to adhere to the preferred license, there are exceptions, which are handled on a case-by-case basis. For example, the Linux kernel patches are under the GPLv2 license with system exceptions, which can be found on kernel.org.'
51. *Oracle America, Inc. v. Google, Inc.*, No. 17-1118 (Fed. Cir. 2018), at p. 8.
52. *Ibid.*, at p. 9.
53. *Ibid.*, at p. 3.
54. *Ibid.*, at p. 51.

important decisions, namely a decision holding that the structure, sequence and organization ('SSO') of the Java API packages are entitled to copyright protection[55] and a decision holding that Google's use of the Java API packages was not fair as a matter of law notwithstanding Google's claims to the opposite.[56] By means of its second decision, the US Court of Appeals for the Federal Circuit remanded for a trial on damages to the lower federal court in San Francisco and, since Oracle claims billions in damages, the outcome of this dispute may be devastating for Google and its Android platform.[57]

### *[b] Availability of Open Source Apps at Google Play and App Store*

A number of apps today use OSS.[58] Apps may be open source or might be developed using a combination of OSSs, each governed by a different licence. A legally compliant launch of such an app requires: (i) identifying the different components on the app software, the OSS licence they are based on, and the compliance requirements for each licence, (ii) drafting a terms of use statement that complies with all the required OSS licence requirements, and (iii) identifying those components of the app software over which the developer can exert an exclusive IPR.

App Store and Google Play allow developers to create open source apps (either from the beginning or by combining their code with open source code). The problem, however, arises when developers developing for Apple and Google, that is for distribution via their respective App Stores, violate key obligations required by the open source licences. When developers distribute their open source apps via App Store and Google Play they are liable (a) towards their open source licensors to the extent terms of the open source licence are violated (an open source app may be removed from the App Store by Apple following the complaint of a developer regarding infringement of the open source license) and (b) towards App Stores to the extent the latter ask for warranties that the app submitted does not infringe third-party IPRs and for an indemnity in case that is the case.

It is not uncommon for apps that were determined to be under the GPL to be pulled from the App Store. In one instance, the Free Software Foundation (FSF) stated that the GPL and iTunes Store Terms of Service are not compatible and had an iOS port of their free software game GNU Go (licensed under GPL v2) removed from the platform. That case in particular concerned the purchase of apps and media through the iTunes store using a Mac or Windows desktop/laptop that is the equivalent of

55. *Oracle Am., Inc. v. Google Inc.*, 750 F.3d 1339, 1348 (Fed. Cir. 2014).
56. *Oracle America, Inc. v. Google, Inc.*, No. 17-1118 (Fed. Cir. 2018).
57. Daniel Eran Dilger, *Google Faces $9 Billion in Damages after Ripping Off Java in Android* (AppleInsider.com, 28/3/2018) available at https://appleinsider.com/articles/18/03/28/google-faces-9-billion-in-damages-after-ripping-off-java-in-android (accessed November 2018).
58. An Dev Con Kim Weins, SVP Marketing, OpenLogic, *Open Source in Android Apps: Tips for Becoming a Good Open Source Citizen* (2006) available at http://www.openlogic.com/getattachment/8e06acc2-8718-4ec1-8ebf-b212c63b84e4/Open-Source-Android-App-Tips-Becoming-Good-Citizen?sitename=OpenLogic (accessed November 2018), where it is stated that 'OSS is used in 88% of the Android phones and 41% of the IOS phones'.

purchasing apps through the App Store using an iOS mobile device. According to the FSF, distribution via the App Store was not in compliance with the GNU GPL since Apple imposed numerous legal restrictions on use and distribution of GNU Go through the iTunes Store Terms of Service.[59] Such restrictions were contrary to what is provided for by section 6 of GPL v2, which provides that: '[e]ach time you redistribute the Program (or any work based on the Program), the recipient automatically receives a license from the original licensor to copy, distribute or modify the Program subject to these terms and conditions. You may not impose any further restrictions on the recipients' exercise of the rights granted herein. … .' When the FSF decided to remove its software game from the App Store, back in 2010, it justified its decision by saying that the then applicable App Store Terms of Service provided in section 9(b) ('Usage Rules') that the user acknowledges that apps downloaded from the App Store 'contain security technology that limits … [their] usage … to the following applicable Usage Rules, and, whether or not [apps] are limited by security technology, [the user] agree[s] to use [apps] in compliance with the applicable Usage Rules'.[60] Usage Rules (i) and (iii) provided that the user was required to accept the Terms of Service to use the software and that he/she can may only install the software on five approved devices. Thus, apart from the separate licence provided to the user by the software developer, i.e., the EULA, the App Store Terms of Service imposed on the user usage rules which, according to section 9(c): 'shall govern [his/her] rights with respect to the Products [i.e. apps], in addition to any other terms or rues that may have been established between [the user] and another party'.[61] According to the FSF, Apple's ToS were imposing restrictive limits on the use and distribution for any software distributed through the App Store contrary to what was permitted by the GPL, since the aforementioned Usage Rules effectively were acting as 'Digital Restrictions Management-narrowly limiting what you can do with the software …' in a legal instead of technological way.[62]

Another case of removal of a GPL licensed app from the App Store was that of the VLC media player in which case a developer who worked on the VLC media player project that is licensed under GPL v2 objected to it being available on the App Store (while the VLC project's management had the opposite opinion and believed that the App Store's terms and the GPL v2 were compatible).[63] VLC's core library has since then

59. Brett Smith, *GPL Enforcement in Apple's App Store* (fsf.org, 25 May 2010) available at https://www.fsf.org/news/2010-05-app-store-compliance (accessed November 2018).
60. *Ibid.*
61. *Ibid.*
62. *Ibid.*
63. Richard Gaywood *The GPL, the App Store, and you* (engadget.com, 9 January 2011) available at https://www.engadget.com/2011/01/09/the-gpl-the-app-store-and-you/ (accessed November 2018); Steven J. Vaughan-Nichols, *No GPL Apps for Apple's App Store* (zdnet.com, 8 January 2011) available at https://www.zdnet.com/article/no-gpl-apps-for-apples-app-store/ (accessed November 2018).

been relicensed under the LGPL which may allow mobile apps under App Store compatible licences to be written.[64]

Today, the App Store Terms of Service have not changed much. In particular, under their new title 'Apple Media Services Terms and Conditions', they govern the use of Apple's services, App Store included. The current terms governing use of the App Store provide that the user 'can use Apps on any device that [he/she] own[s] or control[s]' and that an:

> [i]individual acting on behalf of a commercial enterprise, governmental organization or educational institution (an 'Enterprise') may download and sync Apps for use by either (i) a single individual on one or more devices owned or controlled by an Enterprise; or (ii) multiple individuals on a single shared device owned or controlled by an Enterprise. For the sale of clarity, each device used serially or collectively by multiple users requires a separate license.[65]

The Usage Rules applying to 'All Services' provide that the user 'can use Content from up to five different Apple IDs on each device', that he/she 'may not tamper with or circumvent any security technology included with the Services', that he/she 'may access [the] Services only using Apple's software, and may not modify or use modified versions of such software' and that he/she 'may use the Services and Content only for personal, non-commercial purposes' (with the exception mentioned above regarding use by individuals acting on behalf of a commercial enterprise).[66]

With regard to the current EULA, governing the use of any app acquired via the App Store and also 'any content, materials, or services accessible from or purchased within the licensed application as well as upgrades provided by Licensor that replace or supplement the original Licensed Application ... ',[67] it is noted that Apple's Standard EULA includes a special provision for OSS, according to which:

> [e]xcept as provided in the Usage Rules, [the user] may not distribute or make the Licensed Application available over a network where it could be used by multiple devices at the same time. [The user] may not transfer, redistribute or sublicense the Licensed Application and, if [he/she] sell[s] [his/her] Apple device to a third party, [he/she] must remove the Licensed Application from the Apple Device before doing so. [He/she] may not copy (except as permitted by this license and the Usage Rules), reverse-engineer, disassemble, attempt to derive the source code of, modify, or create derivative works of the Licensed Application, any updates, or any part thereof (except as and only to the extent that any foregoing restriction is prohibited by applicable law or to the extent as may permitted by the licensing terms governing use of any-open-sourced components included with the Licensed Application).[68]

---

64. OpenLogic by Perforce, *VLC license Change: A Lesson in Perseverance* (Nov. 30, 2012) available at http://blog.klocwork.com/open-source/vlc-license-change-a-lesson-in-perseverance/ (accessed November 2018).
65. *See* Apple Media Services Terms and Conditions, section entitled 'Services and Content Usage Rules/App Store Content' available at: https://www.apple.com/legal/internet-services/itunes/us/terms.html (accessed November 2018).
66. *Ibid.*
67. *Ibid.*, section 'Licensed Applications End User License Agreement/ section a. Scope of License'.
68. *Ibid.*

The question whether apps distributed through Android and iOS platforms violate OSS provisions, not necessarily because of the existence of restrictive terms of use of the said platforms as discussed above, was examined in a research by OpenLogic which looked at a total of 635 apps across both platforms, namely 112 Android apps and 523 iOS apps.[69] It was concluded that most of open source Android and iOS open source apps (71% of the app using open source licences that were examined) were violating GPL/LGPL requirements such as providing a copy of the licence and the source code or an offer to get the source code, or the requirement to provide a copy of the licence, and also Apache software licence requirements to provide a copy of the licence along with any notices or attributions required by the licensed code. Generally, code that is licensed under the more permissive open source licences, such as BSD and Apache, is likely to encounter fewer problems with regard to its appearance on the App Store and Google Play.

#### *[6] Software-as-a-Service and Apps*

In the case of Software-as-a-Service (SAAS), users are able to access software applications over the cloud. In the case of SAAS, both users and competitors have access only to GUIs and do not access or copy the code. SAAS does not involve a licence agreement per se but, instead, a contractual arrangement since it is a per se contract for the provision of services. Since SAAS gives rise mainly to questions concerning contract law, consumer protection law, etc., and has little to do with copyright law and licensing agreements, a short reference will only be made here concerning, in particular, reverse engineering.

The relationship between SAAS and reverse engineering is an interesting one. 'Black box' reverse engineering refers to a process where systems are observed without having access to the internal components of a computer program as expressed in source code format, whereas 'white box' reverse engineering involves such an inspection.[70] Since computer programs are released into the market in object code format, developers who want to study them perform a process known as 'decompilation/disassembly' in the context of which they recreate the original source code of a computer program after having analysed the program, generated an intermediate product description and produced product specifications based on such description.[71] In order to avoid copyright infringement of the program's code, developers follow a 'clean room/Chinese wall' technique, which entails two teams of computer engineers; the first team studies the code of the original program and converts it from an object code format into a source code format and describes what the

69. An Dev Con Kim Weins, *supra* n. 58; Maxim V. Tsotsorin, *Open Source Software Compliance: The Devil Is Not So Black As He is Painted*, 29 Santa Clara High Tech. L.J. 559–602 (2012), at p. 562; *see also* Ons Mlouki, Foutse Khomh and Giuliano Antoniol, *On the Detection of Licenses Violations in the Android Ecosystem*, Proceedings of the 23rd IEEE International Conference on Software Analysis, Evolution, and Reengineering (SANER), Osaka, Japan, 16–18 March 2016, available at https://publications.polymtl.ca/2124/1/2016_OnsMlouki.pdf.
70. Shemtov, *supra* n. 26, p. 71.
71. For a detailed description of the process, *see ibid.*, at p. 73.

program does without reference to the code, while the second team produces a new program with the same features and functional specifications of the original one. In that way, no copying of the code of the original program takes place and, accordingly, no copyright infringement.

Black box reverse engineering is permitted under Article 5(3) Software Directive which provides that:

> [the] person having a right to use a copy of a computer program shall be entitled, without the authorization of the rightholder, to observe, study or test the functioning of the program in order to determine the ideas and principles which underlie any element of the program if he does so while performing any of the acts of loading, displaying, running, transmitting or storing the program which he is entitled to do so.

According to Article 8 Software Directive, contractual provisions to the contrary shall be null and void. With regard to white box reverse engineering and decompilation/disassembly, a narrow exception to copyright infringement is provided for in Article 6(1) of the Software Directive which provides that reproduction of code and translation to a human readable format when it is:

> indispensable to obtain the information necessary to achieve the interoperability of an independently created computer program with other programs, provided that the following conditions are met: (a) those acts are performed by the licensee or by another person having a right to use a copy of a program, or on their behalf by a person authorised to do so; (b) the information necessary to achieve interoperability has not previously been readily available to the persons referred to in point (a); and (c) those acts are confined to the parts of the original program which are necessary in order to achieve interoperability.

It has been noted that while white box reverse engineering cannot take place in the case of SAAS this is not the case with black box reverse engineering.[72] White box reverse engineering, in particular, cannot take place in the case of SAAS since the product's code is not distributed and thus cannot be found on the user's hard drive while, instead, it resides on the cloud. By way of contrast, since black box reverse engineering could be carried out remotely even without access to the target program's object code, this type of reverse engineering can take place in a cloud environment in the case of SAAS.[73]

## §3.03 ANTI-CIRCUMVENTION LEGISLATION

An important aspect of 'openness' in the case of App Stores concerns the private distribution of apps via third-party websites, thus, bypassing App Stores. Although Google allows that tactic, Apple, does not allow users to engage in it with the exception of enterprise level distribution for in-house staff. The fact that this is done effectively by

72. *Ibid.*, p. 101.
73. *Ibid.*

the means of TPMs backed by restrictive licensing terms highlights the importance of TPMs in the context of app distribution.

This issue is also closely linked to the phenomenon of app piracy which is on the rise as evidence shows.[74] App piracy can be best understood if broken down to the following four categories:[75] (1) 'mobile app piracy', that is the 'unauthorized use or reproduction of mobile apps in order to circumvent payment or to manipulate features',[76] (2) 'jailbreaking', that is 'the process of gaining access to the operating system of a computing device, such as a smartphone or tablet, to install and execute software that could not otherwise be installed or run on that device, or to remove pre-installed software that could not otherwise be uninstalled',[77] (3) 'cracking', that is to 'disable unwanted features on premium software, such as copy protection or payment requirements',[78] (4) 'clone', that is an 'exact replica of an app made by an unrelated third-party developer'.[79]

Once a user powers the iPhone, the phone's bootloader program loads the operating system into its main memory for operation. In this context, users found a way to jailbreak iPhone by installing a modified bootloader (i.e., anti-circumvention software). Jailbreaking Apple's iPhone allows apps from stores other than iStore to run on an iPhone. Jailbreaked iPhone could install Cydia, an unauthorized alternative to Apple's App Store. One of the most popular services available through Cydia was Hackulous which allowed the user to download 'cracked' apps from Apple's App Store though its program, Installous, for free. Moreover, Cydia offered apps that were unauthorized by Apple or unavailable in the Apple Store. Cydia recently shut down.[80]

As a general observation, contrary to the InfoSoc Directive that prohibits the act of circumvention of TPMs for whatever reason, the Software Directive, which is *lex specialis* compared to the InfoSoc Directive as far as the protection of software is

---

74. John Koetsier, *The Mobile Economy Has A $17.5B Leak: App Piracy* (2 February 2018, Forbes.com) available at https://www.forbes.com/sites/johnkoetsier/2018/02/02/app-publishers-lost-17-5b-to-piracy-in-the-last-5-years-says-tapcore/#7dd548ac7413 (accessed November 2018).
75. For this categorization, *see* IronSource, Free Guide – e-book, *How to Protect Your App from Hackers and Pirates*, available at: https://www.ironsrc.com/ebooks/how-to-protect-apps-hackers/.
76. *Ibid.*
77. Definition in Library of Congress, Copyright Office, 37 CFR Part 201 [Docket No. 2014-07] Exemption to Prohibition on Circumvention of Copyright Protection Systems for Access Control Technologies. Federal Register/Vol. 80, No. 208/Wednesday, October 28, 2015/Rules and Regulations, 65952.
78. IronSource, *supra* n. 75.
79. *Ibid.* As evidence shows, piracy is more than IPRs infringement nowadays since more and more pirates are starting to target freemium apps and their underlying in-app purchases (IAP) and takes the following forms: impersonating attacks, replay attacks, bypassing the validation server, refund fraud, trainers (external software that allow pirate users to modify an app's memory, their most common usage being to increase virtual currency without paying for it), mods (APK (Android Package Kit) and change the values in the code to their advantage). App piracy stretches from the simple downloading an app for free on the web to the unauthorized use or reproduction of mobile apps in order to circumvent payment or manipulate features (the latter instance differentiate it from music and film piracy).
80. Kevin Rogers, *Jailbroken: Examining the Policy and Legal Implications of iPhone Jailbreaking*, 13 Pittsburgh Journal of Technology Law and Policy (Spring 2013).

concerned, permits the circumvention of TPMs for purposes of achieving interoperability.

In particular, Article 6(1)-(3) the InfoSoc provides that:

> 1. Member States shall provide adequate legal protection against the circumvention of any effective technological measures, which the person concerned carries out in the knowledge, or with reasonable grounds to know, that he or she is pursuing that objective. 2. Member States shall provide adequate legal protection against the manufacture, import, distribution, sale, rental, advertisement for sale or rental, or possession for commercial purposes of devices, products or components or the provision of services which: (a) are promoted, advertised or marketed for the purpose of circumvention of, or (b) have only a limited commercially significant purpose or use other than to circumvent, or (c) are primarily designed, produced, adapted or performed for the purpose of enabling or facilitating the circumvention of, any effective technological measures.

Under the InfoSoc Directive, the expression 'technological measures' refers to any technology, device or component that, in the normal course of its operation, is designed to prevent or restrict acts, in respect of works or other subject matters, which are not authorised by the rightholder of any copyright or any right related to copyright as provided for by law or the sui generis right provided for in Directive 96/9/EC (Databases Directive). Technological measures shall be deemed 'effective' where the use of a protected work or other subject matters is controlled by the rightholders through application of an access control or protection process, such as encryption, scrambling or other transformation of the work or other subject matter or a copy control mechanism, which achieves the protection objective.

In the context of the Software Directive, the protection of TPMs applied to software concerns only trafficking and not circumvention as provided for in Article 7 Software Directive according to which:

> Member States shall provide, in accordance with their national legislation, appropriate remedies against a person committing any of the following acts: ... (c) any act of putting into circulation, or the possession for commercial purposes of, any means the sole intended purpose of which is to facilitate the unauthorized removal or circumvention of any technical device which may have been applied to protect a computer program. ... .

Moreover, the Explanatory Memorandum of the Software Directive Part II Article 6(2) stipulates that:

> many programs are marketed with a technical protection system which prevents or limits their unauthorized use or reproduction. If such systems are used by rightholders to protect their exclusive rights, it should not be legally possible to remove or circumvent such systems without the authorization of the rightholder. The term 'deal with' should be taken in this context to include sale, offer or advertise for sale, transmit, store or receive such means.

Therefore, arguably, the lawful user is allowed to circumvent a TPM applied on software in order to engage into lawful activities. The term 'unauthorized' both in Article 7 and in the Explanatory Memorandum may imply that copyright or contract law gives the rightholder the right to prohibit circumvention on a basis other than the anti-circumvention legislation and that there should be a link between copyright infringement and infringement of the anti-circumvention provisions and, thus, exceptions to copyright should be regarded as prevailing over the anti-circumvention norms established by the Software Directive.

Since the InfoSoc Directive has no effect on software protection, the main anti-circumvention EU instrument in the case of TPMs applied to apps is the Software Directive, with the exception, however, of GUIs which are not considered an expression of software but are protected under the InfoSoc Directive instead (*BSA* case[81]).

The relationship between the anti-circumvention provisions of the two Directives in the area of mobile apps and app stores may not be considered clear-cut, however, since (a) the purpose of the anti-circumvention software found on mobile phones (e.g., iPhone) is not directed towards preventing someone from copying the software code found in the mobile phone (iPhone) but, instead, towards preventing a user from using apps not sanctioned or provided by the developer of the digital distribution platform (Apple), and given that this is the case the question is whether such anti-circumvention software is protected under existing anti-circumvention legislation; and (b) the anti-circumvention provisions of the InfoSoc Directive are inconsistent to a certain extent with the mandatory interoperability provisions of the Software Directive (provided for in Article 6(1) of the Software Directive according to which reproduction of code and translation to a human readable format is allowed strictly for interoperability purposes). The relationship between the anti-circumvention provisions of the two Directives has been at the centre of the discussion in the case of *Nintendo v. PC Box* in which Nintendo argued that the TPM it uses to protect its video game consoles (portable and fixed) were circumvented by means of products enabling users to play illegal copies of Nintendo video games on Nintendo consoles. CJEU held that the anti-circumvention provisions of the InfoSoc Directive also apply to portable equipment or devices allowing access to the copyrighted work.[82]

In the US, in the Context of the Digital Millennium Copyright Act 1998 (DMCA), that is the US anti-circumvention legislation, a process for the triennial review of the

81. Case C-393/09, *BSA v. Ministerstvokulturi*, (2011) 3 ECDR 70, OJ C 11.
82. Case C-355/12, *Nintendo Co. Ltd and Others v. PC Box Srl and 9Net Srl*. The Court also held that:

> [i]t is for the national court to determine whether other measures or measures which are not installed in consoles could cause less interference with the activities of third parties or limitations to those activities, while still providing comparable protection of the rightholder's rights. Accordingly, it is relevant to take account, *inter alia*, of the relative costs of different types of technological measures, of technological and practical aspects of their implementation, and of a comparison of the effectiveness of those different types of technological measures as regards the protection of the rightholder's rights, that effectiveness however not having to be absolute. That court must also examine the purpose of devices, products or components, which are capable of circumventing those technological measures. In that regard, the evidence of use which third parties actually make of them will, in the light of the circumstances at issue, be particularly relevant. The national court may, in particular, examine how often those devices, products or components are in fact used in disregard of copyright and how often they are used for purposes which do not infringe copyright.

exemptions to the circumvention legislation is provided.[83] Section 1201 of the DMCA, 17 U.S.C. §1201, makes it a violation to 'circumvent a technological measure that effectively controls access' to copyrighted works. Every three years, the Librarian of Congress, following the recommendations of the Register of Copyrights the Librarian of Congress, reviews the DMCA and its exceptions to determine whether they are, or are likely to be, adversely affected by the prohibition against circumvention. Eventually, the Librarian of Congress publishes a modified list of classes of copyrighted works that are included in the DMCA exemption, which applies until the subsequent review.

In the 7th triennial proceedings in 2018, the Librarian of Congress adopted exemptions to the provision of the DMCA that prohibit circumvention of technological measures that control access to copyrighted works, codified in section 1201(a)(1) of title 17 of the United States Code. The final regulations were adopted by the Librarian of Congress after careful consideration of the Register of Copyrights Recommendation.[84] Paragraph (b) ('Classes of copyrighted works') of section 201.40, among others, therefore, was amended to provide that the anti-circumvention provisions shall not apply in the case of non-infringing uses of several classes of copyrighted works, the most relevant to our discussion being the following:

> Computer programs that operate [:] cellphones, tablets, mobile hotspots, and wearable devices to allow connection to a wireless network ('unlocking'); ... smartphones and all-purpose mobile computing devices, to enable interoperability or removal of software applications ('jailbreaking'); ... smart TVs for the purpose of enabling interoperability with computer programs on the smart television; Computer programs that enable voice assistant devices to enable interoperability or removal of software applications; Computer programs contained and controlling function of motorized land vehicles to allow diagnosis, repair, or modification of a vehicle function; Computer programs that control smartphones, home appliances, or home systems to allow diagnosis, maintenance, or repair of the device or system; ... .[85]

In the context of the discussion whether the anti-circumvention software installed on mobile phones should be or not protected by the anti-circumvention legislation, reference should be made to the *Lexmark US* case.[86] In Lexmark, the Sixth Circuit held that section 1201 of the DMCA did not apply to efforts to circumvent a program containing an authentication sequence called a 'Toner Loading Program' controlling access to Lexmark's printers' software. The program was located in a microchip attached to the company's toner cartridge allowing Lexmark's cartridge to

83. United States Digital Millennium Copyright Act 1998 (DMCA), signed into law by President Clinton on 28 October 1998, amending U.S. Copyright Act (*see* U.S. Code, Title 17), Pub. L. No. 105-304, 112 Stat. 2860.
84. Library of Congress, U.S. Copyright Office, Exemption to Prohibition on Circumvention of Copyright Protection Systems for Access Control Technologies, Final Rule, 37 CFR Part 201 [Docket No. 2017–10].
85. This summarized list is by M. Scheid, *2018 DMCA Section 1201 Exemptions Announced*, Ohio State University, University Libraries, Copyright Corner (March 2019), available at: https://library.osu.edu/site/copyright/2019/03/20/2018-dmca-section-1201-exemptions-announced/#more-1246.
86. *Lexmark International, Inc. v. Static Control Components, Inc.*, 387 F.3d 522 (6th Circuit 2004).

work in Lexmark's printers, while on the contrary, a Lexmark printer would not function without the authentication program located on a cartridge. As already mentioned, section 1201 of the DMCA makes it illegal to circumvent technology that 'effectively controls access to a work', i.e., access to the actual subject matter of the copyright, that is in the present case access to the code of the printer's software/operating system itself. The court held that the authentication program was required to make the printer function but was not required to display the actual software code of the printer itself.

## §3.04 ISSUES OF SECONDARY INFRINGEMENT

Traditionally, primary liability (for substantive relief such as compensation) is different from secondary liability (for injunctive relief) in that the former depends on the 'commission of an act reserved exclusively to another party' while the latter depends on 'the satisfaction of criteria additional to this, including typically proof of a certain intention of knowledge and/or breach of a general legal duty of care to the relevant rights owner'.[87] According to the Software Directive, a secondary infringer is a person committing 'any act of putting into circulation a copy of a computer program knowing, or having reason to believe, that it is an infringing copy' (Article 7(1)(a)) or being in 'possession, for commercial purposes, of a copy of a computer program knowing, or having reason to believe, that it is an infringing copy' (Article 7(1)(b)). Moreover, Article 8 of the InfoSoc Directive provides that: 'Member States shall ensure that rightholders are in a position to apply for an injunction against intermediaries whose services are used by a third party to infringe a copyright or related right.'

The two main app distribution platforms, that is, App Store and Google Play, not only distribute their own apps on their platforms but also allow third-party developers to offer their apps directly to end users through these platforms. App stores, in their capacity as information society service providers (ISPs), that is providers of information society services,[88] may fall foul of secondary liability for the copyright infringing file-sharing apps and/or the pirated apps they host in case they cannot qualify for the 'safe harbour' provisions for the intermediaries under the E-Commerce Directive and the DMCA in the US.

Article 12 of the E-Commerce Directive provides that, in the case that the service offered by the service provider consists of the transmission in a communication network of information provided by a recipient of the service or the provision of access to a communication network, the service provider is not liable for the information transmitted, on condition that the provider does not initiate the transmission, does not select the receiver of the transmission and does not select or modify the information

87. Justine Pila & Paul Torremans, *supra* n. 36, p. 238.
88. Article 2(a) of Directive 2000/31 provides that: 'information society services' means services within the meaning of Article 1(2) of Directive 98/34 as amended by Directive 98/48/EC. Article 1(2) of Directive 98/34 provides that an information society service is: 'any service normally provided for remuneration, at a distance, by electronic means and at the individual request of a recipient of services'.

contained in the transmission ('mere conduit exemption'). Article 13 provides that in the case of 'caching', i.e., intermediate, automatic and temporary storage of transmitted information in order to increase efficiency, the service provider should not be held liable for the information stored on condition that several conditions are met ('caching exemption'). Finally, Article 14 provides that in case the provider does not have actual knowledge of illegal activity or information or the provider, upon obtaining such knowledge or awareness, acts expeditiously to remove or to disable access to the information, then he is not liable for the information stored at the request of a recipient of the service, when the information society service provided consists of the storage of information provided by a recipient of the service ('hosting exemption').

In the US, the Digital Millennium Copyright Act also includes a set of provisions commonly known as the DMCA Safe Harbors (17 U.S.C. § 512) resembling the aforementioned European provisions in that they are designed to protect online service providers from liability from copyright claims arising out of their end-users' allegedly infringing conduct. The US safe harbour provisions cover the following situations: Hosting, storing and making infringing matter available if it was stored at the direction of users (the Storage Safe Harbor, 17 U.S.C. § 512(c)); Transmitting, routing or providing connections (e.g., telephone lines) for digital online connections for infringing material transmitted by users (the Transmission Safe Harbor, 17 U.S.C. § 512(a)); Caching infringing material on a system or network, when the material was initially made available by someone else (the Caching Safe Harbor, 17 U.S.C. § 512(b)); or providing links or referred users to online locations containing infringing matter or activity (the Search Engine or Information Location Tools Safe Harbor, 17 U.S.C. § 512(d)).

The characterization of the main two app stores as 'hosts' of content having developed and maintaining an online app store to which users are directed, shall depend on their special characteristics: more specifically, Apple (1) has turned the App Store into a closed system that Apple heavily regulates and developers must obtain Apple's approval to develop and place their app on the App Store,[89] (2) requires use of iTunes software as a gateway, i.e., it does not permit a user to visit any other website in order to purchase Apple apps without downloading or accessing iTunes via a mobile device[90] and (3) does not allow third parties to sell Apple compatible apps on their own websites. By way of contrast, Google (1) has not developed a closed system heavily regulated by it and, in such a context, apps published on the Android app store do not need approval by Google,[91] (2) uses a website for the Android App Store, Google Play, that can be accessed by any user without being redirected through an intermediate

89. App Store Review Guidelines, App Store Resource Center, available at: https://developer.apple.com/app-store/review/guidelines/ (last visited September 2018).
90. App Store on iTunes Preview, available at: https://itunes.apple.com/us/genre/ios/id36?mt = 8 (last visited September 2018).
91. Developer Program Policies, available at https://play.google.com/about/developer-content-policy/#!?modal_active = none (last visited September 2018).

platform (such as iTunes)[92] and (3) allows third-party developers to sell Android apps on other websites outside the Android App Store.[93]

Until recently, ISPs have avoided primary liability due to their passive role, as opposed to being active infringers.[94] Recently, the scope of secondary liability seems to have been amended both by means of CJEU's jurisprudence and the new DSM Directive.[95] In terms of jurisprudence, the CJEU held that hyperlinking infringes the making available right in case it enables access to works or subject matter by means or a public not authorized by the rightholder[96] or in case the link-provider knew or ought reasonably to have known that the work or subject matter had been posted on the third party's website unlawfully; this will be the case when hyperlinking was profit motivated and the link-provider did not confirm the rightholder's consent to the work or subject matter being posted.[97] With regard to the DSM Directive, it exposes ISPs that host large volumes of protected works of subject matter uploaded by users of their services to primary liability for the actions of their users. 'Online content-sharing service providers', that is 'any provider of an information society service of which the main or one of the main purposes is to store and give the public access to a large amount of copyright-protected works or other protected subject matter uploaded by its users, which it organizes and promotes for profit-making purposes' (Article 2(6)) communicates such works and/or subject matter to the public within the meaning of Article 3(1) InfoSoc Directive (Article 17) and is expressly held that in such an instance 'the limitation of liability established in Article 14(1) of Directive 2000/31/EC shall not apply' (Article 17(3) DSMD). Therefore, subject to the limitations and exceptions found in Article 17, ISPs are now required to ensure content shared by users of their services it is not infringing and, if it is infringing, to obtain the necessary permissions by the rightholders. The Directive was adopted on 17 April 2019, and Member States have until 7 June 2021 to transpose and implement it. It is expected that any ambiguities and nuances of Article 17 will be clarified by means of guidance which shall be issued by the Commission on application of Article 17 of the Directive.

## §3.05 DATABASE RIGHT

There are apps, like Flipboard, Youtube, Spotify, etc., the core component of which are databases, such as a collection of songs, videos, news, books, etc., while all apps need

92. *Ibid.*
93. Android.com, *Publish your app - Releasing through a website*, available at: https://developer.android.com/studio/publish/ (last visited September 2018).
94. CJEU decision of 23 March 2010 in Joined Cases C-236/08 to C-238/08, namely *Google France SARL and Google Inc. v. Louis Vuitton Malletier SA (C-236/08), Google France SARL v. Viaticum SA and Luteciel SARL (C-237/08) and Google France SARL v. Centre national de recherche en relations humaines (CNRRH) SARL and Others (C-238/08)*, ECLI:EU:C:2010:159.
95. Directive (EU) 2019/790 of the EU Parliament and of the Council of 17 April 2019 on copyright and related rights in the Digital Single Market and amending Directives 96/9/EC and 2001/29/EC.
96. Case C-466/12, *Svensson v. Retriever Sverige AB*, [2014] EUECJ.
97. Case C-527/15, *Stichting Brein v. Wullems (t/a Filmspeler)*; Case C-160/15, *GS Media v. Sanoma Media Netherlands*, BV EU:C:2016:644.

databases to store and retrieve data such as the app's users. Moreover, there are apps the core components of which are databases - sub-products of another activity of a database producer whose main investments relate to another economic activity and do not directly concern the creation of the database, such as the apps of airlines permitting for the booking of flights. Last but not least, there are the so-called mobile databases, as opposed to external databases, which play an important role in mobile app development because they ensure that an app still works when a mobile computing environment encounters operation problems, they solve problems regarding routing and query processing, they ensure that an app can also work offline, and generally ensure that an app operates seamlessly.

According to Recitals 9, 10 and 12 of the Databases Directive, the purpose of the Directive is to stimulate the creation of data storage and processing systems in order to contribute to the development of an information market against a background of exponential growth in the amount of information generated and processed annually in all sectors of activity and to protect the creation of material capable or being collected in a database. Databases are not protected as literary or any other existing type of works but, instead, they are defined as 'a collection of independent works, data or other materials arranged in a systematic or methodical way and individually accessible by electronic or other means' (Article 1(2) of the Directive). Protection is not afforded to databases which are created or operated by computer programs or algorithms (Article 1(3)) and to software used to create the database or the material contained therein.

The notion of 'independent materials' of a 'database' within the meaning of the above definition has been interpreted by the Court in *Fixtures Marketing Ltd v. Organismos prognostikon agonon podosfairou AE (OPAP)* case, where it was clarified that independent materials within the meaning of Article 1(2) of the Directive are those which are separable from one another without their informative, literary, artistic, musical or other value being affected and, consequently, have an autonomous informative value.[98]

The notion has been further clarified in the *Freistaat Bayern v. VerlagEsterbauer GmbH* case[99] where the cause of the dispute was the unauthorized scanning of the Land of Bavaria's topographic maps and the subsequent extraction and reuse of geographical information by a third-party publisher for the creation of his own maps. The Court was asked to elucidate whether the geographical data extracted from the topographic map

98. Case C-444/02, *Fixtures Marketing Ltd v. Organismos prognostikon agonon podosfairou AE (OPAP)*, [2004] I-ECR 10549, where it was held that:

> [t]he term 'database' as defined in Article 1(2) of Directive 96/9/EC of the European Parliament and of the Council of 11 March 1996 on the legal protection of databases refers to any collection of works, data or other materials, separable from one another without the value of their contents being affected, including a method or system of some sort for the retrieval of each of its constituent materials. A fixture list for a football league such as that at issue in the case in the main proceedings constitutes a database within the meaning of Article 1(2) of Directive 96/9.

99. Case C-490/14, *Freistaat Bayern v. Verlag Esterbauer GmbH*, [2010] ECR I-02417.

retained, after extraction, sufficient informative value so as to be held to be 'independent material' of a 'database' (within the meaning of the definition in Article 1(2)). The Court affirmed that analogue topographic maps are protected as databases irrespective of whether their separable pieces of geographical information lose all or part of their individual informative value after having been extracted; the value of those pieces of information to the users of sub-products of the initial database made by third parties is what matters. The evaluation of the informative value of the materials should be flexible and take into consideration the collective informative value of the pieces of information which have been reused. The Court asserted that not only an individual piece of information but also a combination of pieces of information can constitute 'independent material' within the meaning of Article 1(2) of Directive 96/9. Therefore, the combination of those two pieces of information can have an autonomous informative value, since those combined data convey relevant information to the customers of the third party who has selectively extracted them from the maps. In order to reach this conclusion, the Court interpreted the concept of 'informative value' broadly by disconnecting it from common value standards, such as the principal intended use, and it seems that for the Court it is sufficient that the subsequent reuse of the data has a certain independent commercial value. The Court's approach seems to be in line with the intention of the EU legislature to ensure a broad definition of the term 'database' (paragraph 26 of the judgment).

### [A] Copyright in Databases

The Directive provides protection to databases by means of copyright and the so-called sui generis right. Copyright protection is afforded only to the structure of a database. Article 3 provides that copyright protection is afforded to databases which 'constitute the author's own intellectual creation' 'by reason of the selection or arrangement of their contents'.[100] Moreover, Recital 16 provides that 'no criterion other than originality in the sense of the author's intellectual creation should be applied to determine the eligibility of the database for copyright protection, and in particular no aesthetic or qualitative criteria should be applied'.

100. *See also* the Berne Convention for the Protection of Literary and Artistic Works (Paris Act, 1971) which states in Article 2(5) that '[c]ollections of literary or artistic works such as encyclopaedias and anthologies which, by reason of the selection and arrangement of their contents, constitute intellectual creations shall be protected as such, without prejudice to the copyright in each of the works forming part of such collections'. Similarly, the TRIPS Agreement provides in Article 10 that '[c]ompilations of data or other material, whether in machine readable or other form, which by reason of the selection or arrangement of their contents constitute intellectual creations shall be protected as such. Such protection, which shall not extend to the data or material itself, shall be without prejudice to any copyright subsisting in the data or material itself.' Finally, the WIPO Copyright Treaty (WCT) provides in Article 5 that '[c]ompilations of data or other material, in any form, which by reason of the selection or arrangement of their contents constitute intellectual creations, are protected as such. This protection does not extend to the data or the material itself and is without prejudice to any copyright subsisting in the data or material contained in the compilation.'

Copyright in the database's contents is afforded only in accordance with traditional copyright law as the Directive explicitly provides in Article 3(2), according to which, '[t]he copyright protection of databases ... shall not extend to their contents and shall be without prejudice to any rights subsisting in those contents themselves'. Similarly, Recital 15 provides that 'the criteria used to determine whether a database should be protected by copyright should be defined to the fact that the selection of the arrangement or the contents of the database is the author's own intellectual creation; ... such protection should cover the structure of the database'.

The issue of copyright protection of databases was discussed in *Football Dataco & Ors v. Yahoo! & Ors.*[101] In the said case, the applicant was creating lists of all the fixtures to take place yearly in English and Scottish football leagues while the defendant was using those lists in their commercial activities which were news reporting, betting, etc. In the context of this dispute, CJEU was asked whether football fixtures are copyright protected databases under the Databases Directive. The Court held that in order for copyright to subsist in a database, the structure of the database must constitute the 'original expression of the creative freedom of its author', free from technical or other restraints[102] and that a database is protected by copyright provided that the selection or arrangement of its data amounts to an original expression of the creative freedom of its authors, which is a matter for the national court to determine; consequently, (a) the intellectual effort and skill of creating that data are not relevant in order to assess the eligibility of that database for copyright protection,[103] (b) it is irrelevant, for the purpose of assessing the eligibility of that database for copyright protection, whether or not the selection or arrangement of that data includes the addition of important significance to that data,[104] and (c) the significant labour and skill required for setting up that database cannot as such justify such a protection if they do not express any originality in the selection or arrangement of the database's data.[105]

### [B] Sui Generis Right

The sui generis protection afforded by the Database Directive concerns the contents of the databases and is not granted on the basis of originality but, instead, on the basis of a 'substantial investment' in either obtaining, verification or presenting the contents of the database. Article 7(1) of the Directive provides that protection is afforded when 'there has been qualitatively and/or quantitatively a substantial investment in either the obtaining, verification or presentation of the [database's] contents to prevent extraction and/or re-utilization of the whole or of a substantial part, evaluated qualitatively and/or quantitatively, of the contents of that database'. Not only substantial parts are protected against extraction and re-utilization but also insubstantial parts as well to the extent extraction and re-utilization are systematic and 'conflict with a

101. Case C-604/10, *Football Dataco & Others v. Yahoo! & Others*, [2012] 2 CMLR 24.
102. *Ibid.*, paras 38, 39.
103. *Ibid.*, paras 42, 46.
104. *Ibid.*, paras 35, 41.
105. *Ibid.*, paras 42, 46.

normal exploitation of that database or ... unreasonably prejudice the legitimate interests or the maker or the database ... ' (Article 7(5) of the Directive).

Article 8(1) of the Directive on 'rights and obligations of lawful users' provides that a lawful user of the database may not be prevented by the maker of the database 'from extracting and/or re-utilizing insubstantial parts of its contents, evaluated qualitatively and/or quantitatively, for any purpose whatsoever'. Article 8(2) provides that a lawful user of a database 'may not perform acts which conflict with normal exploitation of the database or unreasonably prejudice the legitimate interests of the maker of the database' while Article 8(3) provides that he/she 'may not cause prejudice to the holder of a copyright or related right in respect of the works or subject matter contained in the database'.

The exceptions to the sui generis rights can be found in Article 9 of the Directive and concern: (1) extraction for private purposes of the contents of a non-electronic database, (2) extraction for the purposes of illustration for teaching or scientific research, as long as the source is indicated and to the extent justified by the non-commercial purpose to be achieved and (3) extraction and/or reutilization for the purposes of public security or an administrative or judicial procedure.

In the *Fixtures Marketing Ltd* cases,[106] the Court held that:

> [t]he expression 'investment in ... the obtaining ... of the contents' of a database in Article 7(1) of Directive 96/9/EC ... must be understood to refer to the resources used to seek out existing independent materials and collect them in the database. It does not cover the resources used for the creation of materials which make up the contents of a database. In the context of drawing up a fixture list for the purpose of organising football league fixtures, therefore, it does not cover the resources used to establish the dates, times and the team pairings for the various matches in the league.[107]

In C-203/02 *British Horseracing Board (BHB) v. William Hill (WH)* case,[108] the applicant's database was comprised by a huge number of records relating to horseracing (names of horses, owners, trainers, jockeys, fixture lists) and the applicant claimed that the defendant's use of the fixture lists on the latter's internet betting site was infringing its database rights in fixture lists. The CJEU stipulated that database rights did not exist in the BHB database and, accordingly, WH did not infringe those rights by extracting or re-utilizing either a substantial part or insubstantial parts of the 'database'. The Court found, in particular, that the resources deployed by BHB in relation to the selection of the horses admitted participating in each race concerned the creation of the data and not the database itself.[109] Although the process of entering a horse in a

106. Case C-46/02, *Fixtures Marketing Ltd v. Oy Veikkaus Ab*, [2004] ECR 1-10365; Case C-338/02, *Fixtures Marketing Ltd v. Svenska Spel AB*, ECLI:EU:C:2004:696; Case C-444/02, *Fixtures Marketing Ltd v. Organismos prognostikon agonon podosfairou AE (OPAP)*, [2004] I-ECR 10549.
107. Case C-444/02, *Fixtures Marketing Ltd v. Organismos prognostikon agonon podosfairou AE (OPAP)*.
108. Case C-203/02, *The British Horseracing Board (BHB) and Others v. William Hill Organisation Ltd* (WH), [2004] ECR I-10415.
109. *Ibid.*, paras 38–41.

race requires an investment with regard to the checking of the identity of the person making the entry, the horse, its owner and the jockey, this investment is linked to the resources necessary to create the database. Accordingly, it was held that, notwithstanding the fact that the applicant's data were vital to the organization of horse races, the defendant could not have taken a quantitative or qualitative substantial part of the database since the data taken was not of the right sort, i.e., was data created rather than data collected.[110]

The court clarified another important issue, that is the issue of whether the concepts of extraction and re-utilization concern only such actions in relation to the original database or not (given that some of BHB's data used by WH were published in newspapers prior to the races). In that respect, the Court held that these concepts:

> cannot be exhaustively defined as instances of extraction and re-utilisation directly from the original database at the risk of leaving the maker or the database without protection from unauthorized copying from a copy of the database. That interpretation is confirmed by Article 7(2)(b) of the [Database] directive, according to which the first sale of a copy of a database within the Community by the rightholder or with his consent is to exhaust the right to control 'resale', but not the right to control extraction and re-utilisation of the contents, of that copy within the Community.[111]

In other words, the concepts of extraction and re-utilization 'do not imply direct access to the database concerned'.[112]

The Court also clarified the issue of whether materials derived from a database constitute or not a part, substantial or insubstantial, of that database, 'where their systematic or methodical arrangement and the conditions of their individual accessibility have been altered by the person carrying out the extraction and/or re-utilisation'.[113] The Court answered that question negatively and explicitly held that '[t]he change made by the person making the extraction and re-utilisation to the arrangement or the conditions of individual accessibility of the data affected by that act cannot, in any event, have the effect of transforming a part of the contents of the database at issue which is not substantial into a substantial part'.[114] In other words, the alteration of the systematic or methodical arrangement and individual accessibility or works, data or other materials derived from a database by the person extracting and re-utilizing such materials do not affect the characterization of the part of the database extracted and re-utilised as either substantial or insubstantial.

In relation to the preliminary question concerning Article 7(5) of the Directive, i.e., to what extent the repeated and systematic extraction and/or re-utilization or insubstantial parts or the contents of a database is permitted, the Court held that such acts are forbidden when they, according to Article 7(5) of the Directive:

110. *Ibid.*, para. 80.
111. *Ibid.*, para. 52.
112. *Ibid.*, para. 67.
113. *Ibid.*, para. 68.
114. *Ibid.*, paras 22(1) and 81.

'conflict with a normal exploitation of that database or [when they] unreasonably prejudice the legitimate interests of the maker of the database', that is they are 'unauthorized actions for the purpose of reconstituting, through the cumulative effect of acts of extraction, the whole or a substantial part of the contents of a database protected by the sui generis rights and/or making available to the public, through the cumulative effect or acts of re-utilisation, the whole or a substantial part of the contents of such a database, which seriously prejudice the investment made by the maker of the database'.[115]

### [C] Databases Not Protected by Copyright or Sui Generis Right

Databases may not always be protected under the Database Directive, in particular when they are sub-products of another activity of a database producer whose main investments relate to another economic activity and do not directly concern the creation of the database, such as the apps of airlines permitting for the booking of flights.

In *Ryanair Ltd v. PR Aviation BV* case,[116] the CJEU held that owner of an online database not protected by copyright or sui generis right may restrict its use by contract. This case concerned a defendant operating a website allowing consumers to search through the flight data of low-cost air companies in the context of which it obtained the necessary data to respond to queries automatically from a dataset linked to the applicant's website (Ryanair). Access to applicant's website presupposed acceptance of its general terms and conditions by ticking a box to that effect. According to these general terms and conditions, the information contained on the site could be used only for private and non-commercial purposes and the use of automated systems or software to extract data from the site for commercial purposes ('screen scraping') was prohibited, unless the third party has directly entered into a written licence agreement with the applicant. The applicant claimed that the defendant had infringed copyright law and the database sui generis right and that it had acted contrary to the terms and condition of use of its website.

After having its claims dismissed by both the Rechtbank Utrecht and the Court of Appeal of Amsterdam, Ryanair appealed against the judgment of the Court of Appeal of Amsterdam before the Netherlands Supreme Court. The Netherlands Supreme Court decided to stay the proceedings and to refer the following question to the CJEU for a preliminary ruling: Does the operation of the Directive 96/9 also extend to online databases which are not protected by copyright and also not by a sui generis right, in the sense that the freedom to use such databases may not be limited contractually?

The Court held that in case a database is not protected by copyright or the sui generis right then the provisions of the Database Directive are not applicable to it and, accordingly, the author or producer of such a database is not precluded from laying down contractual limitations on its use by third parties, in accordance to the national law. In other words, in such a case there is no need to safeguard the minimal level of

115. *Ibid.*, para. 89.
116. Case C-30/14, *Ryanair Ltd v. PR Aviation BV*, ECLI:EU:C:2015:10.

free use of the database contents for the database's users, such as the right for a lawful user to extract and reuse an insubstantial part of the database's contents for any reason, even for non-commercial purposes. Accordingly, in case of databases – sub-products of another activity of a database producer whose main investments relate to another economic activity and do not directly concern the creation of the database – this decision affirms that in case a database does not merit protection under the Database Directive then contractual freedom prevails over the provisions of the Databases Directive, Articles 6(1) and 8 of the Databases Directive included.

## §3.06 PATENTS

Apps make phones function in a certain way by running a process on a mobile phone that connects to a remote server containing data that either stores the data or processes it to be used on the mobile phone. Therefore, apps are functional in nature and also are part of the methods of interaction, i.e., they determine to an extent how a smartphone/smartwatch, etc. functions. In technical terms, it has been argued that:

> mobile device apps exist in two parts, i.e. there is an app which runs on the user's device, and a remote server which may retain persistent user information and/or other data, or act as a processing centre or a conduit for communications between end-users. Any of the interactions and processing occurring at the mobile device(s), or at a server, or indeed any unique client/server transactions which take place, may form the basis for a patentable claim.[117]

Accordingly, several aspects of mobile apps can be patented such as server and mobile interaction and processing, interaction between servers and devices, database creation and user identification processes, transaction processes, etc.

Patentability requirements of smartphone apps resemble patentability requirements of computer-implemented inventions. Products, processes or products derived from a specific process can be patented. Computer code can be possibly patentable to the extent it executes a process. Thus, although computer code that runs the software is not patentable, computer-related inventions can be.

The European Patent Convention (EPC) provides a legal framework for the granting of European patents, via a single harmonized procedure before the European Patent Office (EPO). The eligibility and validity of patents are decided both at the EPO level, in relation to European patents, and at domestic level, in relation to national patents. Article 52(1) of the EPC provides that 'European patents shall be granted for any inventions, in all fields of technology, provided that they are new, involve an inventive step and are susceptible of industrial application.' Subject matter that are not considered 'inventions' are 'mathematical methods ... schemes, rules and methods for performing mental acts, playing games or doing business, and programs for computers ... presentations of information' (Article 52(2)). Finally, it provides that the said

117. Mark Sumerfield, *Can – And Should I – Patent my Smartphone App?*, posted on Patentology Blog on 04.10.2012 available at https://blog.patentology.com.au/2012/10/can-i-and-should-i-patent-my-smartphone.html (accessed December 2018).

exclusions 'shall exclude the patentability of the subject-matter or activities referred to therein only to the extent to which a European patent application or European patent relates to such subject-matter or activities as such' (Article 52(3)).

As confirmed in the EPO decision in *Comvik, Two Identities* case[118] regarding the patentability of software, patent claims may contain not only technical but also non-technical features within the meaning of Article 52(2) EPC. Thus, although a technical character is required for patentability, only the methods that do not solve a technical problem are excluded from patentability.[119]

Situations in which an excluded from patentability subject matter is claimed 'as such' have been discussed at the EPO at several instances. In the *Vicom* case, it was held that an invention is patentable if it satisfies the normal requirements for patentability under the EPC and should not be rejected because its implementation requires a computer program. It was expressly stated that 'decisive is what technical contribution the invention as defined in the claim when considered as a whole makes to the known art'.[120] In the *Pension Benefit* case,[121] the claims concerned a computer-implemented method of doing business excluded from patentability by means of Article 52(2) EPC. The Board of Appeals of EPO held that, one should ask whether the claimed subject matter, as a whole, has a technical character. Accordingly, a computer system must be regarded as a concrete technical apparatus rather than a non-technical method for doing business as such (that is excluded from patentability). In the particular case, the fact that the said computer system was simply a general-purpose computer programmed to execute a business method was irrelevant for assessment under Article 52. However, although the apparatus claims were found to constitute an invention within the meaning of Article 52(1), the method claims were found to describe a 'method-of-doing-business'. In the cases of *Hitachi*[122] and *Microsoft/Data Transfer,*[123] it was held that since apparatus claims in the case of computer-implemented inventions may not infringe Article 52(2), the corresponding method claims should not be excluded where they involve technical means. In the *Circuit Simulation/Infeneon Technologies* case[124], the Board held that the modelling methods the simulation of which were computer-implemented (the patent application concerned the simulation) contributed to the technical character of the claimed subject matter, an essential pre-requisite for the assessment of inventive step.

Finally, the landmark US decision of the Supreme Court in *Alice Corp. Pty. V. CLS Bank Int'l* (hereinafter 'Alice')[125] regarding patentability of software related inventions

118. OEB, T-641/00, 26 September 2002.
119. In the said case, it was held that the claimed concept of selectively distributing the costs for service and private calls or among different users does not make a contribution to the technical character of the invention and the patent application does not provide any technical contribution that could be the basis for an inventive step and the patent awarded was revoked.
120. Vicom/Computer-Related Inventions [1987] OJ EPO 14.
121. Pension Benefit Systems (T931/95) OJ EPO 441.
122. Auction Method/HITACHI (T 258/03) [2004] OJ 2004, 575.
123. Microsoft/Data Transfer (T424/03) [2006] 40 EPOR 533.
124. T-1227/05, *Circuit Simulation/Infeneon Technologies*, [2007] OJ EPO 574.
125. 134 S. Ct. 2347 (2014).

concerned a computerized trading platform eliminating the risk in financial transactions between two parties by using a natural third party, operating as an escrow safeguarding that both parties meet their respective obligations. The Supreme Court held that the particular patent claims were merely referring to a generic computer implementation of the covered abstract idea and not to an eligible subject matter. The Court held that one should ask three things to conclude whether the claims involve an abstract idea or not: (a) whether the claim concerns a process, machine, manufacture, or composition of matter; in case the answer is negative, the claim does not involve an eligible subject matter. In case the answer is positive, it should be asked (b) whether the claim is directed to a law of nature, natural phenomenon or an abstract idea; if the answer is negative, the claim is patentable. If the answer is positive, it should be asked (c) whether the claim is not caught by any judicial exceptions; if yes, the claim involves a patent-eligible subject matter while if no, the claim does not involve an eligible subject matter. In the case at hand, it was decided that the claims passed the first preliminary question but not the second and third.

## §3.07 TRADEMARKS

In the area of mobile apps, trademarks can play an important role since they can be registered for any signs and also for GUIs or GUIs' features whether they are static or animated. In 2015, took place an EU trademark reform: the harmonized law of registered trademarks across the EU was updated by means of new Trade Mark Directive 2015/2436,[126] while the law governing the EU trademark was updated by means of the European Union Trade Mark Regulation 2015/2424.[127]

Trademark protection is awarded following prior registration which must clearly and precisely define the subject matter for which protection is sought. Animated GUIS and/or GUI features are now easier to protect in the form of animated multimedia trademarks. The reformed trademark provisions amended the requirement of graphic representation on the Register and provide that a sign should be permitted to be represented in any appropriate way while there are more technological options available to register signs (Recital 13 of the Directive, Recital 10 of the Regulation). Such options may include audio files, video files and a series of images in a sequence representing the movement for which protection is sought.[128]

For trademark protection to be awarded a certain distinctiveness threshold must be passed, i.e., the mark to be registered must not be descriptive and must have some

126. Directive (EU) 2015/2436 of the European Parliament and of the Council of 16 December 2015 to approximate the laws of the Member States relating to trade marks, OJ L 336, 23.12.2015, pp. 1–26.
127. Regulation (EU) 2015/2424 of the European Parliament and of the Council of 16 December 2015 amending Council Regulation (EC) No. 207/2009 on the Community trade mark and Commission Regulation (EC) No. 2868/95 implementing Council Regulation (EC) No. 40/94 on the Community trade mark, and repealing Commission Regulation (EC) No. 2869/95 on the fees payable to the Office for Harmonization in the Internal Market (Trade Marks and Designs), OJ L 341, 24.12.2015, pp. 21–94.
128. Justine Pila & Paul Torremans, *supra* n. 36, p. 350.

distinctiveness instead and, accordingly, denote origin. In relation to GUIs, it has been argued that this is not an easy task since: 'consumers are less accustomed to consider interfaces as indicating origin and are more likely to treat them simply as aesthetic, functional or arbitrary features' and, as a result:

> it is more likely that an applicant will have to show that the GUI or features thereof have acquired a distinctive character through use, as opposed to being inherently distinctive. Effectively, this means that ... the applicant might have to rely on the prior use where consumers are educated to view the GUI at issue as indicating source rather than merely enabling interaction with a device.[129]

Apart from the distinctiveness feature, the product feature for which protection is sought should not fall under the functionality exception and/or the exception concerning signs which consist exclusively of characteristics which give substantial value to the goods. Under the functionality exception, product features whose objective is functional or technical cannot be awarded trademark protection. In particular, the Trademark Directive in Article 4(1)(e)(ii) provides that signs which consist exclusively of 'the shape, or another characteristic, of goods which is necessary to obtain a technical result' shall not be registered. It has been argued that the functionality exception is particularly relevant in the context of the GUIs whose main purpose is to enable users to interact with mobile phones and which, as a result, may not be eligible for trademark protection.[130]

Regarding the exception concerning signs which consist exclusively of characteristics which give substantial value to the goods, the Trademark Directive provides in Article 4(1)(e)(iii) that a sign that consists exclusively of the shape, or another characteristic, which gives substantial value to the goods, is precluded from registration.

## §3.08 UNFAIR COMPETITION

Both the external aspects of an app, i.e., the GUIs, and the functional elements of an app, whether considered as unregistered trademarks or not, could be protected by unfair competition law.

At an international level, Article 10*bis* of the Paris Convention Paris Convention for the Protection of Industrial Property (as amended on 28 September 1979) provides that unfair competition requires acting in such a way as to cause confusion 'by any means whatever with the establishment, the goods, or the industrial or commercial activities, of a competitor' (Article 10*bis*(3)(i)), as to damage competitors' goodwill or reputation (Article 10*bis*(3)(ii)), or as to 'mislead the public as to the nature, the manufacturing process, the characteristics, the suitability for their purpose, or the quantity of the goods' (Article 10*bis*(3)(iii)). These three categories operate in the broader definition of unfair competition in the form of '[a]ny act of competition contrary to honest practices in industrial or commercial matters' (Article 10*bis*(2)). In

129. Shemtov, *supra* n. 30, p. 45.
130. *Ibid.*

this context, WIPO undertook the initiative and prepared a study on protection against unfair competition reflecting the world situation in 1994[131] and also drafted the WIPO Model Provisions on Protection Against Unfair Competition in 1996.[132]

At the EU level, there is no single instrument dealing with competition law and the only areas where there is legislative intervention is comparative and misleading advertising and unfair commercial practices. The Comparative Advertising Directive 2006/114/EC[133] applies to advertising that explicitly or implicitly identifies a competitor or goods or services offered by a competitor (Article 2(c)). Unfair Commercial Directive 2005/29/EC[134] applies to 'any act, omission, course of conduct or representation, commercial communication including advertising and marketing, by a trader, directly connected with the promotion, sale or supply of a product to consumers' (Article 2(d)). According to Article 5(2):

> [a] commercial practice shall be unfair if: (a) it is contrary to the requirements of professional diligence, and (b) it materially distorts or is likely to materially distort the economic behaviour with regard to the product of the average consumer whom it reaches or to whom it is addressed, or of the average member of the group when a commercial practice is directed to a particular group of consumers.

Apart from the international and European developments mentioned above, unfair competition provisions are jurisdiction-specific. Regarding the civil law model of unfair competition law, broadly speaking, there has been developed a tort of unfair completion that does not require consumer deception. On the contrary, in common law countries there has been developed a stricter tort of passing-off by misrepresentation requiring consumer deception.

In the case of unregistered trademarks, imitation which could give rise to confusion as to the app's origin or affiliation is required. Finally, with regard to emulated features of apps, one must be careful not to fall within the functionality exception present under many unfair competition laws, according to which functional features are not protectable. In order not to fall within such an exception, it has been argued that it must be shown that: 'the manner in which the concept was put into effect in the emulated input and output resulted from arbitrary choices made by the original developer, rather than from functionality-related constraints'.[135]

131. WIPO publication No. 725, *Protection Against Unfair Competition – Analysis of the Present World* (Geneva 1994).
132. WIPO, *Model Provisions on Protection Against Unfair Competition* (1996), available at https://www.wipo.int/publications/en/details.jsp?id=3227&plang=EN (last accessed: 20 December 2019).
133. Directive 2006/114/EC of the European Parliament and of the Council of 12 December 2006 concerning misleading and comparative advertising, OJ L 376, 27.12.2006, pp. 21–27.
134. Directive 2005/29/EC of the European Parliament and of the Council of 11 May 2005 concerning unfair business-to-consumer commercial practices in the internal market and amending Council Directive 84/450/EEC, Directives 97/7/EC, 98/27/EC and 2002/65/EC of the European Parliament and of the Council and Regulation (EC) No 2006/2004 of the European Parliament and of the Council, OJ L 149, 11.6.2005, pp. 22–39.
135. Shemtov, *supra* n. 30, p. 56.

CHAPTER 4

# Protection of Users

*Eleftheria Papadimitriou*

*Mobile applications have raised critical legal issues pertaining to consumers' protection under EU consumer protection law. The consumer acquis is being challenged and consequently, the EU legislation needs to adapt to the digital era. The Consumer Rights Directive (CRD) and the Unfair Commercial Practices Directive (UCPD) have been amended to fit the technological progress and the new business models that have emerged. In this chapter, the complex legal framework of user protection in digital content is examined under the light of the aforementioned Directives. The intricacies of the traders' general precontractual, contractual and post-contractual information obligations are analyzed with respect to mobile applications. The withdrawal right is examined with reference to the case study of the two main App Distribution Platforms, that is, Google Play and Apple App Store. Unfair commercial practices, misleading and aggressive, are viewed with respect to the "average consumer" notion adopted by the European Court of Justice, while attention is given to special group of consumers, namely children that are more vulnerable than average consumers. The information obligation provided by the Regulation on consumer ODR and the Directive on consumer ADR is presented with reference to case law. Finally, conclusions are drawn, taking into consideration the new enforcement measures adopted by the Directive 2019/2161 in EU's attempt to achieve better enforcement and modernize Union's consumer protection rules.*

## §4.01 INTRODUCTION

The use of mobile devices has increased dramatically worldwide, during the last few years. In 2017, the time spent on the internet was more on mobile devices rather on desktops.[1] From the consumers' point of view, there is a clear preference on mobile apps in comparison to mobile sites.[2] This tendency highlights the importance for the examination of mobile apps under the prism of consumer protection. Thus, in this chapter, the protection provided to consumers, mainly by the Consumer Rights Directive (CRD)[3] and the Unfair Commercial Practices Directive (UCPD), will be presented.[4] The recent amendments by the Directive (EU) 2019/2161[5] are also taken into consideration. The Regulation on online dispute resolution for consumer disputes (Regulation on consumer ODR)[6] and its complementing Directive on alternative dispute resolution for consumer disputes (Directive on consumer ADR)[7] shall be examined in the same vein.

## §4.02 THE COMPLEX LEGAL FRAMEWORK OF USER PROTECTION IN DIGITAL CONTENT CONTRACTS[8]

The examination of users' protection in the digital content contracts area presupposes an in-depth understanding of digital content and of its legal treatment. Contracts for the provision of digital content are highly regulated by a number of Directives, that is, CRD

1. The 62% of the time spent on the internet was on mobile devices, available at https://www.ofcom.org.uk/research-and-data/multi-sector-research/cmr/cmr-2018/summary.
2. According to statistics on consumer mobile usage, more than 80% of the time spent in mobiles is spent in apps, available at https://www.smartinsights.com/mobile-marketing/mobile-marketing-analytics/mobile-marketing-statistics.
3. Directive 2011/83/EU of the European Parliament and of the Council of 25 October 2011 on consumer rights, amending Council Directive 93/13/EEC and Directive 1999/44/EC of the European Parliament and of the Council and repealing Council Directive 85/577/EEC and Directive 97/7/EC of the European Parliament and of the Council, OJ L 304/64, ELI: http://data.europa.eu/eli/dir/2011/83/oj.
4. Directive 2005/29/EC of the European Parliament and of the Council of 11 May 2005 concerning unfair business-to-consumer commercial practices in the internal market and amending Council Directive 84/450/EEC, Directives 97/7/EC, 98/27/EC and 2002/65/EC of the European Parliament and of the Council and Regulation (EC) No. 2006/2004 of the European Parliament and of the Council ("Unfair Commercial Practices Directive"), OJ L 149, 11.6.2005, pp. 22–39, ELI: http://data.europa.eu/eli/dir/2005/29/oj.
5. Directive (EU) 2019/2161 of the European Parliament and of the Council of 27 November 2019 amending Council Directive 93/13/EEC and Directives 98/6/EC, 2005/29/EC and 2011/83/EU of the European Parliament and of the Council as regards the better enforcement and modernisation of Union consumer protection rules, OJ L 328, 18.12.2019, pp. 7–28, ELI: http://data.europa.eu/eli/dir/2019/2161/oj.
6. Regulation (EU) No. 524/2013 of the European Parliament and of the Council of 21 May 2013 on online dispute resolution for consumer disputes and amending Regulation (EC) No. 2006/2004 and Directive 2009/22/EC (Regulation on consumer ODR), OJ L 165, 18.6.2013, pp. 1–12, ELI: http://data.europa.eu/eli/reg/2013/524/oj.
7. Directive 2013/11/EU of the European Parliament and of the Council of 21 May 2013 on alternative dispute resolution for consumer disputes and amending Regulation (EC) No. 2006/2004 and Directive 2009/22/EC (Directive on consumer ADR), OJ L 165, 18.6.2013, pp. 63–79, ELI: http://data.europa.eu/eli/dir/2013/11/oj.
8. Section §4.02 is written by Vassiliki Samartzi.

2011/83/EU,[9] E-Commerce Directive 2000/31/EC,[10] UCPD 2005/29/EC,[11] InfoSoc Directive 2001/29 which has been recently amended by the Directive on Copyright in the Digital Single Market 2019/790,[12] Software Directive 2009/24/EC[13] and recently adopted by the European Council Digital Content Directive (DCD).[14]

"Digital content" can be tangible or intangible, depending on the way it is supplied and can be accessed, that is, through a tangible medium or not. The CRD defines "digital content" as "data which are produced and supplied in digital form" (Articles 2, 11 of CRD) and also provides that "digital content means data which are produced and supplied in digital form, such as computer programs, applications, games, music, videos or texts, irrespective of whether they are accessed through downloading or streaming, from a tangible medium or through any other means" (Recital 19 of the CPD). Similarly, the DCD defines "digital content" as "data which is produced and supplied in digital form" (Article 2(1) of the DCD).

Notwithstanding their common definition of "digital content," the aforementioned two Directives treat "digital content" differently although for the DCD the distribution channel (i.e., online, offline, tangible, intangible) is irrelevant for the legal treatment of "digital content," the CRD provides that different rules apply depending on whether the digital content is supplied on a tangible or an intangible medium. Moreover, according to the DCD, digital content shall be subject to an agreement concluded between the supplier and the consumer no matter the counter-performance of the consumer while, by way of contrast, the CRD applies only to sales and services contracts between the supplier and the consumer where the counter-performance of the consumer is constituted to the payment of the price thereof. The fact that the DCD applies, irrespectively of whether the counter-performance of the user is the payment of a price or the processing of his personal data or other data, underlines the

9. Directive 2011/83/EU of the European Parliament and of the Council of 25 October 2011 on consumer rights, amending Council Directive 93/13/EEC and Directive 1999/44/EC of the European Parliament and of the Council and repealing Council Directive 85/577/EEC and Directive 97/7/EC of the European Parliament and of the Council Text with EEA relevance, OJ L 304, 22.11.2011, pp. 64–88.
10. Directive 2000/31/EC of the European Parliament and of the Council of 8 June 2000 on certain legal aspects of information society services, in particular electronic commerce, in the Internal Market, OJ L 178, 17.7.2000, pp. 1–16.
11. Directive 2005/29/EC of the European Parliament and of the Council of 11 May 2005 concerning unfair business-to-consumer commercial practices in the internal market and amending Council Directive 84/450/EEC, Directives 97/7/EC, 98/27/EC and 2002/65/EC of the European Parliament and of the Council and Regulation (EC) No. 2006/2004, OJ L 149, 11.6.2005, pp. 22–39.
12. Directive (EU) 2019/790 of the European Parliament and of the Council of 17 April 2019 on copyright and related rights in the Digital Single Market and amending Directives 96/9/EC and 2001/29/EC.
13. Directive 2009/24/EC of the European Parliament and of the Council of 23 April 2009 on the legal protection of computer programs, OJ L 111, 5.5.2009, pp. 16–22.
14. Directive of the European Parliament and of the Council on certain aspects concerning contracts for the supply of digital content, available online at https://data.consilium.europa.eu/doc/document/PE-26-2019-INIT/en/pdf.

importance of data protection for the users of mobile apps and, accordingly, the necessity to examine the particular field of law in relation to the issue we analyze in the present work, that is, the protection of users of mobile apps.

Regulation of digital content is closely connected to regulation of products, consumer goods, digital goods, digital services and sales contracts, service contracts, and contracts for the supply of digital content not supplied on a tangible medium (sui generis contract). A "product" is defined in the UCPD as "any goods or service including immovable property, rights and obligations" (Article 2(c)), and this definition applies equally to tangible and intangible digital content. A "consumer good" is defined in the Sales of Consumer Goods Directive 1999/44/EC as "any tangible moveable item" (*see also* CRD, Article 2(3)) and, thus, it can be plausibly argued that this Directive does not apply in the case of intangible digital content.

Regarding that notion of "service," the DCD defines "digital service" as "(a) a service that allows the creation, processing or storage of data in digital form, where such data are uploaded or created by the consumer, or (b) a service that allows the sharing of, and any other interaction with, data in digital form that has been uploaded or created by the consumer or by other users of the service, or both" (Article 1a of the DCD). In relation to the notion of "goods," the CRD provides that "if digital content is supplied on a tangible medium, such as a CD or a DVD, it should be considered as goods" (Recital 19). What is more, the CRD contains provisions referring to "contracts for the supply of digital contents which is not supplied on a tangible medium," that is, sui generis contracts since they are neither sales contracts (i.e., contracts for the supply of digital content which is supplied on a tangible medium, as per Article 2(5) of CRD) nor services contracts (i.e., "any contract other than a sales contract under which the trader supplies or undertakes to supply a service to the consumer and the consumer pays or undertakes to pay the price thereof" as per Article 2(6) of CRD). In this case it is not required that the counter-performance of the user is the payment of a price.

It is apparent that the current framework as described above is complex and has certain weaknesses which must be kept in mind before we proceed with the analysis of the information requirements and the withdrawal right, and which can be summarized as follows: (1) the distinction between digital content supplied on a tangible medium or not triggers the application of different provisions, since in the first case there is a sales of goods contract and in the second case there is a contract for the supply of digital content not supplied on a tangible medium; (2) the fact that the CRD sales and services contract provisions apply only when the user pays for the content and the DCD applies even when the content is free leads to the application of different provisions in case there is a download of an app for free or in exchange for payment.

## §4.03 THE CRD

### [A] The Right to Information

#### *[1] General Precontractual Information*

The CRD's scope of application refers to any contract that is concluded between a trader and a consumer.[15] The CRD does not apply to contracts for social services, healthcare, gambling, financial services, the creation, acquisition or transfer of immovable property or of rights in immovable property, the construction or conversion of building or rental of accommodation for residential purposes, passenger transport services, etc.[16] Within the scope of the CRD fall service contracts where the trader supplies or undertakes to supply to the consumer a service, including digital service[17] and the sale of digital goods.[18] Digital content means data which are produced and supplied in digital form, while the digital service is defined as a service that allows the consumer to create, process, store or access data in digital form or a service that allows the sharing of or any other interaction with data in digital form uploaded or created by the consumer or other users of that service.[19]

Digital content, as defined in Directive (EU) 2019/2161, refers to a single act of supply, a series of individual acts of supply or continuous supply over a period of time (e.g., web-streaming, video clips).[20] Digital services are for instance video and audio sharing services, file hosting, word processing, games offered in the cloud, cloud storage, webmail and cloud application.[21] Mobile applications may offer digital content or/and digital services. Therefore, they fall within the scope of the CRD.

Consumers are entitled to general information when a distance or off-premises contract is in place. This information includes the main characteristics of the goods or services offered,[22] the identity of the trader,[23] the geographical address at which the

15. Article 3(1) CRD.
16. Article 3(3) CRD.
17. Article 2(6) CRD, as amended by the Article 4 of the Directive (EU) 2019/2161.
18. Article 2(5)(b) Directive (EU) 2019/771 of the European Parliament and of the Council of 20 May 2019 on certain aspects concerning contracts for the sale of goods, amending Regulation (EU) 2017/2394 and Directive 2009/22/EC, and repealing Directive 1999/44/EC, OJ L 136, 22.5.2019, pp. 28–50, ELI: http://data.europa.eu/eli/dir/2019/771/oj. *See also* B. Hayward, What's in a Name? Software, Digital Products, and the Sale of Goods, 2016, Sydney Law Review (2016) 38:441, about the taxonomy problem of "digital goods."
19. Article 2(1)(2) Directive (EU) 2019/770 of the European Parliament and of the Council of 20 May 2019 on certain aspects concerning contracts for the supply of digital content and digital services, OJ L 136, 22.5.2019, pp. 1–27, ELI: http://data.europa.eu/eli/dir/2019/770/oj. Under the CRD, goods may also be "goods with digital elements" or else digital goods.
20. Recital 30, Directive (EU) 2019/2161. Continuous supply does not necessarily mean long-term supply.
21. Recital 30, Directive (EU) 2019/2161. The CRD applies to contracts for the supply of digital content not supplied on a tangible medium such as online digital content even when this is for free in exchange for his personal data when they are processed for reasons not related to the contract (e.g., for marketing purposes). The same should apply for digital services as well. *See* Recital 33, Directive (EU) 2019/2161.
22. Article 6(a) CRD.
23. Article 6(b) CRD.

trader is established or his place of business (in case these two differentiate), the trader's telephone number, fax number and email address,[24] the total price of the goods or services,[25] the arrangements for payment, delivery and performance of the contract, the trader's complaint handling policy,[26] information about the right of withdrawal,[27] the cost for returning the goods,[28] any legal guarantee,[29] after-sales services,[30] the duration of the contract,[31] the minimum duration of the consumer's obligations,[32] the out-of-court complaint and redress mechanism that may be in place,[33] etc. These are the main precontractual information that should be provided to the consumer by the trader in plain and intelligible language.[34]

Nevertheless, the European legislator had not in mind mobile apps when introducing this information obligation. However, even in the case of mobile apps, all this information has to be provided to the consumer, despite the space limitation issues. The trader has to provide at least the minimum required information and refer the consumer to another source of information that may be a toll-free telephone number, a hypertext link or a webpage of the trader where the consumer will be able to find all the above information easily and directly.[35] Usually, in practice, app stores provide the name of the app provider, his email and geographical address, a description with the main characteristics of the app, the total price (where applicable) including VAT, the refund policy and additionally links for the privacy policy and the app developer's website where the consumer can find the rest of the required information. By and large, there is a compliance with the general precontractual information obligations that are set out by the CRD.

### *[2] Pricing Information*

The trader has to be more meticulous with regard to the information about the price. In case the consumer is under an obligation to pay, he has to be informed explicitly and before placing his order about the main characteristics of the contract, the total price, the duration of the contract, the conditions for its termination and the minimum duration of the contract as well.[36] The consumer not only has to be informed as above but also has to be allowed to verify his order "directly before" placing it.[37] Additionally, all the relevant information to the purchase should be displayed to the consumer in

24. Article 6(c), (d) CRD.
25. Article 6(e) CRD.
26. Article 6(g) CRD.
27. Article 6(h) CRD.
28. Article 6(i) CRD.
29. Article 6(l) CRD.
30. Article 6(m) CRD.
31. Article 6(o) CRD.
32. Article 6(p) CRD.
33. Article 6(t) CRD.
34. Article 8 para. 1 CRD.
35. Recital 36 CRD and Article 8 para. 4 CRD.
36. Article 8 para. 2 CRD.
37. Article 8 paras. 2 and 9 CRD which is without prejudice to Articles 9 and 11 of the Directive 2000/31/EC about the conclusion of e-contracts and the placing of e-orders.

"close vicinity" to the confirmation requested.[38] In practice, this means that the consumer should be allowed to check his shopping basket before he gives his order[39] and get all the relevant information without having to navigate away from the order page.[40]

Finally, when the consumer decides to place his order, he should be fully aware that he is entering into an e-contract by clicking the "order button." The latter has to explicitly inform the consumer that he is ordering with the obligation to pay, e.g., by being labeled as "buy now," "pay now" or "confirm purchase" and not merely as "register," "confirm" or "order now."[41] Last, but not least, the consumer has to receive a confirmation that the contract has been concluded on a durable medium.[42] A "durable medium" can be except from paper, a USB stick, a CD-ROM, a DVD, a memory card or a computer hard disk, or even an email,[43] but not a hyperlink to the trader's website.[44]

All the above information has to be provided when a consumer downloads a mobile app. However, in the app environment, the obligation of the trader to offer transparency about the pricing has an additional meaning. An app may be provided in a certain price or for free. Thus, there is the "*paidium*" business model where the consumer pays for the app, hence to update the up or for additional content has to pay additionally. There is also the "freemium" business model, where the consumer can download the app for free, however, there are advertisements within the app. In both cases, consumers have to be informed about in-app payments and advertising content before downloading the app.[45]

### *[3] Certain Information for Apps Offering Digital Content*

The general precontractual information and the main contractual information apply to all distance and off-premises contracts, including the contracts for digital content. However, in the case of apps offering digital content, the CRD sets to the traders two more information obligations. The first concerns information about the functionality of

38. Recital 39 CRD.
39. DG Justice Guidance Document concerning the Consumer Right Directive, available at https://ec.europa.eu/info/sites/info/files/crd_guidance_en_0.pdf, p. 32.
40. *Id.* 20.
41. *Id.* 20.
42. Article 8 para. 7 CRD.
43. Recital 23 CRD.
44. *See* CJEU C-49/11 of July 5, 2012, *Content Services Ltd v. Bundesarbeitskammer*, ECLI: EU:C:2012:419. This case concerned the Distance Selling Directive 97/7/EC, where the Court of Justice ruled that a website cannot be regarded as "durable medium" within the meaning of Article 5(1) as the information is neither "given" nor "received" by the consumer.
45. *See* Markou, Christiana and Riefa, Christine, App-solutely Protected? The Protection of Consumers Using Mobile Apps in the European Union (July 1, 2015). John A. Rothschild (ed.), Research Handbook on Electronic Commerce Law (Cheltenham, UK and Northampton, US: Edward Elgar 2016). Available at SSRN: https://ssrn.com/abstract=2668977, about in-app purchases and the "freemium model."

the digital content[46] and the second concerns the interoperability of the digital content with hardware and software.[47] The first set of information refers to the use of the digital content. In this respect, the app user should be aware for example if the digital content has any technical restrictions or is protected via Digital Rights Management or region coding.[48] On the other hand, the second set of information that applies specifically to digital content refers to the standard hardware and software that is compatible with the digital content, e.g., the compatible operating system, the required version or certain hardware features.[49] The consumer has to be informed about any possible incompatibilities that will restrict him from using the digital content.

### [B] The Withdrawal Right

#### *[1] Calculation of the Fourteen-Day Period*

A pivotal right for the protection of consumers for distance and off-premises contracts is the right of withdrawal.[50] When the consumer has the right to withdraw from the contract with the trader, at which point of their contractual relationship, under which conditions and when is this right lost, are few of the issues that will be examined in the context of mobile applications purchases.

Article 9 of the CRD provides that the consumer has the right to withdraw from a distance and off-premises contract within a period of fourteen days without giving any reason for the withdrawal and without bearing any costs other than the direct costs of returning the goods and the supplementary costs that will not be reimbursed by the trader.[51] The starting point of this fourteen-day period depends on the type of the contract, i.e., whether there is a service or a sales contract. In the first case the withdrawal period will expire after fourteen days from the conclusion of the contract, while in the latter from the day that the consumer or a third party other than the carrier will acquire physical possession of the goods.[52] What happens, however, in the case of mobile apps, that is, when a digital content contract is in place? As will be analyzed, the type of the contract (sales, service or digital content) is rather crucial for many reasons and not just for the deadline of the fourteen-day period.

For the first time the CRD not only regulates explicitly the sale of digital content but also makes the distinction between digital content that is supplied on a tangible

46. Article 6(1)r CRD, where in the meaning of "functionality" the applicable technical protection measures are included.
47. Article 6(1)s CRD.
48. Recital 19 CRD.
49. Recital 19 CRD.
50. *See* M. Loos, Right of Withdrawal—Interoperability of Directives, Centre for the Study of European Contract Law Working Paper Series, No. 2013-11, published in E. Terryn, G. Straetmans & V. Colaert (eds.), Landmark Cases of EU Consumer Law, in Honor of Jules Stuyck, Cambridge/Antwerp/Portland: Intersentia, pp. 545–558 about the withdrawal right.
51. Articles 9 para. 1, 13 para. 2 and 14 para. 1 CRD.
52. Article 9 para. 2 CRD with its variations in subparas. i-iii when there are multiple goods to be delivered, the delivery of goods consists of multiple lots or pieces or the goods have to be delivered during a defined period of time.

medium and digital content that is not. In the first case, when digital content is supplied on a tangible medium (e.g., on a CD or DVD), digital content is considered by the CRD as goods.[53] Therefore, the classification of digital content as "contract for online digital content," which is neither a sales nor a service contract, applies only to digital content that is supplied in a nontangible medium. In this case and with respect to the withdrawal deadline, the CRD follows the same approach as for service contracts. Thus, the fourteen-day withdrawal period starts from the conclusion of the contract.[54]

The time of expiration of the withdrawal right depends also on the way these fourteen days shall be calculated. According to Recital 41 CRD, "all periods contained in the CRD should be understood to be expressed in calendar days." The fourteen calendar days start from the day following the conclusion of the contract and include public holidays, Sundays and Saturdays as well.[55] However, in the case that the withdrawal period ends on public holiday, Sunday or Saturday, the last day of the withdrawal period shall be the first following working day.[56]

### *[2] The Exception for Online Digital Content*

Nevertheless, the CRD follows a different approach on the issue of the exceptions from the withdrawal right. According to Article 16 of the CRD, in service contracts, the consumer loses his right to withdraw from the contract after the service has been fully performed by the trader.[57] Contrariwise, the withdrawal right is not provided to the consumer in the supply of digital content that is supplied on a nontangible medium when two conditions are met: (1) the consumer has given his prior express consent to the trader to begin the performance of the contract and (2) he is fully aware that by consenting he loses his right to withdraw.[58] The application of this approach on the purchase of apps can prove to be rather problematic. Analyzing the above requirements there shall be an attempt to evaluate whether this provision is for the benefit of the app user on not.

When buying an app from an app store, the performance of the contract starts immediately[59] after the purchase of the digital good (music, play, game, etc.). This means that the consumer, contrary to a sales or service contract, has no time at all at

53. Recital 19 CRD.
54. Article 9 para. 2.c. CRD.
55. Recital 41 CRD and Council Regulation No. 1182/71 of 3 June 1971 determining the rules applicable to periods, dates and time limits.
56. Article 3 para. 4 Council Regulation No. 1182/71 of 3 June 1971 determining the rules applicable to periods, dates and time limits.
57. Article 16 para. 1.a. CRD.
58. Article 16 para. 1.m. CRD, Recital 19 CRD.
59. Usually, the performance of a digital contract starts immediately after the purchase, e.g., with the download or streaming of a video or an audio file. However, in the case there is a link that leads the consumer to the downloading or streaming page, the link has to be first activated for the performance to start. *See* DG Justice Guidance Document concerning the Consumer Right Directive, available at https://ec.europa.eu/info/sites/info/files/crd_guidance_en_0.pdf, p. 65. *See also* Recital 38 of the Directive (EU) 2019/2161. The provision was amended in order to make clear that it is relevant only when the consumer is under an obligation to pay under the contract.

his disposal to test the digital content as there is no withdrawal period granted to him.[60] Therefore, it is on the application store or the app developer to deprive the consumer this "testing right" by depriving him of the withdrawal right by providing the proper information and the proper way to the consumer to give his consent. As the CRD requires the express consent of the consumer, it would seem more appropriate for the trader to seek for the consumer's explicit consent by asking him to proceed to a positive action. The exclusion of the withdrawal right in the Terms of Service and/or in a pre-ticked checkbox where the consumer supposedly waives his right of withdrawal would not satisfy the above requirements.[61]

However, the consumer's express consent alone does not deprive him of his withdrawal right. The trader, additionally, has to provide him with a copy of the contract on a durable medium (e.g., an email) which will also include both a confirmation of his prior express consent and acknowledgement that he waives his withdrawal right.[62] Therefore, the app consumer may lose his withdrawal right by buying a digital good (which he would not have in a sales or service contract), however, there is at least a minimum level of protection offered to him that he can take advantage of.

In case the formal requirements for the exception of the withdrawal right are not met, then the consumer gets to keep and exercise his right to withdraw from the contract. If the trader has provided the obligatory information with regard to the withdrawal right[63] there is a fourteen-day period available to the consumer to withdraw, otherwise he is granted an extension of twelve months from the initial withdrawal period.[64]

Supposedly, the consumer has bought a game app, has enjoyed his game for thirteen days and without any specific reason he wishes to "return" the app and get his money back. The application store neither obtained his express consent nor informed him about waiving his withdrawal right by using the app. Is the trader entitled to compensation for the use of the digital good he offered these thirteen days to the consumer? The CRD is quite explicit on this matter concerning digital goods:

> The consumer shall bear no cost for the supply, full or in part, of digital content which is not supplied on a tangible medium where: (i) the consumer has not given his prior express consent to the beginning of the performance before the end of the

60. DG Justice Guidance Document concerning the Consumer Right Directive, available at https://ec.europa.eu/info/sites/info/files/crd_guidance_en_0.pdf, p. 64.
61. DG Justice Guidance Document concerning the Consumer Right Directive, available at https://ec.europa.eu/info/sites/info/files/crd_guidance_en_0.pdf, where a modal statement declaring the consumer's express consent and acknowledgment is provided as follows "[] I hereby consent to immediate performance of the contract and acknowledge that I will lose my right of withdrawal from the contract once the download or streaming of the digital content has begun."
62. Article 7 para. 2. CRD and Article 8 para. 7.b.
63. Article 6 para. 1.h. CRD. The obligatory information, includes the conditions, the time limit, the procedures and the model withdrawal for the exercise of the withdrawal right. However, it should be noted that the provision of the model withdrawal form is excluded from the information the trader has to provide when the contract is concluded through a means of distance communication (Article 8(4) CRD), as in this case this is technical impossible. *See* Recital 41 Directive 2019/2161. Therefore, the same should apply in apps as well.
64. Article 10 para. 1 CRD.

> 14-day period referred to in Article 9, (ii) the consumer has not acknowledged that he loses his right of withdrawal when giving his consent or (iii) the trader has failed to provide confirmation in accordance with Article 7(2) or Article 8(7).[65]

Therefore, if the trader fails to provide to the consumer the required confirmation, the consumer not only keeps his withdrawal right intact, but also, he can exercise it without paying any cost for the performance that already has taken place.

### *[3] The Withdrawal Right in Practice*

With regard to the withdrawal right, the CRD provides traders with all the necessary guidance to comply with their obligations toward consumers, offering them all the useful tools such as modal statements and modal forms. However, what does the practices shows? Do the app distribution platforms and app developers put all that knowledge into practice? Let us examine the examples of Google Play and App Store.

#### *[a] Google Play*

Google is very explicit on the withdrawal policy that does not apply. According to the terms of service of Google Play, all sales are final.[66] This means that Google Play does not provide consumers with a right to withdraw from their purchases. However, there is a refund policy in place. According to Google Play's refund policy, consumers can get their money back; hence, this is the exception and not the rule. The refund policy depends on the kind of the purchase. Different requirements apply when the purchase concerns movies, music (including subscriptions), individual songs and albums, books, newsstand, subscriptions, gift cards, gifts, etc. For each category different refund time applies as well, which can range from one business day to two months.[67] However, a basic requirement that has to be met is that the refund request has to be made within forty-eight hours since the consumer made the purchase.

What is notable is that Google takes a different approach on consumers located in the European Economic Area and made a purchase after March 28, 2018 and on consumers located within the European Union. In the first case, consumers can request a refund from Google Play (within the forty-eight hours timeframe) or get support from the developer of the app, who is going to apply his own policies and the law applicable with regard to the withdrawal right. On the other hand, if the consumer is located in EU, there is an explicit referral to the withdrawal right. If the consumer has bought digital content, such as in-app items, apps, games, music or movies, he waives

65. Article 14 para. 4.b.i-iii. CRD.
66. *See* Google Play terms of service, version of February 5, 2018, available at https://play.google.com/intl/en-us_us/about/play-terms.html.
67. *See* Google Play refund policy available at https://support.google.com/googleplay/answer/2479637?hl=en.

"automatic" the withdrawal right and the standard Google Play's, refund policy comes in place. If the consumer has bought a service from a developer or a third party, then Google declares that has no authority and responsible for the withdrawal right is the seller, even if the purchase was made on Google Play.[68] In the above manner, Google informs consumers about their withdrawal right.

However, this is the information provided to the consumer when reading the English version of the terms and services. What happens if the consumer chooses to learn more about Google Play's policies? In this case, he is directed again to Google Play terms of service. However, he is directed to the version of the terms of services that corresponds to his IP address. For example, when accessing the terms of service from a Greek IP address, then the Greek version of Google Play's terms of service comes automatically in place.[69] In this case, the EU consumer receives different information with regard to his withdrawal rights. Specifically, he is informed about his withdrawal right when the purchase concerns digital content and when the purchase concerns services. In the first case, Google informs the consumer that when buying digital content, he agrees having immediate access to the digital content (even if he does not) and for that reason he automatically waives his withdrawal right. On the other hand, if he has purchased a service, he is informed of having fourteen days to exercise his withdrawal right by contacting the company (Google Commerce Limited). The postal address of the company is provided and not an email address and additionally a link where the consumer can supposedly find a model withdrawal form, hence he finds more guidelines and a Google's form where he can describe his problem.

#### *[b] Apple's Media Services Terms and Conditions*

Apple, on the other hand, is very clear on the policy that applies with respect to the withdrawal right. According to Apple's media services terms and conditions, all transactions are final.[70] The only remedy the consumer has is to ask for a replacement of the content purchased or a refund of the price paid. It will be at Apple's discretion to grant the replacement or the refund. Thus, the consumer, especially the EU consumer, has neither a right to withdraw from his purchase, nor he is informed about his withdrawal right in any fashion.

68. *See* Google Play refund policy available at https://support.google.com/googleplay/answer/2479637?hl=en.
69. *See* the Greek version of Google Play's terms of service, version March 28, 2018, available at https://play.google.com/about/play-terms.html. This is the version corresponding to the English version of February 5, 2018.
70. *See* Apple's media services terms and conditions, version September 17, 2018, available at https://www.apple.com/ca/legal/internet-services/itunes/ca/terms.html.

## §4.04 THE UCPD

### [A] Scope of Application

The UCPD[71] applies in B2C commercial practices when the transaction is related to a product.[72] Product is defined as any goods or service including immovable property, right and obligations.[73] Digital content and digital services even not explicitly included in products, fall within the scope of the UCPD. However, the UCPD's amendments introduced by the Directive 2019/2161[74] made it clear that the UCPD applies for digital content and digital services as well. Therefore, providers of mobile apps have to engage in fair commercial practices and to abide by the UCPD's provisions, as long as they act as traders.

The definition of the trader in the UCPD is almost identical with the one given in the CRD. The concept of "trader" is defined in Article 2 of the UCPD as meaning "any natural or legal person acting for purposes related to his trade, business, craft or profession and anyone acting in the name of or on behalf of a trader." Advocate General in the case *Zentrale zur Bekämpfung unlauteren Wettbewerbs* expressed the opinion that even public law bodies fall within the meaning of traders when they engage in commercial practices.[75] In the case *Evelina Kamenova* on the other hand, the Advocate General held the opinion that the publication at an online platform of eight advertisements for the sale of different products, new and used, did not suffice to classify the defendant as "trader" within the meaning of the UCPD and the CRD.[76] Other factors

71. Directive 2005/29/EC of the European Parliament and of the Council of 11 May 2005 concerning unfair business-to-consumer commercial practices in the internal market and amending Council Directive 84/450/EEC, Directives 97/7/EC, 98/27/EC and 2002/65/EC of the European Parliament and of the Council and Regulation (EC) No. 2006/2004 of the European Parliament and of the Council ("Unfair Commercial Practices Directive"), OJ L 149, 11.6.2005, pp. 22–39, ELI: http://data.europa.eu/eli/dir/2005/29/oj. The UCPD follows a "three level approach" in order to combat unfair practices. There is the general clause forbidding unfair commercial practices (Article 5), the second level lies in the prohibition of misleading actions (Article 6), misleading omissions (Article 7), aggressive practices (Article 8) and harassment (Article 9) and the third level refers to the Annex I which includes commercial practices that are considered unfair under all circumstances. *See also* Directorate-General for Internal Policies, Policy Department C, Citizens' Rights and Constitutional Affairs, Extent of Harmonization in Consumer Contract Law, 2010, p. 13, available at http://www.europarl.europa.eu/RegData/etudes/note/join/2010/432728/IPOL-JURI_NT%282010%29432728_EN.pdf. *See also* on this H.-W. Micklitz et al., Understanding EU Consumer Law, Antwerp/Oxford/Portland: Intersentia, 2009, pp. 81–82.
72. Article 3(1) UCPD.
73. Article 5(c) UCPD.
74. Directive (EU) 2019/2161 of the European Parliament and of the Council of 27 November 2019 amending Council Directive 93/13/EEC and Directives 98/6/EC, 2005/29/EC and 2011/83/EU of the European Parliament and of the Council as regards the better enforcement and modernisation of Union consumer protection rules, OJ L 328, 18.12.2019, pp. 7–28, ELI: http://data.europa.eu/eli/dir/2019/2161/oj.
75. *See* Advocate General Bot's Opinion in *BKK Mobil Oil Körperschaft des öffentlichen Rechts v. Zentrale zur Bekämpfung unlauteren Wettbewerbs eV*, Case C-59/12, EU:C:2013:450, points 40–44.
76. *See* Advocate General Szpunar's Opinion in *Komisia za zashtita na potrebitelite v. Evelina Kamenova*, Case C-105/17, EU:C:2018:378, points 48–49.

have to be evaluated as well, depending on the factual grounds of each case.[77] All in all, the classification as a "trader" requires a case-by-case approach.

In online platforms and in particular app stores (e.g., Google Play, Apple App Store, Amazon App Store) the platform provider is regarded to act for purposes related to its business when charging on the transactions between suppliers and users a commission, when other additional services are provided under payment or when there are revenues from targeted advertisement.[78] A relevant case was the case of TripAdvisor Italy where the Autorità Garante della Concorrenza e del Mercato held that TripAdvisor acted as professional, as the company provided comparison services and not mere information of tourist facilities.[79] Traders are responsible toward consumers for the commercial practices they are employing and cannot invoke on this matter Article 14(1) of the E-Commerce Directive,[80] that is, claiming that they acted just as intermediaries providing hosting services and for that reason they should not be held liable for third-party illegal content.[81] The obligation posed on online platforms to take appropriate measures under the UCDP does not, however, amount to a general obligation to monitor or carry out fact finding as set out in Article 15(1) of the E-Commerce Directive.[82] Thus, as the classification of an online platform or an app provider as a trader will not be always apparent, the best practice for them would be to provide to consumers this piece of information along with the rest of the obligatory information. This would enhance legal certainty and promote consumers' trust both on the app providers and the app stores.

77. Such factors may be the organization of the online platform to make profit, the duration and frequency of the sales, whether the seller is subject to VAT, etc.
78. *See* Guidance on the implementation/application of Directive 2005/29/EC on Unfair Commercial Practices, SWD (2016) 163 final, p. 110.
79. *See* Autorità Garante della Concorrenza e del Mercato Decision PS9345 Tripadvisor of December 19, 2014, paras. 87–89.
80. Directive 2000/31/EC of the European Parliament and of the Council of 8 June 2000 on certain legal aspects of information society services, in particular electronic commerce, in the Internal Market ("Directive on electronic commerce"), OJ L 178, 17.7.2000, pp. 1–16, ELI: http://data.europa.eu/eli/dir/2000/31/oj.
81. Guidance on the implementation/application of Directive 2005/29/EC on Unfair Commercial Practices, SWD (2016) 163 final, p. 111. Also relevant cases of the European Court of Justice interpreting Article 14(1) of the e-Commerce Directive, Joined Cases C-236/08 to C-238/08, *Louis Vuitton* (paras. 113–119) and Case C-324/09, *L'Oreal* (paras. 123–124). As the interpretation of Article 14(1) of the E-Commerce Directive requires a case-by-case approach in national level, there are conflicting decisions. This is the case with the German Federal Court of Justice judgment *Stokke v. eBay*, I ZR 216/11, 16 May 2013 and the Leeuwarden Court of Appeal judgment *Stokke v. Marktplaats B.V.*, 106031/HA ZA 05211, of 22 May 2012. The national Courts had opposing opinions on the role (active or neutral) of the online market place even though the circumstances were identical. *See also* the decision of the French Supreme Court, Cass. Com. 4 décembre 2012, 11-27729, *Publicité Sté Pewterpassion.com c/ Sté Leguide.com*, available at https://www.legifrance.gouv.fr/affichJuriJudi.do?idTexte=JURITEXT000026742544 and German Federal Court of Justice, I ZR 94/13, March 19, 2015.
82. Guidance on the implementation/application of Directive 2005/29/EC on Unfair Commercial Practices, SWD (2016) 163 final, p. 114.

The UCPD is a directive of horizontal maximum harmonization.[83] This means that Member States may not deviate from the Directive's provision by setting less or more stringent requirements with respect to unfair commercial practices. Annex I black list of unfair commercial practices is therefore exhaustive and not indicative. However, UCPD is not always applicable. Issues pertaining to the validity, formation or effect of a contract are governed by national contract law.[84] The same applies with respect to national rules related to health and safety aspects of products[85] and rules regulating specific aspects of unfair commercial practices.[86] Financial services as defined in the Directive 2002/65/EC and immovable property may be subject to more restrictive or prescriptive measures than those imposed by the UCPD.[87]

In the case of mobile apps the ground rule should be the application of the UCPD but without prejudice to the above-mentioned exceptions. This may be the case when the commercial practice relates to a health mobile application or a financial mobile application. Another issue is of the validity of the transaction, as an unfair commercial practice within an app may not render the whole transaction void in favor of the consumer. In mobile applications, the unfair commercial practice may refer to the sale of the mobile application, the supply of the digital content provided by the mobile app, the invitation to purchase[88] a mobile app, the after-sales period, the promotion or even the advertisement and marketing of a mobile app. After the Directive 2019/2161, online market places, such as App Stores fall explicitly within UCPD's ambit.[89]

### [B] Misleading Actions and Omissions as Unfair Commercial Practices

According to the UCPD, a commercial practice is regarded as unfair when two conditions are met: when the commercial practice is contrary to the requirements of professional diligence and additionally if materially distorts or is likely to materially distort the economic behavior of the average consumer.[90] Professional diligence means the standard of special skill and care, which a trader may reasonably be expected to exercise toward consumers, commensurate with honest market practice and/or the general principle of good faith in the trader's field of activity.[91] This means, however, that the trader's lack of professional diligence has to be able to distort the economic

83. *See* Van Boom, Willem H., Unfair Commercial Practices (November 1, 2015). Available at SSRN: https://ssrn.com/abstract=2709911 or http://dx.doi.org/10.2139/ssrn.2709911 for a more detail analysis of the maximum harmonization principle applying in the UCPD.
84. Article 3(2) UCPD.
85. Article 3(3) UCPD.
86. Article 3(4) UCPD.
87. Article 3(9) UCPD.
88. Article 2(i) UCPD, where invitation to purchase means the commercial communication indicating the characteristics of the product and the price that is provided to consumer in order to make a purchase.
89. Article 3 Directive 2019/2161.
90. Article 5(4)(a), (b) UCPD.
91. Article 2(h) UCPD.

behavior of the consumer by impairing his ability to make an informed decision and making him to take a transactional decision, he would not have taken otherwise.[92]

A commercial practice, most likely, will be unfair if it is misleading or aggressive.[93] Misleading the consumer can take place by act or omission.[94] Commercial practice should not contain false or untruthful information about the existence or the nature of the product, the main characteristics of the product, the trader's commitments, the price or the manner the price is calculated, the need for a service, part, replacement or repair, the nature, attributes and rights of the trader and the consumer's rights. On the opposite case, the relevant practice is regarded as misleading action.[95] Material information such as the main characteristics of the product, the geographical address and identity of the trader, the price, the payment, delivery, and performance arrangements, the complaint handling policy and the right of withdrawal should be provided to consumers in a clear, intelligible, unambiguous and timely manner; otherwise, the omitted or hidden information shall be regarded as a misleading omission.[96]

In mobile apps one could argue that omitting information, that is, providing to consumers less information than the legislation requires, is not a misleading but a necessary omission. The medium offers too little space to include all the abovementioned material information. Even so, the trader has to override space (or time) medium limitations and employ other means to make the necessary information available to consumers.[97] In-game apps for example, only games that in-app payments are optional can be presented as "free," otherwise the app store or the app provider will be in breach both of Article 7(4)(c) and number 20 of the Annex I.[98]

### [C] Aggressive Commercial Practices

A commercial practice is deemed aggressive when harassment and coercion take place with the use of physical force or undue influence, which impairs to a significant degree the consumer's ability to choose freely.[99] An aggressive commercial practice is unfair as is likely to cause the consumer to take a transactional decision he would not have

92. Article 2(e) UCPD.
93. Article 5(2)(a), (b) UCPD.
94. *See* H.-W. Micklitz et al., Understanding EU Consumer Law, Antwerp/Oxford/Portland: Intersentia, 2009, p. 95, where three elements are extracted from CJEU's established practice on the term "misleading": (a) The informed consumer is required to obtain missing information (CJEU C-220/98, *Lifting*), (b) true information must not be withheld from the consumer (CJEU C-362/88, *GB-Inno*) and (c) the reasonable consumer is required to identify objectively false information (CJEU C-470/93, *Mars*).
95. Article 6(1)(a-g) UCPD.
96. Article 7(4)(a-e) UCPD.
97. Article 7(3) UCPD.
98. *See* Guidance on the implementation/application of Directive 2005/29/EC on Unfair Commercial Practices, SWD (2016) 163 final, p. 118. *See also* European Commission's press release on July 18, 2014, "In-app purchases: Joint action by the European Commission and Member States is leading to better protection for consumers in online games," available at https://ec.europa.eu/commission/presscorner/detail/en/IP_14_847.
99. Recital 16 UCPD.

taken otherwise.[100] For the harassment, coercion and undue influence, certain criteria apply such as, among others, the timing, location or persistence of the trader's practice, the use of threatening or abusive language or behavior or the use of onerous or disproportionate noncontractual barriers with regard to consumers' rights. For instance, contractual terms imposing barriers to consumers who want to exercise their contractual right of terminating the contract or switching to another trader, qualify as an aggressive commercial practice.

Requiring the mandatory registration to the trader's online platform in exchange for consumer's personal data may constitute an aggressive commercial practice as well. That was the case with the commercial practice of Samsung Electronics Italia S.p.A. in 2017. The Italian Competition Authority held that the subsidiary of the Samsung Group in Italy, was infringing the national consumer protection law and Articles 8 and 9 of the UCPD as the company forced consumers, after buying the promotional offer, to register to the Samsung People online platform and provide their personal data. The latter were used by Samsung for marketing purposes not linked with the promotional offer of the product they had bought. The Authority assessed this commercial practice as aggressive and imposed to Samsung Electronics a fine of EUR 975.000.[101]

In mobile apps that are most likely to appeal to children, the app store or the app provider has to abstain from using direct exhortation to children to buy additional in-game items; otherwise, Article 5(3) and point 28 of the UCPD are violated.[102] Gaming apps that appeal to children should not exploit a child's inherent inexperience, vulnerability or credulity. On the contrary, these gaming apps have to be child friendly and not aggressive. Even language, design, visual interface and structure should be considered more carefully in gaming apps addressed to children.[103]

### [D] The Average Consumer

The characterization of a commercial practice as unfair, however, depends on the probability of this commercial practice to materially distort the average consumer's ability to make an informed decision. How is the average consumer defined and which consumer is regarded as vulnerable[104]? Does the notion of the average consumer or the average member of a particular group of consumers apply in the case of mobile apps?

100. Article 8 UCPD.
101. *See* Press release February 10, 2017 of Autorità Garante della Concorrenza e del Mercato, "Unfair Promotions: Sanctions Issued Against Samsung Electronics Italia for over Three Million Euros," available at https://en.agcm.it/en/media/press-releases/2017/2/alias-2414.
102. *See* Guidance on the implementation/application of Directive 2005/29/EC on Unfair Commercial Practices, SWD(2016) 163 final, p. 118.
103. *See* Office of Fair Trading (OFT), Children's Online Games, report and consultations, p. 20, available at https://assets.publishing.service.gov.uk/media/53330c4de5274a5660000005/oft1506.pdf.
104. *See* R. Incardona et al., The Average Consumer, the Unfair Commercial Practices Directive, and the Cognitive Revolution, J Consumer Policy (2007) 30:21–38, where the notion of the vulnerable consumer is characterized as superfluous and paternalistic introducing uncertainties and confusion in the assessment of commercial practices as unfair by national authorities.

The European Court of Justice has defined the average consumer as "the reasonably well informed and reasonably observant and circumspect consumer."[105] As the notion of the average consumer is not a statistical one,[106] problems in defining the average consumer usually raise in practice.[107] Social, linguistic and cultural factors have to be taken into consideration as well.[108]

There are also categories of consumers with certain characteristics that make them more vulnerable to direct purchase exhortations or advertisement, children being one of them. For instance, a direct exhortation in an advertisement addressed to children to buy advertised products, or persuade their parents to buy advertised products for them, qualifies as an aggressive commercial practice.[109] As a great number of mobile applications and especially game apps are addressed to children, the average consumer in that case will not be any consumer but the average member of the particular group of consumers, that is, the average child. Nevertheless, even in the case of apps that are addressed to consumers in general, there are still issues raised as there are consumers who are less tech-savvy. The latter are more susceptible to unfair commercial practices and need greater protection.

## §4.05 ONLINE DISPUTE RESOLUTION

### [A] The Informational Obligation to the EU's ODR Platform

On January 9, 2016[110] the Commission launched a new redress mechanism for consumer disputes. The European Union's platform for the online dispute resolution of consumer disputes, hereinafter referred as the ODR platform, has been introduced by the Regulation on consumer ODR which is complemented by the Directive on consumer ADR[111] (the "Directive"). In both legal instruments, there is a new obligation imposed on the trader when engaging in electronic transactions.

105. *See* CJEU Case C-210/96, *Gut Springenheide and Tusky*, ECLI:EU:C:1998:369, para. 31, Case C-220/98, *Estée Lauder*, ECLI:EU:C:2000:8, para. 27, Case C-44/01, *Pippig Augenoptik*, ECLI: EU:C:2003:205, para. 55.
106. *See* A. Tor, Some Challenges Facing a Behaviorally-Informed Approach to the Directive on Unfair Commercial Practices, in T. Toth (ed.), Unfair Commercial Practices, The long road to harmonized law enforcement, Pazmany Press, 2013. p. 11 about the "framing effects" characterizing phenomena that make consumers deviate from a rational choice. This means that the empirical definition of the average consumer may prove even more difficult in practice.
107. *See* H-W. Micklitz et al., Understanding EU Consumer Law, Antwerp/Oxford/Portland: Intersentia, 2009, pp. 87–88, about the "average consumer" and vulnerable groups of consumers, where he points out the problematic on the evaluation of the spill-over effect when advertisements reach children even if they originally are addressed to adults. *See also*, about average and vulnerable consumer, C. Poncibo et al., The EU Unfair Commercial Practices Directive: A Faltering First Step, London Law Review (October 2005), 1(2):317–337.
108. Recital 18 UCPD.
109. *See* Annex I (28) UCPD.
110. However, the ODR platform became fully operational as of February 15, 2016.
111. *See* Directive 2013/11/EU of the European Parliament and of the Council of 21 May 2013 on alternative dispute resolution for consumer disputes and amending Regulation (EC) No. 2006/2004 and Directive 2009/22/EC (Directive on consumer ADR), OJ L 165/63.

According to Article 14 of the Regulation on consumer ODR ("the Regulation") the traders offering online sales or services bear the responsibility of informing the consumers that they can have recourse to an online dispute resolution tool in order to resolve their dispute, that is, the ODR platform, by providing an electronic link to the latter.[112] The Regulation does not mention digital content contracts per se, however, as long as digital content is offered online, it falls within the scope of the Regulation.[113] Likewise, Article 13 of the Directive provides that the trader shall inform the consumers about the ADR entity which is committed or obliged to use to resolve his disputes.[114] One could argue that the legislation is clear, simple and easy to be followed by the trader. Is this, however, the case? What are the possible pitfalls that a trader has to avoid?

To begin with, if the trader is committed voluntarily or compulsory to use the ADR services of a specific ADR provider, he should provide this piece of information at his website. However, he does not extricate himself from the duty to include the relevant link to the ODR platform.[115] The next question refers to the way the trader has to provide this piece of information. According to the Regulation, it should be provided with an electronic link to his website or if he makes his offer by an email, he has to provide the relevant link in that email.[116] The mere inclusion of the link in the terms of service does not seem to suffice.[117] Additionally, the link placed has to link to the ODR platform and not just refer to the latter. Finally, if the trader offers his goods or services through a market platform such as Amazon or eBay it would be advisable to place the link both on his own website and on the website of the marketplace.[118]

In the Facebook's app case, for instance, there is no such link on the mobile app before the consumer proceeds to the download. On the contrary, the consumer has to follow the link of the refund policy, to find the link to the terms of service and then look for the governing law and courts clause.[119] Therefore, the informational obligation in this case does not seem to apply.

## §4.06 CONCLUSIONS

Consumer protection in the digital world and specifically in mobile apps seems a hard task for traders. App platforms and app providers have to comply with a wide set of

112. Article 14 Regulation on consumer ODR.
113. Recital 14 Regulation on consumer ODR clarifies that the definition of "online sales or service contract" covers also cases where the consumer accesses a website or other information society service through a mobile device.
114. Article 13 Directive on consumer ADR.
115. Article 14(3) Regulation on consumer ODR clearly states that the application of the Regulation is without prejudice to Article 13 of the Directive on consumer ADR.
116. Article 14(2) Regulation on consumer ODR.
117. Recital 47 Directive on consumer ADR, where the argument is draw upon the fact that the relevant information about the ADR entity should be provided on the trader's website and where applicable in the terms and conditions.
118. *See* OLG Dresden, 11.08.2017—14 U 732/17, where according to the court's ruling, the display of a link to the ODR platform at the website of the market place is not compulsory.
119. *See* at https://policies.google.com/terms?hl=en.

precontractual, contractual and post-contractual obligations. If one general principle would have to characterize these obligations (informational, withdrawal right, commercial practices, complaint handling polices and online dispute resolution) that would be transparency.

In mobile apps this principle may prove even harder to apply due to technical restrictions. In any case, failure to comply with consumer protection legislation would be (and was until recently to a certain degree) a void letter. The lacuna in the enforcement of consumer protection law was filled eventually by the Directive (EU) 2019/2161. For the first time penalties are introduced in European consumer protection legal instruments. Both the CRD and the UCPD were amended to include enforcement measures. EU Member States will have to apply onwards certain criteria on the imposition of penalties.[120] Common enforcement rules on consumer protection law may be the key in achieving greater degree of harmonization and legal certainty in the field of consumer protection in EU. The future will tell whether these provisions will be a potential game changer in consumer protection law.

120. Articles 3 and 4 of the Directive (EU) 2019/2161.

# CHAPTER 5
# Data Protection

*Ioannis Iglezakis*

*Mobile apps collect and process a great mass of personal data, including data from the device and from various sensors, in order to provide services to users. Processing of personal data by app developers and third parties which gain access to personal data in mobile devices, e.g., for advertising purposes, may result in significant risks for the privacy of app users. The main data protection risks to app users are the lack of transparency, poor security measures, data maximization and noncompliance with the principle of purpose limitation. In the EU, the General Data Protection Regulation (GDPR) has been enacted to address these issues, while the ePrivacy Directive is also relevant. In this chapter, we examine the application of the data protection legislation to apps and furthermore, the role and responsibilities of the various actors in the app ecosystem, the legal grounds of the processing of personal data by apps, the application of general principles of data protection, as well as the new obligations introduced in the GDPR, that is, accountability, data protection by design and by default, security and data protection impact assessment.*

## §5.01 DATA PROTECTION RISKS IN THE USE OF APPS

### [A] General Overview

Personal data are the commodity of the twenty-first century and, as such, they play a key role in the global digital economy.[1] This stands also for mobile applications when

1. P. Voigt& A.v.d. Bussche, *The EU General Data Protection Regulation (GDPR): A Practical Guide*, 2017, p. 1.

offered for free, as app providers and third parties use the personal data of app's users for marketing purposes.[2] In general, apps collect and process a great mass of personal data to provide tailored services to users and, therefore, app developers or providers in their capacity as data controllers or processors must comply with data protection standards which have become more strict under the General Data Protection Regulation (GDPR).[3] The GDPR harmonizes data protection law in all EU Member States, adapting the legal framework to modern technological developments such as the internet, social media and smartphones, and providing data subjects with enhanced rights.[4] Thus, within the EU, the processing of personal data by mobile apps is governed by GDPR, which has entered into force on May 25, 2018.

The GDPR is a major step toward greater harmonization of data protection law in the EU Member States, as it is a single set of applicable rules which is directly binding. It will, thus, bring about the simplification and reduction of costs for companies operating in different EU Member States.[5] This applies also for companies offering online content, such as mobile apps. The Regulation also strengthens the position of app users, as it applies not only to the processing of personal data by a company acting as a data controller or data processor established within the EU, but also where this company offers services to data subjects within the Union (Article 3 GDPR).

### [B] Data Protection Risks in Particular

In today's world, modern smartphones and other mobile devices have seen widespread use, as the use of mobile services provide many benefits.[6] However, the use of app-enabled mobile devices raises new privacy risks, as the former are collecting huge amounts of personal information and mobile apps gain access to user information and content stored in the device (location data, photos, videos, text messages, emails, calls and calendar logs, contacts, passwords, financial data, etc.), to which not only many companies but also pubic authorities seek to have access.[7]

Data protection risks are essentially multiplied in the apps' environment, as apps gain access to big quantities of data which are stored in the device or data collected by the various sensors of the device.[8] It is notable that smart devices may have various sensors, including a gyroscope, a magnetometer (digital compass), accelerometer, front and rear cameras, microphone, proximity sensors, GPS, ambient light sensors,

2. *See* Baumgartner, "Apps und Datenschutzrecht," in: *Apps und Recht*, C.H. Beck 2013, p. 57.
3. Regulation (EU) 2016/679 of the European Parliament and of the Council of 27 April 2016 on the protection of natural persons with regard to the processing of personal data and on the free movement of such data, and repealing Directive 95/46/EC (General Data Protection Regulation, OJ L 119, 4.5.2016, ELI: http://data.europa.eu/eli/reg/2016/679/oj.
4. *See* A. Murray, *Information Technology Law: The Law & Society*, 4th edn., 2019, 568.
5. P. Hustinx, "EU Data Protection Law: The Review of Directive 95/46/EC and the Proposed General Data Protection Regulation," available online at: https://edps.europa.eu/data-protection/our-work/publications/speeches-articles/eu-data-protection-law-review-directive_en.
6. *See* Chapter 1.
7. *See* J.M. Urban, C.J. Hoofnagle & S. Li, *Mobile Phones and Privacy*, Berkeley Consumer Privacy Survey BCLT Research Paper, July 11, 2012.
8. *See* Article 29 WP, Opinion 2/2013 on apps on smart devices, pp. 4 et seq.

fingerprint sensors, pedometer, QR Code sensors, barometer, heart rate sensor, etc.[9] All these sensors are used to collect data from the environment concerning the user of the device. Mobile devices also connect to networks or to other devices through interfaces such as Wi-Fi, Bluetooth, NFC, and their location can be acquired through geolocation services.[10] Through application programming interfaces (APIs), app developers gain access to device sensors and data stored in the device, which is not always based on consent and prior information of the data subject.

A data protection scandal was revealed in 2012, as many popular iOS applications, such as Facebook, Twitter, Instagram, Foursquare, etc. have transmitted names, email addresses and/or phone numbers from the device's internal address book to their server for matching purposes, i.e., to search for friends using the app and generate friend suggestions, without informing and/or receiving consent of the app user.[11] It, thus, becomes evident that apps are exploiting smartphones' functionalities to gain access to personal data of users without obtaining prior consent and/or providing appropriate information.

It is also notable that smartphones and other smart devices lack data security software and are thus vulnerable to cyber-attacks and other security threats such as malicious applications and spyware.[12] Furthermore, insufficient data security could result into unauthorized processing of users' personal data, in case of a data breach.[13] It becomes, therefore, evident that security issues which may occur in connection with the use of mobile apps may endanger the privacy of app users.[14]

The absence of comprehensive information on the processing of personal data leads to a lack of transparency which is detrimental for the app user. Many apps, and not only free ones, do not have a privacy policy or do not inform users about the personal data that the app is processing and about the purpose of processing.[15] Where the legality of processing is based on the consent of the data subject, this is equally uninformed and free, and presented on a "take or leave it" basis, insofar the end-user is given merely the option to accept the terms and conditions of the app, following its downloading by the user.[16]

Recently, a face-aging app has sparked a lot of polemic, for it was alleged that the app provider, a Russian-based company, uploaded users' photographs to the cloud or that these were transferred to Russia, and users were not informed that processing is

9. M. Priyadarshini, "Which Sensors Do I Have In My Smartphone? How Do They Work?," September 25, 2018, https://fossbytes.com/which-smartphone-sensors-how-work/.
10. Article 29 WP, *supra*, 4.
11. *See* J.V. Grove, "Your Address Book Is Mine: Many iPhone Apps Take Your Data," *VENTUREBEAT*, Feb. 14, 2012, available at http://venturebeat.com/2012/02/14/iphone-address-book/.
12. *See, e.g.*, J. Wright, M. Dawson & M. Omar, "Cyber Security and Mobile Threats: The Need for Antivirus Applications for Smart Phones," *Journal of Information Systems Technology and Planning*, 5 (2012), 40–60.
13. *See* Article 29 WP, *supra*, p. 6.
14. *See* Chapter 1, §1.04.
15. *See* FPF, *June 2012 Mobile Apps Study*. Available at: http://www.futureofprivacy.org/wp-content/uploads/Mobile-Apps-Study-June-2012.pdf.
16. *See* Article 29 WP, *supra*.

not taking place on their device.[17] The terms of service of this app contributed to this misapprehension, as they provided that by agreeing, the user grants "a perpetual, irrevocable, nonexclusive, royalty-free, worldwide, fully-paid, transferable sub-licensable license to use, reproduce, modify, adapt, publicly perform and display the user content and any name, username or likeness provided in connection with the user content in all media formats and channels now known or later developed, without compensation to the user."[18]

Personal data collected for a specific purpose may be transmitted to third parties by app developers or app service providers to gain an economic benefit. Since many apps and apps services are offered for free, app developers and service providers rely on advertising to finance their services, as mentioned above, but that may lead to significant risks to privacy of users of apps' services. This is also the result of fragmentation among the various actors in the app development environment. Data processed by an app may be transmitted to third parties for further processing or be copied between chains of third parties, including advertising companies.[19]

Stiftung Warentest, a German consumer organization and foundation, conducted a survey of sixty-three apps in 2012, concluding that thirty-seven apps were problematic, as they either transferred personal data not anonymized/encrypted to the main or other servers, or sent personal data which are excessive and not necessary, without informing users.[20] Only twenty-six apps operated according to users' expectations, i.e., they did not transfer any personal data or transferred only necessary data. More particularly, social networking apps gained access to contact data of the device to find connections between users, failing partly to inform users about such processing. In a more recent survey which examined more than 500 apps, it was found that many apps transfer more user data than necessary and often unencrypted, e.g., telephone provider of the user, device-id or its location. Forty percent of those apps were characterized as problematic in the aspect of data protection.[21]

Previous work on mobile privacy issues by the Federal Trade Commission (FTC) in the United States has focused on the privacy disclosures on the major app platforms—Apple and Google.[22] The key issues emerging from panel discussions were the following: (a) lack of consumer awareness and understanding, i.e., that consumers do not know or understand current information collection and use practices occurring on mobile devices, (b) importance of design to address limitations of small screens: the space limitations on mobile devices and the limited attention spans of consumers

17. *See, e.g.*, N. Lomas, *FaceApp Responds to Privacy Concerns*, available at: https://techcrunch.com/2019/07/17/faceapp-responds-to-privacy-concerns/.
18. *See* R. Christ, *FaceApp Was a Test. We Didn't Pass*, available at: https://www.cnet.com/news/faceapp-privacy-concerns/.
19. *See* Article 29 WP, *supra*, 5.
20. *See* Datenschutz bei Apps. Welche Apps Ihre Daten ausspähen, 31.05.2012, https://www.test.de/Datenschutz-bei-Apps-Welche-Apps-Ihre-Daten-ausspaehen-4378643-0/.
21. *See* Apps sollen Nutzer künftig weniger ausspionieren, 14.04.2017, https://www.test.de/Datenschutz-Apps-sollen-Nutzer-kuenftig-weniger-ausspionieren-5163737-0/.
22. FTC Staff report, Mobile Privacy Disclosures. Building Trust Through Transparency, 2013, 9 et seq., https://www.ftc.gov/reports/mobile-privacy-disclosures-building-trust-through-transparency-federal-trade-commission.

restrict privacy disclosures, (c) key role of platforms: it was emphasized that the platforms possess considerable control over information which is conveyed to consumers and also, significant influence over app developers.

To mitigate the data protection risks related to mobiles apps, data processing must comply with the applicable rules in this field, i.e., the GDPR in the EU. In this chapter, we will examine the legal framework which applies to personal data processing in the development, distribution and usage of mobile apps under the scope of the GDPR.

## §5.02 APPLICATION OF THE DATA PROTECTION LEGISLATION

### [A] Territorial Application

Where personal data are processed with the use of mobile apps, i.e., following the downloading and installation of apps in mobile devices, the rules of data protection law will apply to the processing of data by a data controller or processor. If the processing falls within the field of application of the GDPR, then its rules will apply, otherwise, the rules of data protection law of a third country are applicable. Many apps are provided by app developers or providers with a seat in the USA or in a third country (e.g., China, Vietnam) and therefore, it should be examined whether EU law is applicable as far as the use of apps in the EU Member States and the EEA EFTA states is concerned.[23]

The GDPR applies to the processing of personal data in the context of the activities of an establishment of a controller or processor in the Union, in accordance with Article 3(1) GDPR. In contrast to the EU Directive 95/46, which referred to data controllers only, it also applies where personal data are processed by a data controller, as may be the case with some actors involved in the processing of personal data.[24] Therefore, the distinction between a data controller and a processor is not crucial for the application of the GDPR.

This provision of the GDPR lays down the establishment principle, according to which the application law depends on where an entity is established.[25] Thus, it does matter if the processing takes place within the EU, but for the GDPR to apply, it is required that the data controller or processor is established in the EU.[26] The requirement of establishment means that an entity has an effective and real exercise of activity through stable arrangements. These are not determined by their legal form, and it does not matter whether the entity is a branch or a subsidiary with a legal personality.[27] The place of establishment is surely not the place of registration of a company, but this is

23. The General Data Protection Regulation (GDPR) (EU) 2016/679 entered into force in the EEA EFTA states, i.e., Iceland, Liechtenstein and Norway on July 20, 2018, with the adoption of the Decision of the EEA Joint Committee No. 154/2018 of 6 July 2018.
24. *See infra*, §5.03.
25. *See* G.-J. Zwenne, W. Steenbruggen, in: T. dreier, C. Gielen & R. Hacon, *Concise European Data Protection, E-Commerce and IT Law*, 3rd edn., 2018, p. 68.
26. P. Voigt, A.v.d. Bussche, *supra*, 21 et seq.; Recital 22 GDPR.
27. Recital 22 GDPR.

an indication for the former.[28] Stability of an arrangement is determined according to the nature of economic activities offered.[29] So if a company offers mobile apps, the existence of an arrangement involved in offering or administrating such services in an EU Member State would be regarded as an establishment.[30] The establishment must not carry out any data processing activities, since data processing is required only to take place "in the context of the activities" of the establishment. Consequently, there must be a connection between the economic activity of the establishment and the data processing.[31]

The GDPR also applies to the processing of personal data subjects who are in the Union by a controller or processor not established in the Union, where the processing activities are related to the offering of app services irrespective of whether a payment of the data subject is required, to such data subjects in the Union (Article 3(2) lit. a GDPR). The extraterritoriality effect of this provision is aimed at providing protection to data subjects who are in the EU and whose personal data are processed by a data controller or processor not established in the EU.[32]

To determine whether a company is offering online services to data subjects in the Union, it should be apparent that it envisages offering such services to data subject subjects in one or more EU Member States.[33] As it is pointed out in the Preamble of the GDRP, "the mere accessibility of the controller's, processor's or an intermediary's website in the Union, of an email address or of other contact details, or the use of a language generally used in the third country where the controller is established, is insufficient to ascertain such intention." Factors indicating that a company is targeting EU consumers are the use of a language or a currency generally used in one or more Member States with the possibility of ordering goods and services in that other language, or the mentioning of customers or users who are in the Union, the accepted languages, especially the Euro, the domain name of the website referring to European countries, etc.[34] These factors should be taken into account as far as the distribution of mobile apps directly through app providers is concerned. Insofar as apps are offered by app stores, it is evident that they are targeted at EU consumers, as app stores are intended to provide services to users worldwide and in European countries as well.

The GDPR applies, furthermore, to the processing of personal data of data subjects who are in the Union by a controller or processor not established in the Union, where the processing activities are related to the monitoring of their behavior as far as their behavior takes place within the Union, pursuant to Article 3(2) lit. b GDPR. In order to determine whether a processing activity can be considered to monitor the behavior of data subjects, it should be ascertained whether natural persons are tracked on the internet including potential subsequent use of personal data processing techniques which consist of profiling a natural person, particularly in order to make

28. CJEU, C-230/14 (*Weltimmo*), Recital 29.
29. *Ibid.*
30. *Ibid.*
31. CJEU, C-131/12 (*Google Spain*), Recital 52.
32. Recital 23 GDPR.
33. *Ibid.*
34. *Ibid.*; CJEU, C-585/08 and C-144/09, recs 80–84; P. Voigt, A.v.d. Bussche, *supra*, 26.

decisions concerning her or him or for analyzing or predicting her or his personal preferences, behaviors and attitudes.[35] Any form of web tracking, e.g., cookies, etc. will be considered as monitoring,[36] and thus, advertising companies involved in the distribution of mobile apps and companies providing data analytics will fall under the scope of the GDPR.

### [B] Material Scope

The GDPR applies to the processing of personal data wholly or partly by automated means, according to Article 2(1). This refers to the processing of personal data through computers and software, thus including mobile devices using microchips, and mobile apps which is essentially, software.[37] The Regulation also applies to non-automatic processing, but this is not the case with mobile apps.

The Regulation lists a number of exceptions from its material scope, referring to: (a) activities outside the scope of Union law, (b) activities in relation to the common foreign and security policy of the Union, (c) purely personal or household activities and (d) processing by competent authorities for the purposes of the prevention, investigation, detection or prosecution of criminal offences or the execution of criminal penalties, including the safeguarding against and the prevention of threats to public security (Article 2 section 2 GDPR). None of these exceptions, however, is relevant to data processing by mobile apps.

The Regulation applies to the processing of data which are "personal," that is, if the information relates to an identified or identifiable individual, according to Article 4 No. 1 GDPR. It does not apply to anonymous information, i.e., information which does not relate to an identified or identifiable natural person or to personal data rendered anonymous in such a manner that the data subject is not or no longer identifiable.[38] Personal data is identifiable if a natural person can be detected, directly or indirectly, by reference to an identifier such as a name, an identification number, location data, an online identifier or to one or more factors specific to the physical, physiological, genetic, mental, economic, cultural or social identity of that natural person (Article 4 No. 1 GDPR).

The novelty of the GDPR is that a person is considered identifiable, if it can be associated with online identifiers. Recital No. 30 states that:

> Natural persons may be associated with online identifiers provided by their devices, applications, tools and protocols, such as internet protocol addresses, cookie identifiers or other identifiers such as radio frequency identification tags. This may leave traces which, in particular when combined with unique identifiers and other information received by the servers, may be used to create profiles of the natural persons and identify them.

35. Recital 24 GDRP.
36. P. Voigt, A.v.d. Bussche, *supra*, 28.
37. G.-J. Zwenne, W. Steenbruggen, *supra*, p. 65.
38. Recital 26 GDPR.

Thus, the field of application of GDPR clearly covers the processing of personal data of individuals taking place through the use of apps on smart devices. This includes data stored on a smart device or data generated by the device. Such data are considered personal data if they related to an identified or identifiable natural person, regardless if this is the owner of the device or any other individual, since the definition of personal data in the GDPR is broad and includes location data and online identifiers. It should be noted that data can be automatically generated by the device, according to the settings of the operating system and/or those of the manufacturer or the mobile telephony provider, such as geolocation data, network settings, IP address; they are also generated by the user through apps, e.g., contact lists, notes, photos; and finally, data are produced by the apps, e.g., browsing history. Those data can be collected and processed on the device or they may be transferred to app developers' or third parties' servers, through the connection to an external API.[39]

In particular, the Article 29 Working Party mentions specific examples of personal data which are collected and stored on the device, and namely the following: location, contacts, IMEI (International Mobile Equipment Identity), IMSI (International Mobile Subscriber Identity), UDID (Unique Device Identifier), mobile phone number, identity of the data subject, identity of the phone, credit card and payment data, phone call logs, SMS or instant messaging, browsing history, email, information society service authentication credentials, pictures, videos and biometrics (facial recognition and fingerprint templates).[40]

## §5.03 ACTORS IN THE APP ENVIRONMENT AND THEIR RESPONSIBILITIES

The actors involved in the development, distribution and functioning of mobile apps are many and assume diverse roles (*see* Figure 5.1).[41] Apps are produced by app developers or are commissioned by app right holders. Operating system (OS) and device manufacturers which process users' personal data necessary for the operation and security of the device play a crucial role. The developer of an app enters into a contract directly with an app store or indirectly through an app provider, who is the rights holder and is responsible for the distribution of the app. The app store distributes the apps, making them available online and enters into an agreement (subject to general terms and conditions) with end-users. The app developer or provider may also sell the app individually, without the involvement of the app store. In many cases, the role of the OS manufacturer and of the app store coincide, as the former controls the latter.

39. Article 29 WP 202, p. 8.
40. *See* Article 29 WP, *supra*, pp. 8 et seq.
41. *See* Article 29 WP, Opinion 2/2013, pp. 9 et seq.; Baumgartner/Ewald, *Apps und Recht*, 58.

End-users may also qualify as data controllers in case they use an app, e.g., a social networking app, to make information public on the internet, since this does fall within the household exception of Article 2(2) lit. c GDPR.[42]

*Figure 5.1 Relations of Actors Involved in the Distribution of Apps*

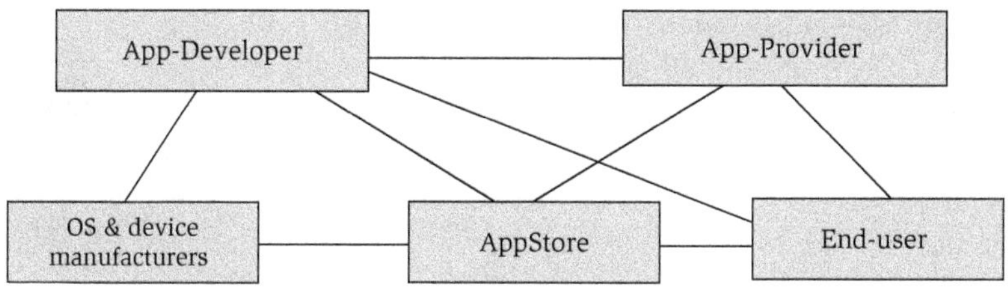


The end-user is certainly the data subject in the sense of Article 4 No. 1 GDPR, in case it is a natural and not a legal person, as his/her personal data are being processed by automated means, that is, they are collected by the app or via the API or are stored in the device, and are then processed by the various actors involved in the distribution of the app, and transmitted to third parties, including advertising companies.

Consequently, it should be determined whether the other actors involved qualify as data controllers or processors in the sense of Article 4 Nos 7 and 8. The burden to comply with data protection rules lies mainly with the controller, pursuant to Article 24 GDPR and forth, while the processor must implement appropriate technical and organizational measures in such a manner that processing will meet the requirements of the regulation and ensure the protection of the rights of the data subject, pursuant to Article 28(1) GDPR.

The definition of "controller" is laid down in Article 4 No. 7 GDPR, which provides that: "controller" means the natural or legal person, public authority, agency or other body which, alone or jointly with others, determines the purposes and means of the processing of personal data; where the purposes and means of such processing are determined by Union or Member State law, the controller or the specific criteria for its nomination may be provided for by Union or Member State law. On the other hand, the processor is defined as meaning a natural or legal person, public authority, agency or other body which processes personal data on behalf of the controller, according to Article 4 No. 8 GDRP.

App developers and app providers produce and distribute mobile apps to app users, and thus determine the purpose of collection and processing of personal data, as well as the categories of personal data collected and processed, and the recipients of data, in case of data transmission.

Third parties assume involved in apps' data processing undertake different roles than the one of the data controller. The most discernible case is when the app developer delegates parts or the whole data processing to a third party, rendering that

42. *See* European Court of Justice, Case C-101/01 (*Bodil Linqvist*), 47; Case C-73/07 (*Satamedia Oy*), 62.

third party "a data processor" and thus, making applicable the rules of Article 28 GDPR. Accordingly, the app developer/provider must choose a processor providing sufficient guarantees to implement appropriate technical and organizational measures in such a manner that processing will meet the requirements of the law and ensure the protection of the rights of the data subject. Additionally, processing must be governed by a contract or other legal act stipulating the terms of Article 28(3) GDPR. Cloud computing is also relevant in this case, even if it concerns the use of external data storage, i.e., the app developer/provider should be considered as a data controller and the cloud provider as a provider, since the former determines the ultimate purpose of the processing and decides on the outsourcing of processing to the latter.[43]

It is doubtful whether third parties accessing user data are to be considered as recipients of data, as suggested by Article 29 WP.[44] In our view, they should be regarded as data processors or as joint controllers if they process personal data for their own purposes and should define their respective responsibilities for compliance with the obligations of the GDPR as provided for in Article 26.

Furthermore, in case an app developer uses third-party libraries with software providing common functionalities, e.g., a library for a social gaming platform, users must be informed about any processing carried out by these libraries and, if necessary, provide their consent to it.[45]

OS and device manufacturers could also be regarded as data controllers or joint controllers, if they process personal data for their own purposes, such as security. Processing includes user generated data, such as the user details provided at the registration, data automatically generated by the device or data resulting from the installation or use of the apps.[46] The OS manufacturer is the data controller with regard to data processed to provide geolocation information to apps, when access to geolocation is required.

The OS and device manufacturer are, furthermore, responsible for APIs enabling the processing of personal data by apps on the device. As they determine access to data on the device by apps, they must ensure that the app developer has access only to those data that are necessary for the app to function.[47]

App stores are hubs which facilitate the distribution of apps. Users can buy apps directly from an app store and payments are processed by app stores. In-app purchases are also processed and such processing necessitates registration of users, which must provide their name, address and means of payment, e.g., credit card information. For the processing of such information, app stores are considered as controllers, and eventually, as joint controllers with app providers, as they report such information to the latter.[48]

Third parties may also qualify as data controllers or processors, depending on the function which they achieve. In particular, advertising is provided by advertising

43. *See* Article 29 WP, Opinion 05/2012 on cloud computing.
44. *See* Article 29 WP, Opinion 2/2013, p. 10.
45. *Ibid.*
46. *Ibid.*
47. *Ibid.*, p. 11.
48. *Ibid.*, pp. 11–12.

networks and other intermediaries, which use cookies or other online identifiers to provide personalized or behavioral advertising. Since advertising network providers determine the purposes and the means of the processing of data, they qualify as data controllers.[49]

## §5.04 THE LEGAL GROUNDS OF PROCESSING

### [A] Legitimation of Processing of Personal Data

The processing of personal data requires a legal basis, in accordance with Article 5 GDPR, providing that personal data shall be processed lawfully (principle of lawfulness). The legal grounds for data processing, laid down in Article 6 GDPR, are the following: (a) the data subject's consent for one or more specific purposes, (b) the necessity for the performance of a contract to which the data subject is party or at its request prior to entering a contract (c) the necessity for compliance with a legal obligation to which the controller is subject, (d) the necessity to protect the vital interests of the data subject or of another natural person, (e) the necessity for the performance of a task carried out in the public interest or in the exercise of official authority vested in the controller and (f) the necessity for the purposes of the legitimate interests pursued by the controller or by a third party, except where such interests are overridden by the interests or fundamental rights and freedoms of the data subject which require protection of personal data, in particular where the data subject is a child.

The processing of personal data by apps can rely mainly on the consent of the user in accordance with Article 6(1) lit. a GDPR. Such consent is provided during installation of the app, and it should have the qualities provided for in Article 4 No. 11 GDPR, which reads as follows:

> "consent" of the data subject means any freely given, specific, informed and unambiguous indication of the data subject's wishes by which he or she, by a statement or by a clear affirmative action, signifies agreement to the processing of personal data relating to him or her.

It is made clear from the above that consent should be given by an act indicating the data subject's agreement to the processing data relating to him/her. In the context of apps, it can be given by clicking a button or ticking a box on the website of the app provider or the app store. Silence, pre-ticked boxes or inactivity do not constitute consent.[50]

Moreover, the provision of Article 7(1) GDPR stipulates that "the controller shall be able to demonstrate that the data subject has consented to processing of his or her personal data." This means that the controller must prove that consent has been granted by data subjects and it is, therefore, required to keep proof of actual provided agreements of data subjects.

49. WP29 Opinion 2/2010 on online behavioral advertising.
50. Recital 32 GDPR.

In addition, if an app needs to access personal data stored on the device such as contacts in the address book, videos or pictures, or place information on it, it is required to obtain consent from the user, pursuant to Article 5(3) of the ePrivacy Directive, which provides that: "the use of electronic communications networks to store information or to gain access to information stored in the terminal equipment of a subscriber or user is only allowed on condition that the subscriber or user concerned is provided with clear and comprehensive information in accordance with Directive 95/46/EC, inter alia about the purposes of the processing, and is offered the right to refuse such processing by the data controller."[51] The consent requirements imposed by the GDPR and the ePrivacy Directive are different, and thus, they can only be obtained separately, even though they can be merged in practice.[52]

To illustrate the difference in obtaining consent under the GDPR and the ePrivacy Directive, an example might be helpful: an app which provides taxi services requires consent in order to be installed on a mobile phone. The app has a feature which allows finding of the actual location of the customer to provide customized services. To enable this feature, the app needs to have access to the GPS of the user's device and, therefore, it should require consent by the app user to access the geolocation.

The consent for the processing of personal data must be "informed," which means that the app user should be informed about the processing before agreeing to it. Informing the user on the basic characteristics only of an app before its installation does not qualify as valid.[53] Instead, the user must be provided with information conforming to the requirements of Article 13 GDPR.

Also, the consent must be "freely given." This means that the app user must be given the opportunity to accept or refuse the processing of his/her personal data and thus, only giving the option of accepting and not the option of cancelling the installation of an app is contrary to the explicit requirements for consent according to the GDRP. Consent should not be regarded as freely given if the data subject has no genuine or free choice or is unable to refuse or withdraw consent without detriment.[54] Consent is presumed not to be freely given if it does not allow separate consent to be given to different personal data processing operations despite it being appropriate in the individual case.[55] Consent should be "granular," in the sense that users must be given the option to provide consent to the each of the subprocessing operations carried out by an app.[56]

Consent is also presumed not to be freely given if the performance of a contract, including the provision of a service, is dependent on the consent despite such consent not being necessary for such performance, pursuant to Article 7(4) GDPR.[57] This does

51. Directive 2002/58/EC of the European Parliament and of the Council of 12 July 2002 concerning the processing of personal data and the protection of privacy in the electronic communications sector, OJ L 201, 31.7.2002, 37–47.
52. Article 29 WP, Opinion 2/2013, p. 14.
53. *See* WP29 Opinion 15/2011 on the definition of consent (WP 187).
54. Recital 42 GDPR.
55. Recital 43 GDPR.
56. Article WP 187, *supra*, p. 18.
57. *See also* Recital 43 GDPR.

not mean, however, that it is contrary to the GDPR to cancel the installation of an app in case the user does not agree to the processing of his/her personal data and consent is the principal legal basis.

If the data subjects whose personal data are processed by apps are children, Article 8 GDPR applies, which states that the processing of data of a child will be lawful provided that the child is at least 16 years old. If the child is below that age, such processing will be lawful only if and to the extent that consent is given or authorized by the holder of parental responsibility over the child. Under the national laws of EU Member States implementing the GDPR, the age limit can be lower, but it should not be below 13 years. To ensure that consent by a child is informed, any information addressed to a child, should be in such a clear and plain language that the child can easily understand.[58]

Consent must also be "specific," which means practically that it must refer to the specific category of data or data processing. It is for this reason that it is suggested to provide the ability to users of giving a granular consent, that is, to consent separately to each specific category of personal data the app needs to access.[59] For example, to install an app providing social networking services, the user provides his/her consent, but access to the address book of the device which is carried out by the app to provide friends' suggestions is only legitimate if the user provides *additional* consent. Furthermore, the user should have the possibility to select the contacts that he/she wishes to communicate with, rather than granting access to his/her entire address book.[60]

The requirement of specific consent means that it must be limited to the specific purpose for which data are collected and processed. So, e.g., an app requiring access to geolocation data of a device to provide taxi services is not permitted to continuously collect geolocation data; instead, this further processing requires the consent of the app user.

Apps preinstalled on a device should provide a possibility of genuine consent, if processing of personal data by means of the app is based on consent. More precisely, with the first running of such apps, consent must be required from the user and such consent must be informed, that is, the user must be adequately informed before clicking a button indicating agreement.

In accordance with Article 7(3) GDPR, the data subject has the right to withdraw his or her consent at any time, as easily as giving consent. In case of apps, this may take place with uninstalling the app or certain features of it. Certainly, the withdrawal of consent does not affect the lawfulness of processing based on consent before its withdrawal.

Subsequently, during the operation of an app, the legality of the processing of personal data can be based on another legal basis, rather than consent. In particular, the processing could be necessary for the performance of a contract with the data subject, if there is such a contractual relationship. So, for example, the user of a banking app would not be required to provide additional consent in order to disclose

58. Recital 58 GDPR.
59. *See* Article 29 WP, Opinion 2/2013, p. 15.
60. *Ibid.*

his or her name and bank account number to a third person to whom a payment is made, since this processing is necessary to perform the contract with this particular user.

### [B] Processing of Special Categories of Personal Data

Mobile apps are also used for health and fitness purposes.[61] In this case, apps process health data which are sensitive and enjoy enhanced protection, since the risks for natural persons are higher. Article 9 GDPR provides that generally the processing of special categories of data including health is prohibited, save that one of the requirements in section 2 is met. As far as the processing of health data is concerned, processing will be lawful if the data subject has given explicit consent (section 2 lit. a) or if it is necessary for the purposes of preventive medicine, medical diagnosis, and the provision of health care (section 2 lit. h), provided that data are processed by or under the responsibility of a professional subject to the obligation of professional secrecy (Article 9 section 3 GDPR). However, in the case of mobile health apps the latter requirement cannot be met, since personal data are then stored on the device or on the server of the app provider, and not under the responsibility of a physician, and also, the app determines the scope of the processing.[62]

Consent by the data subject in the processing of health data must be explicit, according to the regulation. "Explicit" consent is not defined in the GDPR, and thus, reference to the interpretation given by the Article 29 WP is needed. Namely, they explain that this term refers to the way consent is expressed by the data subject.[63] Hence, this could be a written statement given by the data subject, preferably signed, which would be considered to be explicit. In a digital or online context, consent may be given with a statement of the data subject, that is, by filling in an electronic form, by sending an email, by uploading a scanned document carrying the signature of the data subject, or by using an electronic signature.

### [C] Transfer of Personal Data to Third Countries and to Third Parties

App developers and providers may be established in a third country, i.e., any country that is not an EU Member State or a member of the European Economic Area or store personal data in third countries, e.g., when using cloud services. In both cases, the data transfer is subject to the provisions of Chapter V of the GDPR, to ensure that the level of data protection guaranteed by the regulation is not undermined (Article 44 GDPR).

The transfer may take place on the basis of an adequacy decision, according to Article 45 GDPR, i.e., if the EU Commission has decided that the third country in question ensures an adequate level of protection. The criteria for an adequacy decision

61. *See* T. Mulder, Health Apps, Their Privacy Policies and the GDPR, *EJLT* 10(1) (2019).
62. *Ibid.*, p. 4.
63. Article 29 WP, Guidelines on consent under Regulation 2016/679, WP259 rev.01, April 10, 2018, p. 18.

are laid down in Article 45 section 2 GDPR,[64] including the third country's data protection legislation, implement and supervision and its international assurances. The EU Commission adopts an adequacy decision on the basis of Article 45 GDPR.[65] The transfer of personal data to the United States is based on the Privacy Shield certification system. The EU has adopted an adequacy decision on the EU-US Privacy Shield on July 12, 2016, allowing the transfer of data to companies in the US which are certified under the Privacy Shield.[66] This decision has replaced the previous Safe Harbor system which was declared invalid by the CJEU decision in the case *Maximillian Schrems v. Data Protection Commissioner*.[67] If a third country does not ensure an adequate level of protection, the transfer is subject to appropriate safeguards, in accordance with Article 46, including binding corporate rules, standard data protection clauses, approved codes of conducts and approved certification mechanisms. As these are not relevant for data processing by mobile apps, in our view, the controller should request the consent by the data subject, in accordance with Article 49 section 1 lit. a GDPR.

In case app developers or providers outsource data processing to a third party acting as a processor, including the use of a cloud computing provider (e.g., for data storage), the former should comply with the requirements of Article 28 GDPR. Accordingly, the controller is obliged to use only processors providing sufficient guarantees to implement appropriate technical and organizational measures so that processing complies with the GDPR. In particular, the processing by a processor must be based on a contract, binding on the controller with regard to the controller, defining the subject matter and details of the processing and include the provisions of Article 28 section 3 lit. a-h GDPR.

### [D] Online Tracking

Where app developers use cookies or similar devices to monitor users' behavior, this is only permitted on condition that the app user has given his/her consent, having been provided with clear and comprehensive information, according to Article 5 section 3 of the ePrivacy Directive.[68] The proposal for a regulation on Privacy and Electronic Communications provides also for an opt-in for tracking cookies in Article 8 section 1.[69]

Where app developers use APIs to collect personal data stored on the user's device, this is conditional, *inter alia*, on the consent of the user, according to Article 8 section 2 of the proposal, which provides that the collection of information emitted by

64. *See* CJEU, Decision of October 6, 2015, *Maximilian Schrems v. Data Protection Commissioner*, C-362/14.
65. *See* https://ec.europa.eu/info/law/law-topic/data-protection/international-dimension-data-protection/adequacy-decisions_en.
66. Commission Implementing Decision (EU) 2016/1250 of 12 July 2016 pursuant to Directive 95/46/EC of the European Parliament and of the Council on the adequacy of the protection provided by the EU-US Privacy Shield (notified under document C(2016) 4176, C/2016/4176, OJ L 207, 1.8.2016).
67. *See supra* n. 64.
68. Directive 2002/58/EC of July 12, 2002, amended by Directive 2006/24/EC of March 15, 2006 and Directive 2009/136/EC of November 25, 2009.
69. *See* the Council draft of the proposal as of September 18, 2019.

terminal equipment of the end-user to enable it to connect to another device and/or to network equipment shall be otherwise prohibited. Consent must be informed in this case; in particular, a clear and prominent notice must be displayed, informing of, at least, the modalities of the collection, its purpose, the person responsible for it and the other information required under Article 13 GDPR, as well as any measure the end-user of the terminal equipment can take to stop or minimize the collection (Article 8 section 2a). To this end, information may be provided in combination with standardized icons (Article 8 section 3).

## §5.05 APPLICATION OF GENERAL PRINCIPLES OF DATA PROTECTION

### [A] Article 5 GDPR

The Regulation establishes in Article 5 basic principles of data processing, which are important for data processing in mobile apps. These are the following principles: (a) lawfulness, fairness and transparency, (b) purpose limitation, (c) data minimization, (d) accuracy, (e) storage limitation, (f) integrity and confidentiality and (g) accountability of the controller. These are enforceable provisions but can also be used to interpret the other provisions of the GDPR.[70]

The principle of lawfulness, fairness and transparency requires that there is a legal basis for the processing of personal data, as has already been mentioned above. It also provides that data subjects must be properly informed about the processing of their data, and that app developers and providers should implement appropriate mechanisms to allow data subjects to exercise their rights, e.g., right to access, to rectification, erasure, data portability, etc.

The purpose limitation principle provides that personal data be collected for specified, explicit and legitimate purposes and not further processed in a manner that is incompatible with those purposes (Article 5 section 1 lit. b GDPR). Therefore, the purpose of processing with regard to the functioning of apps should be defined before the data processing takes place. Any subsequent changes to the purposes of processing are not allowed and can only be considered as lawful if the data controllers manage to obtain additional consent from data subjects.

For example, if an app initially had access to the GPS of mobile devices to provide hotel and restaurant reviews to subscribers, depending on their location, but the developer changes the purpose of processing and chooses to use the location information to send direct messages to users with reviews which are near their current location. This processing is not compatible with the original purpose of processing and, thus, the app developer should ask users for their consent, before sending them any messages.

In the same vein, the principle of data minimization which provides that data must be adequate, relevant and limited to what is necessary in relation to the purposes for which they are processed must be respected. This calls for an evaluation of the

70. P. Voigt, A.v.d. Bussche, *supra*, p. 87.

proportionality of the processing activities, so that it is determined which data are necessary vis-à-vis the purposes of processing.[71] Thus, app developers must design their software products in such a way that unnecessary data processing is prevented.

For example, apps should not require billing information from their users who download the app from an app store, since billing is carried out by the app store. The address of a user is also not necessary, except where product delivery has to take place.

The purpose limitation and the data minimization principle must be applied more strictly in the case of children's data processing by an app. In such case, a data controller should not process data for behavioral advertising, as this will be outside the scope of children's understanding.[72]

The above principles must also be respected by third parties which obtain access to user data through the apps.[73]

Furthermore, the OS and device manufacturers should provide APIs to app developers with precise controls, to make sure that they can request access only to those data which are strictly necessary for the app operation. Article 29 WP proposed different mechanisms to achieve control over the access to data stored in the device: (a) OS and device manufacturers and app stores define rules that apply to submit apps in their app store: app developers must respect these rules or risk not being available in these stores, (b) OS' APIs define standard methods to access the data stored in the telephone to which apps have access. They also have an impact on the collection of data on the server side, (c) Ex-ante controls—controls in place before installing an app, (d) Ex-post controls—controls implemented after having installed an app.[74]

The accuracy principle is also relevant, as it provides that personal data must be accurate and, where necessary, kept up to date, while personal data that are inaccurate, having regard to the purposes for which they are processed, should be erased or rectified without delay. Consequently, processes of erasure or rectification of personal data must be introduced in the apps.

The storage limitation principle obliges the data controller to define retention periods with regard to data collected with apps. Therefore, data must be stored only for a certain period of time as regards non-active users. It would be advisable, where a user has not used the app, e.g., for a period of three years, to delete his or her personal data, after warning the user that his/her account will be deleted. When the data have been used to carry out a financial transaction, they should be stored for as long as there is a legal obligation to retain the data for control on the part of a competent authority.

The principle of integrity and confidentiality furthermore requires that app developers and providers should ensure appropriate security of personal data, including protection against unauthorized or unlawful processing and against accidental loss, destruction or damage, using appropriate technical or organizational measures.

---

71. *Ibid.*, p. 80.
72. *See* Article 29 WP, Opinion 2/13, *supra*, p. 26.
73. *Ibid.*, p. 17.
74. *Ibid.*, p. 18.

### [B] Transparency

Transparency is an important principle which is established as a general principle in Article 5(1) lit. a GDPR (*see above*) and as a specific requirement, according to Article 12 GDPR, which states that information provided to data subjects must be made in a concise, transparent, intelligible and easily accessible form, using clear and plain language, in particular for any information addressed specifically to a child.

To ensure that the data subject is informed about the processing and is able to provide an informed consent, it is crucial to make available the information in Article 13 GDPR. This includes information on the following points:

- the identity and the contact details of the controller;
- the contact details of the DPO, if one is appointed;
- the purposes of processing;
- where processing is necessary for the legitimate interests pursued by the controller or by a third party, these interests;
- the recipients or categories of recipients of the personal data, if any;
- where applicable, the fact that the controller intends to transfer personal data to a third country or international organization and the existence or absence of an adequacy decision by the Commission, or the appropriate or suitable safeguards and the means by which to obtain a copy of them or where they have been made available;
- additionally, the storage period, the right to request access, the right to withdraw consent, the right to lodge a complaint with a supervisor, etc.

Information to data subjects should be provided before and after app installation, to make sure that data processing is transparent. App stores must also provide information about personal data processing to users, as they are joint controllers.[75] Information according to Article 13 GDPR can be provided by the app developer or provider through a privacy policy which must meet the requirements of Article 12 section 1 GDPR, i.e., it must be drafted in a concise, transparent, intelligible and easily accessible form, using clear and plain language. This information can also be provided in combination with standardized icons in order to provide an overview of the processing (Article 12 section 7 GDPR).[76] App stores should also provide a link to the privacy policy of apps, allowing users to review the permissions required by apps and the information about personal data processing. The most renewed app stores, i.e., Apple's App Store[77] and Android's Play Market[78] require applications to have a privacy policy. For instance, the App Store provides that all apps must include a link to their privacy policy in the App Store Connect metadata field and within the app in an easily accessible manner. The privacy policy must clearly and explicitly: (a) identify what

75. *See, e.g.*, https://policies.google.com/privacy.
76. *See* Privacy Icons: A Risk-Based Approach to Visualisation of Data Processing, *EDPL* (3/2019), 352.
77. https://developer.apple.com/app-store/review/guidelines/.
78. *See* Play Console Help, shorturl.at/bovV1.

data, if any, the app/service collects, how it collects that data, and all uses of that data, (b) confirm that any third party with whom an app shares user data—such as analytics tools, advertising networks and third-party SDKs, as well as any parent, subsidiary or other related entities that will have access to user data—will provide the same or equal protection of user data as stated in the app's privacy policy and required by the App Store's Guidelines, (c) explain its data retention/deletion policies and describe how a user can revoke consent and/or request deletion of the user's data.

An impediment to providing information exists because mobile devices have small screens, and this means that there are space limitations, while the attention spans of consumers are limited. To address this issue, it is proposed to develop shorthand, consistent disclosures, which will include the use of icons, short form privacy notices and layered notices.[79] In particular, layered notices can increase the level of transparency of information to data subjects.[80] This means that minimum information required by the GDPR is provided to data subjects, in a concise and user-friendly manner, which fits in the small screen of mobile devices, while additional information via a link to the entire data protection policy is provided to those who require further clarification.[81] This approach to informing data subjects can be combined with the use of icons, images, video and audio, and with providing real time notification when an app gains access to the address book or photos stored on the device.[82]

### [C] Rights of Data Subjects

Pursuant to Article 12 section 2 GDPR, data controllers, i.e., app developers and other actors in the app ecosystem, must facilitate the exercise of the data subjects' rights under Articles 15–22. The GDPR has strengthened the legal position of the data subject by introducing new rights and enhancing existing ones. Articles 15–22 include, namely, the following rights: (a) right of access by the data subject, (b) right to rectification, (c) right to erasure ("right to be forgotten"), (d) right to restriction of processing, (e) right to data portability, (f) right to object and (g) automated individual decision-making including profiling.

To facilitate the exercise of these rights and give control to users over their right, app developers must inform the users of their apps about the existence of these rights and provide them with secure online tools for this purpose. Such tools could be available within the app or via a link to an online mechanism for exercising the right to access by the app user. In this case, the app developer must provide information to the user about the processing details, in accordance with Article 15 section 1 GDPR. If the controller employs automated decision-making, including profiling, he should provide meaningful information about the logic involved, as well as the significance and the

79. *See* FTC staff report Mobile Privacy Disclosures, Building Trust Through Transparency, February 2013, http://www.ftc.gov/os/2013/02/130201mobileprivacyreport.pdf, FTC staff report Mobile.
80. Article 29 WP, Opinion 15/2011, p. 20; Opinion 03/2013, p. 16.
81. Article 29 WP, Opinion 03/2013, *ibid.*; Article WP 29 Opinion 10/2004 on More Harmonised Information Provisions.
82. Article 29 WP, Opinion 03/2013, p. 24.

envisaged consequences of such processing for the data subject (lit. h). These online tools must also allow app users to require rectification, blocking or deletion of personal data concerning them, objecting to the processing or requiring data portability.

App users must be provided with the right to withdraw their consent at any time, as easily as they give consent, pursuant to Article 7 section 3 GDPR. Thus, consent withdrawal could be facilitated with online tools, as mentioned above. Uninstalling an app is also a way of withdrawing consent and it should result in removing all personal data from the device and the servers of the app provider. When a user uninstalls an app, the OS manufacturer should enable signaling to the app developer to delete all personal data.[83]

## §5.06 ACCOUNTABILITY, DATA PROTECTION BY DESIGN AND BY DEFAULT, SECURITY AND DATA PROTECTION IMPACT ASSESSMENT

The GDPR introduces the general principle of accountability in Article 5 section 2 GDPR, which stipulates that the controller is responsible for the compliance of the processing with the GDPR and that the controller should be able to prove compliance to supervisor authorities.[84] App providers and other actors in the app ecosystem who are considered controllers or processors must, therefore, maintain records if processing activities in accordance with Article 30 GDPR and keep them updated, so that they can make them available to supervising authorities, once the latter request them for monitoring. The controller is obliged to implement data protection policies, where this is proportionate in relation to processing activities, according to Article 24 section 2 GDPR. Thus, it is suggested to implement a Data Protection Management System (DPMS) which effectively implements appropriate technical and organizational measures in compliance with the GDPR. The DPMS should include policies for data security, a data security plan and a data recovery plan, in order to comply with the requirements of Article 32 GDPR regarding security of processing. The controller must also have in place a policy and procedures for the notification of personal data breaches to the supervisory authorities, in accordance with Article 33 GDPR; if the personal data breach is likely to result in a high risk to the rights and freedoms of natural persons, the controller should communicate the data breach to the users of apps, according to Article 34 GDPR.

It may also be mandatory for data controllers and processors to designate a Data Protection Officer (DPO). The obligation to designate a DPO is conditional on the type of processing activities. Private entities are obliged to designate a DPO in any case where: (a) the core activities of the controller or the processor consist of processing operations which, by virtue of their nature, their scope and/or their purposes, require regular and systematic monitoring of data subjects on a large scale or (b) the core activities of the controller or the processor consist of processing on a large scale of

83. *Ibid.*, p. 25.
84. P. Voigt, A.v.d. Bussche, *supra*, pp. 31 et seq.

special categories of data. Thus, most of the apps employing data processing on a large scale and monitoring users, as well as health and fitness apps processing health data, will be subjected to the obligation to designate a DPO. Apps which are only presenting information, e.g., news or information apps, will not be imposed to such obligation. In case they cooperate with advertisers who track users, the former will be obliged to designate a DPO, not the app providers. Where the designation of a DPO takes place, the controller or processor must publish the contact details of the DPO and communicate them to the supervisory authority (Article 37 section 7 GDPR).

Article 25 GDPR introduces the principles of data protection by design and by default which are essential for mobile apps. Privacy by design implies that privacy considerations should be taken into account throughout the system development lifecycle.[85] It is a rather fuzzy concept and the regulation does not make it precise enough, as Article 25 section 1 GDPR reads that "taking into account the state of the art, the cost of implementation and the nature, scope, context and purposes of processing as well as the risks of varying likelihood and severity for rights and freedoms of natural persons posed by the processing, the controller shall, both at the time of the determination of the means for processing and at the time of the processing itself, implement appropriate technical and organisational measures, such as pseudonymisation, which are designed to implement data-protection principles, such as data minimisation, in an effective manner and to integrate the necessary safeguards into the processing in order to meet the requirements of this Regulation and protect the rights of data subjects."

In November 2017, the European Agency for Network and Information Security (ENISA) issued a study, in which it addresses data protection goals (unlinkability, transparency, intervenability) and privacy design strategies.[86] Such strategies include: (a) the limitation of the processing of personal data as possible (minimize), (b) the prevention of correlation of personal data by separating the processing logically or physically (separate), (c) the limitation as much as possible of the amount of personal data being processed (abstract), (d) the prevention of personal data becoming public (hide), the provision of data subjects with adequate information about what personal data is processed, how it is processed, and for what purpose, (e) to provide data subjects mechanisms to control the processing of their personal data (control), (f) to commit to a privacy-friendly way of processing personal data and enforce this (enforce), and (g) to provide evidence that you process personal data in a privacy-friendly way (demonstrate). For example, to limit the processing of personal data, apps should limit their access to sensors and locally stored data to the minimum and only to the extent that it is relevant for the functioning of the app. So, e.g., a weather app may ask permission to access geolocation information to provide local weather information. Furthermore, mobile devices could process data locally instead of uploading them to a central server. To hide personal data, apps should encrypt communications and other techniques such as certificate pinning (or preinstalled keys) to prevent man-in-the-middle attacks. To demonstrate that the processing of personal data is carried out in a

85. A. Cavoukian, *Privacy by Design—The 7 Foundational Principles*, 2011.
86. ENISA, Privacy and data protection in mobile applications. A study on the app development ecosystem and the technical implementation of GDPR, November 2017.

privacy-friendly way, it is suggested to track all processing of data, without revealing personal data, securing and reviewing the information gathered for any risks, to examine day-to-day activities and report, i.e., analyze collected information on test, audits and logs periodically.[87]

Data protection by design and by default can be integrated into the processing of personal data by apps with data protection impact assessments (DPIAs). A DPIA is mandatory, according to Article 35 GDPR, if based on a risk analysis, the processing of personal data is likely to result in a high risk to the rights and freedoms of natural persons. Regarding risk management as a component of the GDPR legal framework, Recital 75 GDPR states the following:

> The risk to the rights and freedoms of natural persons, of varying likelihood and severity, may result from personal data processing which could lead to physical, material or non-material damage, in particular: where the processing may give rise to discrimination, identity theft or fraud, financial loss, damage to the reputation, loss of confidentiality of personal data protected by professional secrecy, unauthorised reversal of pseudonymisation, or any other significant economic or social disadvantage; where data subjects might be deprived of their rights and freedoms or prevented from exercising control over their personal data; where personal data are processed which reveal racial or ethnic origin, political opinions, religion or philosophical beliefs, trade union membership, and the processing of genetic data, data concerning health or data concerning sex life or criminal convictions and offences or related security measures; where personal aspects are evaluated, in particular analysing or predicting aspects concerning performance at work, economic situation, health, personal preferences or interests, reliability or behaviour, location or movements, in order to create or use personal profiles; where personal data of vulnerable natural persons, in particular of children, are processed; or where processing involves a large amount of personal data and affects a large number of data subjects.

Privacy risk management is important for mobile app providers and developers, as this is needed to address the various privacy risks inherent to processing of personal data. A DPIA is, thus, useful, as it reviews the risks or the users of the apps and addresses measures to mitigate those risks, by introducing data protection requirements by design and by default.[88] A DPIA should be carried out prior to data processing, and in an early phase of the system design. It contains at least: (a) a systematic description of the intended processing and the purposes of the processing, (b) an assessment of the necessity and proportionality of the processing operations, (c) an assessment of the risks to the rights and freedoms of data subjects and (d) the measures envisaged to address the risks, including safeguards, security measures and mechanisms to ensure the protection of personal data and to demonstrate compliance with the GDPR (Article 35 section 7).

87. *Ibid.*, pp. 51 et seq.
88. *Ibid.*, p. 23.

## §5.07 DATA PROTECTION AND PRIVACY IN APP STORES

Platforms not only play a key role in the dissemination of information to consumers regarding apps' services, but also possess influence over app developers which rely on them in order to have their apps presented to the public.[89] They are the gatekeepers in the app ecosystem and have the ability to define conditions for the participation in their platform and even reject apps that do not meet the conditions. It thus becomes apparent that app stores can play a proactive role in advancing app developers' compliance with data protection rules. In their developer agreements and app store review guidelines, app stores define the legal requirements for apps including data protection requirements, which must be met by app developers.

The App Store provides Guidelines for app developers which are responsible to make sure that their apps comply with them.[90] It is highlighted that the protection of user privacy is paramount in the Apple ecosystem and that developers should use care when handling personal data to ensure that they have not only complied with privacy best practices, which are compiled in official documents, i.e., Guidelines from Government Industry Sources,[91] applicable laws and the terms of the Apple Developer Program License Agreement,[92] but also meet customer expectations.

The Guidelines require that all apps include a link to their privacy policy in the App Store and within the app in an easily accessible manner, which must clearly and explicitly: (a) identify what data, if any, the app/service collects, how it collects that data, and all uses of that data, (b) confirm that any third party with whom an app shares user data (in compliance with these Guidelines)—such as analytics tools, advertising networks and third-party SDKs, as well as any parent, subsidiary or other related entities that will have access to user data—will provide the same or equal protection of user data as stated in the app's privacy policy and required by the Guidelines and (c) explain its data retention/deletion policies and describe how a user can revoke consent and/or request deletion of the user's data.

Furthermore, they provide that apps that collect user or usage data must secure user content for that collection, that data minimization should be respected, as well as user's permission settings, and that account sign-in should not be required if not

89. *See, e.g.*, FTC Staff Report, pp. 11, 14.
90. https://developer.apple.com/app-store/review/guidelines/?fbclid=IwAR2CTtYdoCDspcUyrmwuKAf7gblm-Ot15UZhh2FU56nTbcZ5Pme5oAiNHIw#legal.
91. The following documents are mentioned: (a) Mobile Privacy Disclosures: Building Trust Through Transparency. The Federal Trade Commission's report on mobile privacy, (b) Opinion 02/2013 on Apps on Smart Devices. The EU Data Protection Commissioners' opinion on data protection for mobile apps, (c) Privacy on the Go: Recommendations for the Mobile Ecosystem. The California State Attorney General's recommendations for mobile privacy, (d) Smartphone Privacy Initiative (2012) in English or Japanese and Smartphone Privacy Initiative II (2013) in English or Japanese. The Japanese Ministry of Internal Affairs and Communications' Smartphone Privacy Initiatives. *See* https://developer.apple.com/documentation/uikit/protecting_the_user_s_privacy.
92. *See* https://developer.apple.com/register/agree/?successURL=services-account%2Fdownload%3Fpath%3D%2FDocumentation%2FLicense_Agreements__Apple_Developer_Program_ADPLA1028%2FApple_Developer_Program_License_Agreement_20191028.pdf.

necessary. Data sharing and transmission should be based on user's consent, and purpose limitation should be strictly applied; in particular, (a) data collected for one purpose may not be processed for another purpose without further consent unless otherwise explicitly permitted by law, (b) apps should not attempt to surreptitiously build a user profile based on collected data and may not attempt, facilitate or encourage others to identify anonymous users or reconstruct user profiles based on data collected from Apple-provided APIs or any data that has been collected in an "anonymized," "aggregated," or otherwise non-identifiable way, (c) information from Contacts, Photos or other APIs that access user data should not be used to build a contact database owned by the app developer or for sale/distribution to third parties, and information should not be collected about which other apps are installed on a user's device for the purposes of analytics or advertising/marketing, (d) apps should not contact people using information collected via a user's Contacts or Photos, except at the explicit initiative of that user on an individualized basis, (e) data gathered from different APIs may not be used for marketing, advertising or use-based data mining, including by third parties and (f) apps using Apple Pay may only share user data acquired via Apple Pay with third parties to facilitate or improve delivery of goods and services.

Particular reference is made to health and health research, since the relevant data are especially sensitive, while particular care is suggested when dealing with personal data from kids. And finally, location services should be used in an app only when it is directly relevant to the features and services provided by it and if consent is obtained by the app developer. Location-based APIs should not be used to provide emergency services or autonomous control over vehicles, aircraft, and other devices, except for small devices such as lightweight drones and toys, or remote control car alarm systems, etc.

Google Play also requires from app developers to publish a privacy policy, which should comprehensively and accurately disclose an app's privacy practices, and also comply with applicable laws and regulations.[93] The reasons for that requirement are according to Google the following:

> Privacy disclosures—made via a privacy policy and in-Action conversations—help users understand what data you collect, why you collect it, and what you do with it. The disclosures should be comprehensive, accurate, and easy to understand by users. Users will have an opportunity to review the policy when they browse actions in the Directory, and we encourage developers to make it available on their website and other convenient places.

In the Developer Policy Center's User Data Guidelines,[94] app developers are addressed to as follows:

> You must be transparent in how you handle user data (e.g., information provided by a user, collected about a user, and collected about a user's use of the app or device), including by disclosing the collection, use, and sharing of the data, and

93. https://developers.google.com/assistant/console/policies/privacy-policy-guide.
94. https://play.google.com/intl/en-US/about/privacy-security-deception/user-data/.

> you must limit use of the data to the description in the disclosure. If your app handles personal or sensitive user data, there are additional requirements described below. This policy establishes Google Play's minimum privacy requirements; you or your app may need to comply with additional restrictions or procedures if required by an applicable law.

An app privacy policy, according to Google, should answer three questions: (1) what information do you collect? (2) how do you use the information and (3) what information do you share? Additionally, a developer may choose to add information regarding information security practices, or inform users how to change or delete their data and how long their data are retained.[95]

Google Play requires, specifically, that a link to a privacy policy is visible on the app's store listing page, in a website and within the app itself,[96] in cases where: (a) an app handles personal or sensitive user data[97] or (b) an app is in the "Designed for Families" program.[98] In the first case, the disclosure: (i) must be within the app itself, not only in the play listing or a website, (ii) must be displayed in the normal usage of the app and not require the user to navigate into a menu or settings, (iii) must describe the data being collected, (iv) must explain how the data will be used, (v) cannot only be placed in a privacy policy or terms of service and (vi) cannot be included with other disclosures unrelated to personal or sensitive data collection. Google also requires that user consent has certain qualities. In particular, the app's request for consent must present the consent dialog in a clear and unambiguous way, and require affirmative user action (e.g., tap to accept, tick a check box, a verbal command, etc.) in order to accept, etc.

## §5.08 CONCLUSION

Mobile apps present high risks to data protection, since the processing of personal data through apps is in many cases not transparent for users, who are often unaware of the processing carried out by apps. In addition, the lack of appropriate security measures, invalid consent and noncompliance with important data protection principles such as purpose limitation and data minimization endanger the privacy of data subjects. These data protection issues should be addressed by the various actors in the app ecosystem and not only by app developers. App stores can also play an important role in requiring that app developers and providers publish a privacy policy and comply with applicable data protection legislation.

95. *See supra* n. 93.
96. https://support.google.com/googleplay/android-developer/answer/113469?hl=en&visit_id=636733945304418846-2175441800&rd=1#privacy.
97. https://play.google.com/intl/en-US/about/privacy-security-deception/user-data/.
98. https://play.google.com/intl/en_us/about/families/.

# CHAPTER 6
# EU Medical Device Legislation and the Safety Implications for App Users

*Maria K. Sheppard*

*As a relatively new technology 'health' apps are included in different EU legal and regulatory mechanisms to ensure the safety of patients and consumers. Depending on whether an app is classified as a medical or as a fitness or well-being app the required safety standards vary: the latter are subject to EU consumer regulation whereas the former to the EU medical device regulation (MDR). Drawing a clear distinction between these two types of apps is, however, difficult apparent from the additional interpretative guidelines issued by the EU Commission as well as from Court of Justice of the European Union (CJEU) case law. As a consequence, app developers might flout the restrictions of medical device law with potential safety risks for users or they might err on the more restrictive side thus hampering innovative advances. However, there are examples of healthcare institutions of Member States adjusting their strategies and approving non-medical apps for inclusion in their healthcare baskets available to patients. In this, the consideration of patient safety and improved outcome trumps the restrictive interpretation of medical apps as medical device.*

## §6.01 INTRODUCTION

The origin of apps dates back to 2008 when the Apple iTunes Apps Store was launched, followed later the same year by Google Play. With the proliferation of smartphones, apps as software products of physical products or services have since evolved to play an increasingly important role in everyday life.[1] This is also the case in the area of health in its widest sense[2] with many smartphone users using inbuilt smartphone health-related apps or downloading lifestyle and well-being apps and medical apps.[3] Medical apps, in particular, have emerged as powerful tools for health-information transfer as they support medical practice, health-information delivery, patient screening, monitoring of physiological signs, direct care, and patient education by healthcare professionals and also encourage self-care by the patient. According to Research2guidance there were more than 300,000 medical as well as health and fitness apps available in 2017[4] including both patient/consumer-facing apps and those which target health professionals enabling quicker access to patient information and triaging, patient monitoring and medical information. A still higher figure of 350,000 health and fitness apps available from the major apps stores of Apple, Google and Windows/Microsoft has been cited more recently.[5]

As relatively new technology, medical and fitness and well-being apps are included in different EU legal and regulatory mechanisms to ensure user safety. Depending on whether an app is classified as a medical or mHealth app or as a fitness and well-being app the legally required safety standards vary. This is because apps outside the medical context are subject to ordinary consumer regulation[6] whereas apps defined as medical or mHealth apps are subject to the European medical device regulations, the Medical Device Directive (MDD)[7] and from 26 May 2020 the Medical Device Regulation (MDR).[8] However, drawing a clear distinction between these two types of apps can be fraught with difficulty apparent both from the additional interpretative guidelines issued by the EU Commission as well as from Court of Justice of the European Union (CJEU) case law.

As a consequence, app developers might flout the restrictions of medical device law with a potential risk for user safety or they might err on the more restrictive side when developing their software thus reducing innovative advances. It is argued that to reduce this conflict some healthcare institutions of EU Member States, whether based on taxation or on statutory health insurance, are adjusting their strategies regarding apps approved for inclusion in the healthcare baskets available to patients.

1. M Szczepański, *European App Economy: State of Play, Challenges and EU Policy* (2018) European Parliament, Brussels, at http://www.europarl.europa.eu/RegData/etudes/BRIE/2018/621894/EPRS_BRI(2018)621894_EN.pdf.
2. The Preamble to the Constitution of the World Health Organization as adopted by the International Health Conference, New York, 19–22 June 1946, provides this wider definition of health as 'a state of complete physical, mental and social well-being and not merely the absence of disease and infirmity'.
3. S Castle-Clarke and C Imison, *The Digital Patient: Transforming Primary Care?* (2016) Nuffield Trust, at https://www.nuffieldtrust.org.uk/files/2017-06/1497259872_nt-the-digital-patient-web-corrected-p46-.pdf.
4. https://research2guidance.com/325000-mobile-health-apps-available-in-2017/.
5. T Mulder, *Health Apps, Their Privacy Policies and the GDPR* 10(1) 2019 European Journal of Law and Technology 2.
6. Directive 2001/95/EC of the European Parliament and of the Council of 3 December 2001 on general product safety (General Product Safety Directive).
7. Medical Device Directive 2007/47/EC (MDD).
8. Regulation (EU) 2017/745 on MDR.

Thus, the consideration of improved patient outcome and patient safety trump the narrow legal interpretation of medical apps as medical devices. The chapter first discusses the applicable safety regulations for mHealth apps before discussing the approach to the safety requirements for non-medical apps by EU Member States using the healthcare systems of the UK and Germany as examples.

## §6.02 APPLICABLE SAFETY REGULATIONS

It is questionable whether there are definite regulations regarding the safety and performance of apps which purely support well-being and lifestyle. This is because the General Product Safety Directive (GPSD)[9] refers to general *product* safety rules *before* a product is placed on the market or brought into use for the first time. It establishes a general obligation upon manufacturers to ensure that their products, which do not fall within the scope of sectoral legislation or national regulations covering product safety, are manufactured in compliance with the GPSD safety requirements. Software is unlikely to be covered as a product by the GPSD as it refers to producers and distributors,[10] to product characteristics, including product composition, packaging and instructions for assembly.[11] According to the Commission Staff Working Document the GSPD applies to *manufactured* products so that lifestyle and well-being apps must be excluded.[12] Even if the GSPD applied to such apps the level of safety requirements would likely be inadequate. This is because a safe product is interpreted by the GPSD as one that 'under normal or reasonably foreseeable conditions of use does not present any risk or only the *minimum risks compatible with the product's use, considered to be acceptable*.'[13]

While the lack of enforceable safety regulations for wellness and fitness apps depends on the definition of what constitutes a *product*, medical device law has taken cognisance of the safety requirements of software from its inception. Thus even the original MDD (93/42/EEC) referred to software defining a medical device as being hardware with or without a software element.[14] The later MDD (2007/47/EC) classified certain stand-alone software as an active medical device (and therefore as a product), a definition which has not been materially changed by the new MDR:

> 'Medical device' means any instrument, apparatus, appliance, **software**, material or other article, whether used alone or in combination ... .[15]

9. *Supra* n. 6.
10. *Ibid.*, Article 13.
11. *Ibid.*, Article 2.
12. European Commission (2014) *Commission Staff Working Document on the existing EU legal framework applicable to lifestyle and wellbeing apps accessed,* at https://ec.europa.eu/digital-single-market/en/news/commission-staff-working-document-existing-eu-legal-framework-applicable-lifestyle-and, p. 3.
13. *Ibid.*
14. European Council, Council Directive 93/42/EEC Concerning Medical Devices, 14 June (1993).
15. *Supra* n. 7, Article 1(2)(a).

The classification as an active medical device makes the software subject to the specific safety requirements of medical device law. Generally, the safety requirements for medical devices encompass a need for clinical performance studies as evidence that their safety and performance is proportionate with the associated risk. They also include a risk stratification of the devices into four risk classes determining which conformity assessment procedures for market access have to be followed. The lowest risk category, Category I, rests on self-certification whereas the higher categories necessitate increasingly more thorough reviews by Notified Bodies to obtain a CE mark showing conformity with European Regulations.[16]

Smartphone apps are governed by the MDD and from May 2020 by the new medical device legislation, the MDR,[17] as long as they are identified as medical or mHealth apps rather than as fitness or wellness apps.[18] The MDR establishes a still more robust framework than the MDD in order to ensure better protection of patient safety with consequences for the risk classification of apps.[19] It also adds a new Rule 11 classification on the use of information obtained for decisions with diagnostic or therapeutic purposes[20] which is likely to lead to many apps being classified as higher risk thus requiring a more stringent market authorization.[21] Still, app developers for medical apps that are of low or Class I risk, even though much fewer in number in future, may continue to carry out the market authorization procedure themselves.

However, a major difficulty exists in that the distinction between a medical and non-medical app is not always easy to draw.[22] The medical device regulations under both the MDD and MDR refer to two essential elements in the definition of a mHealth app, namely the *objective* element of medical *function* that the software needs to fulfil and the *subjective* element of the manufacturer's *intent* to produce a software to serve a medical purpose.

Thus, a medical device is defined as software that is:

> intended by its manufacturer to be used specifically for diagnostic and/or therapeutic purposes and necessary for its proper application, intended by the manufacturer to be used for human beings for the purpose of:
>
> - diagnosis, prevention, monitoring, treatment or alleviation of disease,
> - diagnosis, monitoring, treatment, alleviation of or compensation for an injury or handicap,
> - investigation, replacement or modification of the anatomy or of a physiological process,

16. *Ibid.*, Annex VI.
17. *Supra* n. 8.
18. *Supra* n. 7, Recital 6 states that: 'it is necessary to clarify that software in its own right, when specifically intended by the manufacturer to be used for one or more of the medical purposes set out in the definition of a medical device, is a medical device. Stand alone software for general purposes when used in a healthcare setting is not a medical device.'
19. *Supra* n. 8, Article 51.
20. *Ibid.*, Annex VIII Ch. 3 rule 11.
21. A van Drongelen et al., *Apps under the Medical Devices Legislation* (National Institute for Public Health and the Environment, 2019), p. 18.
22. *Ibid.*, p. 16 with research showing that apps are often wrongly categorized by the app developers with mistakes erring in favour of categorization as lifestyle or fitness app.

- control of conception

  and which does not achieve its principal intended action in or on the human body by pharmaco-logical, immunological or metabolic means, but which may be assisted in its function by such means.[23]

Some help in clarifying the *objective* aspects of what constitutes stand-alone software as a medical device is provided by the European Commission with MEDDEV 2.1/6 (the MEDDEV guidance) according to its own terms a non-legally binding guidance.[24] The MEDDEV guidance which has been updated several times provides a decision diagram to assist objective qualification of software as medical device and must be read together with the Borderline Manual.[25] A special EU task force was set up to facilitate a consistent approach in the interpretation of the regulations to ensure consistency in their application.[26]

Subject to the above, the Member States determine the classification of an app as a medical device but the Commission can on request by a Member State decide after consultation with the Medical Device Coordination Group whether a specific device (or app) falls within the MDR.[27] Guidance documents for app developers in the form of decision trees have been published by the regulatory authorities in the Member States, e.g., by the UK MHRA.[28]

According to the MHRA guidance decision, support software is usually considered a medical device when it applies automated reasoning such as a simple calculation, an algorithm or a more complex series of calculations, e.g., dose calculations, or symptom tracking or clinicians' guides helping with decision-making. In contrast, decision support software would not usually be considered a medical device if it is for the monitoring of general fitness, general health and well-being or exists only to provide reference information to enable a healthcare professional to make clinical decisions. Contrarily, if the software performs calculations or interprets or interpolates data and the healthcare professional does not review the raw data, then this software may be considered a medical device.[29]

There is a grey area with many apps available on the market designed for a wide range of health-related issues or purposes, including diet and exercise, pregnancy, mental health and self-monitoring of conditions. Although they are not legally considered medical devices if they do not perform action on data and therefore unlikely to be subject to any safety regulations they target users' health and may provide advice that

23. *Supra* n. 7, Article 1(2)(a).
24. European Commission, *Guidelines on the qualification and classification of standalone software used in healthcare within the regulatory framework of medical devices*, MEDDEV 2.1/6, July 2016, p. 1.
25. Manual on borderline and classification in the community regulatory framework for medical devices version 1.18 (12-2017).
26. https://www.camd-europe.eu/mdr-ivdr-implementation/about-implementation-taskforce/; n. 29, p. 23.
27. *Supra* n. 8, Recital 8.
28. MHRA, *Guidance: Medical Device Stand-Alone Software Including Apps (Including IVDs)*. Version 1.04, September 2017, at https://www.gov.uk/government/publications/medical-devices-software-applications-apps.
29. *Ibid.*

is incomplete, misleading or wrong.[30] Interestingly, a Dutch study found that approximately 20% of all apps investigated by the authors should objectively have been classified as medical devices using the decision rules of the current MDD as they might be related to medical decisions or measurements.[31] Moreover, further vagueness may arise when during one of the regular updates apps that were not medical devices originally, become so because of the addition of new features. This reclassification would then necessitate the involvement of notified bodies to obtain market authorization for the updated app.[32]

Apart from the objective element, the definition of stand-alone software as medical device includes a subjective element. The MEDDEV guidance defines the term 'software as a medical device' as software *intended* to be used by the manufacturer for one or more medical purposes that perform these purposes without being part of the hardware of a medical device. The original MDD[33] already defined an intended purpose as 'the use for which the device is *intended* according to the data supplied by the manufacturer on the labelling, in the instructions and/or in promotional materials'. This subjective element of the definition has come under scrutiny by the CJEU in the case of *Brain Products GmbH v. BioSemi VOF and Others*.[34]

The CJEU determined that the fact that a device not explicitly conceived as medical can be put to a medical use is not sufficient to attribute a medical device status. The manufacturer's explicit intent remains a leading factor. The case concerned the product ActiveTwo, a biopotential measurement system manufactured by BioSemi, that recorded electrical signals from the brain, heart and muscles. According to BioSemi, the product was not designed for use in medical diagnosis or treatment but was used by researchers for used for human beings for the purposes of investigating a physiological process without being intended for a medical purpose. Brain Products marketed a similar product for clinical purposes which had a CE marking in accordance with the MDD. The company had alleged that, regardless of its intended use, the system manufactured by BioSemi must be regarded as a medical device for the purposes of the directive and, accordingly, must be certified as such. Nevertheless, it is interesting that the CJEU's finding contrasted with the opinion of the Advocate General that 'any product, which by its very nature, is clearly intended to be used solely for a purpose of a medical nature will have to be regarded as a medical device'.[35]

Importantly, the CJEU judgment does not account for the possibility of app developers acting arbitrarily. Developers may make the disclaimer that that despite appearances an app is not intended for medical use in order to avoid the application of the stricter regulations of the MDD or MDR. Since medical device law is harmonized EU legislation valid in all Member States excluding the applicability of medical device law

30. A Ferretti et al., *From Principles to Practice: Benchmarking Government Guidance on Health Apps* 1(2) (2019) The Lancet p. 55.
31. *Supra* n. 21, p. 23.
32. *Ibid.*, p. 26.
33. *Supra* n. 14.
34. CJEU, C-219/11, para. 34.
35. *Ibid.*, The Advocate General Mengozzi's opinion was delivered in this case on 15 May 2012, para, 63.

by using a disclaimer as to medical purpose will enable considerable cost savings. Specifically, there will then be no need for the prerequisite CE marking.

The role of CE marking was a consideration in the case of *Snitem and Philips France*.[36] The CJEU reiterated that software only constitutes a medical device for the purposes of the MDD if it satisfies the two cumulative conditions.[37] First, software is a medical device in its own right when specifically intended by the manufacturer to be used for one or more of the medical purposes set out in the definition of a medical device.[38] Second, the subjective element must be given, as set out in the *Brain Products* case,[39] namely it is also necessary that the intended purpose, defined by the manufacturer, is specifically medical. Once a specific software or part of software was defined as a medical device and had received the CE marking of conformity no further certification was necessary in any Member State. The product may be placed on the market and circulate freely in the European Union without having to undergo any additional procedure.[40]

The judgment extended the definition of software as a medical device from that given in the *Brain Products* case. Namely, software falls within the meaning of the provisions of the MDD, even if that software does not act directly in or on the human body. Specifically, software, of which at least one of the functions makes it possible to use patient-specific data for the purposes, *inter alia*, of detecting contraindications, drug interactions and excessive doses, is in respect of that function a medical device.[41]

Interestingly, the CJEU referred to their interpretation of the MDD as being based on MEDDEV 2.1/6,[42] thus in effect elevating these guidelines to legal principles. Accordingly the CJEU found that these guidelines indicate that software also constitutes a medical device where it is intended to create or modify medical information, in particular by means of calculation, quantification or comparison of the recorded data against certain references, in order to provide information about a particular patient.[43] In contrast, software that only performs an action limited to storage, archiving or simple search and functions as a digital library and makes it possible to find information from metadata, without modifying or interpreting it, should not be considered a medical device.[44]

What could add to further difficulty for app developers is the reference in *Snitem* to software modules which are medical devices and others that are not. In that regard and following the Commission's Guidelines, where software is composed of modules which satisfy the definition of 'medical device' and others which do not, only the former must bear the CE marking; the others are not subject to the provisions of the

36. C-329/16 EU.
37. *Ibid.*, para. 22.
38. *Ibid.*, para. 23.
39. *Ibid.*, para. 24.
40. *Ibid.*, para. 35.
41. *Ibid.*, para. 21.
42. European Commission, *Medical Devices Guidance Document: Qualification and Classification of Stand alone Software*, July 2016.
43. *Supra* n. 36, para. 33.
44. *Ibid.*

directive.[45] It is the responsibility of the manufacturer to identify the limits and interfaces of the different modules which, in the case of modules subject to Directive 93/42, must be clearly identified by the manufacturer and based on the use which will be made of the product. The risk of non-compliance, either knowingly or inadvertently, by app developers is undoubtedly given.

## §6.03 A CHANGE IN APPROACH TO THE SAFETY REQUIREMENTS FOR NON-MEDICAL APPS

As has been explained, from a regulatory standpoint drawing a clear distinction between an app with a medical purpose and a general health and well-being apps can be difficult but will have potential safety implications for the user. App developers may not necessarily be aware of the distinction between mHealth Apps and non-medical apps and the different regulations which apply. Missing or unnecessary CE marking of apps were evidence of this problem in the Dutch study.[46]

With this in mind, it should not be surprising that the access to apps as part of the healthcare basket has been handled by some Member States in a more patient friendly and more safety conscious manner. The healthcare systems of the UK and Germany serve as examples with the former being taxation based with a national health service (NHS) whereas the latter is based on social health insurance offered by an array of stakeholders. The NHS system has implemented a consistent regulatory approach in this field since 2015 with the aim of harnessing digital technology that improves health and well-being and empowers the person while at the same time reassuring users that the app is safe, secure and effective.[47] After initial teething problems the NHS has developed an apps library with available apps including those that would not be classified as medical devices but which are nevertheless subject to the NHS assessment process. Apps in this library have the benefit of reaching a larger number of people and patient uptake also increased since the NHS Apps Library is signposted from relevant health and well-being pages across the NHS website.[48]

In contrast, Germany with its multitude of insurance funds has recently passed a draft law dealing with apps, namely the Digital Care Act[49] which is intended to enter into effect in early 2020. This law would make apps, mainly mHealth apps in the risk Classes I or IIa, available on prescription by physicians thus making them part of standard medical care. The German regulatory authority, BfArM,[50] is to be responsible for quality control of this software with a new directory for digital health apps being established. It seems likely that some of these apps will include apps for patient self-monitoring, supporting treatment or with diary functions so that it is dubious

45. *Ibid.*, para. 37, referring to Title 4 entitled 'Modules'.
46. *Supra* n. 21, p. 26.
47. NHS Apps Library, at https://digital.nhs.uk/services/nhs-apps-library.
48. NHS Digital, *Get Your Health App Assessed,* at https://digital.nhs.uk/services/nhs-apps-library/guidance-for-health-app-developers-commissioners-and-assessors/get-your-health-app-assessed.
49. Digitale Versorgungsgesetz, first reading on 27 September 2019.
50. Bundesinstitut für Arzneimittel und Medizinprodukte (BfArM).

whether all such apps fall under the MDR. It therefore remains to be seen whether the statutory health insurance funds will reimburse the cost of apps which improve patient care but are outside the definition of the EU medical device legislation whether or not they have the CE marking. Criticism of the draft law has been raised by both the sickness insurance funds and the German medical association regarding the potential problems with app safety and effectiveness.[51]

Maybe because of the grey interpretative zone around non-medical apps there appears to be a trend in both healthcare systems to go beyond what is demanded by the law. Both are concerned about the safety of all health apps used in the medical context even those which are not classified as medical devices. Both also emphasize the need for the app to be of benefit to patients and improve patient outcomes. To this end the UK NHS, together with the National Institute for Health and Care Excellence (NICE), has developed an evidence standards framework which, *inter alia*, stratifies technologies into evidence tiers based on the potential risk to users and is independent of any need for CE marking under the MDR.[52]

The evidence level needed for each tier is proportionate to the potential risk to users so that even simple self-monitoring apps are graded as more than low risk.[53] In its statement concerning the draft German Digital Care Act the German Institute for Quality and Economics in Healthcare, IQWiG, suggested that non-medical apps should be included in the assessment process and that the BfArM ought to follow the NICE evidence standards framework because of its greater competence and practical experience in patient care.[54] Although less evidence was needed for apps which are not medical devices the IQWiG argued that it was still necessary to assess them: low risk according to the MDR classification could still have considerable medical and financial consequences.[55] Furthermore, reimbursement of prescribed apps should not depend on the definition of apps as medical device. It remains to be seen whether this advice will be heeded.

## §6.04 CONCLUSION

With the complexity of the legal distinction between mHealth apps and wellness and fitness apps a potential negative effect on the safety of patients and consumers is

51. Aerzteblatt, *Digitale-Versorgung-Gesetz: Experten sehen noch Nachbesserungsbedarf* (October 2019) at https://www.aerzteblatt.de/nachrichten/106722/Digitale-Versorgung-Gesetz-Experten-sehen-noch-Nachbesserungsbedarf.
52. NICE, Evidence standards framework for digital health technologies (2019) at https://www.nice.org.uk/Media/Default/About/what-we-do/our-programmes/evidence-standards-framework/digital-evidence-standards-framework.pdf, pp. 7-10.
53. *Ibid.*
54. Institut für Qualität und Wirtschaftlichkeit im Gesundheitswesen (IQWiG), *Stellungnahme des IQWiG zum Referentenentwurf des Bundesministeriums für Gesundheit (BMG) eines Gesetzes für eine bessere Versorgung durch Digitalisierung und Innovation*, at https://www.iqwig.de/de/projekte-ergebnisse/publikationen/iqwig-stellungnahmen/stellungnahme-des-iqwig-zum-referentenentwurf-des-bundesministeriums-fuer-gesundheit-bmg-eines-gesetzes-fuer-eine-bessere-versorgung-durch-digitalisierung-und-innovation-digitale-versorgung-gesetz-dvg.12041.html.
55. *Ibid.*

foreseeable. Healthcare systems in some Member States are attempting to overcome this interpretational problem by including apps not classified as medical devices in their assessment process making them available to patients free of charge or on a reimbursement basis. These apps will need to reach a standard of effectiveness demonstrating a positive health benefit for the patient, an effect which is the objective of many well-being apps. At the same time, a risk stratification of all apps in the health field will increase the safety of the end users without stifling innovative advances in this field. It is debatable whether EU legislation regarding apps is adequate in terms of patient safety or more concerned with the furtherance of the internal market. However, while the MDD and the MDR together with MEDDEV and the case law of the CJEU define what constitutes an app as a medical device some Member States already appear to go beyond the requirements of the law to ensure patient safety.

CHAPTER 7

# Fitness or Wellness Apps

*Efmorfia (Efi) Tziva*

*Mobile Fitness or Wellness Applications (Apps) have made their appearance some years ago, and since then they have created a real huge business worldwide. These apps, together with health apps and wearable devices, offer a parallel path for the consumers in seeking their health and well-being, with the use of personalized and low-cost means, alongside the typical medical care providers and other relative commercial channels. This new trend has many aspects, such as social, ethical and legal ones. According to some studies, fitness apps, especially these which have been developed as mobile games, have made physical activities fun and have promoted a healthy lifestyle for everyone who owns a smartphone but probably has not the means or the time to visit public or private services providers offering similar services. Besides the obvious advantages of "using" fitness apps, such as especially the improvement of a persons' health, behavioral changes, social interactions, etc., there are many legal issues that remain open, mainly concerning consumer protection and data protection. This chapter discusses the main legal issues arising from Mobile Fitness or Wellness Apps' design and use and the relevant EU legislative endeavors in this domain.*

## §7.01 INTRODUCTION

One distinct category of apps, amongst the millions of mobile applications available on the market,[1] downloaded daily by users worldwide on Android (Google Play)[2] or on

1. *See* N.P. Terry & L.F. Wiley, "Liability for Mobile Health and Wearable Technologies," (2016) 25 Annals Health L. 62, p. 2 (available on WESTLAW).
2. Google, Google Play, https://play.google.com/store/apps/category/HEALTH_AND_FITNESS?hl=en (accessed December 2, 2019).

iOS (App Store)[3] or using other multiple platforms, are the so-called Fitness Apps. There is a wide range of such apps including those improving fitness activities, nutrition and diets, solutions for sleep disturbances, relaxation, general healthcare information and even medicines.[4] Since fitness prescribes the state of being physically fit and healthy, through exercise, diet and sleep habits, being so closely related to health, most of the fitness or wellness apps are also considered as mobile health applications. In spite of the similarities, though, it is important to notice the differences, existing in the fitness applications, in particular regarding their content and the relationship with the health sector. It is important first to identify the key features of the respective apps in order to identify their legal nature and adopt the appropriate legal approach.

Most of the popular fitness apps focus on fitness and self-monitoring and assist healthcare providers in measuring health and fitness parameters.[5] However, their purpose is not the provision of health services. Their role, in most of the cases, seems to be mainly advice-giving or a role auxiliary to dealing with patients and consumers, in general, regarding their health (e.g., obesity, sleep disorders, depression, etc.) and lifestyle problems (e.g., lack of activity, even loneliness). These apps are either free or "sold" at a price, usually lower, comparing to other services, offered online and offline.

## §7.02 LEGAL DEFINITIONS

The so-called fitness or wellness apps, as it was mentioned above, are apps that are addressed to users, giving them the opportunity to solve, with their help, problems regarding their status of health and their lifestyle, in general. The content of these apps is, for example, diet and exercise programs, behavioral and mental health coaches, sleep and relaxation aids, even advices on various diseases and chronic conditions. Some of these apps are simply informational but others offer more to users, by being for example interactive.[6] Users participate in a program (diet or gymnastic), and according to some studies this kind of apps have the capacity to facilitate behavioral change, especially in the field of nutrition and physical activity.[7] Besides that, apps whose intervention concludes goal-setting, self-monitoring and individual-tailored feedback provide the opportunity to the people involved to socialize which is of a great importance in our everyday life.

The big differences in the content and in the conditions of use of fitness apps make a coherent legal approach of the issue quite difficult, but in most cases, the main characteristics are basically the same. They use smartphone technology, including the Global Positioning System, accelerometer, microphone and other tools in order to

3. *See* category Health and Fitness at https://apps.apple.com/us/genre/ios-health-fitness/id6013 (accessed December 2, 2019).
4. *See* J.P. Higgins, "Smartphone Applications for Patients' Health and Fitness," 29 The American Journal of Medicine p. 11 (p. 13) (2016).
5. *Ibid.*, at 11.
6. https://privacyrights.org/consumer-guides/mobile-health-and-fitness-apps-what-are-privacy-risks.
7. *See* J.P. Higgins, *supra*, p. 12.

measure some physical activities and give the necessary instructions on adopting a healthy lifestyle. Many of these apps involve virtual coaches that talk and inspire the users and others to use the so-called "gamification," that is, they adopt methods and games in order to make sport activities fun[8] and encourage the motivator for wellness habits.[9]

Summarizing these main characteristics of fitness or wellness apps we could attempt to give a legal definition, in accordance with Article 2(2) of the Directive 2019/770 on Digital Content (DCD): these applications constitute digital services, such as those belonging to both or to one of the categories: (a) services that allow the consumer to create, process, store or access data in digital form or (b) services that allow the sharing of or any other interaction with data in digital form uploaded or created by the consumer or other users of that service.

## §7.03 THE MAIN LEGAL ASPECTS OF FITNESS APPLICATIONS

The immense "presence" and use of fitness apps have provoked serious concerns, while users/consumers use their smartphones to achieve the improvement of their health and fitness. These apps use the data given by the users or collected from the smartphones inbuilt tools, then analyze them and devise personalized programs, based on everyone's goals, they provide feedback and help also the socialization between the persons using the same apps.

Their multifaceted nature has as result the emergence of legal issues related to consumer protection, unfair commercial practices, right of cancellation of contracts, and problems concerning e-payments and the entire system of digital contracts.

Despite the fact that in the last decades a lot of Directives and Regulations were issued at the EU level and they have been transposed in national law of EU Member States, there is always the fear that the consumers do not share, equally with the traders and other sellers, the benefits of the digital economy. Notwithstanding the legal obligations of the traders and other suppliers for providing effective and vast information before, during and after the duration of the contractual relationship, still there is a gap of knowledge, even for the so-called average consumer.

This notion appears in the text of Directives, such as the Directive 2005/29/EC on unfair commercial practices, according to which a commercial practice is unfair if it is included in its "black list" or if it is generally aggressive or misleading or if it fails to

8. *See* some examples in Yu Chen & Pearl Pu, Healthy Together: Exploring Social Incentives for Mobile Fitness Applications, available at: https://www.researchgate.net/publication/2665700, such as UbiFitGarden, that visualizes users' daily steps by the growing status of plants(!). The authors developed a mobile application, called Healthy Together, that allows two person groups (namely dyads) to participate in daily physical exercises as a game, focus on the social interaction, finding out that the cooperation and sometimes the competition play a great role to the success of relative applications, games, especially when users play games together.
9. *See* T. Campbell, B. Ngo & J. Fogarty, Game Design Principles in Everyday Fitness Applications, CSCW '08, November 8-12, 2008, pp. 249-252, who are the creators of the Kukini, which provides one fitness game every day in which players explore the world by running between towns across a variety of terrain. The team insists that thanks to this game the players have created social contacts and interacted with other players cooperatively and competitively.

meet the standard of "professional diligence," given that it materially impairs an average consumer's ability to make an informed decision. According to CJEU case law, the average consumer is considered to be reasonably well informed, reasonably observant and circumspect.[10] The CJEU developed a concept of the consumer by emphasizing his own responsibilities in the market, although recently there are some objections about the energetic role of the consumer as an "economic factor," according to the so-called behavioral studies.

Especially in the field of commercial practices, it is remarkable that many of Fitness Apps' practices could be considered misleading or aggressive according to Articles 6–8 of the Directive 2005/29/EC, since they contain information which is deceiving or which is likely to deceive the average consumer and cause him to make a transactional decision that he would not have taken otherwise, or at least is contrary to professional diligence and materially distorts the economic behavior of the average consumer (Article 5 of the Directive) as could be seen in two examples listed below:

> If you've wanted to eat better, get fitter, feel less stressed, or take any other steps toward living a healthier life, odds are you've looked to brands or personalities to help guide you on your journey. And there's a very strong chance those people are on our annual list of the most influential people in health and fitness.

or:

> In addition to guided meditations, visual aids, and stress-reducing games, this app gives you a five-minute daily routine to reduce stress and increase happiness. Created by scientists, cognitive behavioral therapists, and breathing specialists, these quick exercises help ease anxiety and refresh your mind.
>
> The best feature: A space to write your crappier thoughts and burn them! Don't worry, your phone won't go up in smoke, but watching those limiting beliefs burn in the digital flames is oddly satisfying.

## §7.04 CONSUMER PROTECTION

The necessity for consumer protection in the digital economy has led to the creation of new concepts and has given rise to novel questions requiring an immediate response. Several EU Directives,[11] which are applicable also in the environment of the various and different sectors of the digital economy, including mobile apps, guarantee a sufficient status of protection but recently some authors—as well as the European Commission—have argued that the problem in the legislation on consumer protection "is not the design of the rules, but their enforcement." So, the emphasis should be placed in finding out in which way could the enforcement be more effective and

10. C-210/96 of July 1998, *Gut Springenheide GmbH and Rudolf Tusky* κατά *Oberkreisdirektor des Kreises Steinfurt—Amt für Lebensmittelüberwachung*, para. 31.
11. *See, e.g.*, Directive 93/13 of 5 April 1993 on unfair terms in consumer contracts, OJ L 95/29; Directive 2005/29 of the European Parliament and of the Council of 11 May 2005 concerning unfair business-to consumer commercial practices in the internal market, OJ L 149/22; Directive 2011/83 of the European Parliament and of the Council of 25 October 2011 on consumer rights, OJ L 304/64.

probably a third avenue would be preferable that is based on technology such as moving the rules from the legislative code to the computer code, using the right technologies in order these rules to be incorporated in the personalized communication between the traders and the users, even in the form of algorithms.[12]

Another solution for an effective consumer protection should be the "privatization" of the enforcement of the applicable legislation by introducing informative campaigns in the EU and by the creation of an EU database with the relevant legal provisions. Also, the harmonization of the conditions to receive damages in case of consumer rights infringements seems necessary, in the same way as it was already done in 2014 for competition law infringements by the Directive 2014/104 on certain rules governing actions for damages under national law for infringements of the competition law provisions.[13]

## §7.05 THE DIRECTIVE 2019/770 ON CERTAIN ASPECTS CONCERNING CONTRACTS FOR THE SUPPLY OF DIGITAL CONTENT AND DIGITAL SERVICES

Recently, on May 2019, the Directive 2019/770 of the European Parliament and of the Council on certain aspects concerning contracts for the supply of digital content and digital services was released, which should be implemented by the Member States by July 1, 2021 (Article 24).

In comparison with other Directives this seems to be closer to the main issues concerning the use of apps, in general, fitness apps included.

The aim of this legislative effort, that is prescribed in the preamble of the Directive, Recital 3, is of a great importance. Accordingly, it is provided that:

> certain aspects concerning contracts for the supply of digital content or digital services should be harmonized, taking as a base a high level of consumer protection, in order to achieve a genuine digital single market, increase legal certainty and reduce transaction costs, in particular for small and medium-sized enterprises.

As normally happens to all the sectors of the single market of goods and services, the legislator tries to establish a balance between the interests of the enterprises and the free movement of goods, on the one hand, and the users, especially those who act at the same time as consumers,[14] on the other, focusing on some of the aspects, such as it is impossible to reach an holistic approach to all the matters of the "new" contracts.

---

12. *See* Al. de Streel, *A European Agenda for Smart Consumer Protection Rules for Digital Services*, Intereconomics 2017 (pdf), pp. 226–229.
13. *Ibid.*, at p. 229.
14. Consumer, according to the European and Greek legislation (L. 2251/1994, Article 1α), is any natural person who in relation to contracts is acting for purposes which are outside the person's trade, business, craft or profession, *see more* N. Reich & H.-W. Micklitz (eds.), *Europäisches Verbraucherrecht*, 1997; E. Perakis & Ch. Livada, in *Consumer Law* (El. Alexandridou ed., 2018), Article 1a. Despite the relative legislation and the case law of the Court of Justice of the European Union in some cases it is still discussable the notion of the consumer, *see more*, in detail, J.S.

The four main pillars of the Directive, according to Article 1, are: (1) the conformity of digital content or a digital service with the contract, (2) the remedies in the event of a lack of such conformity or a failure to supply, (3) the modalities for the exercise of those remedies and (4) the modification of the digital content or digital service. The European legislator tries, by means of eighty-seven recitals in the preamble to the Directive, to summarize the main problems of the digital services and explain the content of the twenty-six articles.

The consumers in the European Union are not, in general, confident when they buy products or services online because they feel the uncertainty about their contractual rights or they have doubts about the quality of the digital content or service and about the right way to ask for compensation in a case of financial and non-financial detriment.

Besides the protection of consumers and businesses, especially the SMEs who are involved in the digital economy, it should be stressed out that the national law of the EU Members States is not harmonized as regards the rules on the formation, validity, nullity or effects or even the legality of the digital content or the digital service. So, the specific directive could not have the character of a full harmonization in all the elements, but only for some key rules that have not been regulated until now at Union or at national level (Recital 9 of the Preamble).

These key rules refer to some specific obligations of the traders, such as the supply[15] of the digital content or digital service without delay after the conclusion of the contract, unless something different has been agreed (Article 5), specific subjective and objective requirements for conformity (e.g., "be of the description quantity and quality and possess the functionality, compatibility, interoperability and other features, as required by the contract,", "be fit for any particular purpose for the consumer requires it ...,", "be fit for the purposes for which digital content or digital services of the same type would normally be used ..." etc.) (Articles 7, 8), the relative liability of the trader,[16] the burden of proof for the trader that the digital content or digital service was in conformity at the time of supply or, in the event of continuous supply, during the duration of the contract (Article 12).

Other important issues of the Directive 2019/770 are the right of the consumer to terminate the contract and the relative obligations of the trader as well as of the consumer (Articles 15–18), the modification of the digital content or digital service, the

---

Hedegaard, *The Notion of Consumer under EU Legislation and EU Case Law: Between the Poles of Legal Certainty and Flexibility* (2016).

15. Supply especially for the applications means accessing or downloading the digital content mainly in virtual vision.
16. The trader, according to the Article 2(5) of the Directive, is any natural or legal person, irrespective of whether privately or publicly owed, that is acting, including through any other person acting in that natural or legal person's name or on that person's behalf, for purpose relating to that person's trade, business, craft or profession, in relation to contracts covered by the Directive. It is also declared by the Directive that trader could be a platform provider as far as the provisions should apply to any contract whereby the trader supplies or undertakes to supply digital content or digital service and much more gives the opportunity to the Member States to extend the application to platform providers, even these who do not fulfill the requirements for being considered traders under the Directive (Recital 18 of the Preamble).

coexistence and complementation of the Directive with other Directives and especially with the Directive 2019/771, which laid down new rules on the sale of goods. This means that the Directive 2019/770 should apply when the digital content is supplied in a tangible medium, such as DVD, or USB sticks, but instead of the trader's obligation to supply, should apply the provisions of the Directive 2011/83/EU, on obligations related to the delivery of goods and remedies in the event of the failure to deliver. This has as result that the right of withdrawal and the nature of the contract under which these goods are supplied should also continue to apply to such tangible media including the digital content (Recital 20 of the Preamble).

Directive 2019/771 applies to contracts for the sale of goods, including also goods with digital elements, which means goods that incorporate or are interconnected with digital content or digital service, in such a way, that the absence of the digital content or digital service would prevent the goods from performing their functions and for this reason are provided with the goods under one unique sales contract. In the preamble of the Directive the following examples are mentioned:[17]

> If, for example, a smart TV were advertised as including a particular video application, that video application would be considered to be part of the sales contract. This should apply regardless of whether the digital content or digital service is pre-installed in the good itself or has to be downloaded subsequently on another device and is only inter-connected to the good.

For example, a smartphone could come with a standardized pre-installed application provided under the sales contract, such as an alarm application or a camera application. Another possible example is that of a smart watch. In such a case, the watch itself would be considered to be the good with digital elements, which can perform its functions only with an application that is provided under the sales contract but has to be downloaded by the consumer onto a smartphone; the application would then be the interconnected digital element. This should also apply if the incorporated or interconnected digital content or digital service is not supplied by the seller itself but is supplied, under the sales contract, by a third party. In order to avoid uncertainty for both traders and consumers, in the event of doubt as to whether the supply of the digital content or the digital service forms part of the sales contract, Directive (EU) 2019/771 should apply.

In contrast, if the absence of the digital content or digital service does not prevent the specific good to perform its function, or the consumer concludes a contract for the digital content of digital service which does not form a part of a sales contract concerning goods, this contract should be considered to be separate and fall within the scope of the Directive 2019/770 on digital content and digital service. As it is mentioned in the preamble of the Directive, "... if the consumer downloads a game application from an app store onto a smart phone, the contract for the supply of the game application is separate from the contract for the sale of the smart phone itself."[18]

17. Recital 21.
18. Recital 22.

The Directive 2019/770 takes also in account that there are so many different categories of digital content, digital services and their applications. For this reason, the Directive provides an indicative catalog of the contents and services, which are covered by the specific rules, such as computer programs, applications, video files, audio files, digital games, etc. It is also mentioned that the provisions of the Directive apply independently of the medium used for the transmission of, or for giving access to the digital content or digital service, e.g., transmission on a tangible medium, downloading by the consumers on their devices etc.

Another focal point of the Directive 2019/770 has to do with the protection of personal data. According to the Recital 37 of the Preamble, the Directive is without prejudice to the Regulation 2016/679 and the Directive 2002/58/EC, therefore in case of conflict between Directive 2019/770 and European law on the protection of personal data the latter should prevail.

Last, but not least, it should be mentioned that, according to the Recital 29 of the Preamble, the Directive 2019/770 should not apply to healthcare as defined in Directive 2011/24/EU on the application of patients' rights in cross-border healthcare and also to the sector of the medical devices as described in the relevant Directives 93/42/EC, 98/79/EC and recently in the Regulations 2017/745 (medical devices) and 2017/746 (*in vitro* diagnostic medical devices),[19] that replaced the relevant Directives. From the above-mentioned sectors are excluded health apps that can be obtained by the consumer without being prescribed or provided by a health professional, which means that all these apps are governed by the Directive 2019/770, and specifically, fitness apps, whose connection with health seems to be indirect.

The most characteristic element which distinguishes fitness apps from other apps is that they are designed by their manufacturer to be used for the improvement of the physical and mental status of users and not for medical purposes and also that access to these apps depends on free human will and not on the prescription by a health professional. Besides that, their use is not similar to the medical devices, as this function is strictly described by the relevant legislation. For example, fitness apps have not been designed by their manufacturers to be used for diagnosis, prevention, monitoring, prediction, prognosis, treatment or alleviation of disease,[20] so they do not need certification which is required for medical devices and in general they do not have to meet all the necessary high standards for these products.[21]

## §7.06 CONCLUSIONS: SUGGESTIONS

It is obvious that the widespread use of the so-called fitness apps and their big variety pose certain legal problems. Besides that, the different entities involved in the design

19. Implementation date of both of the Regulations is May 26, 2020.
20. *See* Article 1(2)(a) of Directive 93/42 and now the Article 2(1) of the Regulation 2017/745.
21. According to the Judgment of the Court of Justice of EU of Nov. 22, 2012, C-219/11, *Brain Products GmbH v. BioSemi VOF et al.*, Article 1(2)(a) of Directive 93/42 must be interpreted as meaning that the concept of 'medical device' covers an object conceived by its manufacturer to be used for human beings for the purpose of the investigation of a physiological process only if it is intended for a medical purpose.

and the commercialization of these apps, the personal differences and objectives of users and all the other factors of the phenomenon pointed out in this chapter make the legislative task in this area really difficult. Especially the need for transparency, consumer information, and protection of consumer data[22] are factors to be considered in order to have in place a proper legal framework.

The European legislator seems to have in mind the multifaceted and various issues emerging through the use of apps and other wearable devices in the health and life style sector and has taken the first steps in the direction of a safe and effective use of them for the benefit of consumers, as well as competitors.

Serious concerns arise from the collection and processing of consumer-generated health and sensitive data, through mobile apps,[23] especially because of the transmission of personal data among apps and different traders, insurance companies, health professionals, etc.[24] The information provided to consumers do not meet in many occasions the legal requirements and safeguarding of their rights is not guaranteed. There are various legal approaches to these issues, but these in fact remain inapplicable in the market for apps. There is need for an effective collaboration of the policymakers, not only in European Union but worldwide, to create the necessary conditions for ensuring consumer privacy, freedom of competition and for the free and at the same time safe movement of mobile app services.

22. "...[T]he ways that consumer-generated, and sometimes sensitive personal information, is shared and passed on within the mobile ecosystem is far from transparent ... ." is mentioned by T. Dehling, J.-T. Prieto and G. Weber, "Tracing the Potential Flow of Consumer Data: A Network Analysis of Prominent Health and Fitness Apps," (2017) 19(6) Gunther Eysenbach, Journal of Medical Internet Research e233.
23. Once the user has downloaded the app, he is obliged to give the basic data, such as gender, date of birth, weight, height in order to form the adequate program for him/her or to give the necessary instructions.
24. Most of the health and fitness apps allow also the users to share their accomplishments on social media (Facebook, Twitter, etc.), *see* J. Higgins, *supra* p. 13.

CHAPTER 8

# Cybercrime in the Smartphone and Apps' Environment

*Philippe Jougleux*

*This chapter discusses smartphone and app related cybercrime. It distinguishes between attacks against smartphone and attacks committed via smartphone. In the first part of the chapter, it is demonstrated that, while Directive 2013/40 on cyber-attacks and Directive 2019/713 on cyber-fraud are well-designed repressive tools that are appropriate for fighting against cyber-attacks targeting smartphones, they do little to hinder the exponential growth of smartphones' vulnerabilities. In the second part of the chapter, the analysis focusses on the broadcasting function of the smartphone through the scope of EU criminal media law and also refers to the recent phenomenon of digital pickpocket. In the last part, it is concluded that effective protection of the users of smartphones cannot be solemnly based on repression and coordination of police services. Therefore, the author proposes that a better accountability of intermediaries based on the example of the cybersecurity's strategy (NIS Directive) and the development of a system of cybersecurity certification (based on Regulation 2019/881) are mandatory in order to carry an effective policy of mobile devices' cybersecurity.*

## §8.01 INTRODUCTION

Apple has recently announced that it would give a one-million-dollar reward for a single attack technique that a researcher discovers and shares discretely with the company.[1] At the same time, the Google's project zero (a team of security's researchers dedicated to ferreting out bugs, exploits, and vulnerabilities) discovered a really frightening vulnerability in iPhone's software: when surfing on specific websites, the user maybe the victim of hacking, since the integrity of the smartphone's data could be comprised. A virus is installed in the RAM memory of the phone and data about messages, password and contacts are collected and sent to a remote server.[2] The victims of this hack could have been millions, and it seems that, actually, it enabled a kind of surveillance in China.

Generally, stories about cybersecurity issues related to mobile devices can often make newspapers' headlines. The two examples cited above are related to Apple devices, but that does not mean that Android devices are more secure. For instance, it has recently been found that one very popular app on the official Google platform (PlayStore) with millions of positive reviews called "CamScanner" had a trojan malware hidden in its code.[3] The CamScanner app was actually a legitimate app when it was launched, using ads for monetization, and the virus was injected during an update.

These various scandals shed light upon an actual crisis in the field of cybersecurity. People have never been so dependent on their smartphones, and these have never been so sophisticated and, therefore, vulnerable. The importance of smartphones in the society, as well as the function which they perform, grows exponentially. The smartphone is a communication tool that accumulates various functions: calling, messaging, sending of emails, using social media, video calling and communicating using dating services. As an entertainment device, the smartphone is connected to applications and gaming platforms; it also offers audiovisual services, by streaming or through download. As an instrument of economic life, a two-step verification procedure is enforced regarding most online commercial operations, in accordance with the PSD2 Directive.[4] Usually the second verification stage involves a smartphone, through SMS or automatic call. In addition, smartphones have been upgraded to autonomous electronic payment devices. For billions of people a smartphone is also a watch, an alarm-clock, a health monitor, a camera, a driving assistant, a compass, a remote control, an e-book reader, a document editor, a translator, a converter, a storage device, etc.

Criminal law does not grasp this new reality, i.e., the omnipresence of mobile devices. European criminal law makes no reference to smartphones. This small device that has such importance in our daily life seems irrelevant from a legal point of view. This is the result of a very clever technology-neutral approach in the domain of

1. Zack Whittaker, "Apple Expands Its Bug Bounty, Increases Maximum Pay Out to $1M," *Techcrunch*, August 8, 2019.
2. Ian Beer, "A Very Deep Dive into iOS Exploit Chains Found in the Wild," googleprojectzero.blogspot.com, August 29, 2019.
3. Jordan Valinsky, "Google Pulls a Popular App after It Was Found Spreading Malware," *CNN Business*, August 30, 2019.
4. Directive 2015/2366/EU of the European Parliament and of the Council of 25 November 2015 on payment services in the internal market, amending Directives 2002/65/EC, 2009/110/EC and 2013/36/EU and Regulation (EU) No. 1093/2010, and repealing Directive 2007/64/EC.

cybercrime, as further analyzed below. However, smartphones have become the preferred entry point for all digital activities and cumulate the two identities of computer tool and media service. No other object has ever been so closely associated with the individual, his body, but also his personality, in history of humanity. Therefore, the smartphone functions as a digital extension of the individual himself and is, therefore, the target of multiple attacks (*see* §8.02). In parallel, and like every other technology, it has also been weaponized and has become a tool of realization of criminal activities (*see* §8.03). These both aspects of the cybersecurity's framework of mobile devices are analyzed through the perspective of European law, and it has to be noticed that the European legislator has been active and even proactive in these fields, with attempts of harmonization of substantive criminal law and creation of multiple cooperation tools. It is at the same time clear that the EU legislator's strategy in the field of cybersecurity does not apprehend the mobile devices' peculiar situation (*see* §8.04).

## §8.02 THE ATTACKS AGAINST THE SMARTPHONES

The last three decades have seen the emergence of a new discipline of criminal law related to cyber activities. This field was originally referred to as "cybercrime," but that expression was too imprecise and, as a result, it was subsequently rejected. In its place, a classification that distinguishes between cyber-assisted, cyber-enabled, and cyber-dependent crimes is proposed[5] and the specific field of cyber-attacks has to be seen as synonym of this category of cyber-dependent crimes.[6] In other words, if by "cyber-crime" is understood the sum of criminal behaviors through digital means, the distinction has to be made between crimes committed in the analogic world that are transferred to the digital world and crimes that appeared exclusively in the digital world and threaten the mobile device's integrity. The term "cyber-attacks" refers exclusively to the second situation.

EU criminal substantive law on this aspect has constantly developed (§8.02[A]) and can apply to mobile devices (§8.02[B]). However, new forms of cyber-attacks constantly emerge, that cannot be tackled by criminal law (§8.02[C]).

### [A] Overview of the Cyber-Attacks' Legislation: The Cyber-Attacks Classification in EU

Before analyzing the EU legislation related to cyber-attacks against smartphones, it should be stressed out that the European legislator inherited most of the basic notions and key mechanisms of the legal framework from a previous and much larger attempt

5. David S Wall, *Cybercrime: The Transformation of Crime in the Information Age* (Polity, 2007); David S Wall, "Crime, Security and Information Communication Technologies: The Changing Cybersecurity Threat Landscape and Implications for Regulation and Policing," in: R. Brownsword, E. Scotford & K. Yeung (eds.), *The Oxford Handbook of the Law and Regulation of Technology* (Oxford University Press, 2017), pp. 1075–1096.
6. *See* Philippe Jougleux, "Criminalization of Attacks Against Information Systems," in: Ioannis Iglezakis (ed.), *The Legal Regulation of Cyber Attacks* (Wolters Kluwer, 2016).

of harmonization at the international level: the Convention of Europe's international convention on cybercrime,[7] also called Convention of Budapest. This international mechanism can be seen as an ambitious project to create a common legal framework on cybercrime. The Cybercrime Convention establishes a general framework, focusing mainly on the definition of substantial offenses, but also on regulating the correlated aspects of procedure and international cooperation. It adopts a wide approach on the notion of cybercrime, which is characteristic of a first period of cybercrime law. Subsequently, it addresses the offenses against the confidentiality, integrity and availability of computer data and systems (which will become later the cyber-attacks' field, in the EU legislation), the "computer related" offenses (fraud and forgery in the online environment) and content related offenses, such as child pornography or copyright law infringement. Notably, the Convention missed the opportunity to include in this over reaching approach other cybercriminal behaviors such as identity theft, child grooming or massive spam.[8]

The Convention was programmed to enter into force in 2004, but the European Union did not wait long before using its prerogative to build on the acquis of this international mechanism and propose a legal framework. In particular, Council Framework Decision 2005/222/JHA of 24 February 2005 on attacks against information systems was adopted in 2005.[9] It followed a Communication on cybercrime in 2007[10] that discussed the various developments in this sector, which led to the adoption in 2013 of Directive 2013/40 on cyber-attacks.[11]

It would be vain to search in the Budapest Convention—but also in the 2013/40 Directive—for a reference to smartphones. The strength of this legal framework, addressing an ever-changing digital landscape of changes and evolution, resides in the strategy of adopting a technology-neutral approach. Therefore, the only subject matter of the legislation is the "information system." Information system is defined by Article 2(b) of the Directive as "*a device or group of inter-connected or related devices, one or more of which, pursuant to a programme, automatically processes computer data, as well as computer data stored, processed, retrieved or transmitted by that device or group of devices for the purposes of its or their operation, use, protection and maintenance.*" Consequently, the notion of information system encompasses two alternative definitions: it is either an electronic device of data processing (the smartphone, without any ontological difficulty, enters into this category), or a network of such devices (which could be, for instance, a phone network).

The Directive 2013/40 introduces a list of offences against the information system: illegal access to the system (Article 3), illegal system interference (Article 4), illegal data interference (Article 5), illegal interception (Article 6), production or

7. Convention on cybercrime (ETS N° 185), Budapest, November 23, 2001.
8. J. Clough, "A World of Difference: The Budapest Convention of Cybercrime and the Challenges of Harmonisation," *Monash UL Rev.*, 40 (2014), 698.
9. OJ L 69, 16.3.2005, pp. 67–71.
10. Communication from the Commission to the European Parliament, the Council and the Committee of the Regions—Towards a general policy on the fight against cyber crime (SEC(2007) 641) (SEC(2007) 642), COM/2007/0267 final.
11. OJ L 218, 14.8.2013, pp. 8–14, ELI: http://data.europa.eu/eli/dir/2013/40/oj.

distribution of tools designed to commit cyber-attacks or of sensitive information such as access code facilitating the cyber-attack (Article 7) and the incitement, aiding and abetting and attempt to cyber-attacks (Article 8).

Therefore, the two mostly known in practice cyber-attacks against smartphones, namely hacking and virus/malware injection, are regulated through this approach: the hacking is considered as an illegal access to the system, defined by the Directive 2013/40 as the intentionally access without right, to the whole or to any part of an information system by infringing a security measure, at least for cases which are not minor, while the virus or malware injection is considered as illegal data interference (deleting, damaging, deteriorating, altering or suppressing computer data on an information system, or rendering such data inaccessible, intentionally and without right).

### [B] Specific Cyber-Attacks Against the Smartphones

A large variety of cyber-attacks specifically target smartphones. The motives are diverse: access to personal data theft, identity theft, copyrighted work theft, direct economic gain through surtaxes call or SMS, privacy intrusion for personal reasons or as a mean for blackmail, exploitation of the device's computing capacity or network's access for personal use, distribution of ideological or commercial messages, etc. There were even cases of attacks against smartphones for military purposes. One attack recently took the form of an infiltration into US soldiers' smartphones with the aim to steal their GPS position.[12] These motives can be organized in two rough categories: targeted attacks against an individual and general attacks against any individual.

In the first category, the targeted attacks, we can mention, first, the attack through "*telephony Denial of Service*" or *TDoS attack*.[13] This attack is the cousin of the famous *DDOS* ("Distributed Denial of Service") attacks used mainly against internet servers. The principle is indeed the same: by multiplying the access requests, the criminal successes in blocking the availability of a service. However, whereas the *DDOS* attack aims to multiply the attempts of connection to a server through the help of a "botnet"[14] (a network of "infected" devices that are under his control due to massive hacking attacks), for a *TDoS* attack to occur the attacker needs to occupy lines continuously by means of automatic calls. The criminal may achieve this result by transferring genuine consumers' calls to the target's line, for instance, by creating a false consumer service page where he suggests to contact the victim's phone number or by directly hacking the internet consumer service page of the victim. He may also just use a botnet of devices in order to continually contact the phone service of the victim through the communication page of the victim's website. In any case, as a result,

12. Thomas Grove, Julian E. Barnes, "Drew Hinshaw, Russia Targets NATO Soldier Smartphones, Western Officials Say," *The Wall Street Journal*, 04/10/2017.
13. Y.G. Dantas, M.O. Lemos, I.E. Fonseca & V. Nigam, "Formal Specification and Verification of a Selective Defense for TDoS Attacks," International Workshop on Rewriting Logic and ts Applications April 2 2016 (pp. 82–97) Springer, Cham.
14. D. Barroso (2007). *Botnets—The Silent Threat*. European Network and Information Security Agency (ENISA), 15 (2007), 171.

all communications of the victim are jammed. Motives for such a cyber-attack are several. This operation is intended as a political act per se for instance, or is used as a means in combination with other elements: as a tool for blackmail or, in the frame of a more complex fraud scheme, as a mechanism prohibiting the bank to contact the genuine victim of an identity theft.

From a legal point of view, the *TDoS* attack enters into the definition of Article 4 of Directive 2013/40: the act of seriously hindering or interrupting the functioning of an information system by inputting computer data, by transmitting, damaging, deleting, deteriorating, altering or suppressing such data, or by rendering such data inaccessible, intentionally and without right constitutes the offense of illegal interference with the system.

Furthermore, an individual can be the victim of "SIM swapping,"[15] which is the smartphone's equivalent to the more general "account takeover" cybercrime category. This attack presupposes that the criminal knows personal information of the victim (through social engineering, hacking, phishing or even nowadays through buying personal data on the darknet). Then, the criminal will impersonate the victim and call his connection provider (or even visit a shop of the provider and scam the personal) in order to ask for a swap, that is a transfer of the connection on a new phone. After that, all calls and text messages will go to the criminal's phone. The utility of this attack in practice is obvious: as the smartphone is often used as the second factor in the two-step verification banking services imposed by the new PSD2 Directive as we already mentioned above, all kinds of illegal transactions and thefts can occur. But the attack can also just be used for a "classic" account takeover and for instance the Twitter's CEO has recently been victim of one of these attacks which aimed to control (for a small amount of time) the Twitter account of the victim.[16]

From a legal point of view, the SIM swapping belongs to the criminal offense of illegal interception of digital communications, as defined by Article 6 of the Directive 2013/40, which states that "*intercepting, by technical means, non-public transmissions of computer data to, from or within an information system, including electromagnetic emissions from an information system carrying such computer data, intentionally and without right, is punishable as a criminal offence, at least for cases which are not minor.*" Also, while identity theft is not itself an offense in EU legislation, the Directive 2013/40 makes it an aggravating circumstance in the context of penalties' estimation.[17]

Individual exploitation of a device, software or network vulnerability is another example of targeted cyber-attack. Illegal interference constitutes also the exploitation

15. Van der Bijl, "C. SIM-Card Swapping, Mobile Phone Banking Fraud and RICA 70 of 2002," *SA Mercantile L. J.* 21(2) (January 1, 2009), 159–173.
16. Eduard Kovacs, "SIM Swapping Blamed for Hacking of Twitter CEO's Account," *Security Week*, 03/09/2019.
17. Article 9(5) of the Directive 2013/40 states that "Member States shall take the necessary measures to ensure that when the offences referred to in Articles 4 and 5 are committed by misusing the personal data of another person, with the aim of gaining the trust of a third party, thereby causing prejudice to the rightful identity owner, this may, in accordance with national law, be regarded as aggravating circumstances, unless those circumstances are already covered by another offence, punishable under national law."

of the "SS7 vulnerability," discovered in 2014 by German researchers.[18] When smartphones' networks communicate between them, they use the SS7 technology. If the criminal already knows the phone number of the victim, and with some relevant equipment, he easily can (since the SS7 technology, somehow old, does not use encryption) intercept all basic communications (phone calls through the provider services and SMS) of the victim.

Apps are also a very common way to identify vulnerabilities in the mobile device's integrity. Such a vulnerability has been discovered in WhatsApp.[19] Exploiting a bug in the code that provokes a leak of memory, a criminal could execute code that would trigger this vulnerability (through a malicious gif picture for instance) and then be able to intercept and tamper with messages, to change the identities of senders, and to send messages labeled as private but actually made available to public groups.

In the same way, an FBI executive recently admitted that the FBI deliberately uses vulnerabilities which it detected in some of the most famous smartphones apps. For instance, the games "candy crush" or "angry bird" were used by the police as means to follow their target through its GPS.[20]

In the second category, the non-targeted attacks, the criminal aims to fish for an unascertainable number of victims, proposing its own malware to be installed through deception. Because smartphones move a lot, by definition, they always search for new networks to connect. Public Wi-Fi can be a real danger, as the victim may automatically connect to an unknown network and unconsciously share with the owner all kind of personal information, including access codes. Conversely, smartphones are specifically vulnerable to man-in-the-middle attacks. The man-in-the-middle attack is a kind of cyber-attack where the criminal intercepts the communication between two systems, working as a kind of malicious proxy. In conclusion, by creating a rogue public Wi-Fi hotspot, the hacker may without effort gain the opportunity of a man-in-the-middle-attack or even use its access in order to inject malware apps.

It has to be noticed that every form of communication through the smartphone is concerned by the non-targeted cyber-attacks. Even the deceptively innocent system of "QR code" where an information is embedded in a square black and white picture, for the smartphone's owner to capture through the device's camera. It has been demonstrated that QR code manipulation could lead to hacking.[21]

In all the cases presented above, it can be concluded that the EU legislator has offered an effective answer: on the substantial law approach, criminal offenses are in place, on the procedural aspect, the Directive 2013/40 also includes mechanisms of cooperation and transfer of information.

18. German researchers discovered a flaw that could let anyone listen to your cell calls, washingtonpost.com, December 18, 2014.
19. Charlie Osborne, "WhatsApp Vulnerability Exploited Through Malicious GIFs to Hijack Chat Sessions," *zdnet*, October 3, 2019.
20. Mathieu Perreault, "Entre ampoules et Candy Crush," *La Presses*, 2017.
21. P. Kieseberg, M. Leithner, M. Mulazzani, L. Munroe, S. Schrittwieser, M. Sinha & E. Weippl, "QR Code Security. In Proceedings of the 8th International Conference on Advances," *Mobile Computing and Multimedia* November 2010, 8 (pp. 430–435) ACM.

### [C] New Uses and New Legal Issues: Case Study of Malicious Cryptomining

Smartphones nowadays are very competitive to classic computer devices such as PC in terms of computing power. They also possess some unique quality: their users rarely switch them off, which means that for a large lapse of time (such as night time for instance), they do not fully use their computing capacity. Their computing resources therefore become increasingly interesting for hackers, not so on an isolated level but when put together in a common pool of resources (as part of a "*botnet*"). In this context, malicious *cryptomining* is a new promising activity for botnet's administrators that offers a way of direct monetization of the botnet and rends them by consequence even more compelling for cyber-criminals.

The notion of malicious mining of cryptocurrency has emerged with the *cryptomining* technology and can be defined as the fraudulent use of third party's computing resource in order to mine cryptocurrency.[22] This practice has recently become more and more popular for some practical reasons. First, the multiplicity of cryptocurrencies offers some opportunity for committing cybercrimes as some new cryptocurrencies have some low level of difficulty and can be easily mined. Second, the miner does not literally steal money from anybody. He just uses the computing resources of someone else in order to pursue mining activities, and this is often perceived as "legal." Third, the anonymous character of transactions, real or assumed, gives more incentive to the hackers. According to data published by Microsoft on March 2018, an average of 644,000 unique computers encountered coin-mining malware in the past months from September 2017 to January 2018.[23]

Using botnets for cryptomining differs from using them for DDoS attacks. In the first case, the creation of a pool of interconnected devices is not illegal per se, on the condition that the devices users are informed and consent to this use. Characteristic of this situation is the case of the Russian developer Alexey Khripkov,[24] who proposed some popular games such as "Puzzle" on the android Google platform. His games, however, gave him the ability to control the smartphone of the player while he/she is not using it, for mining purposes. Some of his games have 10–50 million downloads. The developer, however, considers that his activity is entirely legal, as it is used as a counterpart for in-game bonus. The question is whether the insertion of mining code in the game is considered as silent mining (and, therefore, is malicious according to the definition proposed above) or whether a disclaimer does clearly inform and effectively

22. Cyber "mining" can be defined as the process in which transactions for various forms of cryptocurrency are verified and added to the blockchain digital ledger. As incentive, the mining activity may (more or less randomly and according to his computing power) result in the creation and obtention to the "miner" of cybercurrency's resource.
23. Alden Pornasdoro, Michael Johnson & Eric Avena, "Invisible Resource Thieves: The Increasing Threat of Cryptocurrency Miners," March 13, 2018, https://cloudblogs.microsoft.com/microsoftsecure/2018/03/13/invisible-resource-thieves-the-increasing-threat-of-cryptocurrency-miners/ last accessed March 30, 2018.
24. Thomas Fox-Brewster, "This Russian Has the Power to Turn 100,000 Android Phones into Cryptocurrency Miners," forbes.com., 2017, https://www.forbes.com/sites/thomasbrewster/2017/11/08/google-android-cryptocurrency-miner-launched-by-russian/#690a309056fb.

warn the user that his/her device's computing power will be used for gaining revenues by the game developer.

Maybe the most interesting and disturbing case of malicious cryptomining is the so-called *cryptojacking* activity. It is technically possible in the case of some cryptocurrencies that do not require a lot of computing power to insert mining code directly in the website's code.[25] Two distinct situations can therefore occur: First, *cryptojacking* can be used by the website's owner. The website's owner deliberately inserts mining code in his/her website and, with each visitor's connection, assuming that the visitor remains some time on the website (or that he/she just let the windows open) the user's computer will silently mine cryptocurrency for the benefit of the website' owner. Second, hackers find a vulnerability on the website and successfully inject a mining code into an official and often visited webpage for their own personal financial gain. In both situations, given that nowadays the majority of web's surfing occurs through mobile devices (58% exactly), smartphones are directly concerned.[26]

In the first case of cryptojacking, the website's owner could for instance use a script such as "Tidbit," which was presented by its creators, award-winning students of MIT, as an alternative to advertisement for the purpose of monetizing webpage frequentation rates. It has to be highlighted that Tidbit's creators recently faced judicial charges as the New Jersey division of consumer affairs issued a subpoena against them, asking them to turn over all versions of the source code, all Bitcoin wallets associated with Tidbit, all agreements and communications with third parties, and the names and IP addresses of everyone who mined Bitcoins using Tidbit.[27]

In the second case of cryptojacking, the criminal activity combines bot cryptojacking and hacking and has already taken place in several instances. For instance, in UK in February 2018, journalists revealed that hackers had successfully injected a cryptocurrency mining script into the Information Commissioner's Office website and was mentioned that "*[t]he hijacked website would use the processing power of a visitor's computer to mine cryptocurrencies without the knowledge of the user.*"[28]

From a legal point of view, it is worth mentioning that according to the Recital 5 of the cyber-attacks Directive 2013/40, "*the act of establishing remote control over a significant number of computers by infecting them with malicious software through targeted cyber-attacks*" is covered by the legislation. Malicious *cryptomining* uses specific software that allows the interaction with the ledger of the cryptocurrency. However, Article 7 of the Directive (Tools used for committing offenses) takes a lot of precaution to ensure that only tools that are not only used but really designed with the intent to be used in an illegal way.[29] The offense of illegal access to information system

25. S. Eskandari, A. Leoutsarakos, T. Mursch & J. Clark, "A First Look at Browser-Based Cryptojacking," *arXiv preprint*, 2018, arXiv:1803.02887.
26. Eric Enge, "Where Is the Mobile vs. Desktop Story Going?," *Perficient Digital*, April 11, 2019.
27. Eric Blattberg (2014), "New Jersey Slaps MIT Bitcoin Hackers with Subpoena—And They're Fighting Back," *Venture Beat*, https://venturebeat.com/2014/02/12/new-jersey-slaps-mit-bitcoin-hackers-with-subpoena-and-theyre-fighting-back/.
28. Rory Cellan-Jones, "Hackers Hijack Government Websites to Mine Crypto-Cash, BBC," *bbc.com*, February 11, 2018.
29. "Article 7, Tools used for committing offences: Member States shall take the necessary measures to ensure that the intentional production, sale, procurement for use, import, distribution or

could be relevant only in case where botnets are used to crypto mine. However, in this case, it is not the act of *cryptomining* itself that is covered by the infraction, but the use of a botnet by hacking a group of devices itself. This confusion leads in practice to the misconception that if the botnet is legal, malicious cryptomining is also. Journalists had the opportunity to interview some perpetrators of malicious cryptomining acts and arrived at the conclusion that "*[a]nd by assembling that botnet from cloud accounts rather than hijacked computers, Ragan and Salazar believe their creation may have even been legal.*"[30]

The offense of illegal system interference seems to be the offense committed in case of malicious cryptomining. Indeed, malicious cryptomining implies the use of a mechanism that will severely puncture the computing power of the system in order to mine cryptocurrency and, arguably, interfere with its performance. As already explained above, the application of article 4 of the 2013/40 Directive presupposes the act of "*seriously hindering or interrupting the functioning of an information system by inputting computer data, by transmitting, damaging, deleting, deteriorating, altering or suppressing such data, or by rendering such data inaccessible.*" However, in the majority of cases of malicious cryptomining, the interference is not of such a magnitude as to provoke a situation of interruption or quasi interruption ("seriously hindering") of the system. Based on the above, it can be argued that actual cybercrime legislation does not provide for an adequate legal answer to malicious cryptomining issues.

The European Union had decided in 2015[31] to engage a new discussion on the modernization of its legal framework related to fraud and computer fraud, starting from the idea that new types of fraud appear that use non-cash payment. One of the specific goals of the EU is to update the existing legislation (the 2001 Council Framework Decision on combating fraud and counterfeiting of non-cash means of payments),[32] that no longer reflects today's reality, in order to integrate virtual currencies in this framework. The discussions led to a new Directive, namely the Directive 2019/713.[33] While no explicit reference is made to either cryptocurrencies or

---

otherwise making available, of one of the following tools, without right and with the intention that it be used to commit any of the offences referred to in Articles 3 to 6, is punishable as a criminal offence, at least for cases which are not minor:

(a) a computer programme [sic], designed or adapted primarily for the purpose of committing any of the offences referred to in Articles 3 to 6;

(b) a computer password, access code, or similar data by which the whole or any part of an information system is capable of being accessed."

30. https://www.wired.com/2014/07/how-hackers-hid-a-money-mining-botnet-in-amazons-cloud/.
31. European agenda on security of April 2015, the European Commission, Strasbourg, April 28, 2015, COM(2015) 185 final.
32. 2001/413/JHA: Council Framework Decision of 28 May 2001 combating fraud and counterfeiting of non-cash means of payment, OJ L 149, 02/06/2001 P. 0001 – 0004.
33. Directive (EU) 2019/713 of the European Parliament and of the Council of 17 April 2019 on combating fraud and counterfeiting of non-cash means of payment and replacing Council Framework Decision 2001/413/JHA.

smartphones in this legislation, the Directive uses the more general term of "virtual currencies" and "protected devices."[34]

Specifically, Article 6 is directly related to malicious cryptomining. The said Article, entitled "Offences related to information systems," provides for the first time that the following acts constitute an offence, that is the acts of "[...] *performing or causing a transfer of money, monetary value or virtual currency and thereby causing an unlawful loss of property for another person in order to make an unlawful gain for the perpetrator or a third party is punishable as a criminal offence, when committed intentionally by: (a) without right, hindering or interfering with the functioning of an information system; (b) without right, introducing, altering, deleting, transmitting or suppressing computer data.*" Cryptomining, arguably, exhibits all the characteristics of the said offense given that the malicious mining act intends to transfer virtual currencies through mining, this gain is deemed to be unlawful since no consent is given by the device's owner, and the act is executed through interfering with the functioning of the system, by using its computing power.

However, it is uncertain whether courts will eagerly accept that the use of computing power constitutes a loss of property. On the one hand, the smartphone's longevity (and specifically the battery) suffers from this practice. On the other hand, there is strictly speaking no loss of property, as the smartphone is still in the possession of its owner. At the same time, the main reason malicious cyber-mining is seen as an aggressive and reprehensible conduct is not just related to the clandestine mining itself but to its consequences for the user, which are the misuse of (sometimes precious) computer resources. In other words, the Directive's new offense on Article 6 is based on a specific *mens rea*, the financial gain, while malicious cyber-mining could cover several situations, not all of them directly linked to financial gain. Moreover, one inherent characteristic of cyber-mining is randomness, as it is not possible to predict when and by whom the next "mining puzzle" (algorithm related to the verification process of the ledger) will be solved, and thus the financial gain is randomized. This characteristic could create some difficulties as far as evidence is concerned.

Therefore, *de lege ferenda* the introduction of legislation forbidding the misuse of computer resources should be discussed. This means modifying the existing offense of illegal interference to the information system in order to not only apply to interferences that hinder the system but also to interferences that "steal" computing power from the system as well.

34. Article 2 of the Directive 2019/713 gives some interesting definitions. The "protected devices" are defined as "a device, object or record safeguarded against imitation or fraudulent use, for example, through design, coding or signature." The "information system" as defined by reference to the Directive 2013/40. Finally, "'virtual currency' means a digital representation of value that is not issued or guaranteed by a central bank or a public authority, is not necessarily attached to a legally established currency and does not possess a legal status of a currency or money, but is accepted by natural or legal persons as a means of exchange, and which can be transferred, stored and traded electronically."

## §8.03 THE ATTACKS THROUGH THE MOBILE DEVICE

If the smartphone can be a target, it can also easily become a tool for the commitment of plethora of offenses. For a start, criminal media law is concerned that the smartphone itself constitutes a tiny, but immediate and unfiltered, broadcast device. The smartphone in this aspect is the equivalent of the legendary gun in the classic westerns. With one click/push/slide from its owner, it is possible to record a private conversation, broadcast an event, access illegal online content (§8.03[A]). A specific mention of privacy issues through smartphones is requested (§8.03[B]). Finally, mobile devices can also be cybercrime tools of a new type, as digital pickpocket weapons (§8.03[C]).

### [A] The Heterogeneity of European Criminal Media Law

As a specific kind of computing devices, smartphones are portals to online content. It is therefore possible through smartphone to download or just access online illegal content. First, copyright law is concerned. Even private downloading of a protected work without permission or access through streaming (for instance through apps such as "Popcorn time") is illegal. The European Court of Justice (CJEU) has clearly explained that exceptions to copyright law such as the private copy exception apply only in the case of lawful users.[35] However, infringement of copyright law is an offense, based on the TRIPS Convention,[36] only when it occurs at a commercial scale. Therefore, the mere user with his smartphone would only be concerned with civil remedies, not criminal.

Second, the smartphone is the preferred entry portal to social media services. In January 2019, 96% of active user accounts worldwide accessed Facebook social network via mobile devices.[37] Social networks can be seen as an apparent absolute tool toward freedom of expression, as the average users do not perceive any filter to their freedom to post content or react to others' messages. This illusion creates a false feeling of impunity which leads to an explosion of cases of illegal content broadcasting. This concerns not only messages and pictures, but also live video coverage. The recent attack by a far right extremist against a Muslim church in Austria (the "Christchurch shooting") was seen 4,000 times before the video was removed by Facebook, but later the video was numerously rebroadcasted on other means such as Twitter or even on the same medium.[38]

35. *See* CJEU, C-435/12, *ACI Adam BV and Others v. Stichting de Thuiskopie, Stichting Onderhandelingen Thuiskopie vergoeding*, April 10, 2014 and also more recently CJEU, C-527/15, *Stichting Brein*, April 26, 2017 (*Kodi box* case).
36. Article 61 of the Agreement on Trade-Related Aspects of Intellectual Property Rights ("TRIPS Convention"), January 1, 1995.
37. https://www.statista.com/statistics/377808/distribution-of-facebook-users-by-device/.
38. Jane Wakefield, "Christchurch Shootings: Social Media Races to Stop Attack Footage," *BBC news*, March 16, 2019.

However, in Europe freedom of expression can be restricted in specific circumstances, for legitimate reasons related to the protection of the democratic society.[39] For instance, fake news can be in some European countries an offense, when the news can disrupt the civil order.[40] Hate speech, also, constitutes an offense that is regulated by EU law. It is governed by the additional protocol 189 of the Budapest Convention[41] and at EU level by the Framework Decision 2008/913/JHA of 28 November 2008 on combating certain forms and expressions of racism and xenophobia by means of criminal law.[42] Article 1(a) of the Framework Decision states that it is criminal to intentionally and "*publicly inciting to violence or hatred directed against a group of persons or a member of such a group defined by reference to race, colour, religion, descent or national or ethnic origin.*" Denial of genocide is also criminalized by the same regulation. The hate speech offense has been variously interpreted by the national legislators,[43] as it is not clear what intention is required (intention to provoke violence or just intention to publish the message) and whether the reference to racism per se suffices to establish the incitation to violence or if a specific violent message has to accompany it. In any case, this uncertainty means that people often posts hate speech messages through their mobile devices, without being aware they are engaging in criminal activity.

Third, criminal media law of most European countries includes some offenses related to "incitation." The offense of incitation to terrorism is harmonized by the EU legislation, through the Directive 2017/541.[44] Article 5 of the Directive states that "*Member States shall take the necessary measures to ensure that the distribution, or otherwise making available by any means, whether online or offline, of a message to the public, with the intent to incite the commission of one of the offences listed in points (a) to (i) of Article 3(1), where such conduct, directly or indirectly, such as by the glorification of terrorist acts, advocates the commission of terrorist offences, thereby causing a danger that one or more such offences may be committed, is punishable as a criminal offence when committed intentionally.*"

Finally, it is to be noticed that a certain dichotomy exists as regards defamation law. While defamation is traditionally an offense in Europe, this is seen as anachronistic[45] in the light of the European Court of Human Rights (ECtHR) case law on

39. Zoller E. Foreword, "Freedom of Expression: Precious Right in Europe, Sacred Right in the United States," *Ind. L.J.* 84 (2009): 803.
40. For instance, in Greece, an individual has been condemned for posting on social media anti-vaccination information. *See* Greek first instance Court, Veroia, May 12, 2016.
41. Protocole additionnel à la Convention sur la cybercriminalité, relatif à l'incrimination d'actes de nature raciste et xénophobe commis par le biais de systèmes informatiques, Strasbourg, 28/01/2003, STCE no. 189.
42. Council Framework Decision 2008/913/JHA of 28 November 2008 on combating certain forms and expressions of racism and xenophobia by means of criminal law.
43. Mandola, D2.1: Intermediate Report—Definition of Illegal Hatred and Implications, mandola-project.eu, 2016.
44. Directive (EU) 2017/541 of the European Parliament and of the Council of 15 March 2017 on combating terrorism and replacing Council Framework Decision 2002/475/JHA and amending Council Decision 2005/671/JHA.
45. MLDI, *Freedom of Expression, Media Law and Defamation* (International Press Institute, 2015).

freedom of expression (and specially as regards as the chilling effect theory[46] that states that in this case the idea of a punishment could prevent even legal expressions, through auto censorship). Consequently, defamation law is under decriminalization and constitutes in some EU countries only a civil wrong.

### [B] Smartphones and Criminal Violations of the Right to Privacy

The camera function of the smartphone has transformed each citizen into a film director such as Franzis Ford Coppola, for the best or for the worst. In the second case, the law becomes inevitably involved. First, smartphones have gravely exacerbated issues related to child pornography. Teenagers may have sexual relationships, in accordance with national legislation providing for the age of lawfully engaging in sexual acts. However, they cannot photograph or film record sexual acts, and even less broadcast it, as this can be deemed as a kind of child pornography. Indeed, according to Directive 2011/93,[47] any picture or video representing either a minor in a sexual intercourse, the sexual organs of a minor or a person looking like a minor is a child pornography material.[48]

Generally speaking, the smartphones have largely contributed to the generalization of the phenomenon of "revenge porn." What was originally created by one individual as a private sex tape or as a private erotic online conversation ("sexting") becomes a weapon toward the humiliation of the ex-boyfriend or girlfriend. Smartphones are not the only tool available in this context, and hidden camera may also lead to non-consensual photography or video recording, but here again the smartphone's freedom and ease of use provide the more adequate means for this behavior.

Even if everybody would agree that revenge porn constitutes an "*egregious privacy violation that deserves criminal punishment*,"[49] this situation is more delicate from a legal point of view. It cannot be assimilated to harassment as the repetition element is missing. New legislations are therefore been enacted to criminalize this behavior.[50] However, it has been argued that the revenge porn phenomenon constitutes only the top of the iceberg of a "continuum of image-based sexual abuse."[51]

---

46. Judith Townend, 'Freedom of Expression and the Chilling Effect', in Howard Tumber & Silvio Waisbord (eds), *The Routledge Companion to Media and Human Rights* (Routledge, 2017).
47. Directive 2011/93/EU of the European Parliament and of the Council of 13 December 2011 on combating the sexual abuse and sexual exploitation of children and child pornography, and replacing Council Framework Decision 2004/68/JHA.
48. Article 2(e) states that "'child pornography' means:(i) any material that visually depicts a child engaged in real or simulated sexually explicit conduct; (ii) any depiction of the sexual organs of a child for primarily sexual purposes; (iii) any material that visually depicts any person appearing to be a child engaged in real or simulated sexually explicit conduct or any depiction of the sexual organs of any person appearing to be a child, for primarily sexual purposes; or (iv) realistic images of a child engaged in sexually explicit conduct or realistic images of the sexual organs of a child, for primarily sexual purposes."
49. D.K. Citron & M.A. Franks, 'Criminalizing Revenge Porn', *Wake Forest L. Rev.*, 49 (2014), 345.
50. For instance, in UK, the Criminal Justice and Courts Act 2015, sections 33-35, criminalizes the non-consensual disclosure of private, sexual images with the intention of causing distress.
51. C. McGlynn, E. Rackley & R. Houghton, "Beyond 'Revenge Porn': The Continuum of Image-Based Sexual Abuse," *Feminist Legal Studies* 25(1) (2017), 25-46.

### [C] Smartphone as a Cybercrime Tool: The Digital Pickpocketing

Smartphones are obviously not only social media access devices and cameras. As digital tools, they can be programmed and reconfigured through various means. Even if the term cyber pickpocketing is sometimes used in a broad sense,[52] by digital pickpocketing we will refer here to the specific sense of a use of a smartphone to hack contactless credit card. Potentially, smartphone payment services could also be included in the list of targets, but paradoxically, contactless credit card are much more vulnerable than smartphone payment service. Indeed, the NFC technology of the smartphone is deactivated when the screen shut down and the both Apple and Android payment services work a one-use only temporary card number. At the opposite, contactless credit cards function on the basis of permanent identification codes and also in most countries it is possible to transfer small amount of money (typically up to EUR 20) without identification.

Therefore, we nowadays assist to a reemergence of the traditional pickpocket activities, in the form of digital pickpocket. The criminal bets on the limit of the Radio-frequency identification (RFID) technology. While the RFID chip inserted in the contact less credit card is designed to be activated by a very short radio wave signal,[53] there is no short amount of cases whereas two persons may be found at very close range. It means that, with a specifically programmed mobile device in a bag or a pocket, someone on the bus, in the metro or just waiting in a queue could discreetly steal a small amount of money from his victim. Since modern smartphones have nowadays NFC function (which is a form of RFID), any mobile device has theoretically the ability to read the data on microchip credit card. As a direct transfer from the victim account to the criminal account would be too dangerous, the criminal has alternatively the possibility to just copy the data and then use his own smartphone as contactless payment.[54] Once again, the new Directive 2019/713 relative to cyber-fraud we already referred to (*see* §8.02[C]) will apply. However, cyber pickpocket answers to the same legal issues as his analogue predecessor: it is not so much an issue of substantive law than an issue of enforcement (awareness of the victim, identification of the criminal).

## §8.04 EU CYBERCRIME STRATEGY REGARDING MOBILE DEVICES

### [A] The Need of Redefinition of the Cybersecurity's Strategy

Smartphones are the ultimate outcome of the digital convergence phenomenon that took place over the last two decades. Its revolutionary aspect does not reside in one peculiar technology: it is not its camera, not its internet surfing capacity. It is all of them

52. H.S. Zaytoun, "Cyber Pickpockets: Blockchain, Cryptocurrency, and the Law of Theft," *NCL Rev.* 97 (2018), 395.
53. According to the norm ISO/IEC 14443, the operating range is 10 centimeter, but it is believed the maximum range to exceed this estimation.
54. Matt Markovich, "Digital Pickpockets Using Smartphones to Steal Credit Cards," *Komonews*, May 23, 2013.

together in one mobile device that brings with it new legal and illegal behaviors. In this context, the technology-neutral approach adopted by the EU legislator is necessary but does not suffice in order to adapt the legislation to a fast-evolving cyber-threat landscape. Based on the discussion in this chapter, it can be concluded that, on the one hand, substantive law is essentially (but not completely) ready for the smartphone era and mechanisms of cooperation are already in place, but on the other hand, a smartphones' cyber-attack presupposes the action or the inaction of an intermediate actor, either the smart device's manufacturer, the phone's service provider, the online service provider, the app's creator or the apps' distribution platform. In addition, the multiplication of vulnerabilities, the creation of a black market, and the deep transformation of broadcasting activities, they all show that a mere repressive attitude is not enough in order to neutralize the multiple dangers related to smartphone.

Law must initiate policies and good practices at the same time in the technological sector. This is accomplished since 2016 through the NIS Directive,[55] which concerns the strategy to be adopted against cyber-criminality and the adoption of good cybersecurity practices. However, this directive principally emphasizes the coordination of national services and the protection of critical digital infrastructure. Moreover, the Directive asks for national authorities to define operators of essential services, that is a service essential for the maintenance of critical societal and/or economic activities and dependent on information technology. To the extent described above, the approach of the Directive is not relevant to the smartphones' sector.

Arguably, smartphones have become an essential service for all individuals in general, and therefore, a legislative intervention similar to the NIS Directive is needed. A national plan of action should provide the answer to the challenges of the exponential increase of vulnerabilities of mobile devices, while the autoregulation of live broadcast abuses by the online service providers should be accompanied by a legal framework illustrating their legal obligations and duties.

### [B] The Legal Framework of Cybersecurity Certification

The mandatory evolution of the kind of strategy described above could be implemented by means of the recent Regulation reinforcing the prerogatives of the EU cybercrime agency "ENISA." Indeed, Regulation 2019/881[56] does not only concern the function and the powers of the administrative authority but also covers the issues of cybersecurity certification. Under Article 74 (2) of the Regulation, "*[t]he Union rolling work programme shall in particular include a list of ICT products, ICT services and ICT processes or categories thereof that are capable of benefiting from being included in the scope of a European cybersecurity certification scheme.*" Article 74(3) gives some indications as what kind of ICT products, services or processes may be concerned by a

55. Directive (EU) 2016/1148 on the security of network and information systems across the Union.
56. Regulation (EU) 2019/881 of the European Parliament and of the Council of 17 April 2019 on ENISA (the European Union Agency for Cybersecurity) and on information and communications technology cybersecurity certification and repealing Regulation (EU) No. 526/2013 (Cybersecurity Act).

cybersecurity certification scheme: *"(a) the availability and the development of national cybersecurity certification schemes covering a specific category of ICT products, ICT services or ICT processes and, in particular, as regards the risk of fragmentation; (b) relevant Union or Member State law or policy; (c) market demand; (d) developments in the cyber threat landscape; (e) request for the preparation of a specific candidate scheme by the ECCG."*

The certification's purpose is to inform upon the security of the ICT product (such as a smartphone) or service (such as an ISP), with three indicators: "basic," "substantial" or "high" level of protection, given that the assurance level shall be commensurate with the level of the risk associated with the intended use of the ICT product, ICT service or ICT process, in terms of the probability and impact of an incident.[57]

The various components of the smartphone's sector would greatly benefit of a better co-regulation's policy that would incite the actors to more cybersecurity and the consumer to more confidence and a certification could play this role. For instance, the recent legal battle between the smartphone's company Huawei (world's No. 1 telecom supplier and No. 2 phone manufacturer) and the USA government, as the American government fears possible interference from the Chinese government in the security of the device with the potential consequence of cyberespionage activities,[58] should be very worrying for the EU consumer: is the device really a danger to cybersecurity or is the US government playing a political game of competition to the detriment of the Chinese actors? A certification (or the absence of it) on a specific company's devices would achieve a lot more than the mere declaration to Reuters by EU tech official that "Europe should be wary of Huawei."[59] By extension, the same policy of certification could apply to the app distribution platforms.

## §8.05 CONCLUSION

The EU's answer to cybersecurity's treats related to smartphones is based on a triptych: Directive 2013/40 on cyber-attacks, Directive 2019/713 on cyber-frauds and Directive 2016/1148 on cybersecurity (the "NIS Directive"). As we have seen, other regulations are relevant, such as the Directive 2011/93 on child pornography, Decision 2008/913 on hate speech and Regulation 2019/881 on ENISA and cybersecurity certification. These prolific activities of the EU legislator in this field have been discussed and commented in this chapter, and our conclusion will be based on two additional remarks regarding the said regulations:

First, neither the notion of smartphones nor mobile devices is contained in these legislations (with the exception of the Regulation 2019/881). This technology-neutral approach is certainly the preferred way forward in general. However, mobile devices

57. Article 52 of the Regulation 2019/881.
58. Abrar Al-Heeti, "US Hammers Huawei with 23 Indictments for Alleged Trade Secret Theft, Fraud," *cnet.com*, January 29, 2019.
59. Francesco Guarascio & Foo Yun Chee, "Europe Should Be Wary of Huawei, EU Tech Official Says," *Reuters*, December 7, 2018.

may be under new threats (such as stealing of computing power or digital pickpocketing) that would need new sector-specific legislative intervention.

Second, no question for a preliminary reference regarding these legislations has ever been before the CJEU. By that it is not implied that smartphone' criminal law framework is exempt of ambiguity or that the particular issues are not of great interest to individuals and society. More probably, the fact that very few cases are brought before the courts is due to the fact that there is a general lack of digital evidence and lack of awareness from the cybercrime victim. In conclusion, repressive policy in this sector has to be accompanied by preventive policy, such as a development of certifications under the authority of ENISA.

# CHAPTER 9
# Competition Law Issues

*Eleni Tzoulia*

*This chapter reviews competition law issues surrounding the operation of mobile apps as components of the common digital market. It examines from the perspective of EU competition law: (a) the monopolization of mobile OSs and app stores by specific companies, (b) the vertical integration of mobile platform owners into downstream markets associated to their platform, (c) the role of personal data and user traffic as marketable commodities and sources of economic power within mobile industry, and (d) certain concentrations between mobile service providers. The chapter draws conclusions as to which practices are currently considered to distort competition within the mobile economy, and which are not. It also highlights inadequacies of current EU competition law standards when confronted with the particularities of the mobile ecosystem.*

## §9.01 INTRODUCTION

Both end-users and traders are increasingly engaged in mobile networks today.[1] This incites investments in the development of products and services which are meant to support and facilitate mobile activity, interactions and transactions. Hence, a new

1. By the end of 2018 5.1 billion people subscribed to mobile services and approximately 3.6 billion made use of mobile internet. These numbers are expected to rise to 5.8 billion and 5 billion respectively by 2025. This means that in the next seven years more than 65% of the global population will participate in the market of mobile technologies and services. Groupe Speciale Mobile Association (GSMA), *Mobile Economy 2019*, available at: https://www.gsma.com/r/mobileeconomy/, accessed January 1, 2020.

profitable industry has emerged[2] which shows trends of further expansion due to certain technological advances.[3]

In the above context, mobile apps represent distinct commercial goods of significant value. Regardless of their independent marketability, however, mobile apps remain intricately linked to other products and services related to the mobile industry, such as mobile operating systems (OSs), app stores, marketing tools and analytics. This group of utilities, often referred to as "mobile ecosystem," bears several features of interest to competition law.

First, certain undertakings show strong presence in the market of various mobile goods. For instance, companies owning the currently predominant mobile OSs also administer the distribution channels of the latter's matching mobile apps.[4] Besides, providers of mobile apps which operate as two- (or multi-) sided networks,[5] tend to expand their business in downstream markets associated to their platform. Cross-market integration results in a company offering at some level competing services over businesses, which at other levels are its own suppliers or customers. This sets under scrutiny the trading and pricing terms and conditions it imposes on its vertical competitors.

Moreover, online intermediaries typically apply an open access system toward end-users to boost their visitation and utilize end-user data to optimize their services. In this way, they can attract more vendors and/or advertisers aspiring to use their platform to reach the consumer. Such business models result in user traffic and the availability of big data flows being handled as commercial assets within mobile economy. For instance, personal data are required in return for access to services, while the provision of user traffic is redeemed by the supply of free online content. Under these circumstances, the concept of market power acquires new dimensions, while certain conflicts arise between competition, data protection and intellectual property law.

Finally, the presence of big players makes classic digital markets, like the one of internet search, social networking services, etc., stagnant with high entry barriers. Therefore, start-uppers endeavoring to penetrate the mobile industry commonly compete by innovation. Namely, they release pioneering products and services by which they found new markets. Well-established vendors wishing to conquer new territory, commonly seek to acquire control of their developing rivals. Such collaborations may seem competitively harmless, when it comes to the enlargement of market shares and the increase of profits. However, they often entail the concentration of

2. The economic value of mobile goods accounts to around 4.6% of the GDP globally today and is expected to rise to 4.8% by 2023. GSMA, *supra* n. 1.
3. Such as new generation mobile networks (5G), the booming of artificial intelligence, the Internet of Things (IoT) and the blockchain.
4. In order to be functional on a portable device, mobile apps must be compatible with its native OS.
5. Such networks enable direct interactions between two (or more) distinct user groups. For instance, through the app stores app developers are connected to mobile device owners. By the same token, social networking apps connect end-users and advertisers, mobile marketplaces link retailers with customers, while search engines bring together end-users, website owners and advertisers.

critical inputs and the monopolization of customer bases. Therefore, they are particularly likely to annihilate competition to the detriment of the consumer.

The issues of concern illustrated above will be examined herein from the perspective of EU competition law. To this end, the study begins with a brief overview of the pertinent legal framework. Subsequently, it reviews relevant case law, with the objective to indicate how the EU competition authorities and the equivalent bodies in the national legal orders of EU Member States interpret and apply the provisions in force regarding its subject of scrutiny. It further seeks to identify gaps and deficiencies in the legislation and judicial reasoning under consideration and to comment upon the challenges they reserve for the effective functioning of the digital single market.

## §9.02 EU LEGAL FRAMEWORK ON FREE COMPETITION

The objective to establish free and undistorted competition in the internal market has been initially proclaimed by Article 3(f) EEC. Since the entry into force of the Treaty of Lisbon, it is provided in Article 3(3) TEU in conjunction with Article 3 (1c) TFEU. At a primary EU law level, substantive provisions on the functioning of competition within the internal market are incorporated in Articles 101–109 TFEU. These rules are divided into two parts, one dealing with anticompetitive business practices, which covers Articles 101–106 TFEU, and another referring to State aid, which includes Articles 107–109 TFEU. Secondary EU law further specifies and supplements these provisions.[6] Regulation (EC) 1/2003 assigned the European Commission with quasi-judicial powers regarding the implementation and enforcement of the above legal framework. Regulation (EC) 773/2004 further governs the conduct of Commission-led proceedings pursuant to Articles 101 and 102 TFEU. Commission decisions are subject to judicial review by EU courts according to Articles 261 and 263 TFEU.

### [A] The Practice of Abusing a Dominant Position (Article 102 TFEU)

The financial strength enjoyed by an undertaking which enables it to have significant impact on the conditions under which competition is developed in a market and to act largely indifferently to it, is characterized as a "dominant position." Its existence derives from a combination of factors, which, when taken separately into account,

6. For instance, Regulation No. 19/65/EEC on application of Article 85 (3) of the Treaty to certain categories of agreements and concerted practices, Regulation (EC) No. 139/2004 on the control of concentrations between undertakings, Regulation (EU) No. 330/2010 on the application of Article 101(3) of the Treaty on the Functioning of the European Union to categories of vertical agreements and concerted practices, Regulation (EU) No. 316/2014 on the application of Article 101(3) of the Treaty on the Functioning of the European Union to categories of technology transfer agreements.

would not necessarily be decisive.[7] However, the possession of a particularly significant market share[8] justifies the rebuttable presumption that an undertaking has established dominant position in the respective market.[9] In accordance with CJEU case law, any market share of 50% or more is regarded as particularly significant.[10]

The dominant position of an undertaking is evaluated in relation to a specific market, the so-called relevant market, which is defined by criteria mainly qualitative and geographical. In qualitative terms, the relevant market is determined by the products or services offered by the undertaking concerned. These belong to the same distinct market as all competing products and services, to which they are largely similar regarding their physical or technical characteristics, price and intended use, so that they can be mutually interchanged or substituted by the consumer.[11] In geographical terms, the relevant market comprises the region where the objective conditions of competition are alike for the traders concerned.[12]

According to Article 102 TFEU:

> Any abuse by one or more undertakings of a dominant position within the internal market or in a substantial part of it shall be prohibited as incompatible with the internal market in so far as it may affect trade between Member States.

As examples of such an abuse are further cited:

> a) directly or indirectly imposing unfair purchase or selling prices or other unfair trading conditions, b) limiting production, markets or technical development to the prejudice of consumers, c) applying dissimilar conditions to equivalent transactions with other trading parties, thereby placing them at a competitive disadvantage and d) making the conclusion of contracts subject to acceptance by the other parties of supplementary obligations which, by their nature or according to commercial usage, have no connection with the subject of such contracts.

In broad terms, the above provision prohibits a dominant undertaking from resorting to methods other than those, which commonly govern efficient competition between goods or services, with a view to hinder the maintenance or development of competition in a market where, precisely because of the presence of the dominant

7. *See* Case C-250/92 of 15.12.1994, *Gøttrup-Klim e.a. Grovvareforeninger v. Dansk Landbrugs Grovvareselskab AmbA*, ECLI:EU:C:1994:413, rec. 47.
8. Market shares represent the portion of a market's total sales that is earned by a company over a specified time period.
9. *See* Cases C-85/76 of 13.02.1979, *Hoffmann-La Roche v. Commission*, EU:C:1979:36, rec. 41; T-65/98 of 23.10.2003, *Van den Bergh Foods v. Commission*, EU:T:2003:281, rec. 154.
10. *See* Cases C-62/86 of 03.07.1991, *AKZO Chemie BV v. Commission*, ECLI:EU:C:1991:286, rec. 60; T-79/12 of 11.12.2003, *Cisco Systems, Inc. and Messagenet SpA v. Commission*, EU:T:2013:635, rec. 65; T-340/03 of 30.01.2007, *France Télécom SA v. Commission*, EU:T:2007:22, rec. 100; T-336/07, *Telefónica SA v. Commission*, EU:T:2012:172, rec. 150.
11. *Commission notice on the definition of relevant market for the purposes of Community competition law*, 97/C372/03 (1997), para. 7. Available at: https://eur-lex.europa.eu/legal-content/EN/TXT/HTML/?uri=CELEX:31997Y1209(01)&from=EN, accessed January 1, 2020.
12. *See* Cases C-27/76 of 14.02.1978, *United Brands v. Commission*, EU:C:1978:22, rec. 44; C-322/81 of 09.11.1983, *Michelin v. Commission*, EU:C:1983:313, rec. 26.

undertaking, the degree of competition has already been significantly weakened.[13] Intention on the part of the dominant undertaking is not required,[14] although it may be taken into account when determining abuse.[15] Moreover, the potential distortion of competition suffices for the application of Article 102 TFEU, i.e., the establishment of abuse does not presuppose that the practice in question has already had a concrete effect on the market concerned.[16]

Legal theory distinguishes between "exploitative," "anticompetitive" and "reprisal" abuses of a dominant position, as well as between pricing and non-pricing ones. The competent judicial and quasi-judicial EU bodies have further indicated a range of "nominate" practices with potentially anticompetitive effect, such as exclusivity agreements, practices of tying and bundling, refusing to sell or supply, and the one of margin squeeze. According to the CJEU, however, the designation of a practice as abusive depends on substantive criteria, which are examined ad hoc in any given case.[17] Consequently, there is no need for a practice to fall under one of the above categories in order to be banned.[18] In any case, the above categories intersect with each other, and it is possible that the same practice fits into more than one category.

### [B] Anticompetitive Business Collaborations

#### *[1] Coordination of Business Practices*

Article 101 paragraph 1 TFEU prohibits any type of cooperation between independent undertakings, which either by object or by effect may prevent, restrict or distort competition within the internal market. The distinction between 'infringements by object' and 'infringements by effect' in this provision implies that certain forms of collusion between undertakings can be regarded as being injurious to the proper functioning of normal competition by their very nature.[19] Such character is attributed to practices like fixing prices, restricting output, sharing markets and limiting parallel

---

13. *See* Cases C-52/07 of 11.12.2008, *Kanal 5 Ltd and TV 4 AB v. Föreningen Svenska Tonsättares Internationella Musikbyrå (STIM) upa.*, ECLI:EU:C:2008:703, rec. 25; C-52/09 of 17.02.2011, *Konkurrensverket v. TeliaSonera Sverige AB*, ECLI:EU:C:2011:83, rec. 27; C-202/07P of 02.04.2009, *France Télécom v. Commission*, ECLI:EU:C:2009:214, rec. 106; C-549/10P of 19.04.2012, *Tomra Systems ASA and Others v. European Commission*, EU: C: 2012:221, rec. 17; C-457/10P of 06.12.2012, *AstraZeneca AB and AstraZeneca plc v. European Commission*, EU:C:2012:770, rec. 74.
14. Case T-128/98 of 12.12.2000, *Aéroports de Paris v. Commission*, ECLI:EU:T:2000:290, rec. 170.
15. Case C-549/10P, *Tomra Systems ASA and Others v. European Commission*, recs. 1–22.
16. Cases T-201/04 of 17.09.2007, *Microsoft Corp. v. Commission*, ECLI:EU:T:2007:289, rec. 1089; C-457/10P, *AstraZeneca, supra* n. 13, recs. 109 and 111; T-286/09 of 12.06.2014, *Intel Corporation v. Commission*, EU:T:2014:547, rec. 186.
17. Case C-95/04P of 15.03.2007, *British Airways v. Commission*, ECLI:EU:C:2007:166, rec. 67; C-549/10P, *supra* n. 13, rec. 18.
18. Case T-286/09, *supra* n. 16, recs. 219–220.
19. For instance, their content or their objectives taking into account the economic and legal context of which they form a part.

trade.[20] Where coordination has not a per se anticompetitive object, one should determine its actual and potential effects on competition.[21] In this respect, Article 101 TFEU precludes the creation of competitive conditions which do not correspond to the normal conditions of the market in question, by evaluating the nature of the products or services offered, the size and number of the undertakings involved and the volume of the said market.[22]

Anticompetitive coordination of business practices may be achieved through formal or informal agreements,[23] decisions by trade associations,[24] as well as concerted practices. The latter term refers to any form of parallel conduct between competitors, which does not result explicitly from a mutual agreement or common decision but furnishes proof of tacit concertation and consensus.[25] Anticompetitive coordination of business behavior is equally conceivable between entities that operate at the same or at different levels of supply.[26]

Article 101 applies only where competition is "appreciably" restricted by a strategic alliance.[27] Thus, a "de minimis" doctrine is applied, which relates in the first place to the size of the collaborating undertakings' market shares (quantitative criterion). For agreements surpassing the established quantitative thresholds and,

20. Alison Jones and Brenda Surfin, *EU Competition law* (4th edn, Oxford University Press 2011) 171. *See also* Peter Roth, "The continual evolution of competition law" (2019) 7 J Antitrust Enforcement 6, 31 et seq.
21. *See* Cases C-32/11 of 14.03.2013, *Allianz Hungária Biztosító Zrt, et al., v. Gazdasági Versenyhivatal*, ECLI:EU:C:2013:160, recs. 33 and 34; C-67/13P of 11.09.2014, *Groupement des cartes bancaires (CB) v. European Commission*, ECLI:EU:C:2014:2204, rec. 53.
22. Cases C-194/99P of 02.10.2003, *Thyssen Stahl AG v. Commission of the European Communities*, ECLI:EU:C:2003:527, rec. 83; C-49/92 of 08.07.1999, *Commission of the European Communities v. Anic Partecipazioni SpA*, ECLI:EU:C:1999:356, rec. 117.
23. For instance, no-challenge clauses: Case C-65/86 of 27.09.1988, *Maschinenfabrik Hennecke GmbH and Heinz Süllhöfer*, ECLI:EU:C:1988:448; Gentlemen's agreements: Case C-41/69 of 15.07.1970, *ACF Chemiefarma NV v. Commission of the European Communities*, ECLI: EU:C:1970:71.
24. This term covers any rules the members of a trade association must abide by, e.g., the regulations governing its operation, recommendations it issues, and binding agreements concluded under its auspices. *See* Richard Whish and David Bailey, *Competition law* (9th edn, Oxford University Press 2018) 114; Case C-250/92 of 15.12.1994, *Gøttrup-Klim Grovvareforening and Others and Dansk Landbrugs Grovvareselskab AmbA (DLG)*, ECLI:EU:C:1994:413, rec. 35.
25. The tacit acceptance without protest of a restrictive conduct being systematically repeated on the same conditions by a supplier toward its customers, constitutes an "agreement": Case C-277/87 of 11.01.1990, *Sandoz prodotti farmaceutici SpA v. European Commission*, ECLI:EU:C:1990:6. A single meeting among competitors may fall under the concept of concerted practice: Case C-8/08 of 04.06.2009, *T-Mobile Netherlands BV et al. v. Raad van bestuur van de Nederlandse Mededingingsautoriteit*, ECLI:EU:C:2009:343. *See also* Case T-53/03 of 08.07.2008, *BPB plc v. European Commission*, ECLI:EU:T:2008:254, recs. 143–144; *Communication from the Commission—Guidelines on the applicability of Article 101 of the Treaty on the Functioning of the European Union to horizontal co-operation agreements*, 2011/C 11/01 (2011), paras. 60–63; Whish and Bailay, *supra* n. 24, 115 et seq.
26. *See, for instance,* Cases C-277/87, *supra* n. 25; C-32/11, *supra* n. 21, rec. 43.
27. *See* the landmark Case C-5/69 of 09.07.1969, *Franz Völk v. S.P.R.L. Ets J. Vervaecke*, ECLI-:EU:C:1969:35.

more generally, for the correction of any antinomies, a qualitative assessment may be also conducted (qualitative criterion).[28]

Pursuant to Article 101 paragraph 3 TFEU, anticompetitive business collaborations may be exempt from the above rules if they contribute to improving the production or distribution of goods, or to promoting technical or economic progress, while allowing consumers a fair share of the resulting benefit. For this exception to apply, however, the restrictions imposed by the collusion on the undertakings involved and their competitors are expected to also satisfy the proportionality principle.[29]

### *[2] Concentrations of Undertakings*

In comparison to the above forms of business cooperation, in the context of a "concentration" the firms involved quit their economic independence and come under common management.[30] Therefore, under the concentration concept, fall in principle mergers, acquisitions, takeovers and joint ventures. Initially, such transactions have been scrutinized in the light of Articles 101[31] and 102[32] TFEU. However, the enactment of separate legislation in that regard has been deemed necessary to ensure legal certainty.[33] Currently,[34] mergers, acquisitions and full-function joint ventures are governed by Regulation 139/2004.[35]

The above Regulation applies to concentrations between companies being actual or potential[36] competitors on the same relevant market,[37] or at different levels of the supply chain,[38] as well as to "conglomerate" mergers between companies providing supplementary products.[39] The Regulation empowers the Commission to contest ex-ante such transactions if they, cumulatively, surpass certain turnover thresholds and prove incompatible with the internal market. Article 2 sets out a nonexhaustive list of appraisal criteria, which need to be considered when estimating the competitive

28. *See* the *Commission Notice on agreements of minor importance which do not appreciably restrict competition under Article 101(1) of the Treaty on the Functioning of the European Union (De Minimis Notice)*, 2014/C 291/01 (2014); Whish and Bailey, *supra* n. 24, 147 et seq.
29. *See* Whish and Bailey, *supra* n. 24, 157 et seq.
30. Case C-633/16 of 31.05.2018, *Ernst & Young P/S v. Konkurrencerådet*, ECLI:EU:C:2018:371.
31. Joined Cases C-142 and 156/84 of 17.11.1987, *British-American Tobacco Company Ltd and R. J. Reynolds Industries Inc. v. Commission of the European Communities*, ECLI:EU:C:1987:490, recs. 37–40, 43–45 and 48. *See also* Commission Decision of 13.09.1993, Case No. IV/M.353—BRITISH TELECOM / MCI.
32. Case C-6/72 of 21.02.1973, *Continental Can*, ECLI:EU:C:1973:22, recs. 25–26. *See also* Commission Decision of 10.11.1992, Case No. IV/33.440—*Warner-Lambert, Gillette and Others* and No. IV/33.486—*BIC, Gillette and Others*, OJ L 116, 12/05/1993, pp. 0021–0032.
33. *See* European Commission, *White Paper Towards more effective EU merger control*, com/2014/0449 final (2014), para. 3.1.2.
34. Previously, Regulation (EEC) No. 4064/89 of December 21, 1989 on the control of concentrations between undertakings has been in effect.
35. *See* Article 3 of Regulation 139/2004 and *Commission notice on the concept of full-function joint ventures under Council Regulation (EEC) No. 4064/89*, 98/C 66/01, March 2, 1998.
36. M.7290-*Apple/Beats*, July 25, 2014, paras. 35 et seq.
37. Horizontal mergers.
38. Vertical mergers. *See* Commission Decision of 27 May 1998, Case No. IV/M.993—*Bertelsmann/Kirch/Premiere*, COM(1998) 1439, L 053 (1999), 1-30.
39. Case T-5/02 of 25.10.2002, *Tetra Laval BV v. European Commission*, ECLI:EU:T:2002:264.

effects of a merger. These have been further specified by the European Commission through its guidelines on horizontal[40] and non-horizontal[41] mergers.

Accordingly, a merger may cause either non-coordinated or coordinated foreclosing effects. Horizontal non-coordinated effects relate to any conditions which enable a merged entity to change unilaterally the competitive dynamics in the relevant market, e.g., through the creation or strengthening of a dominant position.[42] By the same token, vertical non-coordinated foreclosing effects occur, for instance, when a merged entity acquires the ability to restrict its downstream competitors' access to an important input or the access of upstream competitors to an adequate customer base.[43] Conglomerate non-coordinated effects are caused when the combination of products in related markets confer on the merged entity the ability and the incentive to leverage a strong market position from the one market to the other.[44] On the other hand, coordinated foreclosing effects relate to conditions facilitating tacit coordination between the merged undertaking and its competitors so that a sustainable oligopoly is constructed. Such effects are more likely to occur in highly concentrated and balanced markets with proportioned market shares and homogeneous products.[45]

## §9.03 THE APPLICATION OF ARTICLE 102 TFEU IN RELATION TO MOBILE APPS

### [A] Providing Mobile App Services as an "Economic Activity"

As noted above, mobile app providers often make their services available free of charge to the user. However, EU antitrust law applies to "undertakings," i.e., any entity which, irrespective of its legal status and means of financing, pursues an economic activity.[46] The latter term refers to the supply of goods or services to a given market with a view, whether exclusive or not, to making profit. Therefore, activities exercised without remuneration, e.g., the ones relating to social service, are not "economic" in the above

40. *See Guidelines on the assessment of horizontal mergers under the Council Regulation on the control of concentrations between undertakings*, 2004/C 31/03 (2004).
41. *See Guidelines on the assessment of non-horizontal mergers under the Council Regulation on the control of concentrations between undertakings*, 2008/C 265/07 (2008).
42. *Guidelines on the assessment of horizontal mergers, supra* n. 40, paras. 4, 28 et seq.
43. *Guidelines on the assessment of non-horizontal mergers, supra* n. 41, para. 30.
44. *Supra* n. 41, paras. 91 and 93.
45. *Ibid.*, paras. 15, 39 and 44–57.
46. Cases C-205/03 P of 11.07.2006, *FENIN v. Commission*, ECLI:EU:C:2006:453, rec. 25; C-35/96 of 18.06.1998, *Commission v. Italy*, ECLI:EU:C:1998:303, rec. 36; C-41/90 of 23.04.1991, *Klaus Höfner and Fritz Elser v. Macrotron GmbH*, ECLI:EU:C:1991:161, rec. 21; Joint cases C-264/01, C-306/01, C-354/01 and C-355/01 of 16.03.2004, *AOK-Bundesverband, etc.*, ECLI: EU:C:2003:304, rec. 46.

sense.[47] In view of the above, it is not self-evident that the provision of non-paid apps constitutes an "economic activity," thus falling under the scope of EU antitrust law.[48]

The European Commission had the opportunity to contemplate this issue in the context of *Google Shopping* case.[49] It concluded that the complimentary provision of general search services over the internet through Google Search constitutes an economic activity in the sense of EU antitrust law. By providing its services free of charge, Google increases its website's traffic and attracts advertisers. Moreover, according to the pertinent terms of service, each user consents to the storage and processing of his/her personal data when using Google Search. These data are then utilized not only to improve the relevance of Google's generic search results with the users' queries, but also to personalize the displayed sponsored links. In this way, Google Search can continually expand its network and optimize its advertising services, thus proportionately increasing its relevant revenues.[50]

More broadly, multisided networks, which provide free services to consumers, are funded by their business users. In such cases, end-users represent a necessary factor in generating profits.[51] Even when they are not monetarily charged, they provide an in-kind consideration in return for using mobile apps, which consists in visitation and personal information.[52] These elements multiply in-app advertisements and increase the provider's advertising revenues. Under these circumstances, the provision and operation of non-paid apps constitutes an ordinary economic activity, which falls under the scrutiny of EU competition law.

### [B] Identifying Separate Markets in the Mobile Ecosystem

When examining whether a firm active in the mobile industry violates Article 102 TFEU, EU competition authorities first identify the relevant market in which it is engaged. As analyzed above, the relevant market is determined by the nature of the economic activity in question and the geographical area where it is exercised. This market encompasses all alternative sources of supply for the customers of the undertaking concerned, in terms both of products/services and of geographic location of suppliers.[53] According to these criteria, the various mobile goods identified above

47. By the same token, the exercise of public authority, as well as activities carried out for the satisfaction of personal needs or in the framework of a dependent job, are not considered to be economic activities either. *See* Jones and Surfin, *supra* n. 20, 124 et seq.
48. *See* on this issue Ruppert Podszun and Benjamin Franz, "Was ist ein Markt?—Unentgeltliche Leistungsbeziehungen im Kartellrecht" (2015) NZKart 121.
49. AT.39740—*Google Search (Shopping)*, June 27, 2017, paras. 157 et seq. Available at: https://ec.europa.eu/competition/antitrust/cases/dec_docs/39740/39740_14996_3.pdf, accessed January 1, 2020.
50. *See* Jay Matthew Strader, "Google, monopolization, refusing to deal and the duty to promote economic activity" (2019) 50 ICC 559, 576.
51. Michael Kummer and Patrick Schulte, "When private information settles the bill: Money and privacy in Google's market for smartphone applications" (2019) 65 Management Science 3470, 3475 et seq.
52. Urs Albrecht Datta and Amit Klein, "Kostenlose Apps—eine vertragsrechtliche Analyse. Warum werbefinanzierte Gratis-Apps nicht verschenkt werden" (2017) 33 CR 174, 178 et seq.
53. *See Commission Notice on the definition of relevant market*, *supra* n. 11, paras. 13 et seq.

compose distinct relevant markets, which cover a broader or narrower geographical area each time.

Regarding mobile OSs,[54] in the first place, the European Commission has distinguished two separate markets,[55] one comprising the licensable OSs[56] and another for OSs used exclusively by vertically integrated programmers.[57] In relation to the above, separate markets are formed by the respective in each case app stores.[58] Moreover, individual markets are shaped by the several services provided through apps in the context of mobile commerce, such as online mapping services,[59] music recognition services,[60] social networking services,[61] etc.

The geographical scope of the above markets is worldwide[62] and certainly extends all over the EEA. The reason is that such markets are occupied by multinational corporations and there are no legal or technical barriers restricting the sale and use of the relevant products with similar quality, price and characteristics state by state.[63] On the contrary, general search engines form markets of national scope, since they are expected to index local businesses in each state and to display search results in the official language of each national territory.[64]

In relation to general search services separate markets are formed by both content sites[65] and specialized search services.[66] All these online search facilities differ in their technical features, rely on different sources of data and serve different purposes.[67] Therefore, they are considered to be complementary for each other and not substitutable ones. By the same token, Facebook as a social network is not placed in the same relevant market with other networks like YouTube, LinkedIn, Xing, Twitter, etc. From

54. OSs for smart devices and OSs for PCs belong to distinct markets, given that both use different hardware and have different performance capacities. *See* Commission decision M.6381 of 13.02.2012, *Google/Motorola Mobility*, paras. 26 and 29–30.
55. AT.40099—*Google Android*, July 18, 2018. Available at: https://ec.europa.eu/competition/antitrust/cases/dec_docs/40099/40099_9993_3.pdf, accessed January 1, 2020.
56. Such OSs can be installed on any manufacturer's portable devices, such as Google's Android OS and Microsoft Windows.
57. Such OSs are installed only on portable devices produced by their own programmer, such as Apple's iOS and Blackberry OS.
58. Supreme Court of the United States, No. 17-204—*Apple Inc. v. Robert Pepper et al.*, September 24, 2018, 3 et seq.
59. England and Wales High Court (Chancery Division), *Streetmap.EU Ltd v. Google Inc. & Ors* [2016] EWHC 253 (Ch) (February 12, 2016).
60. European Commission, M.8788-*Apple/Shazam*, February 6, 2018, paras. 23 et seq.
61. OLG Düsseldorf, VI-Kart 1/19 (V), August 26, 2019.
62. Excluding China as regards the market for licensable smart mobile OSs and Android app stores. Decision *Google Android, supra* n. 55, 92 et seq.
63. *See* European Commission Decisions *Google Android, supra* n. 55, para. 404; M.8788-*Apple/Shazam, supra* n. 60, paras. 25 et seq.; M.7217-*Facebook/WhatsApp*, October 3, 2014, para. 35.
64. *See* decision *Google Android, supra* n. 55, paras. 422 et seq.
65. Namely search functionalities within websites and social networking platforms which return search results from the latter's own content and not from all over the internet.
66. The term refers to search engines which focus on providing specific information or purchasing options in their respective fields of specialization, e.g., for flights, hotels or products.
67. Decision *Google Search (Shopping), supra* n. 49, paras. 163 et seq.

the point of view of private users, these platforms do not provide the same range of services and meet different requirements.[68]

### [C] Establishment of a Dominant Position in Mobile Markets

It has been ruled that Google occupies a dominant position throughout the EEA in several markets linked to mobile economy. This applies for instance to general search services (Google Search),[69] licensable OSs (Android) and the respective app stores (Google Play Store),[70] as well as to online search advertising intermediation.[71] Apple dominates the market of vertically integrated operating systems (iOS) and the respective app stores (Apple Store).[72] Furthermore, the position of Facebook in the market of social networking services has become globally monopolistic ever since the operation of "Google + " has ceased.[73]

In the above cases, the establishment of a dominant position has been mainly justified by the high market share held by the undertaking concerned and its ratio to the market shares of the nearest rivals.[74] Supplementarily, the European Commission takes into account eventual barriers which prevent either potential competitors from having access to or actual ones from expanding their activities on the relevant market. Such barriers constitute, e.g., the technical or economic constraints,[75] as well as the existence of brand effects[76] which prevent users from switching providers. Further barriers to entry or expand are raised by high capital expenditures, network effects and economies of scale[77] that competitors would have to match in order to compete viably in the relevant market.[78]

68. *See Background information on the Bundeskartellamt's Facebook Proceeding* (February 7, 2019), https://www.bundeskartellamt.de/SharedDocs/Publikation/EN/Pressemitteilungen/2019/07_02_2019_Facebook_FAQs.pdf?__blob = publicationFile&v = 6.
69. *Google Search (Shopping), supra* n. 49, paras. 264 et seq.
70. *Google Android, supra* n. 55, paras. 439 et seq.
71. European Commission, Decision AT.40411-*Google Search (AdSense)*, March 20, 2019. Available at: https://europa.eu/rapid/press-release_IP-19-1770_en.htm, accessed January 1, 2020. *See also* the decision EWCH No. 1363, *Unlockd Ltd and others v. Google Ireland Ltd and others*, May 25, 2018.
72. *Apple Inc. v. Robert Pepper et al., supra* n. 58, 8; Daizy Walzel, "Plattformen auf dem Kartellrechtlichen Prüfstand. Grenzen der Selbstbevorzugung (self-preferencing) durch sog. Tech-Giganten" (2019) 35 CR 314, 318.
73. *Supra* n. 68.
74. For instance, Google's market share exceeds 90% regarding general search services, 95% regarding licensable OSs and 70% regarding online search advertising intermediation.
75. *Google Android* case, *supra* n. 55, para. 438.
76. These relate to the strength of a brand which evokes trust and dissuades users from multi-homing. *Ibid.*, paras. 712 et seq.
77. The cost advantages that enterprises obtain due to their scale of operation.
78. *Google Search (Shopping), supra* n. 49, para. 270.

## [D] Abuses of Market Power Related to Cross-Market Integration Within the Mobile Ecosystem

Undertakings with multilevel presence in the digital industry, take advantage of their economic power in the markets which they dominate, in order to consolidate their position in related markets. In broad terms, they exploit their control on critical inputs in the mobile ecosystem to either hinder the release of competing services or downgrade their existing competitors in the retail mobile markets. The following case-law review illustrates in detail how this leveraging has been demonstrated so far within the digital common market and how it has been evaluated by the competent authorities.

### *[1] Exclusivity Agreements Related to Mobile App Services*

When a dominant undertaking exploits its financial strength to impose unfair trading terms on its customers or suppliers thus reaping benefits, which would not be permitted under conditions of functional and effective competition, it infringes Article 102 TFEU by committing an "exploitative abuse." Exclusivity agreements concluded between dominant undertakings and intermediate suppliers may constitute an exploitative abuse in the above sense. Through exclusivity clauses, retailers undertake the commitment, usually for consideration, to purchase goods or services exclusively or principally from the dominant undertaking in lieu of its competitors.

In this context, a dominant undertaking is considered to exercise undue influence on its counterparties, e.g., when it applies punitive measures and reprisals against suppliers refusing to withdraw from commercial relations with its competitors or against those seeking to terminate an exclusivity agreement already in force. Exclusivity agreements may fetter competition in the relevant market, in the sense that only certain undertakings shall survive, those whose behavior depends on the dominant one.[79] This effect is detrimental also to consumers, who are deprived of the opportunity to take full advantage of the competition that is normally possible in that market. The likelihood of anticompetitive foreclosure by exclusive purchasing obligations is conditional upon their duration, the existence of brand effects and the capacities of competitors to supply for each individual customer's entire demand.[80]

In light of the above regime, the European Commission examined Google's conduct to contractually prohibit manufacturers from developing hardware compatible with Android forks and from preinstalling third-party apps on Android devices.[81] According to the Commission, by making the licensing of Android OS dependent on commitments unrelated to the use of the OS itself, Google unduly restricted the financial freedom of hardware manufacturers with a view to consolidate its dominant

79. C-6/72, *supra* n. 32, rec. 26.

80. *Communication from the Commission—Guidance on the Commission's enforcement priorities in applying Article 82 of the EC Treaty to abusive exclusionary conduct by dominant undertakings*, 2009/C 45/02 (2009), paras. 32 et seq.

81. "Anti-Fragmentation Agreements." See *Google Android, supra* n. 55, recs. 157 et seq., 1015 et seq.

position in the markets of licensable OSs and its proprietary mobile apps. In this way, Google also hindered less powerful companies to enter the relevant markets and compete viably, thus causing interference with the structure of competition.[82] By the same token, Google deprived consumers of the opportunity to access any further innovation,[83] defining itself which technologies will be developed and which will not.

In a more recent ruling, the European Commission examined exclusivity obligations imposed by Google in the advertising brokering market, where it also holds a dominant position.[84] Through its AdSense for search platform, Google enables third-party sites and mobile apps to embed Google Search functionalities and profit by exploiting the space next to the search results for the placement of advertisements. Google acts as an advertising broker, mediating between third-party sites and advertisers. From 2006 Google began including in the relevant contracts exclusivity clauses in order to prevent websites using the Google Search AdSense functionality from sourcing advertisements from its rivals. Since 2009, these clauses have been gradually replaced by "Premium Placement" clauses ("relaxed exclusivity" strategy) which obliged counterparty websites to reserve the most visible and profitable advertising space for a minimum number of Google adverts. Google was entitled to even influence how websites would display the adverts of its rivals, e.g., in terms of size, color and font. According to the European Commission, the above conduct conferred on Google competitive advantage over its competitors through non-merit-based measures. Its exclusivity clauses hampered website owners from monetizing freely their advertising space, distorted consumer choice and stifled innovation.

### *[2] The Issue of "Carrier-Bundled" Apps*

According to the European jurisprudence, "tying" occurs when a company makes the purchase of a product or service technically[85] or contractually[86] conditional on the purchase of a second product or service. "Bundling" consists in the practice of offering several goods jointly for sale, as one package. The products concerned must be regarded as distinct from the consumer perspective, i.e., on a regular basis expected to be separately purchased.[87] Article 102 TFEU applies, when the above practices are exercised by a company holding a dominant position in the relevant market of at least one of the products involved in the tie or bundle and are likely to lead to anticompetitive effects in the tied market, the tying market, or both at the same time. Among other parameters, the long duration of such supply strategies, any circumstances preventing competitors from replicating the tie, as well as the condition that the tied market

82. Article 102d TFEU.
83. Article 102b TFEU.
84. Commission decision *Google Search (AdSense)*, *supra* n. 71.
85. This refers to the technical integration of the tying and tied product so that they operate only in conjunction with each other.
86. Contractual tying occurs when the purchase of the tied product is agreed upon as a precondition to acquire the tying product.
87. *EC Guidance on abusive exclusionary conducts*, *supra* n. 80, para. 51; Case T-201/04, *Microsoft Corp. v. Commission*, *supra* n. 16, recs. 872–959.

represents an aftermarket[88] for the tying product, advocate the establishment of anticompetitive foreclosure.[89]

Between 2011 and 2014 the mobile apps "Google Play Store," "Google Search" and "Google Chrome" were set as default in mobile devices running on Android OS and could not be entirely removed unless the user performed root access.[90] This conduct has been scrutinized by the European Commission in light of the above doctrines.[91] In this respect, the offering of Google's proprietary apps as pre-installed software on Android OS devices has been considered in the entire relevant context.

It came to light that, in order to discourage hardware manufacturers from pre-loading competing software on their devices, Google provided significant financial incentives which its competitors were unable to offset. Besides, Google was contractually blocking the release of modified Android versions and corresponding applications. In view of the above, the tying of Google Chrome and Google Search on Android OS devices was found to confer on Google an artificial distribution advantage that other providers could not match. Indeed, Google was already monopolizing the major distribution channel for Android apps, i.e., Android app stores, which enabled it to treat its proprietary applications more favorably than any competing ones. By also occupying the distribution channel of mobile equipment manufacturers, Google was forcing consumers to use its own applications instead of any rival ones.[92] Consequently, it was liable to foreclose competition in the respective markets.

### *[3] Treating Like Mobile Apps in an Unlike Way*

In 2005 Google launched an online mapping service called "Google Maps." Two years later, the company incorporated this service in Google Search by displaying clickable thumbnail maps on top of the search results in response to geographical queries. These thumbnails could lead users to the requested location on Google Maps website. Other hyperlinks brought up in response to the search query, including a blue link leading to the competing online mapping service "Streetmap.EU," were displayed lower down the page of the search results. Streetmap.EU contended before the England and Wales High Court (Chancery Division),[93] that this practice constituted an abusive exploitation of

88. A secondary market or "aftermarket" is a supplementary or subsequent market in relation to a primary one. Aftermarkets are either composed by products used in repair, maintenance or enhancement of a primary product, such as accessories, spare parts, add-ons, etc., or formed when sales in the original market are finished (e.g., aftermarket for second-hand products, videocassette aftermarket for movies).
89. *EC Guidance on abusive exclusionary conducts*, *supra* n. 80, paras. 52–58; Case T-201/04, *supra* n. 16, recs. 976 et seq.
90. Rooting is the process of attaining privileged control over Android OS, which enables the alteration or replacement of system applications and settings that are otherwise inaccessible to Android users.
91. *Google Android* case, *supra* n. 55, paras. 169 et seq. *See also* Commission decision AT.39.530 —*Microsoft (tying)*, December 16, 2009, available at: https://ec.europa.eu/competition/antitrust/cases/dec_docs/39530/39530_2671_5.pdf, accessed January 2, 2020.
92. *Google Android* case, *supra* n. 55, paras. 896 et seq.; *Microsoft (tying)* case, *supra* n. 91, paras. 39–54.
93. EWHC 253 (Ch), *Streetmap.EU Ltd v. Google Inc. & Ors*, February 12, 2016.

Google's dominant position in the market of general search services, which enabled Google to leverage its position in the associated market of online maps. By privileging its own mapping service on Google Search, Google was allegedly hindering its competitors' access to consumers, thus ultimately foreclosing competition in the relevant market.

Taking as a starting point the principle, that dominant firms should be encouraged to compete—which inherently entails the preferential treatment of proprietary products or services over competing ones[94]—the court examined whether the contested practice had an appreciable effect on competition in the relevant market. Thus, it applied a de minimis threshold which is in principle engaged by the jurisprudence in the context of Article 101 TFEU on business partnerships.[95] In that respect the court referred to statistics, finding that the online traffic of Streetmap.EU did not originate exclusively from Google's search engine. On the contrary, it was primarily based on unique visitors. Therefore, the traffic of Streetmap.EU was not significantly altered after Google Maps' thumbnails were imported into Google Search. Consequently, the anticompetitive effect of Google's discriminatory practice in favor of its own services was not substantial.

Apart from the above, the court also examined whether Google's conduct was justified by an objective necessity, as well as whether its anticompetitive effects have been counter-balanced by advantages that also benefit consumers.[96] It concluded that Google's thumbnail maps had improved users' experience in the context of geographical search. In pursue of these efficiency gains, the unequal ranking between search results from Google Maps and competing mapping services was indispensable and proportionate. Any attempt for a more equitable positioning of the rival services would have burdened Google with significant expenses and would have encountered technical obstacles.

Contrary to the above, the European Commission imposed a fine of EUR 2.42 billion on Google for abusing its dominant position in the market of general search services, providing unfair competitive advantage to its comparison-shopping service known as "Google Shopping."[97] According to the Commission, the success of price comparison services is largely based on the traffic they attract on their website. A major source of traffic for these services is Google's general search engine. By incorporating Google Shopping in this search engine, Google has diverted user traffic from Google

---

94. *See* Thomas Höppner, "Das Verhältnis von Suchmaschinen zu Inhalteanbietern an der Schnittstelle von Urheber- und Kartellrecht" (2012) WRP 625, 637.
95. According to the court's reasoning, in cases when the anticompetitive effect of an abuse of power is not on the market where the scrutinized undertaking is dominant but on a separate, associated market, it is to be examined whether the degree of that effect is appreciable. The court points to the Advocate General Opinion in the CJEU Case C-7/97 of 28.05.1998, *Bronner v. Mediaprint*, ECLI:EU:C:1998:264, rec. 58. Critical to this approach, Anca D. Chirita, "The rise of big data and the loss of privacy" in Mor Bakhoum, Beatriz Conde Gallego, Mark-Oliver Mackenrodt and Gintarė Surblytė-Namavičienė (eds), *Personal data in competition, Consumer protection and intellectual property law* (Springer Verlag GmbH 2018) 167.
96. Based on *EC Guidance on abusive exclusionary conducts, supra* n. 80, para. 28.
97. *Google Search (Shopping), supra* n. 49, paras. 331 et seq., currently under appeal before the General Court. *See* Case T-612/17 *Google and Alphabet v. Commission* [2017] OJ C 369/37.

Search to its developing price comparison service at the expense of any competing provider.

In more detail, when ranking search results for product queries, Google did not apply merit-based criteria. On the contrary, it positioned prominently on Google Search pages and displayed in rich format its own price comparison service. Competing services would only appear in the generic search results, and their exact position depended on algorithmic assessments. Google Search rankings are based on algorithms which automatically demote websites with low original content. This is however an inherent feature of comparison shopping-services, which therefore would be permanently shown downgraded in the least visible places of the generic search results to the competitive advantage of Google Shopping.

### *[4] Price-Related Abuses of Dominance*

Apple devices are programmed to accept apps coming exclusively from the company's own distribution platform called "App Store." After obtaining an iOS app, all subsequent upgrades or modifications occur using Apple's servers. In case users manage to install unauthorized software,[98] their iPhone warranty will be voided. Under these circumstances, third-party providers wishing to reach iPhone users are obliged to have their apps sold through the App Store.

To gain access to the above platform, developers pay an annual fee of about EUR 99. Besides, Apple charges digital content providers an additional 30% fee for any subscriptions sold through its distribution platform. Moreover, the company obliges third-party providers to select prices for their apps from 0.99 cents and above, in one-dollar increments. The company also retains the right to change the pricing agreement at any time and suspend or terminate the distribution of a given app unilaterally.[99]

The above practices are currently being scrutinized for their anticompetitive effects in both Europe and the USA. On the consumer side, it is alleged that being shielded from competition Apple may charge iOS compatible apps unduly, deriving excessive benefits to their detriment.[100] On the part of mobile app providers, it is argued that Apple exploits its monopolistic position to enforce unfair pricing and distribution terms on third-party apps, thus favoring its own applications, which in many cases are also preinstalled on its devices.

A relevant complaint by Spotify Technology SA against Apple is already pending before the European Commission. It concerns Spotify's competing application for downloading and streaming music called "Apple Music." Allegedly, the successive fees incurred by Spotify for using App Store inflate artificially the selling price of its app. At the same time, Apple's proprietary music streaming service can maintain a lower price, thus gaining a competitive advantage. Spotify also condemns that it is prevented from

98. This practice is known as "jail breaking."
99. *See* case *Apple Inc. v. Robert Pepper, et al.*, *supra* n. 58, 7 et seq.
100. Article 102a TFEU. *See also Apple Inc. v. Robert Pepper et al.*, *supra*, which however examines the admissibility of the claim filed by iPhone users and not the substance of the case.

communicating alternative ways to iPhone users for buying and upgrading its service outside App Store. Besides, upgrades and improvements to Spotify's app are supposed to delay for months within the App Store.[101]

In anticipation of the Commission ruling in the above case, legal theory scrutinizes Apple's contested billing system in light of the jurisprudence on price-related abuses.[102] In principle, any pricing strategy by a dominant undertaking, such as excessive pricing, price discrimination,[103] selling at artificially low prices[104] and rebates,[105] can be deemed contrary to Article 102 TFEU, if it is likely to impede competition in the relevant market. Depending on the type of each price-based conduct, EU competition authorities have determined specific criteria to be considered when assessing the likelihood of such an effect.[106]

Accordingly, whether Apple rips off supra-competitive profits by its pricing policy depends on the real cost and the real value of the services it provides to its counterparties. The economic value of a service is determined by all relevant circumstances, including the pertinent supply-demand ratio.[107] It is argued, however, that monopolistic competition justifies greater billing discretion. Therefore, when it comes to Apple's billing system, the concept of "excess" becomes opaque.[108]

Another pricing abuse, which applies in the context of vertical integration in particular, is the one of "margin squeeze." Such an abuse occurs, when a vertically integrated company sells an upstream input to its downstream rivals under terms and conditions which squeeze their profit margins, thus ultimately driving them off the downstream market. According to the pertinent ECJ doctrine, a margin squeeze presupposes (a) that the vertically integrated undertaking is dominant in the upstream market, (b) that it would not be able to offer its retail services to end-users profitably

101. Philip Blenkinsop, *Spotify files EU antitrust complaint against Apple*, Reuters (March 13, 2019, 12:04 PM), https://www.reuters.com/article/us-apple-spotify-tech-eu/spotify-files-eu-antitrust-complaint-against-apple-idUSKBN1QU18G.
102. *See* Friso Bostoen, "Online platforms and vertical integration: the return of margin squeeze?" (2018) 6 J Antitrust Enforcement 355; Walzel, *supra* n. 72, 318 et seq.
103. *See* respectively Articles 102a and 102c TFEU.
104. *See* Roth, *supra* n. 20, 17 et seq.
105. *See* Cases T-203/01, *Michelin v. Commission*, ECLI:EU:T:2003:250; Case C-85/76, *Hoffmann-La Roche*, *supra* n. 9; C-95/04P, *British Airways*, *supra* n. 17.
106. *See EC Guidance on abusive exclusionary conducts*, *supra* n. 80, paras. 23–27.
107. *See* the case law cited by Sandra Colino, *Competition law of the EU and UK* (Oxford University Press 2019) 364 et seq.
108. Walzel, *supra* n. 72, 316. This approach is in principle followed in the US antitrust policy. Filippo Maria Lancieri, "Digital protectionism? Antitrust, data protection, and the EU/US transatlantic rift" (2019) 7 J Antitrust Enforcement 27, 36 et seq. A method to overcome this impasse could be, to compare Apple's scales of fees with the equivalent rates in the monopolistic market of Android app distribution, by analogy with the ECJ's approach in Case C-177/16 of 14.09.2017, *Autortiesību un komunicēšanās konsultāciju aģentūra/Latvijas Autoru apvienība v. Konkurences padome*, ECLI:EU:C:2017:689, rec. 38; Joined cases C-110/88, C-241/88 and C-242/88, *François Lucazeau and others v. Société des Auteurs, Compositeurs et Editeurs de Musique (SACEM) and others*, ECLI:EU:C:1989:326, rec. 25. Any discrepancies in the charges of the same services within these markets should be justifiable by reference to objective dissimilarities, e.g., the costs borne by the provider or the volume of demand in each case. Otherwise, they may conceal an abuse of dominant position in the form of excessive pricing.

either, if it had to pay its own wholesale prices and (c) that this situation has an exclusionary effect over competitors who are at least as efficient as the dominant undertaking in the downstream market.[109]

The application of the above doctrine in the Spotify case would therefore initially entail the assessment, whether this company is in principle profitable in the music streaming market, and in fact whether it is as profitable as Apple. On a following stage, it should be tested whether Spotify gets objectively prevented from making profits due to the charges imposed by Apple for supplying its upstream input. Decisive in this respect is the question, whether Apple Music itself would be able to compete profitably, if it had to pay 30% of its subscription price to an upstream competitor. If the answer is negative, the concrete effects of Apple's billing system on Spotify's competitive performance must be considered. These are conditional upon, e.g., any options available for Spotify to bypass Apple's fees in order to compete profitably toward iPhone users.

It is observed that neither Spotify nor Apple Music are profitable apps, despite their large scale of paid subscribers. To adapt the margin squeeze doctrine in the particularities of this case, it is therefore suggested to compare these companies' unprofitability and to assess whether App Store charges objectively delay Spotify's prospects to become profitable.[110] It seems however rather more secure to alternatively assess Apple's billing system in light of the case law on anticompetitive leveraging cited above.[111]

According to this approach, it should be investigated whether Apple exploits its dominant position in the upstream market of app distribution services to gain a competitive advantage in the downstream market of music streaming services by non-merit-based measures. To this end, the costs imposed by Apple on its downstream competitors should be weighed in light of all pertinent circumstances. It is of relevance to consider, e.g., the lock-in effects observed within Apple's ecosystem for both users and developers, the occasion that Apple preloads Apple Music on its mobile devices, the ability of music streaming app users to multi-home, any practices exercised by Apple to deliberately harm Spotify's efficiency,[112] etc.

#### *[5] Interim Conclusions*

Any service represented in the mobile ecosystem through mobile apps forms an individual relevant market within the meaning of EU antitrust law. Mobile apps operating as multisided networks, which offer complimentary services to consumers, capitalize on the networks effects of their platform and make profits from vendors and advertisers. As long as the provision of mobile apps serves directly or indirectly speculative purposes, it is an economic activity which falls within the scope of EU antitrust law.

109. Bostoen, *supra* n. 102, 360.
110. *Ibid.*, 369 et seq.
111. *See also* the analysis of Walzel, *supra* n. 72, 318 et seq.
112. Such as blocking its upgrades.

Exclusivity clauses imposed by licensable OS providers on manufacturers with a view to block the development and installation of competing software[113] on smart devices, may distort competition. This practice is considered to impair the economic freedom of hardware manufactures and to erect barriers against technological progress and innovation. On the other hand, the tying between OSs and mobile apps of the same provider is considered anticompetitive, as long as competitors are technically or contractually hindered to replicate the tie and consumers are practically forced to use the tied app regardless of its performance.

The preferential treatment of proprietary applications over competing ones by vertically integrated platform owners is, in principle, legitimate. The impact of the discriminatory conduct on competition must be examined ad hoc in any given case taking into consideration all relevant circumstances. One approach advocated in the jurisprudence suggests that foreclosing effects on downstream competitors must be weighted in light of the "*de minimis*" doctrine and against any benefits derived by the consumers.[114] It is unanimously accepted that measures taken to deliberately downgrade competitors when promoting mobile services of one's own interests, are not permitted.

The billing system of vertically integrated app store providers may conceal an anticompetitive leveraging strategy toward the retail mobile app markets. The competent EU authorities have not yet issued a relevant ruling. However, it follows from the above findings that anticompetitive foreclosure is established in any case, where high charges of upstream inputs are accompanied by targeted exclusionary practices against specific providers of competing apps.

### [E] Abuses of Market Dominance Related to the Exploitation of Network Effects

In economic terms, a "network effect" or "network externality" describes the additional value conferred on multisided platforms by each user joining them. To keep all their sides growing, online platforms reduce the price paid by end-users of their services,[115] thus attracting business users who wish to use them as an input to reach the consumer. User traffic may be cashed through advertisements entrusted to online platforms or transaction fees paid by vendors. Besides, online intermediaries may redeem the traffic they divert to individual websites against free online content.

It has been already implied herein, that network effects within digital platforms are to a large extend data driven.[116] The collection and processing of personal data enable online intermediaries to improve their services toward both end- and business users. User profiling is significant in particular for the promotion of third-party sales. By

113. OSs and mobile apps.
114. By analogy with Article 101 paras. 1 and 3.
115. "Zero price markets" according to Douglas A. Melamed and Nicolas Petit, "The misguided assault on the consumer welfare standard in the age of platform markets" (2019) 54 Rev Ind Organ 741, 754 et seq.
116. *See* on that *European Parliament—Is data the new oil? Competition issues in the digital economy*, PE 646.117 (2020).

optimizing their advertising services, online platforms can increase their revenues. This section deals with anticompetitive practices exercised by dominant platform owners in their effort to use to the best advantage the network effects of their platform.

### *[1] The Data Policy of Multisided Networks under the Scrutiny of EU Competition Law*

The above patterns are also followed by Facebook Inc. which administers the homonymous social networking platform. Facebook's network can be joined online and is also available via a mobile app. To subscribe to these services, users do not have to pay a fee. However, they are required to consent to the company's data policy.

Accordingly, Facebook may collect user personal data from external sources and associate them with the corresponding accounts on its platform. These data will mainly stem from mobile apps managed by Facebook itself, like WhatsApp, Instagram, Oculus and Masquerade. However, they may also originate from third-party sites having installed Facebook add-ons[117] or simply using the Facebook analytics service. In such cases, it suffices for the user to visit the third-party site so that his information is uploaded to the Facebook database. Namely, it is neither necessary that the user activates the add-ons, nor does the user get specifically informed about the transmission of his data to Facebook in each given case.

At the beginning of 2019, the German Competition Authority (Bundeskartellamt) examined the above regime in the light of German and, by extension, EU competition law. The Bundeskartellamt attached importance to the fact that the authorization of such extensive data processing is imposed as a prerequisite for a user to register on Facebook. Accordingly, Facebook has been found to exploit its dominant position in the market of social networking services in order to impose contractual obligations on its users, which violate their rights as data subjects. By this conduct, Facebook users suffered damage in the form of a loss of control on their privacy. In addition, the abuse was likely to foreclose competition in the relevant market.[118]

The above decision has been however overturned by OLG Düsseldorf on August 26, 2019.[119] According to the court, the protection of consumer interests falls in principle under the regulating scope of competition law. Unfair terms of service imposed on consumers may therefore constitute an exploitative abuse in the sense of Article 102a TFEU. This presupposes, however, that a specific influence of the unfair terms on competition in the relevant market is substantiated. Neither the unlawfulness of the terms per se, nor the fact that the consumer's counterparty happens to be a dominant undertaking suffices to identify a competitive abuse. In other words, not every unlawful behavior of a dominant undertaking is anticompetitive. Competition

117. Meaning the Facebook "Like" and "Share" buttons.
118. Decision Bundeskartellamt No. B6-22/16, February 6, 2019, available at: https://www.bundeskartellamt.de/SharedDocs/Entscheidung/EN/Fallberichte/Missbrauchsaufsicht/2019/B6-22-16.pdf?__blob=publicationFile&v=4, accessed January 2, 2020.
119. OLG Düsseldorf, VI-Kart 1/19 (V), *Facebook v. Bundeskartellamt*. English translation available at: https://www.d-kart.de/wp-content/uploads/2019/08/OLG-D%C3%BCsseldorf-Facebook-2019-English.pdf, accessed January 2, 2020.

law entrusts the dominant undertaking with the responsibility to maintain healthy competition in the relevant market,[120] but not with the obligation to uphold the rule of law in general.

In view of the above, the court held that any privacy-related concerns flowing from the increased accumulation of data within the control of Facebook fall in principle within the scope of data protection rules.[121] For competition law to additionally apply, a causal link must be firstly ascertained between Facebook's market-dominating position and the infringement of data protection law. The enforcement of Facebook's unlawful data policy must be namely attributable to its market power. Moreover, a causal connection is necessary between the infringement of data protection law and an impeding influence on the structure and development of competition in the relevant market. By imposing its data policy, Facebook must be namely granted unjustifiable advantages at the expense of current or potential competitors and ultimately the consumer. That the conduct in question fulfills these requirements has not been proven in the given case.

First, there is no evidence to suggest that users are dependent on Facebook at the time they agree to its terms of service, nor that Facebook obtains the users' consent to the contested data policy by unfair means, like coercion or undue influence. Although agreement is a prerequisite for gaining access to the crucial network, a user is free to decide whether to consent or not. Statistics show that most users worldwide still choose not to subscribe to Facebook.

Besides, the contested terms of use do not qualify as unfavorable to consumers. On the consumer side, the requested data stand for consideration in return for using an advert-financed service for free. It has not been substantiated that this consideration is disproportionate in relation to the economic value of the supplied service.[122] Data collected by Facebook do not serve exclusively commercial purposes, but also the optimization of its services and the improvement of user experience on its platform. There is no evidence that the company uses the collected data beyond the agreed scopes.

Moreover, Facebook's data policy has neither been found to foreclose the relevant market for existing competitors nor to erect barriers against new entrants. In the field of social networking services, a crucial input for the usefulness and performance of a product is the number of its users. In this respect, Facebook's competitive edge with around 32 million users per month is enormous. It cannot be concluded,

---

120. *See* on that Cases C-322/81, *supra* n. 12, rec. 57; T-51/89 of 10.07.1990, *Tetra Pak v. Commission*, ECLI:EU:T:1990:41, rec. 23; T-111/96 of 11.07.1998, *ITT Promedia NV v. European Commission*, ECLI:EU:T:1998:183, rec. 139; Joined Cases C-395/96P and C-396/96P of 16.03.2000, *Compagnie maritime belge transports and Others v. Commission*, ECLI:EU:C:2000:132, rec. 37; T-228/97 of 07.10.1999, *Irish Sugar plc v. Commission*, ECLI:EU:T:1999:246, rec. 112; C-209/10 of 27.03.2012, *Post Danmark A/S v. Konkurrencerådet*, ECLI:EU:C:2012:172, rec. 21–23.
121. *See also* Commission decision M.7217-*Facebook/WhatsApp*, *supra* n. 63, para. 164.
122. *See* on that Inge Graef, "How to create synergies between competition, consumer and data protection law in digital markets," in Mor Bakhoum, Beatriz Conde Gallego, Mark-Oliver Mackenrodt and Gintarė Surblytė-Namavičienė (eds), *Personal data in competition, Consumer protection and intellectual property law* (Springer Verlag GmbH 2018), 137 et seq.

however, that Facebook's data policy makes it unreasonably difficult for its competitors to gain equal access to its customer base. On the contrary, subscribers retain the right to further share their personal data in order to gain access to third-party services, even competing ones to Facebook.

The German Competition Authority's decision implied, that in the given case it is the processing and linking of "multi-data" for the purposes of the Facebook's network that influences the possibility of competing providers to enter the relevant market. It appears, however, that the amount of data is not decisive for successfully operating a social network. This has been verified by the fact that Google + had to withdraw from this market although having a data share many times higher than Facebook. On the contrary, it is the scope and quality of user data that matters for determining the consumer's interests and future behavior with the help of algorithms. The contested decision has failed however to substantiate in which sense the additional data retrieved from external sources noticeably increase the quality of Facebook's algorithmic evaluations. What is more, it has not been clarified, to what extent the use of the controversial data could enable Facebook to noticeably increase its advertising revenues and to protect its market position against future market entries.

### *[2] The "Google Snippets" Case*

In 2016 the Landgericht (LG) Berlin had the opportunity to examine in the light of EU competition law Google's practice of featuring short snippets and thumbnails of press products listed in the results of its search engine without compensating the publishers.[123] In August 2013, a new provision on related rights was introduced in Germany[124] prohibiting internet search engines from using newspaper or magazine snippets without the publisher's authorization.[125] Forty-one German publishers, represented by the copyright protection organization "VG Media," initiated proceedings before the competent German authorities seeking to enforce the above provision against Google. In response, Google has asked the claimants to consent to the continuation of their content quotation for free. Google intended not to display snippets from sites asking for reimbursement.

The above practice has been contested before LG Berlin on the ground of constituting a discriminatory abuse according to Article 102 paragraph 2c TFEU. Google was allegedly forcing those publishers having asked for redress through VG Media, to waive their right to compensation for the reproduction of their products. The companies in question would have to comply with Google's illegitimate terms of use,

123. Decision LG Berlin, 92 O 5/14 Kart, February 19, 2016, MMR 2016, 620 et seq.
124. Paragraph 87f of the UrhG titled "Publishers of newspapers and magazines."
125. *See* Case C-299/17 of 12.09.2019, *VG Media Gesellschaft zur Verwertung der Urheber- und Leistungsschutzrechte von Medienunternehmen mbH v. Google LLC*, ECLI:EU:C:2019:716, which declared the disapplication of this provision on the ground of constituting a rule on information society services and, therefore, a "technical regulation" within the meaning of Article 1(11) of Directive 98/34/EC so that its draft should have been subject to prior notification to the Commission.

in order for their site's traffic not to be diminished by not being displayed in the Google Search results.[126]

LG Berlin has ruled, however, that Google did not abuse its dominant position in this case. Article 102 paragraph 2c TFEU prohibits abuses of dominance which consist in applying dissimilar conditions to equivalent transactions thereby placing some trading parties at a competitive disadvantage in relation to others. Subsequently, preferential terms and conditions toward individual trading partners can be considered discriminatory, if they cannot be justified by differentiated economic and competitive circumstances.[127] Conversely, no discriminatory abuse of dominance is established where the treatment of comparable cases is identical. In the given case, Google was applying the contested practice equally to all German publishers, who retained the right to have their content featured for free in Google Search results, or not at all.

Furthermore, Google's requirement to use third-party content for free was not found to constitute an unfair exploitation of foreign assets.[128] The incorporation of website snippets and thumbnails into Google's search results creates a win-win situation for all parties involved. The search engine itself benefits by enhancing user experience on its platform, thus inciting more user traffic. Users benefit by being able to search more accurately for information in the vast web. Third-party websites benefit by attracting more easily user traffic, thus increasing their sales and ad profits. The German publishers' claim that Google pays for displaying excerpts of their texts in the search results would upset the above balances. It would namely oblige a party to pay in order to continue a practice from which the other party is already making a profit.[129]

In a related case, however, the European Commission has regarded as anticompetitive the conduct, which consisted in Google using original material from competing specialized search engines, without the latter's consent or even against their explicit will. Competitors who have objected to the use of their information in Google's specialized search services have been asked to opt out of Google's web search entirely. Such a choice, however, would substantially reduce their visitation and was therefore not sustainable.[130]

According to the Commission's preliminary assessment, Google was abusing its dominant position in the relevant market of general web search, in order to benefit from investments made by competing firms in the associated market of specialized search services.[131] It was namely linking its authorization to use content from

126. Being indexed by Google is nowadays crucial for attracting visitors online. *See* Stephan Ott, "Ich will hier rein! Suchmaschinen und das Kartellrecht" (2006) MMR 195. In this sense, Google is a monopsonist, according to Melamed and Petit, *supra* n. 115, 751.
127. C-27/76, *United Brands v. Commission*, *supra* n. 12, rec. 227.
128. *See also* decision BGH, I ZR 259/00, July 17, 2003, BGHZ 156, 1-19.
129. Critical on this decision Jan Bernd Nordemann and Olaf Wolters, "Google, das Leistungsschutzrecht für Presseverleger und das Kartellrecht" (2016) ZUM 846, 850 et seq.
130. "All or nothing choice." *See* Thomas Höppner, "The EU competition investigation of internet search. Why Google's market tested proposals for re-labelling and opt-out solutions do not suffice" (2013) CRi 107, 112.
131. In favor of this approach also Boris Paal, "Immaterialgüter, Internetmonopole und Kartellrecht" (2013) GRUR 873, 877 et seq.; Boris Paal, "Internet-Suchmaschinen im Kartellrecht" (2015) GRUR-Int. 997, 1001.

third-party sites with the appearance of these sites on its general search results. This practice might suppress its rivals' incentives to invest in the creation of original content and compete. Indeed, if Google's specialized search services contained all information that is posted on the web, users would get demotivated to visit other sites, even those from which the relevant information originated.[132] The Commission has therefore asked Google to sever the above link to restore competitive incentives.[133]

### *[3] Interim Conclusions*

Although online intermediaries offer their services for free to end-users, they monetize their platform's traffic. On the one hand, their visitation is associated with the assignments they get for third-party sales promotion. Thus, it determines their advertising revenues. On the other hand, the traffic they divert to their business users entitles them to ask for free third-party content. In this way, they can enrich their services with fewer input costs. These business models are regarded as in principle legitimate from the perspective of EU competition law. Competitive concerns arise, when platform owners utilize end-user personal data for the purposes of their network, as well as content from business users which are simultaneously their downstream competitors.

The competition authorities having dealt with the above speculations to date acknowledge that the concentration of personal data may confer on an online intermediary competitive advantage over its rivals. This depends on the scope and quality of the accumulated data and relates to their usage for the training of algorithms, according to which the environment of the platform adapts to the user needs and habits, as well as intra-platform advertising gets more personalized and therefore more profitable. Such an advantage is supposed to contradict merit-based competition, when the platform owner exploits its dominant position in the relevant market to obtain user consent to an unlawful data policy, which cannot be implemented by less powerful rivals.

The use of third-party content without reimbursement by vertically integrated online intermediaries is considered anticompetitive in case: (a) the controversial content originates from downstream competitors, (b) its exploitation by the platform owner decreases user traffic toward its original web source, and (c) content owners are not granted a right to opt-out of the above scheme without being entirely denied the upstream input of the intermediary platform.

132. *See Commission seeks feedback on commitments offered by Google to address competition concerns—questions and answers,* MEMO/13/383 (2013), available at: http://europa.eu/rapid/press-release_MEMO-13-383_en.htm, accessed January 3, 2020.

133. *Intellectual property and competition policy,* SPEECH/13/1042 (2013), available at: http://europa.eu/rapid/press-release_SPEECH-13-1042_en.htm, accessed January 3, 2020. Critical on Google's commitment proposals, Höppner, *supra* n. 130.

## §9.04 ACCESS TO DATA RELEVANT FOR COMPETITION IN DOWNSTREAM MARKETS

In July 2019 the European Commission initiated a formal antitrust procedure against Amazon. This company has a dual role as a platform, on the one hand, selling proprietary products on its website as a retailer and, on the other hand, providing a marketplace for other retailers to supply their products to consumers. As a supplier of its downstream competitors, Amazon obtains critical information about their activity on its platform, their products and transactions.[134] Allegedly, third-party seller data[135] can be used by Amazon to identify competitive threats or demand trends and to customize accordingly its own commercial policy.[136]

Through a Communication from 2018,[137] the European Commission acknowledged that where data is generated as a by-product of using a service, there is shared value creation. This implies that both business users and intermediaries contribute to the accumulation of, e.g., ratings and reviews on online marketplaces like Amazon. Therefore, both parties should rip the benefits of gaining access to and making use of such information. The relevant contractual agreements are expected however to protect the commercial interests and secrets of all parties involved, as well as to ensure undistorted competition when exchanging commercially sensitive data.

Based on the above, Amazon's practice to accumulate data of retailers active on its marketplace is in principle legitimate. This is true, even when these data are used for the planning of Amazon's commercial strategies in the retails markets where it competes against its business users. In this respect, Amazon's latitude finds its limits in the general doctrines of EU competition law which prohibit non-merit-based leveraging and constraining collusions. By this token, the European Commission intends to examine the standard trading terms, which entitle Amazon to analyze and use competitively sensitive information about retailers active on its marketplace, in light of

134. The Amazon standard agreement stipulates: "You grant us a royalty-free, non-exclusive, worldwide, perpetual, irrevocable right and license to use, reproduce, perform, display (public communication), distribute, adapt, modify, re-format, create and exploit derivative works of, and otherwise commercially or non-commercially exploit in any manner, any and all of Your Materials." "Materials" are defined as "all Technology, Your Trademarks, Content, Your Product information, data, materials, and other items or information provided or made available by you or your affiliates to Amazon or its affiliates." It follows that the extracted information includes product prices, volume of sales, feedback scores, etc. Georgina Prodhan and Foo Yun Chee, *Explainer: What is the EU's antitrust investigation into Amazon about?*, Reuters (July 17, 2019, 7:55 PM), https://www.reuters.com/article/us-eu-amazon-com-antitrust-explainer/explainer-what-is-the-eus-antitrust-investigation-into-amazon-about-idUSKCN1UC24R.

135. According to the above, the term "data" in this section refers mainly to non-personal information, which pertains to products and services, rather than individuals.

136. *See* Bostoen, *supra* n. 102, 375 et seq.; Inge Graef, "Differentiated Treatment in Platform-to-Business Relations: EU Competition Law and Economic Dependence," (2019) Yearbook of European Law 1, 8.

137. *Communication from the Commission "Towards a common European data space,"* SWD(2018) 125 final (2018), 10 et seq.

both Articles 101 and 102 TFEU.[138] In anticipation of the relevant assessment, this section endeavors to outline the specifications for the application of the above provisions in the given case.

### [A] Access to Competitively Sensitive Information in Light of Article 102 TFEU

Amazon is a vertically integrated online intermediary which competes with business users of its platform in the downstream markets of consumer goods. It is acknowledged that control over online intermediation services gives platform owners an economic incentive and the ability to provide their own offerings with technical or economic advantages which they deny to competing business users. Such differentiated treatment may be facilitated by means of competitively sensitive information generated for and through the provision of online intermediation services. Amazon's self-preferencing usage of foreign information could undermine fair competition and restrict consumer choice in the retail mobile markets.

When assessing whether Amazon's scrutinized practices amount to an infringement of Article 102 TFEU, the competent authorities must first examine whether this company possesses a dominant position in the relevant market of online marketplaces within the EEA.[139] If this is the case, it must be further investigated whether Amazon takes advantage of its market power to enforce illegitimate terms of use on its business users with reference to the handling of their data. To assess the legitimacy of the pertinent terms and conditions, the European Commission may consult the recently adopted Regulation (EU) 2019/1150.[140]

This Regulation serves the objective of guaranteeing fairness and transparency in the commercial relations between online platforms and sellers which offer goods and services to consumers. It shall apply from July 12, 2020. Its substantial provisions refer in particular to the terms and conditions imposed on business users by platform providers (Article 3), the lawful restriction, suspension and termination of business user accounts (Article 4), the parameters determining the latter's rankings (Article 5) and the issue of access to business data obtained for and through the provision of online intermediation services (Article 9).

With regard to the latter issue, the Regulation prescribes the obligation of online intermediaries to thoroughly inform business users about the scope and nature of the accumulated data, the conditions under which business users can gain access to and make use of this information, its eventual transmission to third parties, the purposes

---

138. Pursuant to the relevant press release. *See European Commission—Antitrust: Commission Opens Investigation into Possible Anti-Competitive Conduct of Amazon*, IP/19/4291 (2019), available at: https://europa.eu/rapid/press-release_IP-19-4291_en.htm, accessed January 4, 2020.
139. This will depend on the extent to which other market players such as eBay, AliExpress, Fnac, etc. compete with and restrain the Amazon Marketplace.
140. Regulation (EU) 2019/1150 of the European Parliament and of the Council of 20 June 2019 on promoting fairness and transparency for business users of online intermediation services, OJ L 186, 11.7.2019, pp. 57–79.

served by the transmission, as well as any possibilities for opting-out of this data-sharing. Business users should also be fully informed of any access that providers of online intermediation services maintain to the information provided or generated in the context of their contractual relationship, after the latter has expired.[141] When business data are used by vertically integrated platform owners, these are expected to act in a transparent manner providing an appropriate description of how business data can facilitate the preferential treatment of their proprietary services in the downstream markets of consumer goods.[142]

If the above prerequisites are not met, the competent authorities should examine to what extent business users are dependent on Amazon when consenting to the unlawful use of their information. This relates to the ability of business users to multi-home and even change provider, as well as to the importance of Amazon's marketplace for them entering the downstream retail markets and competing viably toward the consumer.

### [B] Access to Competitively Sensitive Information in Light of Article 101 TFEU

It is acknowledged by well-established case law, that the exchange of competitively sensitive information between competing undertakings, even when it is imposed by one party on the other, may amount to an "agreement" or a "concerted practice" in the sense of Article 101 TFEU.[143] To be banned, such strategic alliances must have the object or effect of appreciably restricting competition, i.e., reducing or removing, on the one hand, uncertainty as to the operation of the market in question and, on the other hand, autonomy as to the determination of one's own economic policy.[144] In the same line, the Communication from the Commission on the application of Article 101 TFEU to horizontal cooperation agreements declares that:[145]

> The exchange between competitors of strategic data, that is to say, data that reduces strategic uncertainty in the market, is more likely to be caught by Article 101 than exchanges of other types of information. Sharing of strategic data can give rise to restrictive effects on competition because it reduces the parties' decision-making independence by decreasing their incentives to compete. Strategic information can be related to prices (for example, actual prices, discounts, increases, reductions or rebates), customer lists, production costs, quantities, turnovers, sales, capacities, qualities, marketing plans, risks, investments, technologies and

141. *See* rec. 32 of the Regulation.
142. *See* Article 7 in conjunction with recitals 30 and 31 of the Regulation.
143. *See* Cases C-238/05 of 23.11.2006, *Asnef-Equifax, Servicios de Información sobre Solvencia y Crédito, SL v. Asociación de Usuarios de Servicios Bancarios (Ausbanc)*, ECLI:EU:C:2006:734, recs. 31–32; C-7/95P of 28.05.1998, *John Deere Ltd v. Commission of the European Communities*, ECLI:EU:C:1998:256, rec. 88.
144. C-194/99P, *Thyssen Stahl AG v. Commission of the European Communities, supra* n. 22, recs. 81 et seq.
145. *Guidelines on the applicability of Article 101 of the Treaty on the Functioning of the European Union to horizontal co-operation agreements, supra* n. 25, para. 86.

R&D[146] programmes and their results. Generally, information related to prices and quantities is the most strategic, followed by information about costs and demand. However, if companies compete with regard to R&D it is the technology data that may be the most strategic for competition. The strategic usefulness of data also depends on its aggregation and age, as well as the market context and frequency of the exchange.

According to the above[147] as well as the preceding analysis of Article 101 TFEU, the compatibility of Amazon's information exchange system with the EU rules on competition depends first on the specific characteristics of this system, such as its purpose and the conditions of access to it. Moreover, the type of the exchanged information,[148] the periodicity of the exchange and its importance for the fixing of prices, volumes or conditions of service[149] are also significant parameters. Finally, the economic conditions on the markets affected by the information exchange are also of relevance. Being aware of the commercial strategy of one's competitors is particularly liable to distort rivalry and facilitate collusion on a highly concentrated market. On the contrary, the dissemination of information within fragmented markets is in principle neutral or even beneficial. This however presupposes that equal accessibility to the crucial information is guaranteed to all operators.[150] Giving the opportunity for a risk assessment to a limited circle of undertakings, leaves the rest at a competitive disadvantage and poses entry barriers in the affected market. It must be reminded that any anticompetitive effects of the investigated information exchange system may be legitimized pursuant to the derogation of Article 101 paragraph 3.[151]

## §9.05 CONCENTRATIONS OF UNDERTAKINGS PROVIDING MOBILE APPS

### [A] The Acquisition of WhatsApp by Facebook

In August 2014 the European Commission received notification of an envisaged merger between Facebook Inc. and WhatsApp Inc.[152] As mentioned above, the online social networking platform constitutes a core service of Facebook Inc., where it also offers online advertising services. However, Facebook is also engaged in the market of

146. The abbreviation stands for the terms "research and development."
147. It is argued, that currently Regulation (EU) 330/2010 sets limits to the application of the above principles by analogy in the exchange of competitively sensitive information which pertains to vertical cooperation. The latter Regulation excludes specific vertical alliances per se from the restrictions of Article 101 TFEU on the grounds of Article 101 para. 3 TFEU. It shall however expire on May 31, 2022. *See* Regulation (EU) 330/2010 of April 20, 2010 on the application of Article 101(3) of the Treaty on the Functioning of the European Union to categories of vertical agreements and concerted practices, L 102/1. Graef, *supra* n. 136, 50.
148. For instance, whether it is public or confidential, aggregated or detailed, historical or current.
149. C-238/05, *Asnef-Equifax, Servicios de Información sobre Solvencia y Crédito, SL v. Asociación de Usuarios de Servicios Bancarios (Ausbanc)*, *supra* n. 143, para. 54.
150. *Ibid.*, para. 58.
151. *Ibid.*, paras. 64 et seq.
152. Commission decision M.7217—*Facebook/WhatsApp*, October 3, 2014.

consumer communications services through Facebook "Messenger," which is a competing service to the standalone app "WhatsApp." Mobile apps providing consumer communications services compose a single EEA-wide market regardless of the OS they are designed for and the several functionalities they support.[153] The Commission examined the possible effects of the proposed merger on this relevant market (horizontal effects), as well as on Facebook's position in both online social networking and advertising services markets (vertical effects).

Post-transaction, the parties' combined market share in the relevant market of consumer communications services would amount to 30%-40%. Despite the merger, there would remain several alternative providers, like Skype, Twitter, iMessage, Viber, etc., each one possessing market shares of about 5%-10%. The proposed merger was not expected to materially influence these market shares. However, the Commission recalled an ECJ assessment according to which the consumer communications sector is a fast-growing sector characterized by short innovation cycles in which large market shares are not necessarily indicative of market power and, therefore, of lasting damage to competition which Regulation No. 139/2004 seeks to prevent.[154] Therefore, the Commission further examined the closeness of competition between the investigated undertakings to assess any competitive constraints exerted on each other pre-merger and the likelihood of the latter being eliminated by the envisaged transaction.

In that regard, the Commission noticed that the merging parties' apps differ in several aspects, e.g., their interface, data policy, sources of contacts, etc. Besides, their networks largely overlap, i.e., they are simultaneously used by the same users. These elements advocate for the assumption that the services in question have been rather complementary than competing ones prior to the merger. Consequently, the competitive conditions resulting from the concentration would not differ significantly from the ones existing at the time of the merger.

The Commission further noticed that the relevant market is open to new entries, since consumer communications apps are increasingly standardized, and their development does not require any significant investment in terms of time and resources. Besides, most communications apps are downloaded and installed for free by the user. Consumers are moreover technically capable to use on the same handset several communications services simultaneously. The merging parties do not control any necessary input, like OSs, software solutions, etc., which would enable them to lock-in users to their applications in lieu of any competing ones. The envisaged merger would therefore not pose significant entry barriers, thus disrupting the expansion of competition in the relevant market.

Regarding the issue whether the envisaged merger could strengthen Facebook's position in the online networking and advertising market, the Commission examined two possible scenarios. On the one hand, whether a potential integration of WhatsApp and Facebook could add users and functionalities to the social network of Facebook.

153. *See* Commission decisions M.6281—*Microsoft/Skype*, October 7, 2011; No. M.7047—*Microsoft/Nokia*, December 4, 2013.

154. T-79/12 of 11.12.2013, *Cisco Systems Inc. et al. v. European Commission*, ECLI:EU:T:2013:635, rec. 69.

On the other hand, whether WhatsApp could serve as a provider of online advertising space and a source of user data in order for the latter to be exploited for advertising purposes by Facebook. The first scenario was deemed unlikely to be implemented due to mainly technical hurdles.[155] The second has been considered likely to change user experience within WhatsApp so gravely that would alienate users and cause their outflow to competing apps. Consequently, the Commission has decided not to oppose the transaction.

### [B] The Acquisition of Shazam by Apple

In 2018 the European Commission received notification of the acquisition by Apple Inc. of sole control of the entire undertaking of Shazam Entertainment Ltd.[156] Shazam is the developer and distributor of music recognition apps for smart devices and personal computers. It generates revenues from the display of online advertising, commissions earned on user referrals to digital music streaming and download services, as well as from licensing of music data and analytics services. Apple is a hardware manufacturer and software developer which, among many other services, offers the music and video streaming service called "Apple Music." According to the Commission, the envisaged concentration constituted a conglomerate merger which was meant to combine complementary services of the parties, i.e., Apple's music streaming services with Shazam's music recognition app.

The Commission identified the following competitive concerns: (a) the merged entity directing Shazam's referrals exclusively to Apple Music, (b) denying access of competing music streaming providers to the Shazam app as advertising tool, (c) integrating exclusively Shazam's music recognition functionalities within Apple Music apps, (d) restricting access of competing music streaming providers to Shazam User Data as an input to improve their services.

The Commission concluded that the merged entity would not have the ability to foreclose competing providers of digital music streaming apps and therefore decided not to oppose the scrutinized transaction.[157] Pre-merger Shazam's significance as a customer acquisition channel, marketing tool and provider of user data for digital music streaming providers has been low in relation, e.g., to search engines and social media, email campaigns and the referral mechanisms of other apps. Moreover, the integration of Shazam's functionalities within Apple Music apps would not deprive competing music streaming providers from alternative music recognition technologies. What is more, Shazam's User Data demonstrate limited variety, velocity, volume and value. Therefore, they cannot qualify as an important input to improve digital music streaming services.

---

155. *See* however M.8228—*Facebook/WhatsApp*, May 18, 2017.
156. Commission decision M.8788—*Apple/Shazam*, September 6, 2018.
157. *See ibid.*, paras. 275 et seq.

### [C] The Acquisition of Deliveroo by Amazon

Currently, the Competition and Markets Authority of the UK (CMA) investigates the anticipated acquisition of a minority shareholding and certain rights of Roofoods Ltd (Deliveroo) by Amazon.com NV Investment Holdings LLC, a wholly owned subsidiary of Amazon.com, Inc. (Amazon). Deliveroo is a UK-based online food delivery company operating as an online delivery platform for restaurants while also offering online convenience grocery delivery. Amazon operated a competing online food platform in the UK until November 2018 and wishes to re-enter that market. It remains active in online convenience grocery delivery services to date. The CMA believes that the envisaged merger will cause horizontal non-coordinated foreclosing effects on the markets concerned.

According to a preliminary assessment published on December 11, 2019,[158] online food delivery markets are highly concentrated and present significant entry-barriers.[159] The envisaged merger will result in the combination of the two largest and best-established suppliers in this field. Therefore, it is likely to lessen competition in the relevant markets by impairing the competitive constraints currently faced by the merging companies. The constraints posed by third parties would be insufficient to mitigate this effect. Consequently, the transaction could have a negative impact on effective competition regarding prices, quality improvements, efficiency enhancements, innovation and choice in the relevant markets to the detriment of the consumer.

### [D] Interim Conclusions

Concentrations between undertakings active on the same mobile market may confer on the merged entity significant economic power and control over crucial inputs, thus enabling it to foreclose competition for existing and future rivals. Within oligopolistic mobile markets in particular, the combination of strong suppliers, which have been in close competition pre-merger, may annihilate essential competitive constrains, thus leaving the merged entity out of control and decreasing consumer choice. When the merging undertakings have been active on separate mobile markets, their combination may confer on the merged entity the ability and the incentive to leverage a strong market position from the one market into the other, in a way that contradicts merit-based competition and poses entry barriers. This is conditional upon the merged entity monopolizing essential inputs post-transaction, like technological facilities, personal data or marketing tools.

158. Competition & Markets Authority of the UK, *Anticipated acquisition by Amazon of a minority shareholding and certain rights in Deliveroo*, ME/6836/19 (2019), available at: https://assets.publishing.service.gov.uk/media/5defd083ed915d15f052f549/Summary_of_decision_-_web_version_-----_pdf.pdf, accessed January 5, 2020.

159. Such as the need to build relationships with vendors, couriers and consumers, and to develop the necessary technology to power the logistics.

## §9.06 CONCLUDING REMARKS AND RECOMMENDATIONS

A major conclusion drawn by the above analysis is that mobile industry is dominated by operators of intermediary platforms, like social networks, online search engines and marketplaces. On such websites, separate markets converge, while the established transactional relations are multileveled and multisided, i.e., platform-to-business (P2B), business-to-consumer (B2C), business-to-business (B2B). Through a Communication from 2016,[160] the European Commission underlined the importance of online platforms for the economic growth and the effective functioning of the digital single market. They are supposed to increase citizens' access to information, as well as consumer choice, and to promote data-driven innovation. However, the Commission acknowledges that online platforms also raise new policy and regulatory challenges.

Regarding the desideratum to maintain free and undistorted competition within the common digital market in particular, the Commission identified as an issue of concern the practice of dual-role platforms to unfairly promote their own services to the disadvantage of competing suppliers using the platform to gain downstream market access. This may occur by means of unfair terms and conditions, untransparent use of data and search results. To address these challenges, the Commission proposed the enactment of a uniform legal framework which takes account of all conflicting interests within mobile economy.

To date, however, no harmonization measures have been adopted in relation to the above. Fragmented EU arrangements in force are argued to have an impact on ensuring transparency and accessibility in mobile markets. Such is for instance the provision of General Data Protection Regulation prescribing data portability,[161] which is supposed to facilitate user multi-homing,[162] as well as the provisions of the Regulation 2019/1150 on promoting fairness and transparency for business users of online intermediation services.

The above legislative instruments do not deal with competition law concerns.[163] The latter is meant to provide a precise and technologically neutral definition of multi-sided networks, which has been long expected.[164] In principle, however, it provides civil law remedies for infringements falling under its application scope. This is limited to unilaterally determined terms of use which govern commercial relations between online platforms and sellers offering goods and services to consumers. Consequently, any negotiable terms of use and any sellers providing goods to business

160. *Communication from the Commission to the European Parliament, the Council, the European Economic and social Committee and the Committee of the Regions, Online platforms and the digital single market, Opportunities and challenges for Europe*, SWD(2016) 172 final, COM(2016) 288 final (2016).

161. Article 20 of Regulation (EU) 2016/679 of the European Parliament and of the Council of April 27, 2016 on the protection of natural persons with regard to the processing of personal data and on the free movement of such data, and repealing Directive 95/46/EC, OJ L 119, pp. 1–88.

162. Lancieri, *supra* n. 108, 51.

163. Graef, *supra* n. 136, 4.

164. Diane Coyle, "Practical competition policy implications of digital platforms," University of Cambridge, working paper 01 (2018), 3 et seq. https://www.bennettinstitute.cam.ac.uk/media/uploads/files/Practical_competition_policy_tools_for_digital_platforms.pdf.

customers are not subject to it.[165] Most importantly, an infringement of this Regulation may give rise to concerns about the functioning of competition in the markets affected but does not in itself constitute an anticompetitive practice. The concurrent violation of EU antitrust law must be specifically justified according to the pertinent regulatory framework.

It is a common perception in the legal literature that the traditional EU competition law cannot cope with the peculiarities of the mobile economy. The above case-law review revealed certain relevant adversities. Conventionally, market power and profitability are measured by economic standards. When it comes to mobile markets, however, which are characterized by dynamic competition and non-monetary gains, such weights and measures seem unreliable. A firm may be influential without significant profits. Besides, dominance may be established through data power. Under these circumstances, current competition law doctrines which are based on quantitative thresholds, like the ones governing pricing abuses and the merger control,[166] are challenged.

In lack of EU initiatives, national legal orders attempt to adapt their domestic competition rules to the particularities of digital industry. A new provision added to the German Competition law (GWB) in 2017[167] has established specific nonexhaustive criteria advocating the acquisition of a dominant position by an undertaking in multi-sided markets and networks. Accordingly, the evaluation of an undertaking's market position in such cases should take account of: *(1) direct and indirect network effects, (2) the parallel use of services from different providers and the switching costs for users, (3) the undertaking's economies of scale arising in connection with network effects, (4) the undertaking's access to data relevant for competition, (5) innovation-driven competitive pressure.*

As shown herein, although at EU level the above parameters have not been laid down and codified,[168] they are considered by the competent authorities where appropriate on a case-by-case basis. Such a compilation of criteria, which are formulated abstractly to fit the assessment of different facts, may guide the judicial reasoning when examining anticompetitive conduct in the digital markets. However they will remain a dead letter until, on the one hand, economic analysis provides the necessary toolkit for a systematic assessment of competition in digital markets[169] and, on the other hand, the EU redefines the goals of its competition policy pertaining to the digital common market.[170]

Indeed, as indicated above, the link between data accumulation and market power remains blur. The same is true considering the significance of personal and

165. *See* recs. 12 and 14 of the Regulation.
166. *See* on that Roth, *supra* n. 20, 24; Christoph Wagner, "Impact of digitalization and convergence on merger control in the media sector. Five suggestions for a more adequate balance and format for merger control in the digital age" (2016) CRi 65.
167. Article 18 para. 3c.
168. *See* on that Tobias Lettl, "Digitale Plattformen: Setzt die 9. GWB-Novelle Maßstäbe für die Europäische Union?" (2018) WRP 145, 147 et seq.
169. Coyle, *supra* n. 164, 1; Ott, *supra* n. 126, 196.
170. Lancieri, *supra* n. 108, 45 et seq.

non-personal data for anticompetitive abuses.[171] OLG Düsseldorf overturned the Bundeskartellamt decision condemning the data policy of Facebook, on the ground that it took the above correlations for granted. Nevertheless, the court did not make a stand about the substance of the pertinent speculations. Therefore, it remains open to clarify the relation between volume, scope and quality of personal data collected by an online platform with its capacity to strengthen or secure its market power and to pose entry barriers in the relevant market.

Similar impasses have been observed in the assessment of leveraging market power from one mobile market onto another. In the *Google Maps* case, the England and Wales High Court has taken a liberal position, by applying a de minimis threshold in relation to foreclosing effects caused by self-preferencing practices of digital platforms. It also weighed foreclosure against consumer welfare. In the *Google Shopping* case, however, European Commission followed a rather "by the book" approach, based on merit-based competition.[172] Opposing views and differing conclusions as regards similar practices taking place in the mobile ecosystem can be also noticed among rulings of national competition authorities in EU Member States.[173] These phenomena bear evidence of legal uncertainty.

Furthermore, when it comes in particular to assessing abuses of monopolistic market power by vertically integrated intermediary platforms, legal literature voices the "refusal to supply" doctrine as the appropriate formula.[174] Such an approach would require the European jurisprudence making a stand as to whether goods, such as user traffic, personal and non-personal data, online intermediary services, etc. represent "essential facilities" in the digital economy. However, to adapt the concept of indispensability in the context of such fluid and dynamic markets, as the digital ones, would entail consistent rationalization based on proactive legopolitical and economic argumentation.

It may be argued that the boom in the mobile industry is a relatively recent phenomenon. In the coming years, EU judicial authorities and lawmakers will have the opportunity to crystallize their attitudes toward competition in the common digital market. In broad terms, it appears that the proper revision of EU competition policy regarding mobile economy necessitates a synergy of economic research, political will and legal instruction.

171. Graef, *supra* n. 122, 137 et seq.
172. Critical analysis by Patrick Todd, "Intra-platform exclusion in software markets" (2018) 6 J Antitrust Enforcement 409, 417 et seq.
173. Coyle, *supra* n. 164, 10 et seq.
174. *See* Paal, *supra* n. 131; Strader, *supra* n. 50, 585 et seq.; Mathew Heim and Igor Nikolic, "A FRAND regime for dominant digital platforms" (2019) JIPITEC 38.

# CHAPTER 10
# Taxation of Mobile Applications

*Georgios Matsos & Paschalis Paschalidis*

*Taxation of mobile applications should be regarded as part of business taxation. In Europe, main taxes regarding business activity are the value-added tax and the income tax. However, the highly mobile character of digital economy has led to the introduction of a 'Mini-One-Stop-Shop' for VAT on digital suppliers, while in income taxation the redistribution of taxing powers according to a 'significant digital presence' or even the imposition of a 'digital tax' are currently hot discussion topics.*

## §10.01 INTRODUCTION

The economy of mobile applications is part of the digital economy. Thus, problems posed by their taxation are in principle the ones posed by digital economy in general.

Compared to traditional economy, digital economy is marked by quasi-unlimited, immediate mobility cross-border mobility. Revenue from mobile applications can be produced from any country, no matter where the creator or owner of such mobile applications may reside. Revenue from mobile applications can be earned mainly in three ways: The first one is by receiving payments for the use of mobile applications, the second is for rendering electronic services through mobile applications and the third one is through other types of digital interaction between mobile applications and their users.

These relatively new phenomena pose significant particularities worldwide. In general, there are two main taxations relevant to all types of economic activity, namely, taxation of consumption and taxation of income. Both these issues pose different problems. The European Union (EU) has sought different types of solutions for each type of taxation.

## §10.02 MAIN BUSINESS TAXES IN EUROPE

### [A] Value-Added Tax

The main *consumption* tax in the EU is the widely harmonised Value Added Tax (VAT). VAT is a general consumption tax, which is imposed on almost every transaction and, in principle, on the supply of goods and of services. Final payer of the tax is the consumer of goods or of services. The tax is imposed only if the seller is a person who carries out an independent economic activity ('*Taxable Person*').[1] Tax rate is calculated on the final price of a good or of a service and is *added* on such final price.[2]

In this way, the consumer finally pays a price, which includes the net price and the VAT. Then the taxable persons forward to the state the sums collected from their customers, to the extent that such sums correspond to the 'added value': As its name suggests, the VAT is not a tax imposed on the full turnover of taxable persons, but only on the added value they create. Such added value is easily calculated, by simply deducting the VAT already paid by the taxable persons for '*goods and services [that] are used for the purposes of the taxed transactions of a taxable person*'.[3] Such right to deduct the VAT goes as far as to entitle the taxable persons to receive paid by the government any VAT that they overpaid, if the VAT, they receive from their customers is lower than the VAT they have already paid. The VAT becomes in this way a truly neutral consumption tax.

The EU has very early harmonised the VAT, so that today quasi all VAT rules derive from EU Law: VAT has been harmonised in Europe mainly through Council Directive 77/778/EEC, which has been in the meantime repealed by Directive 2006/112/EC ('VAT Directive'). The latter is regularly modified by newer Directives, so that all VAT rules are finally codified there.

### [B] Income Tax

Income taxation is imposed on individuals and on legal entities, aiming - as the wording suggests - to tax their income. Such taxable income is overwhelmingly defined according to domestic laws.

Income tax is calculated according to tax rates that are usually progressive when the taxpayer is an individual (i.e., they become higher as income becomes higher) or are flat, when the taxpayer is a company or a legal entity (i.e., they remain stable regardless the amount of taxable income). In most jurisdictions, individuals enjoy a tax-free threshold for their lower block of income.

Income tax on business profits – often called corporate tax, when the taxpayer is a corporation – is imposed on net profits. Net profits are usually calculated based on

---

1. Article 9(1) of the VAT Directive.
2. More details on the VAT in a framework of taxation of mobile applications can be found in Höink, *Umsatzsteuer und Apps*, in Solmeke/Taeger/Feldmann (eds), *Mobile Apps, Rechtsfragen und rechtliche Rahmenbedingungen*, Berlin 2013, pp. 327 et seq.
3. Article 168 of the VAT Directive.

generally accepted accounting rules, as they may be defined in the laws. In this process of calculating profits, gross revenue is added and expenses used for the process of generating income are deducted from the taxable base.

Very often taxable profits are adjusted upwards or downwards according to specific law provisions. The resulting taxable base is subject to taxation according to the applicable tax rate.

## §10.03 CROSS-BORDER EFFECTS OF VAT AND OF INCOME TAXATION

### [A] VAT

As analysed above, VAT is a neutral tax and, thus, ideal for cross-border relations, both when crossing intra-EU or extra-EU borders. Four basic principles apply in cross-border transactions concerning the fundamental question of which jurisdiction is entitled to impose the VAT:

(1) Intra-EU B2C (business-to-consumer) transactions are charged with VAT in the Member State where the seller is located.[4]
(2) Intra-EU B2B (business-to-business) transaction are charged with VAT in the Member State the buyer is located.[5]
(3) Extra-EU outbound transactions ('exports') are VAT-free both for business and consumers.[6]
(4) Extra-EU inbound transactions ('imports') are charged with regular VAT at the point of import both for business and consumers.[7]

These cross-borders VAT rules are oriented towards physical crossing of borders.[8] Physical border-crossing makes it more difficult for taxpayers to take advantage of VAT rules in an abusive way. Thus, different rules had to apply for the much easier 'electronic' border-crossing of digital products and services.

Consequently, the main VAT issue with e-services is that e-commerce and e-services – including mobile apps – can support massive distance sales without any need for physical business presence. This easiness of crossing borders has led the EU to seek new VAT rules about digital products.

4. Article 41 of the VAT Directive when it comes to acquisition of goods and Articles 43 and 45 of the VAT Directive when it comes to supply of services.
5. Article 40 of the VAT Directive when it comes to acquisition of goods and Article 44 of the VAT Directive when it comes to supply of services.
6. Article 58 of the VAT Directive.
7. Article 30 of the VAT Directive when it comes to acquisition of goods and Article 59 of the VAT Directive when it comes to supply of services.
8. Details about the general framework governing cross-border transactions can be found in Höink, *Umsatzsteuer und Apps*, in Solmeke/Taeger/Feldmann (eds), *Mobile Apps, Rechtsfragen und rechtliche Rahmenbedingungen*, Berlin 2013, pp. 331 et seq.

Such new rules are already in place and form the main core of what can be called 'taxation of mobile applications' nowadays in Europe.[9]

### [B] Income Taxation

The main criteria for linking a taxpayer to a tax jurisdiction are residence of the taxpayer and source of income.[10] Both criteria entail wholly different range of taxation: Residents are taxed for their worldwide income. Non-residents pay income tax to a jurisdiction only if they have income from sources situated therein.

Although income taxation is not harmonised in the EU, quasi all Member States use both aforementioned criteria (residence and source of income) for imposing income tax.

The simultaneous application of both the aforementioned criteria leads to obvious conflicts, since the same income is taxed in more than one jurisdiction: The country of residence requires to tax according to the world-income rule and the country of source requires to tax according to the source rule. This is a situation of so-called double taxation.

There are two main ways for resolving such conflict. The first one is to implement national measures for the prevention of double taxation – usually in the country of residence. The second one is the conclusion of (usually bilateral) Double Taxation Conventions (DTCs). The latter assign the taxing powers either to the residence or to the source state, by allocating such taxing powers via criteria like the permanent establishment of an undertaking.

In this way, DTCs not only prevent double taxation in a radical way, but they also do something much more important: They set the tax borders between countries. They regulate when the taxing power of one state stops and when the taxing powers of the other begin.

The DTCs are pretty widely based on a Model Tax Convention on Income and on Capital published and regularly updated by the OECD.[11] In this way a quasi-unified global law of DTCs has emerged, where taxpayers know in advance, which rules may approximately apply, when they seek to exercise cross-border activity – though the final text of each DTC contains individual deviations from the legally non-binding OECD Model text.

Setting tax borders through international conventions leads to a relatively inflexible framework of taxing powers for governments. This enables taxpayers with highly mobile products – like digital products in the era of internet – to use and to abuse such framework in order to reduce their tax burden.

---

9. *See* below §10.05.
10. This is not absolute, however. For instance, the United States of America uses the criterion of nationality for taxing the worldwide income of their citizens.
11. The full text is accessible online on the following link: https://www.oecd.org/ctp/model-tax-convention-on-income-and-on-capital-condensed-version-20745419.htm (assessed: 27 January 2020).

## §10.04 VAT RULES SPECIFICALLY APPLICABLE ON MOBILE APPS

### [A] 'Electronically Supplied' Services or Goods

With the VAT being in principle paid at the country of residence of the supplier, many digital providers became in the past residents of Member States with low VAT rates. In order to avoid such distortions of competition, the EU changed the VAT rules of digital economy.

Thus, since 1 January 2015, VAT on all electronically supplied services[12] is imposed in the country where the consumer is located. According to these rules, if consumers buy a smartphone from an EU country than their country of residence, they must pay the VAT rate of that other country to that other country. However, if they buy a mobile application, then they pay the VAT rate of their country of residence, which the supplier forwards then through the so-called Mini-One-Stop-Shop (MOSS) to the country of residence of the consumer.[13]

This tax treatment concerns *inter alia*: digitised products, services taking place on an electronic network, services automatically generated from a computer via the Internet or an electronic network, internet service packages, website supply, web-hosting, distance maintenance of programmes and of equipment, supply of software and software updates, electronic supply of images, of music of films and of games, as well as distance teaching.

On the contrary, no electronic supply takes place in case of broadcasting and telecommunications services, supply of files in CDs and DVDs, video cassettes, disks and similar tangible media. Since mobile applications are never included in the aforementioned categories, they are always considered electronically provided services. Of course, the same happens for all the services provided through the mobile applications.

It is really important to clarify the distinction between selling a product online and electronically providing services. For example, if people download the application of Facebook on their smartphones, via a marketplace, they purchase a product. This means that VAT must be paid on the country where Facebook company is located. In case the same persons are advertised through Facebook, VAT must be paid on the country where they are located.

### [B] Detection of Customers' Location

As the VAT rate is determined according to the customer's location, it is crucial to identify where customers are located. Customers subject to the VAT are taxed in the country where they are registered or, if they receive goods or services through fixed premises in another country, in the latter country. Consumers not subject to the VAT are taxed in their country of residence.

12. As well as telecommunications and broadcasting.
13. *See* below §10.04[C].

Localising customers correctly is a task sometimes very difficult. For this purpose, the EU sets various (though rebuttable) presumptions. Where the physical location of consumers is necessary for the supply of services, they are identified through their physical presence.[14] For instance, when it is verified that the consumers use a telephone box, a telephone kiosk, a Wi-Fi hot spot, an internet café, a restaurant or a hotel lobby, they are presumed to be established, to have their permanent address and usually reside at the place of that location. In case not such a physical presence is verified, the consumers are located through their fixed landline,[15] the country code of their SIM[16] or their decoder.[17] If none of the aforementioned ways is technologically possible, it is presumed that the customer is located at the place identified as such by the supplier.[18]

In order to reverse a presumption, taxpayers should adduce three items of non-contradictory evidence, which indicate their establishment, permanent address or usual residence. Evidence can be limited to just one piece, in case the total value of the provided services does not exceed EUR 100,000 per year.[19] If it is the tax authorities who attempt to reverse a presumption, they must prove misuse or abuse by the supplier.[20]

### [C] MOSS System

As already stated above, if a customer in the mobile app transaction is not subject to VAT, then the supplier is subject to the VAT in the Member State of the customer. However, as it would be very onerous for suppliers to operate VAT procedures in many or in all EU Member States, since 1 January 2015, providers of digital services and goods may use the so-called MOSS system. Through the MOSS, cross-border providers can comply with the requirement of applying different VAT rates depending upon the customer's location by operating only in one EU Member State – which is the Member State of their tax residence.

MOSS system is available in the form of the Union scheme, for suppliers established in the EU, and in the form of the non-Union scheme, for suppliers not established in the EU.[21]

The use of an MOSS is optional and very flexible, as it automatically applies in all those Member States, in which a supplier has clients. MOSS VAT returns, along with VAT due, are submitted on a quarterly basis. Suppliers must submit their total pre-VAT turnover, applicable VAT rates and total amount of VAT charged to their clients per Member State.

14. Article 24a of the Regulation No. 282/2011.
15. Article 24b, point (a) of the Regulation No. 282/2011.
16. Article 24b, point (b) of the Regulation No. 282/2011.
17. Article 24b, point (c) of the Regulation No. 282/2011.
18. Article 24b, point (d) of the Regulation No. 282/2011.
19. Article 1 of the Regulation No. 2459/2017.
20. Article 24d of the Regulation No. 282/2011.
21. Article 1 para. 3 of the Council Directive 2017/2455.

Registration to the MOSS system does not affect the national VAT status. Taxpayers having already a VAT registration in their Member State of residence simply extend their registration using the same VAT number. If no VAT registration exists already, suppliers can register for a first time specifically under the MOSS rules. Invoicing is subject to the domestic legislation of the supplier and not to the jurisdiction of the customers.[22]

From 1 January 2019, suppliers registered in the MOSS system can unregister, if they fall below an annual turnover threshold deriving from electronically provided below EUR 10,000. If suppliers make use of this option, then they cannot re-register in MOSS for the next two years.

## §10.05 INCOME TAXATION OF DIGITAL ECONOMY: PROPOSED EU-RULES

### [A] Cause and Action Plan about the Taxation

While particularities of the digital economy in the area of the VAT have been adequately dealt with through the introduction of the MOSS system, challenges in the area of income taxation still lie ahead.

High mobility of digital products enables enterprises to easily locate their residence and their development departments in low tax countries, while they can still sell their products across the globe, without having any physical presence. Such a low tax jurisdiction can be situated in the EU or outside the EU. In this way, they make profits taxed with very low rates, if at all, by simply using the standard rules of Double Tax Conventions on business profits.

It has been, thus, clear since many years that income taxation of digital economy - including of course the economy of mobile applications - represents a challenge not easy to confront.

The European Commission has been a pioneer in suggesting solutions, which take into account the specific characteristics of digital economy and create a model of taxation different from the classical source/residence scheme, or even different from classical taxation of business profits through income tax. Two Directive Proposals have been launched in March 2018.

The first Directive Proposal attempts to shift focus from source and residence to the *digital channels*, i.e., to the ways that value is created in the world of digital applications beyond the typical scheme of remuneration for a service or for a product. It is no coincidence that many digital applications, including mobile applications are free of charge for their end users. However, businesses with such free applications are still very lucrative for their suppliers. Google products, to mention a set of mobile applications mostly used, are free, like Android, Gmail, Google Maps and Google Search. However, Google still makes tenths of billions of profits on a global level,

22. Article 1 para. 2 of the Council Directive 2017/2455.

despite its free-of-charge products for the end user. It is exactly this phenomenon that the first Directive Proposal tries to address.

The second Directive Proposal aims to tackle that part of income, which Member States fail to tax via a totally new tax system.

### [B] Corporate Taxation Based on a 'Significant Digital Presence'

The first Directive Proposal of the European Commission aims to draw corporate income taxation of digital business out of the strict territoriality of residence and source. Main goal is to link with the EU taxable profits acquired in the EU through digital interaction, regardless if taxpayers are tax residents of an EU Member State.

Thus, every digital platform is considered linked with a European state, via a '*virtual permanent establishment*', if someone has a '*significant digital presence*' within the EU.[23] Significant digital presence takes place when services are consisted wholly or partially through a digital interface in a Member State of the EU.

Such significant digital presence depends upon the number of *users* of a digital application (including mobile ones). A 'user' is a person using electronic devices in an EU Member State, in order to access a digital interface, through which digital services are supplied.[24] Users are identified on the basis of their IP address or of any other valid method of geolocation.[25] Revenues are assigned to a Member State according to the frequency that devices are used to access a digital interface through which digital services are supplied.[26]

To affirm such 'significant digital presence' at least one out of the following three criteria has to be met:

(a) the proportion of total revenues obtained in that tax period and resulting from the supply of those digital services to users located in that Member State in that tax period exceeds EUR 7,000,000;
(b) the number of users of one or more of those digital services who are located in that Member State in that tax period exceeds EUR 100,000;
(c) the number of business contracts for the supply of any such digital service that are concluded in that tax period by users located in that Member State exceeds EUR 3,000[27]'.

These criteria must be calculated on a consolidated basis for all associated enterprises of a supplier.[28] Member States are free to lower the threshold of revenue or of users, so that they link more digital suppliers to their taxing powers.[29]

23. Article 4 para. 1 of the Directive Proposal.
24. Article 4 para. 4 of the Directive Proposal.
25. Article 4 para. 6 of the Directive Proposal.
26. Article 4 para. 7 of the Directive Proposal.
27. Article 4 para. 3 of the Directive Proposal.
28. Article 4 para. 3 of the Directive Proposal.
29. Article 4 para. 2 of the Directive Proposal.

It is clear that through the criterion of users and the value that such users create, a digital enterprise may be required to pay income tax, although profits are not formally generated within the territory of the European Union!

Profits are attributed to a Member State accordingly to the level of profits that an enterprise would have earned in its territory, in case it was a separate and independent enterprise performing the same or similar activities under the same or similar conditions. To this end, economically significant activities should be taken into account relevant to the development, enhancement, maintenance, protection and exploitation of the enterprise's intangible assets. Such activities could be collection, storage, processing, analysis, deployment and sale of user-level data; collection, storage, processing and display of user-generated content; sale of online advertising space; making available of third-party created content on a digital marketplace.[30]

### [C] Proposal for a Digital Tax

The second Directive Proposal of the European Commission aims to replace classical income taxation in the area of digital economy through a different type of tax, which is widely called 'digital tax' since that Directive Proposal came to surface.[31] The basic idea behind the digital tax is the value creation through algorithms, know-how, sales functions and user data. Under such concept, even a user's 'like' in a social media page can create value, because it increases page traffic.[32]

Unlike the first Directive Proposal, this second one alters fundamentally the object of income taxation. Aiming to combat tax avoidance, tax is not any more imposed on profits, but on gross revenues from certain digital activities, including mobile applications.[33] Groups of companies can choose one group member company to be liable to pay the entire tax burden on behalf of the group.[34]

Crucial about digital tax is the role of internet users in determining value creation. Taxable revenues will be the following:

(a) the placing on a digital interface of advertising targeted at users of that interface;
(b) the making available to users of a multi-sided digital interface which allows users to find other users and to interact with them, and which may also facilitate the provision of underlying supplies of goods or services directly between users;

30. Article 5 of the Directive Proposal.
31. Some European countries have already imposed a digital tax, before the EU decides whether it adopts the second Directive Proposal. *See* a list of such countries in: https://taxfoundation.org/digital-taxes-europe-2019/ (assessed: 27 January 2020).
32. The European Commission estimates that more than EUR 5 billion per tax year can be generated for the Member States of the EU, if the tax rate applied is of 3%.
33. Article 3 of the Directive Proposal.
34. Article 9 of the Directive Proposal.

(c) the transmission of data collected about users and generated from users' activities on digital interfaces.[35]

A person is considered taxable, only if both following criteria are met:

(a) the total amount of worldwide revenues reported by the entity for the relevant financial year exceeds EUR 750,000,000;
(b) the total amount of taxable revenues obtained by the entity within the Union during the relevant financial year exceeds EUR 50,000,000.[36]

The power to collect said tax is attributed to those Member States, in which both above mentioned criteria are met.[37]

Tax rate will be 3% calculated on the gross revenues.[38]

Users will be localised and proportion of an entity's total taxable revenues will be calculated according to the criteria[39] below:

(a) If a digital advertising interface targeted at users of that interface is placed, users are localised when such interface is used on their devices at a time when the device is being used in that Member State in that tax period to access said interface. In this case, taxable revenues will be calculated upon to how often an advertisement has appeared on users' devices in that tax period.
(b) If a multi-sided digital interface is made available to users, allowing them to find other users and to interact with them and which may also facilitate the provision of underlying supplies of goods or services directly between users, they can be localised: (i) If the digital interface enables underlying supplies of goods or services directly between users, then taxable revenues are calculated according to the number of users having used the interface during a taxable period in a Member State to really conclude underlying transactions. Or: (ii) If digital services or products are delivered through a multi-sided digital interface, which users access at least for part of a tax period through an account opened using a device in a Member State, then taxable revenues are calculated according to the number of users holding such an account. The location where that underlying supply takes place is never taken into account.[40]
(c) When data collected about users and generated from their activities on digital interfaces is transmitted, users are localised if data generated from them have used a device in that Member State to access a digital interface. In this case, taxable revenues are calculated according to the number of users from whom data has been generated.

35. Article 3 para. 1 of the Directive Proposal.
36. Article 4 para. 1 of the Directive Proposal.
37. Article 5 para. 1 of the Directive Proposal.
38. Article 8 of the Directive Proposal.
39. Article 5 paras 2 and 3 of the Directive Proposal.
40. Article 5 para. 4 of the Directive Proposal.

According to the Proposal, the place from which payments for taxable service are performed is never taken into account as a criterion to localise users.[41] Localisation is feasible through their IP address or through any other method of geolocation.[42] Data collected should not reach total identification of users,[43] in order to protect anonymity, etc.

When a business entity falls within the scope of the proposed digital tax, it will also be subject to many procedural obligations provided for in the Directive Proposal itself.[44]

## §10.06 CONCLUSION

While in the area of the VAT, taxation of mobile applications has been adjusted on an EU level to the particularities of the digital economy through the MOSS system, allowing easy access to the entire European Market for any digital provider, in the area of income corporate taxation, things have not changed much yet on a *de lege lata* basis.

However, both Directive Proposals aim to change this. The European Commission aims on the one hand to develop the notion of a virtual permanent establishment, so that income is attributed to a jurisdiction solely on the basis of a 'significant digital presence'. On the other hand, the second Directive Proposal aims to fundamentally reform taxation of digital economy, by refocusing from the profits to the gross revenues and having explicitly in mind the digital giants.

Even if the EU as a whole fail in the foreseeable future to adopt the Directive Proposals, it is certain that many individual countries will proceed to the direction either of a digital tax or of the attribution of profits according solely to the digital presence of mobile applications. Future is unknown, but will be for certain exciting.

41. Article 5 para. 4 of the Directive Proposal.
42. Article 5 para. 5 of the Directive Proposal.
43. Article 5 para. 6 of the Directive Proposal.
44. Articles 10 et seq. of the Directive Proposal. However, in case it ceases to be liable to the present tax in the Member State of its choice, then it shall change the Member State of its identification.

CHAPTER 11

# App Stores: Liability Issues and the New Regulatory Framework on Online Platforms

*Ioannis Iglezakis*

*App Stores play a central role in the app ecosystem and, therefore, legal regulations ensuring a fair and transparent treatment for app developers are essential to ensure their success. Not only the case law of the CJEU but also EU Member States' case law has dealt extensively with the issue of online intermediaries liability for the infringement of third-party rights, shaping the limits of liability of Internet intermediaries for hosted and user generated content. Besides the issue of liability of app stores acting as intermediaries, which will be discussed in this chapter, fairness and transparency must be also ensured, to provide legal certainty and an innovation-friendly environment. The recently adopted EU Regulation 2019/1150 introduces new rules, promoting fairness and transparency for business users of online intermediation services which apply effectively to app stores. The Regulation will apply from July 12, 2020. In this chapter, the effect of this new Regulation on app stores and the mobile ecosystem will be examined.*

## §11.01 INTRODUCTION

App stores are online platforms which host third parties' mobile applications, and as such, they have employed a successful new business model, contributing greatly to the creation of the thriving mobile app market. Online platforms, in general, have brought dramatic changes in today's digital society and play a prominent role in the creation of "digital value," and therefore, they are of great importance to the functioning of the digital single market.[1] To reap the benefits of the platform economy, including mobile app economy, it is essential to ensure that a balanced regulatory framework is in place that supports the development and success of online platforms.

Certain legal aspects such as the issue of liability for infringing third parties' rights are subject to existing legislation. Liability for apps is an issue mainly concerning apps developers, app providers and app stores.[2] While the liability issues related to the first two categories is dealt with in Chapters 2 and 3 of this book, the issue of the liability of app stores which publish and offer apps remains to be discussed. App stores play a very important role concerning the marketing of apps and legislation should encourage their efforts to make available innovative technology through their platforms.[3] It should be considered, however, what happens if app stores as intermediaries are infringing upon intellectual property rights or other third-party rights, and whether they can be held liable for such behavior.

An essential factor for the development of a mobile ecosystem, which is competitive, fair and transparent, is the adoption of specific rules on EU level, so that undertakings and particularly, SMEs are benefited, and thus, online platforms cannot behave in an unfair way, damaging to the legitimate interests of business users and consequently, to consumers. For that purpose, the EU has adopted Regulation 2019/1150 "on promoting fairness and transparency for business users of online intermediation services."[4] The regulation provides new rules which give business users of online platforms effective legal protection vis-à-vis online platforms and create a transparent and innovation-friendly regulatory environment in that field. In this chapter we will present the effect of the regulation on app stores.

## §11.02 LIABILITY OF APP STORES UNDER THE E-COMMERCE DIRECTIVE

The general legal framework regulating the liability of intermediary service providers is laid down in the EU E-Commerce Directive,[5] which applies to information society services. The definition of information society services is provided by Directive 2015/1535[6] which states that: "'service' means any Information Society service, that is to say, any service normally provided for remuneration, at a distance, by electronic means and at the individual request of a recipient of services."[7] In addition, according to Recital 18 of the E-Commerce Directive, the concept of information society services

1. European Commission Communication, Online Platforms and the Digital Single Market. Opportunities and Challenges for Europe, COM/2016/288 final.
2. CF Baumgartner, in: U. Baumgartner/Ewald, *Apps und Recht*, 2013, p. 124.
3. *See*, *inter alia*, A. Savin, *EU Internet Law*, 2014, pp. 104 et seq.
4. OJ L 186, 11.7.2019, p. 57, ELI: http://data.europa.eu/eli/reg/2019/1150/oj.
5. Directive 2000/31/EC of the European Parliament and of the Council of 8 June 2000 on certain legal aspects of information society services, in particular electronic commerce, in the Internal Market, OJ L 178, 17/07/2000.
6. Directive (EU) 2015/1535 of the European Parliament and of the Council of 9 September 2015 laying down a procedure for the provision of information in the field of technical regulations and of rules on Information Society services, OJ L 241, 17.9.2015, pp. 1–15.
7. Directive 2015/1535:

include services which represent an economic activity and may extend to services which are not remunerated by those who receive them. Such a case would be where the service provider is remunerated by income generated by advertisement posted on a website (C-291/13).[8]

The CJEU in its *L'Oréal v. eBay* judgment has indicated that "an internet service consisting of facilitating relations between sellers and buyers of goods is, in principle, a service for the purposes of the directive 2000/31."[9] App stores are online market-places, which facilitate the conclusion of contracts between app providers and end-users. Since app stores' services are provided at a distance, by electronic means for the processing and storage of the data, and at the individual request of the recipient of services, they are deemed as information society services.

An app store is a service provider in the sense of E-Commerce Directive even when the use of the platform is provided free of charge. In such a case, the requirement for remuneration is satisfied by revenue coming from advertisements, "publicity or from secondary use of users' data."[10] The above is further supported by the Digital Content Directive which applies to content provided either for money or in exchange of any other counter-performance, including but not limited to access to personal or other data as well.[11]

App stores offer—among others—hosting services to app providers as well as to end-users. They host apps on their servers and at the same time, store data of app providers and platform users, who have opened accounts on the app platform. In addition, they provide payment services and keep account of the transactions conducted via its online platform. Users of app stores upload data or applications on these platforms. As the uploaded content may be unlawful, e.g., contain hate speech or infringe upon third parties' intellectual property rights, the issue which arises is whether operators of app stores can benefit from the liability exemptions provided for in Articles 12–15 of the Directive 2000/31.

---

> For the purposes of this definition: (i) "*at a distance*" means that the service is provided without the parties being simultaneously present; (ii) "*by electronic means*" means that the service is sent initially and received at its destination by means of electronic equipment for the processing (including digital compression) and storage of data, and entirely transmitted, conveyed and received by wire, by radio, by optical means or by other electromagnetic means; (iii) "*at the individual request of a recipient of services*" means that the service is provided through the transmission of data on individual request ... .

8. http://curia.europa.eu/juris/document/document.jsf?docid=157524&doclang=EN. Case C-291/13, *Sotiris Papasavvas v. O Fileleftheros Dimosia Etairia Ltd.*
9. C-324/09.
10. Vassilis Hatzopoulos and Sofia Roma, *Caring for Sharing? Collaborative Economy under EU Law*, Common Market Law Review 54(1): 81–127, February 2017, available online at https://www.researchgate.net/publication/316094932_Caring_for_sharing_The_collaborative_economy_under_EU_law.
11. Proposal for a Directive of the European Parliament and of the Council on certain aspects concerning contracts for the supply of digital content COM/2015/0634 final—2015/0287 (COD), available online at https://eur-lex.europa.eu/legal-content/EN/TXT/?uri=celex%3A52015PC0634.

The E-Commerce Directive grants intermediaries an exemption from liability as regards the following activities: (a) the provision of transmission of information and access to a communication network ("mere conduit"), (b) the automatic, intermediate and temporary storage of information ("caching") and (c) hosting (Articles 12–14). Thus, the exemptions apply to intermediary service providers, not content providers, and to activities of a merely technical, automatic and passive nature.[12] These provisions and Article 15, providing that ISPs are not under a general obligation to monitor unlawful information, are designed to facilitate the provision of information society services by protecting ISPs from civil or criminal liability for the communication of unlawful content provided by third parties.[13] Nevertheless, to strike a balance between the different interests, the Directive recognizes that ISPs have a duty to act, under certain circumstances, with a view to preventing or stopping illegal activities.[14]

Up to date, there is dense case law regarding ISP liability, both from national courts of EU Member States and the CJEU, which also affect the potential liability of app stores. The most relevant cases will be described below.

## §11.03 CASE LAW ON INTERNET PLATFORM LIABILITY

### [A] CJEU Google France and Google[15]

Vuitton, a company selling luxury bags and other leather goods, which is the proprietor of the Community trademark "Vuitton" and of the French national trademarks "Louis Vuitton" and "LV," became aware that the entry, by internet users, of terms constituting its trademarks into Google's search engine triggered the display, under the heading "sponsored links," of links to sites offering imitation versions of Vuitton's products. And also that Google offered advertisers the possibility of selecting also keywords corresponding to Vuitton's trademarks in combination with expressions indicating imitation, such as "imitation" and "copy." Consequently, Vuitton brought proceeding against Google with a view, inter alia, to obtaining a declaration that Google had infringed its trademarks.

In this case it was discussed whether Article 14 of the E-Commerce Directive is to be interpreted as meaning that an internet referencing service such as Google's "AdWords" constitutes an information society service consisting in the storage of information supplied by the advertiser, with the result that that information is the subject of "hosting" within the meaning of that Article and that the referencing service provider therefore cannot be held liable prior to its being informed of the unlawful

12. A. Lodder, "'Directive 2000/31 on Certain Legal Aspects of Information Society Services, in Particular Electronic Commerce', in the Internal Market," in A. Lodder and A. Murray (eds.), *EU Regulation of E-Commerce. A Commentary*, 2017, p. 47.
13. A. Lodder and N. Lodder, Electronic Commerce Directive, in: S. Gijrath, S.v.d. Hof, A. Lodder and G.-J. Zwenne, *Concise European Data Protection, E-Commerce and IT Law*, (3rd ed.), 2018, p. 305.
14. Directive 2000/31, Recital 40.
15. CJEU, Judgment of the Court of March 23, 2010, Joined Cases C-236/08–C-238/08, ECLI: EU:C:2010:159.

conduct of that advertiser. The Court held that in order to establish whether the liability of a referencing service provider may be limited under the hosting exemption, it is necessary to examine whether the role played by that service provider is neutral, in the sense that its conduct is merely technical, automatic and passive, indicating a lack of knowledge or control of the data which it stores.[16] If the service provider has not played such a role, it cannot be held liable for the data which it had stored at the request of an advertiser. The exemption from liability does not apply, however, if the service provider, having obtained knowledge of the unlawful nature of those data or of that advertiser's activities, failed to act expeditiously to remove or to disable access to the data concerned.[17]

### [B] CJEU Case *L'Oréal SA v. eBay*[18]

In this case, the CJEU has dealt with the issue whether the operator of an electronic marketplace can be held liable for trademark infringement by third parties which offer for sale goods on its platform.

L'Oréal brought actions against eBay and sought a ruling, first, that eBay and the individual defendants are liable for sales of seventeen items made by those individuals through the website www.ebay.co.uk. L'Oréal claimed that those sales infringed the rights conferred on it by, *inter alia*, the figurative Community trademark including the words "Amor Amor" and the national word mark "Lancôme." Second, L'Oréal submitted that eBay is liable for the use of L'Oréal trademarks where those marks are displayed on eBay's website and where sponsored links triggered by the use of keywords corresponding to the trademarks are displayed on the websites of search engine operators, such as Google.

The court examined, first, the issue whether the service provided by the operator of an online marketplace falls within the scope of the hosting exemption in Article 14(1) of Directive 2000/31. It held that an internet service consisting in facilitating relations between sellers and buyers of goods is, in principle, a service for the purposes of Directive 2000/31. The definition of "information society service," according to the court, includes services provided at a distance by means of electronic equipment for the processing and storage of data, at the individual request of a recipient of services and, normally, for remuneration. Hence, the operation of an online marketplace can bring all those elements into play.[19]

It is not sufficient that the service by the operator of an online marketplace includes the storage of information transmitted to it by its customers-sellers for that service to fall within the scope of Article 14 of Directive 2000/31. The provider must be an intermediary provider and assume a neutral status as pointed out in the Google France and Google decision. That is not the case where the service provider plays an active role of such a kind as to give it knowledge of, or control over, those data. So, e.g.,

16. *Ibid.*, para. 114.
17. *Ibid.*, para. 120.
18. CJEU, Judgment of the Court of July 12, 2011, Case C-324/09, ECLI:EU:C:2011:474.
19. *Ibid.*, para. 109.

if the operator has provided assistance by way of optimizing the presentation of the offers for sale in question or promoting those offers, then, according to the court, it must be considered not to have taken a neutral position between the customer-seller concerned and potential buyers but to have played an active role, and therefore, it cannot rely on the hosting exemption.[20]

Second, the court went on to examine the existence of "awareness" from the part of the operator of the online marketplace. In particular, according to Article 14(1) of Directive 2000/31, the service provider is exempted from any liability for unlawful data that it has stored on condition that it has not had "actual knowledge of illegal activity or information" and, as regards claims for damages, has not been "aware of facts or circumstances from which the illegal activity or information is apparent" or that, having obtained such knowledge or awareness, it has acted expeditiously to remove, or disable access to, the information.

The court interpreted this requirement as covering every situation in which the provider concerned becomes aware, in one way or another, of facts or circumstances on the basis of which a diligent economic operator should have identified the illegality in question and acted appropriately.[21] The CJEU states, particularly, that:

> The situations thus covered include, in particular, that in which the operator of an online marketplace uncovers, as the result of an investigation undertaken on its own initiative, an illegal activity or illegal information, as well as a situation in which the operator is notified of the existence of such an activity or such information. In the second case, although such a notification admittedly cannot automatically preclude the exemption from liability provided for in Article 14 of Directive 2000/31, given that notifications of allegedly illegal activities or information may turn out to be insufficiently precise or inadequately substantiated, the fact remains that such notification represents, as a general rule, a factor of which the national court must take account when determining, in the light of the information so transmitted to the operator, whether the latter was actually aware of facts or circumstances on the basis of which a diligent economic operator should have identified the illegality.[22]

### [C] CJEU Case *Papasavvas v. Fileleftheros*[23]

This case concerned an action for damages brought against a Cypriot newspaper, the editor-in-chief and journalists in the newspaper for harm caused by articles published on the paper's website that were of an allegedly defamatory nature. The Court held that the limitations of civil liability specified in Articles 12–14 of Directive 2000/31 are capable of applying in the context of proceedings between individuals relating to civil liability for defamation, where the conditions referred to in those articles are satisfied.[24] It clarified, thus, that the field of application of the E-Commerce Directive is wide and

20. *Ibid.*, para. 116.
21. *Ibid.*, para. 121.
22. *Ibid.*, para. 122.
23. CJEU, Judgment of the Court of September 11, 2014, C-291/13, ECLI:EU:C:2014:2209.
24. *Ibid.*, para. 50.

defamation cases are not excluded from its ambit. It also noted that the directive does not preclude the application of rules of civil liability for defamation to information society service providers.[25]

Most importantly, the court dealt with the issue whether the limitations of civil liability specified in Articles 12–14 of Directive 2000/31 are applicable to the case of a newspaper publishing company which operates a website on which the online version of a newspaper drafted by staff or freelance journalists is posted, that company being, moreover, remunerated by income generated by commercial advertisements posted on that website. Additionally, it addressed the issue whether the answer to that question depended on whether or not access to that website is free of charge. The court referred to its previous case law in Google France and Google and mentioned that the exemptions from liability established in that directive cover only cases in which the activity of the information society service provider is of a merely technical, automatic and passive nature, which implies that that service provider has neither knowledge of nor control over the information which is transmitted or stored.

However, since a newspaper publishing company which posts an online version of a newspaper on its website has, in principle, knowledge about the information which it posts and exercises control over that information, it cannot be considered to be an "intermediary service provider," whether or not access to that website is free of charge. Thus, the court came to the conclusion that the safe harbors of Articles 12–14 of the E-Commerce Directive do not apply in that case.

### [D] ECHR Case *Delfi AS v. Estonia*

The decision of the Grand Chamber of the European Court of Human Rights (ECtHR) in the case *Delfi AS v. Estonia* was issued on June 16, 2015,[26] following the Chamber judgment of October 10, 2013. The Court examined a complaint concerning user generated expressive activity on the Internet, but as far as the freedom of expression was concerned. The applicant company, which owned an Internet news portal in Estonia, was held liable for defamatory comments made, following the publication of an article on its portal concerning a ferry company. These comments were posted by users of the portal under the article and essentially constituted hate speech and direct incitement to violence. As a result the company was ordered to pay EUR 320 in damages and consequently, it filed a complaint before the ECtHR. The Chamber of the Court found that there had been no violation of Article 10 ECHR and so, the case was referred to the Grand Chamber at the request of the applicant company.

The Grand Chamber considered that the case concerned the "duties and responsibilities" of Internet news portals, under Article 10 §2 of the Convention,[27] when they provide for economic purposes a platform for user generated comments on previously published content and some users—whether identified or anonymous—engage in clearly unlawful speech, which infringes the personality rights of others and amounts

25. *Ibid.*, para. 36.
26. Case of *Delfi AS v. Estonia*, Application No. 64569/09.
27. *Ibid.*, para. 113.

to hate speech and incitement to violence against them. The Court stressed out that the case was related to a large professionally managed Internet news portal run on a commercial basis which published news articles of its own and invited its readers to comment on them, and not any discussion fore where users can freely discuss their ideas on any topic without any intervention by the forum's manager.

The Court found that, as a professional publisher, the applicant company should have been familiar with the legislation and case law and that the Estonian courts' finding of liability against Delfi was a justified and proportionate restriction on the portal's freedom of expression.[28] It noted that it is not disputed that the comments posted by readers in reaction to the news article published in the comments section on the applicant company's Internet news portal were of a clearly unlawful nature. The applicant company removed the comments once it was notified by the injured party, and described them as "infringing" and "illicit." The Court was of the view that the majority of the impugned comments amounted to hate speech or incitements to violence and as such did not enjoy the protection of Article 10.[29] Therefore, the freedom of expression of the authors of the comments was not in issue in the present case, but rather whether the domestic courts' decisions, holding the applicant company liable for these comments posted by third parties, were in breach of its freedom to impart information as guaranteed by Article 10 of the Convention. The Court observed that, although the applicant company immediately removed the comments in question from its website upon notification by L.'s lawyers, the Supreme Court held the applicant company liable on the basis of the national law, as it should have prevented the publication of comments with clearly unlawful contents.[30] The court found that the applicant company had the technical means to delete the comments posted on the news portal and thus, it was considered to have exercised a substantial degree of control over the comments published on its portal. It thus came to the conclusion that Delfi's involvement in making public the comments on its news articles on its news portal went beyond that of a passive, purely technical service provider.

Consequently, the imposition on the applicant company of an obligation to remove from its website, without delay after publication, comments that amounted to hate speech and incitements to violence, and were thus clearly unlawful on their face, did amount, according to the Court's findings, to a disproportionate interference with its freedom of expression.[31] The court, then, examined whether the applicant company had put in place mechanisms that were capable of filtering comments amounting to hate speech or speech entailing an incitement to violence.

The Court noted that there was a disclaimer on the Delfi news portal stating that the writers of the comments were accountable for them, and that the posting of comments that were contrary to good practice or contained threats, insults, obscene expressions or vulgarities, or incited hostility, violence or illegal activities, was

28. *Ibid.*, para. 115.
29. *Ibid.*, para. 117.
30. *Ibid.*, para. 141.
31. *Ibid.*, para. 119.

prohibited.[32] And also, that the portal had an automatic system of deletion of comments based on stems of certain vulgar words and it had a notice-and-take-down system in place, whereby anyone could notify it of an inappropriate comment by simply clicking on a button designated for that purpose, while occasionally the administrators removed inappropriate comments on their own initiative. However, the automatic word-based filter failed to filter out odious hate speech and speech inciting violence posted by readers and thus limited its ability to expeditiously remove the offending comments, which remained online for six weeks. Thus, the measures taken by Delfi to remove the offensive comments had been clearly insufficient. Finally, the compensation of EUR 320 imposed on Delfi was not to be considered as disproportionate.

By way of conclusion, the Court mentioned that:

> based on the concrete assessment of the above aspects, taking into account the reasoning of the Supreme Court in the present case, in particular the extreme nature of the comments in question, the fact that the comments were posted in reaction to an article published by the applicant company on its professionally managed news portal run on a commercial basis, the insufficiency of the measures taken by the applicant company to remove without delay after publication comments amounting to hate speech and speech inciting violence and to ensure a realistic prospect of the authors of such comments being held liable, and the moderate sanction imposed on the applicant company, the Court finds that the domestic courts' imposition of liability on the applicant company was based on relevant and sufficient grounds, having regard to the margin of appreciation afforded to the respondent State. Therefore, the measure did not constitute a disproportionate restriction on the applicant company's right to freedom of expression.[33]

### [E] German Supreme Court Decision *Marions Kochbuch*

In a decision of the German Supreme Court ("BGH") the issue was whether the operator of a website for cook recipes was liable for infringing third parties' rights, on the grounds that it published and made available to the public information derived from third parties in its website. The Court came to the conclusion that the platform operator was liable because he made the user generated content his own.[34] The criteria employed by the court in this decision were the following:

(1) The user generated data were the core editorial content of the website.
(2) The user generated data were checked before made available to the public.
(3) The third party content was published with the symbol of the platform operator and was integrated in the design of the website.
(4) The user generated data were marked with the logo of the website, while the information of the content provider stood in the background.

32. *Ibid.*, para. 155.
33. *Ibid.*, para. 162.
34. BGH, 12.11.2009, I ZR 166/07—*Marions Kochbuch*.

(5) The platform operator had ensured comprehensive use and exploitation rights over the user content.
(6) The operator makes commercial use of the user generated content in his website.

This decision is of outmost importance for app stores, since they make available third-party content, i.e., apps. Although apps are not typical editorial content, they are the content of app developers which is hosted in the app platforms. Apps are the essential content of app stores, and this is produced from third parties, i.e., app developers. App stores do not check all apps before publishing them, but reserve the right to delete or reject apps that do not meet the requirements of app stores.[35]

### [F] Application of Case-Law Principles to the Issue of Apps' Liability

Apps stores make available third-party content, i.e., apps, and thus, they are acting as intermediaries; therefore, they can rely on the safe harbor of Article 14 of the E-Commerce Directive and escape liability for third-party content, e.g., apps infringing IP rights or privacy rights.

Article 14 of Directive 2000/31 indicates that: "where an information society service is provided that consists of the storage of information provided by a recipient of the service, Member States shall ensure that the service provider is not liable for the information stored at the request of a recipient of the service, on condition that: (a) the provider does not have actual knowledge of illegal activity or information and, as regards claims for damages, is not aware of facts or circumstances from which the illegal activity or information is apparent; or (b) the provider, upon obtaining such knowledge or awareness, acts expeditiously to remove or to disable access to the information."

However, Article 14 is to be construed in a narrow and restrictive way since Recital 42 of the Directive furthers explains that:

> the exemptions from liability established in this Directive cover only cases where the activity of the information society service provider is limited to the technical process of operating and giving access to a communication network over which information made available by third parties is transmitted or temporarily stored, for the sole purpose of making the transmission more efficient; this activity is of a mere technical, automatic and passive nature, which implies that the information society service provider has neither knowledge of nor control over the information which is transmitted or stored." Recital 46 states that "in order to benefit from a limitation of liability, the provider of an information society service, consisting of the storage of information, upon obtaining actual knowledge or awareness of illegal activities has to act expeditiously to remove or to disable access to the information concerned ... .[36]

35. *See* Baumgartner, in: U. Baumgartner/Ewald, *Apps und Recht*, 2013, p. 130.
36. E-Commerce Directive 2000/31, Recital 46.

As pointed out in the Google France and Google and the *L'Oréal SA v. eBay* decisions, to benefit from the liability exemption, app stores must assume a neutral status and not have knowledge of, or control over, the content of apps hosted in their platforms. Thus, the hosting provider, i.e., the app store, cannot rely on the liability exemption in case he has an active role between the two parties (App provider and end-user) and the active role is of such a kind that enables him to have knowledge of or control over those data.[37] App stores must also not exercise any editorial control over apps.

In the *eBay* case, it was highlighted that "the mere fact that the operator of an online marketplace stores offers for sale on its servers, sets the terms of the service, is remunerated for that service and provides general information to its customers cannot have the effect of denying it the exemptions from liability provided for by Directive 2000/31."[38] However, any assistance of the marketplace operator which consists in "optimizing the presentation of the offers for sale ... or promoting those offers, it must be considered not to have taken a neutral position between the customer-seller concerned, and potential buyers but to have played an active role of such a kind as to give it knowledge or control over the data relating to those offers of sale."[39] In addition, the operator of the marketplace should not have been aware of facts or circumstances from which the illegal activity is apparent where a diligent economic operator would have identified the illegality in question based on those facts.[40]

In particular, regarding the criteria established in the *Marions Kochbuch* case, it is obvious that app stores do not brand apps as their own, but mention the app developer in each app. Furthermore, they apply a rating system, such as Android's PEGI and may reject apps that are objectionable. App Store review Guidelines mention objectionable content, such as defamatory, discriminatory content, overtly sexual or pornographic material, inflammatory religious commentary, etc. It also provides rules concerning user generated content and apps designed for children, medical apps, etc.[41]

The fact, however, that app stores may reject apps, following a review process, does not mean that app store can exercise full control over all apps that are published and take full responsibility for their content. This becomes apparent with the terms and conditions of app stores, which mention clearly that the developer is responsible for uploading apps. So, e.g., the Google Play developer agreement mentions the following:[42]

37. C-324/09, C-236/08 to C-238/08 where it is stated "114. Accordingly, in order to establish whether the liability of a referencing service provider may be limited under Article 14 of Directive 2000/31, it is necessary to examine whether the role played by that service provider is neutral, in the sense that its conduct is merely technical, automatic and passive, pointing to a lack of knowledge or control of the data which it stores."
38. C-324/09, para. 115.
39. C-324/09, paras. 113, 114.
40. C-324/09, paras. 120, 122, 124.
41. *See* https://developer.apple.com/app-store/review/guidelines/
42. *See* https://play.google.com/intl/ALL_us/about/developer-distribution-agreement.html.

(...)

4.8 You agree that if You make Your Products available through Google Play, You will protect the privacy and legal rights of users. If the users provide You with, or Your Product accesses or uses, usernames, passwords, or other login information or personal information, You agree to make the users aware that the information will be available to Your Product, and You agree to provide legally adequate privacy notice and protection for those users. Further, Your Product may only use that information for the limited purposes for which the user has given You permission to do so. If Your Product stores personal or sensitive information provided by users, You agree to do so securely and only for as long as it is needed. However, if the user has opted into a separate agreement with You that allows You or Your Product to store or use personal or sensitive information directly related to Your Product (not including other products or applications), then the terms of that separate agreement will govern Your use of such information. If the user provides Your Product with Google Account information, Your Product may only use that information to access the user's Google Account when, and for the limited purposes for which, the user has given You permission to do so.

4.9 You will not engage in any activity with Google Play, including making Your Products available via Google Play, that interferes with, disrupts, damages, or accesses in an unauthorized manner the devices, servers, networks, or other properties or services of any third party including, but not limited to, Google or any Authorized Provider. You may not use user information obtained via Google Play to sell or distribute Products outside of Google Play.

4.10 You are solely responsible for, and Google has no responsibility to You for, Your Products, including use of any Google Play APIs and for the consequences of Your actions, including any loss or damage which Google may suffer.

(...)

From the above terms it becomes apparent that app stores do not assume responsibility for the quality of information provided by apps, despite the fact that they have introduced rules requiring app developers to comply with legal standards and rules, and with the rating system which app stores have put in place.

However, the fact that they explicitly deny responsibility is not decisive. In such a case, we need to first examine the role of an app store, whether it remains within the realm of neutrality or actively engages in the offered services and is not confined only to a mere automatic technical contribution.

App stores are not just mere facilitators between transactions of traditional sellers and buyers. They tend to play an important role in the development of the applications as well, by providing application programming interfaces, software development kits, programming environments, etc. For instance, Apple offers Integrated Development Environment[43] which contains software development tools to develop applications compatible with Apple's operating systems (MacOS, iOS, iPad OS, etc.).[44] Apps are built in a way that is compatible with the standards set by the Apple store. In addition, Apple inspects the applications before being made available on the app store. As a matter of fact, developers must comply with specific documentation and program

43. https://developer.apple.com/xcode/.

44. Wikipedia, Xcode, available online at https://en.wikipedia.org/wiki/Xcode.

requirements determined by Apple when creating applications. When the application is ready and has undergone tests by the developer, the application can be submitted for consideration by Apple and if it fulfills the requirements set, then it is selected for distribution via the app store.[45]

The control exerted by the app stores and the extensive rights they have reserved for themselves as service providers (e.g., setting development standards, defining terms and conditions, exercising control, approval, setting pricing and payment models etc.) may result in weakening the view that they hold a clearly neutral role, so that they benefit from the liability exemption.

Nevertheless, app stores, in accordance with Article 14(1) of the E-Commerce Directive, must act expeditiously to remove or to disable access to unlawful information, upon obtaining such knowledge or awareness. On the aftermath of the ECtHR's *Delfi* decision, it becomes apparent that internet intermediaries should have in place a mechanism allowing users or third parties to report inappropriate content. Such means are included in the presentation of app stores. So, e.g., Google Play provides the means for reporting content issues or violations, allowing internet users to report an app that infringes on a trademark or copyright, to flag apps, games or music as inappropriate, to report problems with family content and report comments and reviews.[46]

## §11.04 EU REGULATION 2019/1150

### [A] A New Regulatory Framework for Online Platforms

Online platforms have become an important distribution channel in today's society, particularly as regards retailers who sell their products via online shops such as Amazon, eBay, etc.[47] The surge of the activities of online platforms presents many benefits for consumers and small and big businesses, since consumers are offered a variety of products in affordable prices, while businesses expand their sale channels and gain online visibility.[48]

The problem with online platforms is that a number of harmful trading practices exist which restrict the ability of businesses to fully exploit the potential of the online platform economy. Such practices include unexplained changes in terms and condition without prior notice, the delisting of goods and services and the suspension of accounts without a clear statement of reasons, lack of transparency concerning the ranking of goods and services and of the company offering them, etc.[49] To address these issues, in view of the fact that the existing acquis was not effective in preventing such practices,

45. Apple Developer Program License Agreement, available at https://developer.apple.com/.
46. *See* https://support.google.com/googleplay/answer/2853570?visit_id = 637149645666505975-3889176557&p = report_content&rd = 1&hl = en.
47. C. Busch, "Towards Fairness and Transparency in the Platform Economy? A First Look at the P2B Regulation," in: De Franceschi/Schulze (eds.), *Digital Revolution—New Challenges for Law*, 2019, 58.
48. European Commission, Press Release of April 26, 2018, MEMO/18/3373.
49. Explanatory Memorandum, Proposal for a Regulation on promoting fairness and transparency for business users of online intermediation services, COM/2018/238 final.

the EU Commission submitted a Proposal for a Regulation on April 26, 2018.[50] The Regulation 2019/1150 "on promoting fairness and transparency for business users of online intermediation services" ("P2B Regulation") was adopted on June 20, 2019, and it shall apply from July 12, 2020.[51]

The aim of this Regulation is to ensure that businesses operating on online intermediation services and general online search engines have greater legal certainty and clarity on the rules which govern their relationships with the platforms and the dispute resolution procedures. In particular, it seeks to contribute to the proper functioning of the EU internal market by laying down rules to ensure that business users of online intermediation services and corporate website users in relation to online search engines are granted appropriate transparency, fairness and effective redress possibilities (Article 1 paragraph 1).

### [B] Scope of the Regulation

The P2B Regulation applies to online intermediation services and online search engines provided or offered to be provided to business users and corporate website users established or residents in the EU, and to consumers located in the EU, irrespective of the place of establishment or residence of the providers of those services and irrespective of the law otherwise applicable (Article 1 paragraph 2). Online intermediation services, according to Article 2(2), are information society services which allow business users to offer goods or services to consumers, with a view to facilitating the initiating of direct transactions between those business users and consumers. The requirement set is that those services are provided to business users on the basis of contractual relationships between the provider of those services and business users which offer goods or services to consumers. Thus, online platform intermediaries include not only third-party e-commerce market places (e.g., Amazon, eBay) but also app stores, and therefore, it should be examined which are the effects of this regulation on them.

### [C] Substantial Requirements

The provision of Article 3 establishing requirements for the terms and conditions of providers of online intermediation services is at the core of the regulation, and they are particularly important for app stores. It provides that they: (a) are drafted in plain and intelligible language; (b) are easily available to business users at all stages of their commercial relationship with the provider of online intermediation services, including in the precontractual stage; (c) set out the grounds for decisions to suspend or terminate or impose any other kind of restriction upon, in whole or in part, the provision of their online intermediation services to business users; (d) include information on any additional distribution channels and potential affiliate programmes

50. *See supra*, n. 35.
51. OJ L 186/57, 11.7.2019.

through which providers of online intermediation services might market goods and services offered by business users; (e) include general information regarding the effects of the terms and conditions on the ownership and control of intellectual property rights of business users (paragraph 1).

In addition, providers of online intermediation services shall notify, on a durable medium, to the business users concerned any proposed changes of their terms and conditions, and these should not be implemented before the expiry of a notice period of at least fifteen days (paragraph 2).

Furthermore, the provision of Article 8 refers to specific contractual terms and provides that providers of online intermediation services shall: (a) not impose retroactive changes to terms and conditions, unless this is required by law or such changes are beneficial for the business user; (b) ensure that their terms and conditions regarding the termination of the contractual relationship between the business users and the service provider; (c) also include a description of the technical and contractual access, or absence thereof, to the information provided or generated by the business user, which they maintain after the expiry of the contract between the provider of online intermediation services and the business user.

Important for app stores is also the requirement that providers of online intermediation services shall ensure that the identity of the business user providing the goods or services on the online intermediation services is clearly visible (paragraph 5). Thus, at each webpage presenting individual apps, the app developer must be clearly indicated.

App stores may suspend or terminate business user accounts and this might prove problematic if it takes place without giving any prior warning or providing meaningful reasons. So, e.g., the Google Paly Developer Distribution Agreement reads that: "Google may terminate this Agreement with You for any reason with thirty (30) days prior written notice. In addition, Google may, at any time, immediately suspend or terminate this Agreement with You if (a) You have breached any provision of this Agreement, any non-disclosure agreement, or other agreement relating to Google Play or the Android platform; (b) Google is required to do so by law; (c) You cease being an authorized developer, a developer in good standing, or are barred from using Android software; or (d) Google decides to no longer provide Google Play."

The P2B Regulation provides in Article 4 that if a provider of online intermediation services decides to restrict or suspend the provision of its online intermediation services to a given business user in relation to individual goods or services offered by that business user, it shall provide the business user concerned, prior to or at the time of the restriction or suspension taking effect, with a statement of reasons for that decision on a durable medium. And in case of termination of the provision of the whole of its online intermediation services to a given business user, it shall provide the business user concerned, at least thirty days prior to the termination taking effect, with a statement of reasons for that decision on a durable medium.

The ranking of apps on an app store is vital for the marketing of apps, as it affects the consumer's decision as to which app is likely to download from an app store.[52] Article 5 of the P2B Regulation requires that providers of online intermediation services state in their terms and conditions the main parameters determining ranking and the reasons for their importance (Article 5 paragraph 1). Such description shall also include the possibilities and effects of any direct or indirect remuneration that may influence ranking (paragraph 3). In particular, the description of the ranking mechanism should include the following: (a) the characteristics of the goods and services offered to consumers through the online intermediation services or the online search engine; (b) the relevance of those characteristics for those consumers; (c) as regards online search engines, the design characteristics of the website used by corporate website users.

At the moment such description is missing from the terms and conditions of app stores examined (Google Play, App Store, Microsoft Store). Regarding the developer content policy, Google Play provides information on user rating, reviews and installs, as well as app promotion,[53] which do not satisfy the requirements of the P2B Regulation.

App stores act not only as intermediaries but also offer their own software products on their platforms.[54] This "dual role" of app stores may create conflicts of interest, e.g., as the app store operator can use the transaction data produced through the app store for its marketing strategies.[55] To deal with this issue, Article 7(1) of the P2B Regulation states that providers of online intermediation services shall include in their terms and conditions a description of any differentiated treatment which they give, or might give, in relation to goods or services offered to consumers through those online intermediation services by, on the one hand, either that provider itself or any business users which that provider controls and, on the other hand, other business users. The above description shall refer to the main economic, commercial or legal considerations for such differentiated treatment.

The P2B Regulation addresses also the issue of who has access and what kind of access to personal data created in online platforms. However, it does not provide a "right to access data," but it rather establishes a transparency requirement regarding access to data.[56] Article 9 introduces the obligation of providers of online intermediation services to provide in their terms and conditions information to business users concerning the fact whether they or the business users have access to personal data or other data or both, which data are provided by users or consumers or are generated through the provision of those services, and if so, to which categories of such data and under what conditions.

Finally, the P2B Regulation includes provisions on an internal complaint-handling system for handling the complaints of business users which shall be easily accessible and free of charge for business users and shall ensure handling within a

52. *See* Busch, *supra* n. 47, p. 66.
53. https://play.google.com/intl/en-US/about/developer-content-policy/.
54. *See, e.g.*, Apple's own apps: https://apps.apple.com/gb/developer/apple/id284417353?mt=12.
55. Busch, *supra* n. 47, p. 68.
56. Busch, *supra* n. 47, p. 70.

reasonable time frame (Article 11). This also includes the obligation of online platforms to provide the possibility of mediation to business users. In addition, Article 14 enables businesses to be represented by associations or organizations in cases against online platform intermediaries to take action before competent national courts in the Union, in order to stop or prohibit any non-compliance by providers of online intermediation services or by providers of online search engines, with the relevant requirements laid down in the Regulation.

## §11.05 CONCLUSION

The P2B Regulation imposes transparency obligations, mainly, which must be observed by the operators of app stores and will lead to changes in the contract terms and conditions of app stores. Apart from the transparency requirements, contracts terms of app stores may be subjected to fairness control in some extent. And also transparency becomes imperative for rankings of products or the right to access to data and for parity clauses. All in all, the Regulation will lead to app stores and online platforms changing their businesses practices, including transparency rules by design and applying ADR and self-regulation mechanisms.

# Bibliography


Acar, Y., Backes, M., Bugiel, S. & Smith, M., 'SoK: Lessons Learned from Android Security Research for Appified Software Platforms', in *IEEE Symposium on Security and Privacy (SP)*, 2016, available online at: https://oaklandsok.github.io/papers/acar2016.pdf.

Article 29 Working Party, Guidelines on Consent under Regulation 679/2016 (WP259 rev.01), 10/04/2018, available at https://ec.europa.eu/newsroom/article29/item-detail.cfm?item_id = 623051.

Article 29 Working Party, Opinion 8/2014 on the on Recent Developments on the Internet of Things (WP223), 16 September 2019, available at https://ec.europa.eu/justice/article-29/documentation/opinion-recommendation/files/2014/wp223_en.pdf.

Au, M. H. & Choo, K.-K.R., *Mobile Security and Privacy, Advances, Challenges and Future Research Directions*, Elsevier, 2016.

Barroso, D. (2007). Botnets – The Silent Threat: European Network and Information Security Agency (ENISA), 15 (2007), 171, available online at: https://www.enisa.europa.eu/publications/archive/botnets-2013-the-silent-threat.

Baumgartner, Ulrich & Ewald, Konstantin, *Apps und Recht* (Beck Verlag 2013).

Bernabe, Jorge Bernal & Skarmeta, Antonio (eds.), *Challenges in Cybersecurity and Privacy: The European Research Landscape* (River Publishers 2019).

Boom, Willem H. van, *Unfair Commercial Practices* (1 November 2015), available online at: https://core.ac.uk/download/pdf/82997754.pdf.

Bostoen, Friso, 'Online Platforms and Vertical Integration: The Return of Margin Squeeze?', Journal of Antitrust Enforcement 6 (2018), 355.

Broekman, Bart & Notenboom Edwin, *Testing Embedded Software* (Addison-Wesley, 2003).

Buhl, Samir, *Der App-Download, Rechtliche Analyse eines Alltagsphänomens unter besonderer Berücksichtigung von Vertragsschluss, Vertragstyp und Vertragsinhalt aus Sicht des Nutzers*, Juristische Schriftnreihe, Band 297 (LIT Verlag 2019).

Busch, C., Schulte-Nölke, H., Wiewiórowska-Domagalska, A. & Zoll, F., 'The Rise of the Platform Economy: A New Challenge for EU Consumer Law?', *Journal of European Consumer and Market Law*, 5 (1/2016).

Busch, C., 'Towards Fairness and Transparency in the Platform Economy? A First Look at the P2B Regulation', in A. De Franceschi & R. Schulze (eds), *Digital Revolution – New Challenges for Law* (C.H. Beck, Nomos, 2019).

Campbell, T., Ngo, B. & Fogarty, J., 'Game Design Principles in Everyday Fitness Applications', CSCW '08, 8-12 November 2008.

Carvalho, J.M., 'Sale of Goods and Supply of Digital Content and Digital Services – Overview of Directives 2019/770 and 2019/771', *EuCML – Journal of European Consumer and Market Law* (5/2019).

Cavoukian, A., *Privacy by Design – The 7 Foundational Principles* (2011), online available at: https://www.ipc.on.ca/wp-content/uploads/resources/7foundationalprinciples.pdf.

Caylor, L. & Martin, K.S. 'In Pari Delicto and Ex Turpi Causa: The Defence of Illegality – Approaches Taken in England and Whales, Canada and the US', *Business Law Journal* 18(3) (September 2017).

Chirita, A.D., 'The Rise of Big Data and the Loss of Privacy', in Mor Bakhoum, Beatriz Conde Gallego, Mark-Oliver Mackenrodt & Gintarė Surblytė-Namavičienė (eds), *Personal Data in Competition, Consumer Protection and Intellectual Property Law* (Springer Verlag GmbH, 2018).

Citron, D.K., & Franks, M.A., Criminalizing revenge porn. Wake Forest Law Review, 49 (2014), 345.

Clough, J., 'A World of Difference: The Budapest Convention of Cybercrime and the Challenges of Harmonisation', Monash University Law Review, 40 (2014), 698.

Colino, S., *Competition Law of the EU and UK* (Oxford University Press, 2019).

Commission Staff Working Document on the existing EU legal framework applicable to lifestyle and wellbeing apps Accompanying the document – Green Paper on mobile Health ('mHealth'), (COM(2014) 219 final), Brussels, 10/04/2014.

Correa, C.M., & Yusuf, A., Intellectual Property and International Trade: The TRIPs Agreement (Rijn: Kluwer Law International, 2008).

Dagan, H. & Heller, M., *The Choice Theory of Contracts* (Cambridge University Press, 2017).

Dantas, Y.G., Lemos, M.O., Fonseca, I.E., Nigam, V., *Formal Specification and Verification of a Selective Defense for TDoS Attacks*. In International Workshop on Rewriting Logic and Its Applications (Springer, Cham, 2016), pp. 82-97.

Datta, U.A. & Klein, A., 'Kostenlose Apps – eine vertragsrechtliche Analyse. Warum werbefinanzierte Gratis-Apps nicht verschenkt werden', CR 33 (2017), 174.

Dehling, T., Prieto, J.-T. & Weber, G., 'Tracing the Potential Flow of Consumer Data: A Network Analysis of Prominent Health and Fitness Apps', Gunther Eysenbach, *Journal of Medical Internet Research* 19(6) (June 2017), e233.

Denker, Hartl & Denker, in C. Solmeck, J. Taeger & T. Feldmann (eds), *Mobile Apps. Rechtsfragen und Rechtliche Rahmenbedigungen* (De Gruyter, 2013).

Domurath, I., 'Platforms as Contract Partners: Uber and Beyond', *Maastricht Journal of European and Comparative Law*, 25(5) (2018).

Lippoldt, D.C. & Stryszowski, P., *Innovation in the Software Sector* (OECD Publishing, 2009).

Drongelen, A. van, et al., *Apps under the Medical Devices Legislation* (National Institute for Public Health and the Environment, 2019).

Eskandari, S., Leoutsarakos, A., Mursch, T., & Clark, J. *A first look at browser-based Cryptojacking* (2018). arXiv preprint arXiv:1803.02887.

European Commission, *Medical Devices Guidance Document: Qualification and Classification of Stand Alone Software* (July 2016).

Ferretti, A., et al., 'From Principles to Practice: Benchmarking Government Guidance on Health Apps' *The Lancet* 1(2) (2019), p. 55.

Mark FBA, F. & Nicola, K., *The Legal Construction of Personal Work Relations, Oxford Monograph on Labour Law* (Oxford University Press, 2011).

Ghose, A. & Han, S.P., 'Estimating Demand for Mobile Applications in the New Economy (January 1, 2014)'. *Management Science* (Forthcoming), available at SSRN: https://ssrn.com/abstract=2378007.

Gijrath, S., Hof, S. v.d., Lodder, A. & Zwenne, G.-J., *Concise European Data Protection, E-Commerce and IT Law*, 3rd edition (Wolters Kluwer, 2018).

Graef, I., 'Differentiated Treatment in Platform-to-Business Relations: EU Competition Law and Economic Dependence', *Yearbook of European Law* 1 (2019).

Graef, I., 'How to Create Synergies Between Competition, Consumer and Data Protection Law in Digital Markets', in M. Bakhoum, B. Conde Gallego, M.-O. Mackenrodt & G. Surblytė-Namavičienė (eds), *Personal Data in Competition, Consumer Protection and Intellectual Property Law* (Springer Verlag GmbH, 2018).

Griffin, James G.H., 'The Interface Between Copyright and Contract: Suggestions for the Future', *European Journal of Law and Technology*, 2(1) (2011), available at http://ejlt.org/article/view/23/110.

Guibault, L. & Helberger, N., *Digital Consumers and the Law: Towards a Cohesive European Framework* (Wolters Kluwer, 2012).

Hamill, L., 'Introduction: Digital Revolution – Mobile Revolution?', in L. Hamill, A. Lasen & D. Diaper (eds), *Mobile World. Computer Supported Cooperative Work* (Springer, 2005).

Hatzopoulos, V. & Roma, S., 'Caring for Sharing? Collaborative Economy under EU Law', *Common Market Law Review* 54(1) (February 2017), 81-127, available at https://www.researchgate.net/publication/316094932_Caring_for_sharing_The_collaborative_economy_under_EU_law.

Hatzopoulos, V., *The Collaborative Economy and EU Law* (Hart Publishing 2018).

Hayward, B., 'What's in a Name? Software, Digital Products, and the Sale of Goods', *Sydney Law Review*, 38 (2016), 441.

Hedegaard J.S. & Wrbka S., 'The Notion of Consumer Under EU Legislation and EU Case Law: Between the Poles of Legal Certainty and Flexibility', in M. Fenwick & S. Wrbka (eds), Legal Certainty in a Contemporary Context. (Springer, 2016).

Heim, M. & Nikolic, I., 'A FRAND Regime for Dominant Digital Platforms, JIPITEC 38 (2019).

Helberger, N., Loos, M., Guibault, L., Mak, C. & Pessers, L. 'Digital Content Contracts for Consumers', *Journal of Consumer Policy* 36 (2003).

Higgins, J.P., 'Smartphone Applications for Patients' Health and Fitness', *The American Journal of Medicine*, 129 (2016).

Holland, J., Burnett, S. & Millington, P., *Employment 2016* (Oxford University Press, 2016).

Höppner, T., 'Das Verhältnis von Suchmaschinen zu Inhalteanbietern an der Schnittstelle von Urheber- und Kartellrecht', WRP (2012), 625.

Höppner, T., 'The EU Competition Investigation of Internet Search. Why Google's Market Tested Proposals for Re-labelling and Opt-Out Solutions Do Not Suffice', CRi (2013), 107.

Beale, H., et al., Cases, *Materials and Text on Contract Law, Ius Commune Casebooks for the Common Law of Europe*, 2nd edition (Hart Publishing, 2010).

Ioannis, I., (ed.), *The Legal Regulation of Cyber Attacks* (Wolters Kluwer, 2016).

Incardona, R., et al., 'The Average Consumer, the Unfair Commercial Practices Directive, and the Cognitive Revolution', *Journal of Consumer Policy* 30 (2007), 21–38.

Jacques Delors Institut, Berlin, Policy Paper No. 227, Online Platforms and How to Regulate Them: An EU Overview, 14 June 2018.

Ruth, J., *Fishing for an Agreement, Data Access and the Notion of Contract*, in Lohsse Sebastian, Schulze Reiner & Staudenmayer Dirk (eds), *Trading Data in the Digital Economy: Legal Concepts and Tools, Münster Colloquia on EU Law and the Digital Economy III* (NOMOS Hart Publishing, 2017).

Jones, A. & Surfin, B., *EU Competition Law*, 4th edition (Oxford University Press 2011).

Pila, J. & Torremans, P., *European Intellectual Property Law*, 2nd edition (Oxford University Press, 2019).

Khan, M.J., 'Mobile App Security Audit Framework', *ISACA Journal: Mobile Apps*, 4 (2016), 14-17.

Kieseberg P., et al. *QR Code Security*. In Proceedings of the 8th International Conference on Advances in Mobile Computing and Multimedia, ACM (2010), \430-435.

Kummer, M. & Schulte, P., 'When Private Information Settles the Bill: Money and Privacy in Google's Market for Smartphone Applications', *Management Science* 65 (2019), 3470.

Lancieri, F.M., 'Digital Protectionism? Antitrust, Data Protection, and the EU/US Transatlantic Rift', *Journal of Antitrust Enforcement* 7 (2019), 27.

Lettl, T., 'Digitale Plattformen: Setzt die 9. GWB-Novelle Maßstäbe für die Europäische Union?', WRP (2018), 145.

Lodder, A. & Murray, A. (eds), *EU Regulation of E-Commerce. A Commentary* (Edward Elgar Publishing, 2017).

Löflig, Nils, *Die App-Ökonomie des Schenkens, Eine rechtsökonomische Analyse zur Haftung von App-Marktplätzen*, Band 49 (Lit Verlag, 2017).

Loos, M., 'Right of Withdrawal – Interoperability of Directives', Centre for the Study of European Contract Law Working Paper Series, No. 2013-11, published in E. Terryn, G. Straetmans, V. Colaert (eds), *Landmark Cases of EU Consumer Law: In Honor of Jules Stuyck* (Intersentia, 1999).

Mandola, D2.1: Intermediate Report – Definition of Illegal Hatred and Implications (2016), available at mandola-project.eu.

Basil, Markesinis S., Hannes, U. & Angus, J.C., *The German Law of Contract: A Comparative Treatise*, 2nd edition (Hart Publishing, 2006).

Markou, C. & Riefa, C., 'App-Solutely Protected? The Protection of Consumers Using Mobile Apps in the European Union', in John A. Rothschild (ed.), *Research Handbook on Electronic Commerce Law* (Edward Elgar, 2016).

McGlynn, C., Rackley, E. & Houghton, R. 'Beyond "Revenge Porn": The Continuum of Image-Based Sexual Abuse', *Feminist Legal Studies* 25(1) (2017), 25-46.

Melamed, D.A. & Petit, N., 'The Misguided Assault on the Consumer Welfare Standard in the Age of Platform Markets', *Review of Industrial Organization* 54 (2019), 741.

Metzger Axel (Dr.), 'Data as Counter-Performance: What Rights and Duties Do Parties Have?', *Journal of Intellectual Property, Information Technology and E-Commerce Law* 8(1) (2017).

Micklitz, H.-W., et al., *Understanding EU Consumer Law* (Intersentia, 2009).

Mulder, T., 'Health Apps, Their Privacy Policies and the GDPR', EJLT 10(1) (2019).

Murray, A., *Information Technology Law. The Law & Society*, 4th edition (Oxford University Press, 2019).

Fabian, N. & Paul, J.-A. (eds), *Rechtsfragen des Cloud Computing, Herausforderungen für die unternehmerische Praxis* (De Gruyter Praxishandbuch, 2014).

Shemtov, N., *Beyond Code: Protection of Non-textual Features of Software*, 1st edition (Oxford University Press, 2017).

Nordemann, J.B. & Wolters, O., 'Google, das Leistungsschutzrecht für Presseverleger und das Kartellrecht', ZUM (2016), 846.

Ott, S., 'Ich will hier rein! Suchmaschinen und das Kartellrecht', MMR (2006), 195.

Paal, Boris, 'Immaterialgüter, Internetmonopole und Kartellrecht', GRUR (2013), 873.

Paal, Boris, 'Internet-Suchmaschinen im Kartellrecht' GRUR-Int. (2015), 997.

Podszun, R. & Franz, B., 'Was ist ein Markt? – Unentgeltliche Leistungsbeziehungen im Kartellrecht', NZKart (2015), 121.

Poncibo, C., et al., 'The EU Unfair Commercial Practices Directive: A Faltering First Step', *London Law Review* 1(2) (October 2005).

Prodhan, G. & Chee, F.Y., 'Explainer: What Is the EU's Antitrust Investigation into Amazon About?', Reuters (17 July 2019, 7:55 PM), available at https://www.reuters.com/article/us-eu-amazon-com-antitrust-explainer/explainer-what-is-the-eus-antitrust-investigation-into-amazon-about-idUSKCN1UC24R.

Mańko, R., 'Contracts for Supply of Digital Content – A Legal Analysis of the Commission's Proposal for a New Directive', European Parliamentary Research Service, available at http://www.europarl.europa.eu/RegData/etudes/IDAN/2016/582048/EPRS_IDA%282016%29582048_EN.pdf.

Reich N. & Micklitz, H.-W (eds), *Europäisches Verbraucherrecht* (1997).

Roth, P., 'The Continual Evolution of Competition Law', *Journal of Antitrust Enforcement* 7 (2019), 6.

Savic, M., 'The Legality of Resale of Digital Content after Used Soft in Subsequent German and CJEU Law', *European Intellectual Property Review* 37 (2015).

Savin, A., *EU Internet Law* (Edward Elgar Publishing, 2014).

Schmidt-Kessel, 'Part 3 – Processing of Personal Data', in A. De Franceschi & R. Schulze (eds), *Digital Revolution – New Challenges for Law* (NOMOS, C.H. Beck, 2019).

Schwarz, Jesko, *Zugang zu App Stores: Eine Untersuchung des Verhältnisses von App Store-Betreibern und Inhalteanbietern nach Wettbewerbs- und Medienrecht* (NOMOS Verlag, May 2017).

Shackelford, Scott J., *Managing Cyber Attacks in International Law, Business, and Relations: In Search of Cyber Peace* (Cambridge University Press, 2014).

Solmecke, C., Taeger, J. & Feldmann, T., *Mobile Apps, Rechtsfragen und rechtliche Rahmenbedingungen* (de Gruyter Praxishandbuch, August 2013).

Solomon, Michael, Russell-Bennett, R. & Previte, J., *Consumer Behaviour (Buying – Having – Being)* (Pearson Education Inc., 2013).

Stathopoulos, Michael & Karampatzos, A.G., *Contract Law in Greece* (Kluwer Law International BV, 2017).

Store, Richard, *The Modern Law of Contract*, 6th edition (Cavendish Publishing Ltd, 2005).

Strader, J.M., 'Google, Monopolization, Refusing to Deal and the Duty to Promote Economic Activity', ICC 50 (2019), 559.

Streel, Al. de, 'A European Agenda for Smart Consumer Protection Rules for Digital Services', *Intereconomics* 52, 4 (2017).

Study Group on the European Civil Code and Research Group on EC Private Law (Acquis Group), Principles, Definitions and Model Rules of European Private Law – Draft Common Frame of Reference (DCFR), Outline Edition, European Law Publishers GmbH, 2009.

Terry, N.P. & Wiley, L.F., 'Liability for Mobile Health and Wearable Technologies', *Annals* Health L. 25, 62 (2016).

Theresia, T. & Eric, M., 'Cooperatives in the Age of Sharing', in Kai Riemer, Stefan Schellhammer & Michaela Meinert (eds), *Collaboration in the Digital Age – How Technology Enables Individuals, Teams and Businesses* (Springer International Publishing AG, 2019).

Todd, P. 'Intra-platform Exclusion in Software Markets', *Journal of Antitrust Enforcement* 6 (2018), 409.

Tor, A., 'Some Challenges Facing a Behaviorally-Informed Approach to the Directive on Unfair Commercial Practices', in T. Toth (ed.), *Unfair Commercial Practices, The Long Road to Harmonized Law Enforcement* (Pazmany Press, 2013).

Townend, J. 'Freedom of Expression and the Chilling Effect in Howard Tumber', in Silvio Waisbord (ed.), *The Routledge Companion to Media and Human Rights* (Routledge, 2017).

Urban, J.M., Hoofnagle, C.J. & Li, S., *Mobile Phones and Privacy*, Berkeley Consumer Privacy Survey BCLT Research Paper, 11 July 2012.

Van der Bijl, C., 'SIM-Card Swapping, Mobile Phone Banking Fraud and RICA 70 of 2002'. *SA Mercantile Law Journal= SA Tydskrif vir Handelsreg* 21(2) (2009), 159-73.

Voigt, P. & Bussche, A. v.d., *The EU General Data Protection Regulation (GDPR). A Practical Guide* (Springer, 2017).

Vorndran, A., *Die Verwendung Allgemeiner Geschäftsbedingungen beim Vertrieb von Apps* (Duncker & Humblot, 2018).

Wagner, C., 'Impact of Digitalization and Convergence on Merger Control in the Media Sector. Five Suggestions for a More Adequate Balance and Format for Merger Control in the Digital Age', CRi (2016), 65.

Wall David, S., *Cybercrime: The Transformation of Crime in the Information Age* (Polity 2007).

Walzel, D., 'Plattformen auf dem Kartellrechtlichen Prüfstand. Grenzen der Selbstbevorzugung (self-preferencing) durch sog. Tech-Giganten', CR 35 (2019), 314.

Whish, R. & Bailey, D., *Competition Law*, 9th edition (Oxford University Press, 2018).

Wright, J., Dawson, M. & Omar, M., 'Cyber Security and Mobile Threats: The Need for Antivirus Applications for Smart Phones', *Journal of Information Systems Technology and Planning* 5 (2012), 40–60.

Zaytoun, H.S., 'Cyber Pickpockets: Blockchain, Cryptocurrency, and the Law of Theft', NCL Rev. 97 (2018), 395.

Zoller, E., 'Foreword: Freedom of Expression: Precious Right in Europe, Sacred Right in the United States', *Indiana Law Journal* 84 (2009), 803.

**Online Sources**

Cavoukian, A., *Privacy by Design – The 7 Foundational Principles (2011)*, available online at: https://www.ipc.on.ca/wp-content/uploads/resources/7foundational principles.pdf

Con Kim Weins, 'Open Source in Android Apps: Tips for Becoming a Good Open Source Citizen' (SVP Marketing, OpenLogic 2006) available at: https://slide player.com/slide/277525/.

Android.com, Publish your app – Releasing through a website, available at https:// developer.android.com/studio/publish/.

App Store on iTunes Preview, available at https://itunes.apple.com/us/genre/ios/id3 6?mt = 8.

App Store Review Guidelines, App Store Resource Center, available at https://develo per.apple.com/app-store/review/guidelines/.

Apple Developer Program License Agreement, available at https://developer.apple. com/terms/.

Apple Media Services Terms and Conditions (Last Updated: September 17, 2018), available at < https://www.apple.com/ca/legal/internet-services/itunes/ca/ terms.html.

Apple Media Services Terms and Conditions, available at https://www.apple.com/ legal/internet-services/itunes/us/terms.html (Last updated: 13 May 2019).

Apps sollen Nutzer künftig weniger ausspionieren, 14.04.2017, https://www.test.de/ Datenschutz-Apps-sollen-Nutzer-kuenftig-weniger-ausspionieren-5163737-0/.

Blenkinsop, Philip, *Spotify files EU antitrust complaint against Apple*, Reuters (March 13, 2019, 12:04 PM), https://www.reuters.com/article/us-apple-spotify-tech-eu /spotify-files-eu-antitrust-complaint-against-apple-idUSKBN1QU18G.

Brett Smith, GPL Enforcement in Apple's App Store (fsf.org, May 25, 2010) available at https://www.fsf.org/news/2010-05-app-store-compliance.

Castle-Clarke, S. and Imison, C., The digital patient: transforming primary care? (2016) Nuffield Trust, at https://www.nuffieldtrust.org.uk/files/2017-06/1497259872_nt-the-digital-patient-web-corrected-p46-.pdf.

Center for Democracy & Technology, Mobile Platforms as Intermediaries: Liability protections in the United States, the European Union and Canada, September 2012, available at https://cdt.org/files/pdfs/Mobile-Platforms-As-Intermediaries.pdf.

Chen, Yu/Pu, P., Healthy together: Exploring Social Incentives for mobile Fitness Applications, available at https://www.researchgate.net/publication/2665700.

Christ, R., *FaceApp was a test. We didn't pass*, available at https://www.cnet.com/news/faceapp-privacy-concerns/.

Coyle, 'Practical competition policy implications of digital platforms', University of Cambridge, working paper 01 (2018), 3 et seq. https://www.bennettinstitute.cam.ac.uk/media/uploads/files/Practical_competition_policy_tools_for_digital_platforms.pdf.

Daniel Eran Dilger, Google faces $9 billion in damages after ripping off Java in Android (AppleInsider.com, 28/3/2018) available at https://appleinsider.com/articles/18/03/28/google-faces-9-billion-in-damages-after-ripping-off-java-in-android.

Datenschutz bei Apps. Welche Apps Ihre Daten ausspähen, 31.05.2012, https://www.test.de/Datenschutz-bei-Apps-Welche-Apps-Ihre-Daten-ausspaehen-4378643-0/.

Developer Program Policies Available at https://play.google.com/about/developer-content-policy/.

ENISA, Privacy and Data Protection in Mobile Applications. A Study on the App Development Ecosystem and the technical implementation of GDPR, November 2017, p. 26, available online at www.enisa.europa.eu.

European Commission, DG Justice Guidance Document concerning directive 2011/83/EC, June 2014, available at https://www.cr-online.de/crd_guidance_en.pdf.

European Consumer Organization, Ensuring Consumer Protection in the Platform Economy - Position Paper, 02/10/2018, available at https://www.beuc.eu/publications/beuc-x-2018-080_ensuring_consumer_protection_in_the_platform_economy.pdf.

European Parliament, Explanatory Statement, included in the REPORT on the proposal for a directive of the European Parliament and of the Council on certain aspects concerning contracts for the supply of digital content (COM(2015)0634 - C8-0394/2015 - 2015/0287(COD)), 27.11.2017, available at: http://www.europarl.europa.eu/sides/getDoc.do?pubRef=-//EP//NONSGML+REPORT+A8-2017-0375+0+DOC+PDF+V0//EN.

Explanatory Notes (UK), Consumer Rights Act 2015, Chapter 3, available at http://www.legislation.gov.uk/ukpga/2015/15/notes/contents.

FTC Staff report, Mobile Privacy Disclosures. Building Trust Through Transparency, 2013, 9 et seq., https://www.ftc.gov/reports/mobile-privacy-disclosures-building-trust-through-transparency-federal-trade-commission.

Google Play Console Help, Service Fees, available at https://support.google.com/googleplay/android-developer/answer/112622?hl=en-GB (accessed on 26 January 2020).

Google Play Developer Distribution Agreement, effective as of 5 November 2019, available at https://play.google.com/intl/ALL_uk/about/developer-distribution-agreement.html.

Google Play Developer Distribution Agreement, effective as of 5 November 2019, available at https://play.google.com/about/developer-distribution-agreement.html.

Google Play Terms of Service, 5 February 2018, available at https://play.google.com/about/play-terms/index.html.

Grove, J. v., 'Your Address Book Is Mine: Many iPhone Apps Take Your Data', *VENTUREBEAT*, 14 February 2012, available at http://venturebeat.com/2012/02/14/iphone-address-book/.

Hacker, Philipp (Dr.), 'Regulating the Economic Impact of Data as Counter-Performance: From the Illegality Doctrine to the Unfair Contract Terms Directive', May 2019, available at https://papers.ssrn.com/sol3/papers.cfm?abstract_id=3391772.

Hustinx, P., 'EU Data Protection Law: The Review of Directive 95/46/EC and the Proposed General Data Protection Regulation', available online at https://edps.europa.eu/data-protection/our-work/publications/speeches-articles/eu-data-protection-law-review-directive_en.

IronSource, Free Guide/e-book, How to Protect Your App from Hackers and Pirates, available at https://www.ironsrc.com/ebooks/how-to-protect-apps-hackers/.

ISACA Study, Mobile Payment Security: Perceptions and Behaviors, 2015, online at: http://www.isaca.org/SiteCollectionDocuments/CSX-Mobile-Payment_whp_eng_0915.pdf.

Koetsier, J., 'The Mobile Economy Has A $17.5B Leak: App Piracy' (Forbes.com, 2 February 2018), available at https://www.forbes.com/sites/johnkoetsier/2018/02/02/app-publishers-lost-17-5b-to-piracy-in-the-last-5-years-says-tapcore/#7dd548ac7413.

Rogers, K., 'Jailbroken: Examining the Policy and Legal Implications of iPhone Jailbreaking', *Pittsburgh Journal of Technology Law and Policy* 13 (Spring 2013).

Khandelwal, S., 'Hackers Used WhatsApp 0-Day Flaw to Secretly Install Spyware on Phones', available at https://thehackernews.com/2019/05/hack-whatsapp-vulnerability.html?source=post_page-----685c2f09e48c----------------------.

Lomas, N., 'FaceApp Responds to Privacy Concerns', available at https://techcrunch.com/2019/07/17/faceapp-responds-to-privacy-concerns/.

Marco, Loos B.M., CSECL et al., Final Report – Comparative Analysis, Law & Economics Analysis, Assessment and Development of Recommendations for Possible Future Rules on Digital Content Contracts, Centre for the Study of European Contract Law (CSECL), Institute for Information Law (IViR), Amsterdam Centre for Law and Economics (ACLE), available at: https://dare.uva.nl/search?identifier=7d3d806d-8315-4aa6-8fb6-1fc565d2b557.

Mark Sumerfield, 'Can – And should I – Patent My Smartphone App?', Posted on Patentology Blog on 4 October 2012, available at https://blog.patentology.com.au/2012/10/can-i-and-should-i-patent-my-smartphone.html (accessed December 2018).

Tsotsorin, V. 'Open Source Software Compliance: The Devil Is Not So Black as He Is Painted, *Santa Clara High Technology Law Journal* 29 (2012), 559-602.

Evan, M. & Andrew, B., '*Will the Real Merchant (Of Record) Please Stand Up?*, May 2019, available at https://www.paymentfacilitator.com/risk-compliance/will-the-real-merchant-of-record-please-stand-up/.

Shemtov, N., *Intellectual Property and Mobile Applications*, WIPO January 2018, available at https://www.wipo.int/export/sites/www/ip-development/en/agenda/pdf/ip_and_mobile_applications_study.pdf.

OECD, *An Introduction to Online Platforms and Their Role in the Digital Transformation*, 13 May 2019, available at https://www.oecd.org/innovation/an-introduction-to-online-platforms-and-their-role-in-the-digital-transformation-53e5f593-en.htm.

Mlouki, O., Khomh. F. & Antoniol, G., On the Detection of Licenses Violations in the Android Ecosystem, *Proceedings of the 23rd IEEE International Conference on Software Analysis, Evolution, and Reengineering (SANER)*, Osaka, Japan, 16-18 March 2016, available at https://publications.polymtl.ca/2124/1/2016_OnsMlouki.pdf.

OpenLogic by Perforce, VLC License Change: A Lesson in Perseverance (30 November 2012), available at http://blog.klocwork.com/open-source/vlc-license-change-a-lesson-in-perseverance/.

Play Console Help, Supported Locations for Developers and Merchant Registration, available at https://support.google.com/googleplay/android-developer/answer/9306917?hl=en&visit_id=637144478542897754-630038059&rd=1.

Principles of European Contract Law, available at https://www.trans-lex.org/400200/_/pecl/#head_22.

Priyadarshini, M., 'Which Sensors Do I Have in My Smartphone? How Do They Work?', 25 September 2018, https://fossbytes.com/which-smartphone-sensors-how-work/.

Richard Gaywood, The GPL, the App Store, and You (engadget.com, 1/9/2011) available at https://www.engadget.com/2011/01/09/the-gpl-the-app-store-and-you/.

Steven J. Vaughan-Nichols, No GPL Apps for Apple's App Store (zdnet.com, 8 January 2011), available at https://www.zdnet.com/article/no-gpl-apps-for-apples-app-store/.

Stykas, V., 'Remote Smart Car Hacking with Just a Phone', available online at https://medium.com/@evstykas/remote-smart-car-hacking-with-just-a-phone-2fe7ca682162.

Szczepański, M., European App Economy. State of Play, Challenges and EU Policy (2018) European Parliament, Brussels, at http://www.europarl.europa.eu/RegData/etudes/BRIE/2018/621894/EPRS_BRI(2018)621894_EN.pdf.

The Play Console ToU, available at https://policies.google.com/terms?gl = GR&hl = en -GB.

Uber Terms and Conditions, Last Updated: 14/03/2018, available online at https://www.uber.com/legal/terms/gb/.

Vaas, L.., Hacking MiSafes' smartwatches for kids is child's play, available online at https://nakedsecurity.sophos.com/2018/11/16/hacking-misafes-smartwatches-for-kids-is-childs-play/?source = post_page-----685c2f09e48c----------------------.

VISA Core Rules and VISA Product and Service Rules, 19 October 2019, available at usa.visa.com.

Wall, D. 'Crime, Security and Information Communication Technologies: The Changing Cybersecurity Threat Landscape and Implications for Regulation and Policing, SSRN research paper (2017), available at https://dx.doi.org/10.2139/ssrn.3005872.

Wikipedia, Xcode, available at https://en.wikipedia.org/wiki/Xcode.

WIPO, Model Provisions on Protection Against Unfair Competition, 1996, available at https://www.wipo.int/publications/en/details.jsp?id = 3227&plang = EN.

WIPO, *Protection Against Unfair Competition – Analysis of the Present World* (WIPO Publication No. 725, Geneva 1994).

# Table of Cases

**European Court of Human Rights**

Case of *Delfi AS v. Estonia*, Application no. 64569/09, 227–229

**EU Courts**

C 291/13, *Sotiris Papasavvas v O Fileleftheros Dimosia Etairia Ltd,* ECLI:EU: C:2014:2209, 223, 226

C-101/01 of 6 November 2003, *Bodil Linqvist,* ECLI:EU:C:2003:596, 119

C-128/2011, *UsedSoft GmbH v Oracle International Corp,* ECLI:EU:C:2012:407, 34

C-131/12 of 13 May 2014, *Google Spain SL and Google Inc. v Agencia Española de Protección de Datos (AEPD) and Mario Costeja González*, ECLI:EU:C:2014:317, 116

C-142 and 156/84 of 17.11.1987, *British-American Tobacco Company Ltd and R. J. Reynolds Industries Inc. v Commission of the European Communities*, ECLI: EU:C:1987:490, 181

C-149/2015, *Sabrina Wathelet v Garage Bietheres & Fils SPRL*, ECLI:EU:C:2006:511, 31, 44, 45

C-194/99P of 02.10.2003, *Thyssen Stahl AG v Commission of the European Communities*, ECLI:EU:C:2003:527, 180, 201

C-202/07P of 02.04.2009, *France Télécom v Commission*, ECLI:EU:C:2009:214, 179

C-203/02, The *British Horseracing Board (BHB) and Others v William Hill Organisation Ltd (WH)*, [2004] ECR I-10415, 82

C-205/03 P of 11.07.2006, *FENIN v Commission*, ECLI:EU:C:2006:453, 182

C-210/96 of 16 July 1998, *Gut Springenheide GmbH and Rudolf Tusky v Oberkreisdirektor des Kreises Steinfurt – Amt für Lebensmittelüberwachung*, ECLI:EU: C:1998:369, 108, 150

C-220/98 of 13 January 2000, *Estée Lauder Cosmetics GmbH & Co. OHG v Lancaster Group GmbH*, ECLI:EU:C:2000:8, 108

C-230/14 of 1 October 2015, *Weltimmo s.r.o. v Nemzeti Adatvédelmi és Információszabadság Hatóság*, ECLI:EU:C:2015:639, 116

**EPO Cases**

**US Cases**

*Feist Pubs., Inc. v. Rural Tel. Svc. Co., Inc.*, 499 U.S. 340 (1991), 57
*Baker v. Selden,* 101 U.S. 99 (U.S. 1880), 58
*Morrissey v. Procter & Gamble Co.*, 379 F.2d 675 (1st Cir. Mass. 1967), 58
*Oracle Am., Inc. v. Google, Inc.* (2014) 750 F. 3d 1339, 1364 (Fed. Cir), 59, 60
*Oracle America, Inc. v. Google, Inc.*, No. 17-1118 (Fed. Cir. 2018), 66, 67
*Lexmark International, Inc. v. Static Control Components, Inc.*, 387 F.3d 522 (6th Circuit 2004), 75
*Alice Corp. Pty. V. CLS Bank Int'l,* 134 S. Ct. 2347 (2014), 86

**European Commission**

European Commission, Decision of 27.06.2017 No. AT. 39740 - *Google Search (Shopping)*, 183
Commission decision of 07.10.2011, No M.6281 - *Microsoft/Skype*, 203
Commission decision of 04.12.2013, No M.7047 - *Microsoft/Nokia*, 203
M.7290-*Apple/Beats*, 25 July 2014, 181
M.6381 of 13.02.2012-*Google/Motorola Mobility*, 184
Decision no. 40099-*Google Android* of 18.07.2018, 184
European Commission, M.8788-*Apple/Shazam* of 6.2.2018, 184, 204
M.7217-*Facebook/WhatsApp* of 03.10.2014, 184, 195, 202
M.8228 - *Facebook/WhatsApp*, 18 May 2017, 204
Decision AT.40411-*Google Search (AdSense)*, 185
Commission decision of 16.12.2009, AT.39530 - *Microsoft (tying)*, 188

**National Courts**

Supreme Court of the United States, Apple Inc. v Robert Pepper et al., No 17-204 of 24.09.2018, p. 3 et sec, 184, 185, 190
*Streetmap.EU Ltd v Google Inc. & Ors* [2016] EWHC 253 (Ch) (12 February 2016), 184, 188
OLG Düsseldorf, VI-Kart 1/19 (V), 26.08.2019, 184
EWCH decision of 25.05.2018, *Unlockd Ltd and others v Google Ireland Ltd and others*, No 1363, 185
OLG Düsseldorf, *Facebook v Bundeskartellamt*, Case VI-Kart 1/19 (V), 194
LG Berlin Decision of 19.02.2016, 92 O 5/14 Kart, MMR 2016, 620 et seq., 196
BGH decision of 17.07.2003, I ZR 259/00, BGHZ 156, p. 1-19, 197
Veroia Court of first instance, 12/05/2016, 169
*Apple Inc. (petitioner) v. Robbert Pepper et al. (respondents)*, In the Supreme Court of the United States, Brief for Respondents, 2018, available online at https://www.supremecourt.gov/DocketPDF/17/17-204/64643/20180924150810273_17-204bs.pdf, 43
Bundesgerichtshof Urt. v. 04.11.1987, Az.: VIII ZR 314/86, available online at https://www.jurion.de/urteile/bgh/1987-11-04/viii-zr-314_86/, 29

Bundesgerichtshof Urt. v. 15.11.2006, Az.: XII ZR 120/04 available online at https://www.jurion.de/urteile/bgh/2006-11-15/xii-zr-120_04/, 29

*Fox v. Amazon.com Inc. et. al*, 2018, US District Court for the Middle District of Tennessee, available online at https://docs.justia.com/cases/federal/district-courts/tennessee/tnmdce/3:2016cv03013/68712/161, 47

*Heather R. Oberdorf v. Amazon.com INC*, On Appeal from the United States District Court for the Middle District of Pennsylvania (D.C. Civil No. 4-16-cv-01127), United States Court of Appeal for the Third Circuit No.18-1041, Argued October 3, 2018, Opinion filed: July 3, 2019, available online at https://www2.ca3.uscourts.gov/opinarch/181041p.pdf., 46

*Milo Gabby LCC, Karen Keller v. Amazon.com Inc. et al*, Decided on 23 May 2017, United States Court of Appeal for the Federal Circuit, http://curia.europa.eu/juris/document/document.jsf?docid = 157524&doclang = EN, 47

*ProCD, Inc. v. Zeidenberg*, 86 F.3d 1447 (7th Cir. 1996), available online at https://www.courtlistener.com/opinion/720542/procd-inc-v-zeidenberg/, 35

*Ryan McDonald v. LG Electronics and Amazon.com Inc*, United States District Court of Maryland, 2016, available online at https://cases.justia.com/federal/district-courts/maryland/mddce/1:2016cv01093/347907/21/0.pdf?ts = 1478870389, 47

BGH, 12.11.2009, I ZR 166/07 – *Marions Kochbuch*, 229

BGH, *Stokke vs eBay*, I ZR 216/11, 16 May 2013, 104

BGH, I ZR 94/13, 19 March 2015, 104

Leeuwarden Court of Appeal, *Stokke vs Marktplaats B.V*, 106031/HA ZA 05211, of 22 May 2012, 104

French Supreme Court, Cass. Com. 4 décembre 2012, 11-27729, *Publicité Sté Pewter-passion.com c/ Sté Leguide.com*, available at https://www.legifrance.gouv.fr/affichJuriJudi.do?idTexte = JURITEXT000026742544

OLG Dresden, 11.08.2017 – 14 U 732/17, 104

**Independent Authorities**

Competition & Markets Authority of the UK, *Anticipated acquisition by Amazon of a minority shareholding and certain rights in Deliveroo*, ME/6836/19 (2019), 205

Bundeskartellamt decision of 06.02.2019, No B6-22/16, 194

Autorità Garante della Concorrenza e del Mercato, Decision PS9345, *Tripadvisor of 19 December 2014*, 104

# Table of EU Treaties and Secondary Legislation and EC Communications

# International Conventions



**US Statutes**

# Index

www.ingramcontent.com/pod-product-compliance
Lightning Source LLC
Chambersburg PA
CBHW071242230926
51849CB00001B/193
*9789403522401*